I AM, ROI

ROI JOSEPH BROWN

TRAFFORD

© Copyright 2005 Roi Joseph Brown.
All rights reserved. No part of this publication may be reproduced, stored in a retrieval system, or transmitted, in any form or by any means, electronic, mechanical, photocopying, recording, or otherwise, without the written prior permission of the auth or.

Note for Librarians: a cataloguing record for this book that includes Dewey Decimal Classification and US Library of Congress numbers is available from the Library and Archives of Canada. The complete cataloguing record can be obtained from their online database at: www.collectionscanada.ca/amicus/index-e.html
ISBN 1-4251-0650-1
Printed in Victoria, BC, Canada

Printed on paper with minimum 30% recycled fibre.
Trafford's print shop runs on "green energy" from solar, wind and other environmentally-friendly power sources.

TRAFFORD

Offices in Canada, USA, Ireland and UK
This book was published *on-demand* in cooperation with Trafford Publishing. On-demand publishing is a unique process and service of making a book available for retail sale to the public taking advantage of on-demand manufacturing and Internet marketing. On-demand publishing includes promotions, retail sales, manufacturing, order fulfilment, accounting and collecting royalties on behalf of the author.

Book sales for North America and international:
Trafford Publishing, 6E–2333 Government St.,
Victoria, BC V8T 4P4 CANADA
phone 250 383 6864 (toll-free 1 888 232 4444)
fax 250 383 6804; email to orders@trafford.com
Book sales in Europe:
Trafford Publishing (UK) Ltd., Enterprise House, Wistaston Road Business Centre, Wistaston Road, Crewe, Cheshire CW2 7RP UNITED KINGDOM
phone 01270 251 396 (local rate 0845 230 9601)
facsimile 01270 254 983; orders.uk@trafford.com
Order online at:
trafford.com/06-2408

10 9 8 7 6 5 4 3 2

Dedicated to my daughter Pamela
and my son Mario

Table of Contents

I.	Foreword	1
II.	Background	4
III.	Distant Thunder	11
IV.	Abandoned in a Violent Storm	16
V.	On Solid Ground	25
VI.	Shipwrecked	39
VII.	Safely Anchored	42
VIII.	No Safe Harbor	94
IX.	Just a Port of Call	116
X.	Ominous Dark Clouds	153
	Picture Gallery	175
XI.	Driven Into the Rocky Shoals	182
XII.	Another Port of Call	223
XIII.	Reaching a Safe Harbor	239
XIV.	Adrift on the High Seas	260
XV.	Taking Over Command	314
XVI.	Detour into the Skies	336
XVII.	My Name	395
XIX.	Afterward	399

– I. Foreword –

For many years people who became acquainted with me and who had listened to me relate some of the unusual incidents from my past suggested that I should write a book detailing my life's story. I, along with my brothers, did live an exciting but often a very turbulent life. We were made to suffer from a lot of pain and disappointment, besides having the insecurity of never acquiring a "place" that we could give an answer to the question of "Where are you from?" For my brothers and me, it was a life where so much of the time we were forced to deal with the unexpected constant change. Often, for us, everything seemed so completely out of control, at least one couldn't consider our way of life to be even somewhat "normal."

When I began writing this, I didn't have any idea what negative effects writing "my story" might have on me. I even had thought that perhaps I should just allow my past to remain as nothing more than occupying that space in my mind that is reserved for such memories. Once I document all of the events in my life and especially my emotions for others to read about, there just isn't much left that remains private.

I am strongly motivated to write "my story," because for more than twenty years I had been possessed with the idea to chronicle everything about my past. I felt that the kind of life that I led was interesting enough to furnish me with more than sufficient material to write about. I wanted to "set the record straight," for my brothers and all others who knew me, to really understand me and who I am. If not a published book, I at least had the strong desire to provide a somewhat comprehensive record of my life to my own children some day. I certainly would have appreciated receiving something similar to this handed down to me from my parents.

Throughout my youth, I always had the feeling that I had an extra burden to carry, just because I was the oldest son. If it wasn't I who wrote it out, would it ever get done? I still feel somewhat compelled to write this because, being the oldest, I am again left with the responsibility of accepting this task, not just for me, but for all of my younger brothers as well. These were some of the reasons that provided me with the stimulus to write this.

I would also like to dedicate this work in memory of my good Christian mother, who had a dreadfully short and difficult life. It was a life that was so often filled with far too much suffering. Some of my efforts here are to be able to recall in writing those nostalgic remembrances of her and, of course, about my past. I do have the fondest desire to share some of *those* wonderful memories with others. I have always missed the much too little time that I had with my mother.

It is my sincere intention to record the events in my life as graphically as I possibly can. It would have demanded much less effort on my part, if I had been fortunate enough to have at least one of my parents as a living resource. I had to predominantly trust my memory as I observed and perceived those events that implicated me. Where possible, I did extensive research to develop a somewhat truthful timeline and also provide accuracy for some of the information included in this work. This is the story about me and all of the other names and places that I have included are real. Even though it may be most desirable to be objective in my reporting, emotions and perceptions make that impossible at times. It is not my intention in writing this to cause harm or to get even with anyone. Everyone, (good or bad), who had an affect on my life in some way helped forge me into the person that I am today.

After living far too many years, I have finally reached what I consider to be an important milestone in my life: I learned to accept and appreciate that person that I have become. I consider myself to be extremely fortunate and to have been blessed with so much during my lifetime. I can still foresee so many more tremendous and wonderful occurrences taking place before the last pages are written to the real ending of my life's story.

If there are any lessons or messages to be realized from reading about my life and I have confidence that at least one lesson would have to be that there is always a reason to be optimistic and forever have the expectation that your present situation will improve. I also believe that if anyone is truly happy, it is because that person really made that a choice and put the effort into being joyful. Although events often go completely contrary to our hopes or expectations and we are sometimes forced into difficult and new directions, there is definitely some divine purpose for everything that occurs in our lives. We must be able to perceive the role we play and accept our own powerlessness, while we learn and grow through our pain.

We must also learn over and over again to trust in others, because most people are good. And it is our higher power that we must turn to when events appear to be more than what we alone are capable of dealing with. Although often times I forget, it is again that I will receive another reminder that there is definitely a God who cares.

- II. Background -

M̲ʏ ʙʀᴏᴛʜᴇʀꜱ ᴀɴᴅ I did get to know and we spent a small amount of time with each of our grandfathers, Joseph Brown and Peter Dufficy. Joseph had been widowed three times and Peter became widowed once. Joseph was physically very strong, quite stern, and what one would consider being an extremely stoic type of person. Peter was almost Joseph's opposite, being very slight in physical build, and he was jovial, kind, and caring.

Even though they were so different from one another I enjoyed the time that I spent with both of my grandfathers. Each one had his own stories he would tell us and talk about those "Good old days," he had experienced. I, however, felt that I had been denied the opportunity to spend nearly the amount of time that I would have liked with them. I especially enjoyed the time that I was with Peter, because he always made everyone feel good who came into contact with him. He was very easy going and he would tease and kid around with my brothers and me. My brothers and I never did get to know any of our grandmothers, because all of them had died many years before I was even born.

My father, Roy Lester Brown, was born on the twelfth of January in Eureka, Wisconsin, in 1906. He was the son of Joseph Brown. His mother was the first of his dad's three wives. My dad became just another member of a very large farm family where he had five brothers and six sisters. My dad was a large man, six feet two inches tall, and he was quite muscular. He had a fair complexion, with blue eyes, and blond curly hair during his youth.

After moving from Wisconsin, his family at one time was considered to be quite affluent, raising grain on the vast plains of North Dakota. I remember many of the stories that my father told me about his youth. He tried to make me understand and visualize the immense size of the farm that he was raised on. He said that when they did their plowing with three horse teams, the fields were so large that they could only make four or five trips around it in a day. He also told me that because of these enormous fields, in late summer they would use as many as thirteen horse-drawn binders going at a time in just one field, to bundle up the grain. Besides their own family members, they even had to hire several other workers to help them during the busy harvest time, placing the bundles into shocks, and then bringing the loads in for threshing.

Everything had been going well for them, and that farm rewarded them well for all of their hard labor. He and his family had become well accustomed to their good fortune.

As proof that one should never take one's wealth for granted and that nothing will last forever, gigantic legions of locusts moved through their state one year. It got so bad that as the devouring insects were advancing, they turned the sky black and made it appear as if the sun had completely disappeared. The locusts quickly consumed every bit of vegetation that stood in their path and then moved on. Their ravishing route included my dad's family farm, where they completely consumed all of the crops. His family had faith that the next year they could recover from that tragedy.

With renewed hope, his family replanted the following year, and they were anticipating a good crop to make up for last year's losses. As the grain was just beginning to show itself, there also appeared, growing right along with it, more bull thistle than could be tolerated. There was no defense against it, because they were living during a period of time before insecticides, pesticides and chemical fertilizers had become commonly used by farmers. The government ordered my dad's father to completely burn their crops, before that bull thistle could reach maturity and have their seeds scattered about to all the other farms.

The next year, believing that their problems were now behind them, they were again expecting to recover from all of their losses. They planted their crops, fully anticipating a good grain yield, but again they were disappointed with having that ugly bull thistle reappear. They were required to set their fields ablaze once more. With that last catastrophe, there wasn't even enough grain left to provide them with the needed seed for the next year.

The family was totally devastated by their loss and destroyed financially. They felt that there was just no hope in trying to continue any longer. They accepted their defeat and auctioned off everything cheaply and they left. Years later they would come to realize that if they could only have stuck it out for one more year, that they probably would have again experienced the prosperity that they had known in the past.

My father and the rest of his family, after leaving that farm, fled in many directions. Each one of them was going to be challenged with an entirely new way of life, because not one would ever return to farming as an occupation. He and most of his brothers and sisters scattered throughout parts of northern Minnesota and Wisconsin.

My father began attending the ninth grade for a short time, but he was unable to complete it because of a greater need for his labor on their farm. It was his family's decision that only his brother Sherman would receive a formal education through high school and even college. My dad therefore lacked a formal education beyond eighth grade, even though he was quite an intelligent man. He was expected to do backbreaking work during his early life on the farm. That and every other line of work that he got into afterwards always required a great deal of strenuous labor. That still seemed to be his calling until he had a near-fatal accident.

My father was an extremely powerful man and I think he felt that he had to frequently demonstrate this physical strength in some manner. A good example is when he was employed by the railroad and his foreman would give him an extra five dollars each time he demonstrated that he could lift an 883-pound section of rail all by himself. It was sometime afterwards that my father discovered that he was only getting half of the ten dollars that his foreman was receiving on the bet that my father could do it.

My dad was quite proud of this family trait, and all of his brothers and sisters were quite large and able-bodied too. The woeful part of all of this is that he and his whole family also seemed to have the predisposition to die at quite an early age.

Before meeting my mother, my father had been in a disappointing marriage, for a few years, which had ended in a divorce. He fathered two sons by that first marriage, Billy and Bobby. So all together my dad ended up with seven boys and I wouldn't wonder that as each one of my brothers came along, he was always hoping for that next one to be a girl. These first two sons of his, as they grew up, were never thought of as an extension of our family. Even though Billy and Bobby were our half-brothers, we were denied the opportunity to become very well acquainted with them.

I had only seen each of my half brothers twice when I was young. We did know that Billy, the oldest, was quite frail and he suffered some severe physical problems as a result of rheumatic fever when he was very young that had left him an invalid. Bobby, on the other hand, was just his opposite at a large six feet four and one half inches in height and he was quite a gifted athlete.

One could tell that my dad was somewhat disappointed with Billy, because we would rarely hear my dad talk about him. It was a hard fact that my dad just seemed to look with disdain on any physical defects that a person may possess. On the other hand, it was surely obvious how proud he was of Bobby, because my dad was always bragging about him, especially when as Bobby got older.

In high school Bobby excelled in track and my dad would tell my brothers and me about his achievements. Dad would even have the clippings that he cut from the Grand Rapids newspaper to show to us. He gave us the news in this same manner when a big article appeared on the front page of the paper, telling about Bobby chasing after and tackling a man who had just robbed the theater in town. He held that man until the police came to pick him up.

My dad was quite severe with himself and with others, always demanding perfection in whatever had to be done. The only one right way of doing something was his way. My dad explained to us that when he was a young lad, his father administered punishment by using a buggy whip on him. In fact his father nearly cut off one of my dad's toes with that buggy whip. My dad learned this lesson well from his father and to a lesser degree he was influenced quite a bit by his father because he was also quite strict. He wouldn't hesitate at punishing my brothers and me with a painful spanking from his "buggy whip" belt. My dad's anger was evidenced with very few words but usually a violent physical reaction against the offending person.

My brothers and I always had a strong fear of our father and we unconditionally obeyed him. We learned at an early age that his authority was never to be questioned. I had to be careful when our dad was around, because I often received punishment from his belt for what I thought were very minor offenses. He would beat me and then he would tell me that I should know better and that I was setting an example for my younger brothers. It always seemed to me that he let trivial things concern him far too much. As I grew older I began to realize that much of my father's anger might be the result of frustration with himself.

I didn't always get on too well with my dad and I felt at times that I might even hate him. I have a long time since come to reconcile myself with him. I came to believe and accept that he was always doing the best that he could within his capabilities.

In many ways he was a good example for my brothers and me to follow, because he didn't smoke or drink and he would never used profanity. He had a strong sense of morality and he was genuinely quite religious, but it seemed that his god was a very strict and an angry god. In fact, those who knew him would have considered my dad to be quite puritanical, although he never belonged to any organized church or religion until shortly before he died. It was then, with the help of a priest in Balsam Lake, Wisconsin, he received a papal dispensation. He then was able to became a Catholic and receive the sacraments. He made it quite obvious to me that he harbored this desire for many years.

My mother was born on the thirty-first day of December in 1915 and was named Martha Theresa Dufficy. She was the daughter of Peter Francis Dufficy, who was descended from an Irish Catholic family that had lived in the poor, forgotten and agricultural county of Roscommon in the province of Connaught in Ireland. We know very little about my mother's mother, except that she had died at the very early age of only twenty-six years from tuberculosis.

My mother did have a younger brother who tragically died at the untimely age of four by drowning in her family's cistern. Because of her mother's early death, my mother was raised by Uncle John and a very strict Aunt Eva on their small farm near Grand Rapids, Minnesota. Her report cards indicated that she was a model student during her years in school. My mother never had the opportunity to go beyond the eighth grade, because her aunt and uncle made strong demands for her labor on their farm. That farm is where my mother was living when she first met and eventually married my father.

My mother stood five feet two inches tall and she was very fine featured, barely weighing a hundred pounds most of her earlier life. She had brown eyes, coal-black hair and a ruddy complexion; and she would have been considered a quite a handsome lady. She must have looked very young for her years, because some even thought when I was in fifth grade and the two of us were together, that she was my sister.

My mother was married to my father in October of 1934. She was ten years younger than my dad and, in many ways; she was just the direct opposite of him. She was a kind, caring and nurturing type of person. She was quite forgiving of other's faults and she would wish or do no harm to anyone.

Although I observed my mother at times feeling frustrated, hurt or upset, I don't recall a time that she ever displayed any indignation towards someone or even raise her voice in anger. My mother was almost always in a good mood, being pleasant and cheerful, and she made others feel that way too and in this regard she was very much like her father. Even when it seemed as though she had nothing to be happy about, she still seemed to be able to find something good in almost everything.

She was an extremely sensitive person, and she was as unassertive as one can possibly be. I sadly observed her crying many times. I can remember at times when I would get hurt and my mother was holding and consoling me, that sometimes she would be shedding far more tears than I. If she knew of someone in need, she would try everything in her power to help. She was as unselfish as one person can be, and she was always concerned about the well-being of others, people and animals, even to the neglect of herself.

I would consider my mother to have been a good example of what a true Christian ought to be. In fact a Catholic priest who knew my mother once referred to her as a "saintly woman and that there is definitely a place reserved for her in heaven." For the amount of time that we spent with her, she was a very good mother to my brothers and me. She was also quite creative, a hard worker and an excellent cook for just as long as she was physically able.

I believe that I owe so much to both my father and mother for bringing me into this world. In spite of all of the difficulties, it was truly worth the adventure. I am also grateful for those qualities that I may have inherited from them, to help to formulate me into the person that I have become.

- III. Distant Thunder -

IN THE NATIONAL NEWS: Social Security was signed into law, Will Rogers and Wiley Post died in an airplane crash in Alaska. The DC-3, or the "Goony Bird," made its maiden flight with 21 passengers, and dust storms devastated the Midwest. A citizen of the United States could expect to live 59.7 years. President Franklin Roosevelt had convinced Americans that this was a year of hope because the economy was improving and the Depression was nearing the end.

"Mutiny on the Bounty" was considered to be the best movie of the year and three of the top songs were "Red Sails in the Sunset," "I'm in the Mood for Love," and "Lullaby of Broadway." The Detroit Tigers won the World Series. The average income was $1,632, a new car cost about $625, a new house was about $3400, a loaf of bread was 8 cents and a gallon of gas was 10 cents. John Deere came out with a new Model BO tractor and claimed that it could pull the same amount as a four horse team. The year couldn't have been too bad if one could buy an Ingersoll Mickey Mouse wristwatch for only $2.95 in 1935.

In spite of all that happened that year the most important event of all for me was on a Thursday the twenty-seventh day of June I became the first child born to my parents who were living at 304 Chestnut Street, Grand Forks, North Dakota. The house we lived in no longer stands and the site is now just part of the parking lot for the United Lutheran Church. The city is situated in the Red River Valley just about 60 miles south of the Canadian border and right next to the state of Minnesota. I did not have a terribly nice introduction to residing outside of the womb and I had an even less chance of continuing that life afterwards.

From the very beginning, things were not good for me. I had a premature birth, and I weighed a little less than four pounds. Immediately afterwards I even began to lose some of that weight. I then began to slowly put on some weight, but I was always quite frail. My digestive system wasn't functioning properly, my heart showed some signs of damage, and I was demanding constant attention. It wasn't until sometime in early August that my parents were allowed to bring me home from the hospital.

I resembled my mother in physical features, being slight in build, and having dark brown eyes, black hair and a ruddy complexion. When I was still young, my mother told me that I was so tiny that I then fit neatly into a shoe box and that a dresser drawer was my first bed. I was told that most babies in my condition, at that time, did not survive for long. That was going to be just the beginning of my struggle for survival.

A little more than Four months after I was brought home, I got quite sick. My parents were extremely worried at that time that I was going to die which motivated them to have me baptized as a Catholic at Saint Michael's Church on 524 5th Avenue North in Grand Forks on the fifteenth of December.

After the quick baptism my parents continued with me from the church to the hospital again. After spending several days there under special supervision, I was taken back home. My parents were required to closely monitor my condition each day, and it was now necessary for me to take some new medicines. Large amounts of a syrupy mixture of dextrose-maltose mixed in my milk had also become a twice daily supplement to my regular daily diet.

On the twenty-sixth of August, 1936, just fourteen months after I was born, my brother Patrick James joined our little family. So I was quickly cheated out of any chance to have the luxury of being the spoiled only child. Patrick was a healthy baby and before he was even two years old, he passed me up in size and strength. He resembled our father with a larger and stouter build, blue eyes and a fair complexion; but he did have our mother's dark hair.

I lived there with my folks in Grand Forks for a little less than two years. The country was still in a depression, and my dad lost his job and he had difficulty finding other work. Because of that, we made a short move to an upstairs apartment at 115 East 4th Street in Crookston, Minnesota, where we lived for less than six months. My dad entered into a partnership agreement with two other men to operate a garage and repair shop for cars and trucks. Because of certain differences, the partnership didn't last long and it was to be just another one of my father's failed attempts at financial security

Crookston turned out to be only a stepping-stone to our next residence in Minneapolis, Minnesota. We lived there for only a few months, and that is where my second brother, Thomas, was born. He was also a nice healthy baby with blue eyes, fair complexion, brown hair and physically resembling our father. I have no memory of anything significant happening while we were living there. As so many others, our father was soon without a job and we were on the move again.

It was in November of 1938 that we moved to 920 ½ E 9th St in Duluth, Minnesota. We made this move because my father was in need of work and he had been promised a job with the MacDonald Motor Co. That job didn't provide enough income and other jobs were quite difficult to find. In the winter the city of Duluth was always in need of truck drivers to deliver coal, so my dad took on the additional job of doing just that, but it only provided work during the winter months.

We lived in an upstairs apartment and it was here at little more than three years of age that I can truly say that I remembered anything from my past. I was one day pushing myself around in my "Kiddie Kart" (a stroller with the foot pan removed) and I guided my cart to the very edge of the stairs.

Now the segment of this particular incident that got firmly planted into my memory was when I had moved my vehicle until one wheel hung over that first step, causing it to tip. That was to be the most unexpected and frightening trip of my short life. I was trapped in my cart and I was violently bouncing, end over end as I was descending those stairs. My father threw himself over the upstairs railing and he came to a landing just in front of me. I, still trapped in my cart, was brought to a sudden halt against his strong body.

I was frightened and still feeling some hurt. My father picked me up and carried me, still wearing the cart, back up the stairs. My mother was really quite anxious and worried that I might have been seriously hurt. I cried as she held me so tenderly and made every attempt to console me. I even recall that she and my dad tried to cheer me up by giving me an ice cream bar.

Normally, my love for the ice cream and especially the chocolate could easily have been used to take away any of the pain that I might have been experiencing, but after this particular "car" accident, I didn't have any taste for it. I wouldn't eat ice cream then and not for several months after that.

I really was able to remember everything as I have just told it here and how it all felt at that time. That event was to be the first that I would have any memory of. I can't recall, firsthand, anything else from my life until almost a year later and again they were to be painful experiences also.

I continued to be quite unwell most of those early years. I nearly died, with my folks and Patrick, in a blizzard in North Dakota which I don't remember, and from a gas leak in the apartment in Duluth which I had to be told about. I was also in a bad car accident when I happened to be traveling alone with my dad one day, but fortunately I only received a broken nose. My dad didn't take me to any hospital for the nose, but just used his fingers to straighten it. Death was calling me on several occasions from my sicknesses, of which I was only able to recollect some of my more terrible experiences.

In the spring of 1939 my dad was no longer needed to deliver coal and he quit the job at the MacDonald Motor Co. He then got a job as a salesman with the Sterling Motor Co. and with the anticipation of better times, we moved to 2713 Helm St. On his new job he was only paid a commission for what he sold. It seemed that hardly anybody had the money to buy so he got behind in the rent at the new house and we had to move again.

Since I was born, economic conditions in the United States were still not very good and the effects of the Depression continued to linger. Decent jobs were difficult to get and hard to keep. Our family was certainly a victim of the times.

My father made attempts at several different schemes to achieve financial success and it seemed that he was always meeting with failure. We were constantly living on the edge and just barely making ends meet. For our family, at least, the *distant thunder* could already be heard, which foretold of the coming misfortunes for us.

- IV. Abandoned in a Violent Storm -

N**OT HAVING STEADY EMPLOYMENT** created a serious financial crisis for my father. My brother Pat just turned three years old and I was four when we were to be affected directly by all of this misfortune. We were taken to an orphanage during the time that our dad was trying to find work, while my brother Thomas was lucky enough to stay with our mother. I had no idea where they went or even if I would ever see them again.

I don't remember anything about how we got there but I had a few strong memories of it after we became residents. That orphanage was really a most detestable place, completely lacking in love or caring for its inmates. The building had only many young boys, the girls were housed elsewhere. All of the matrons were quite strict and some treated us horribly and were quick to discipline. Even though meals were scheduled regularly, we must not have been fed very well, because it was normal for me to go to bed with my stomach aching from hunger. The large, sparsely furnished rooms quite often echoed with the loud screams of the new children that had not yet learned to suppress their cries when being punished.

That home was quite a frightening place for me. I was living in constant fear and even when I went to bed, I always completely covered my head, feeling that would offer me some kind of protection when I slept. I was afraid of the darkness when I could hear the cries of other children. Occasionally and without warning, some sleeping child would be pulled from his bed to be physically punished for something. It was there that I developed the habit of tucking the covers in all around me and covering my head. When I left that home, a great amount of fear obviously remained, because I continued to completely cover myself at night long after I was away from the place.

The most common methods of administering punishment at the orphanage were harsh beatings, restriction of privileges, long periods of sitting on a hard wooden chair and the withholding of meals. There were many times that we would receive brutal beatings, or we weren't allowed to participate during play time, or we might be locked up in cupboards for hours, or we were forced to go without any food for long periods of time. We were hungry almost all of the time. They were extremely strict with us and they wouldn't hesitate, a second, to punish us in the most severe ways. Patrick and I have only dreadfully bad memories of it. I continued to have nightmares about that place for several years after we left.

I can remember one incident which had to do with Pat getting into the refrigerator one morning and taking some food. I think that it was some raw meat because the large matron who caught my brother could easily see the evidence of some blood on his face angrily asked, *"Did you take something from the refrigerator?"*

Obviously filled with fear Pat just responded meekly with a, "No."

She scolded him with, *"I'll show you what happens when you steal food here and lie about it!"* I watched as she then slapped him as hard as she could. The blow was hard enough to knock Pat completely off his feet and I was silently crying for my brother. As Pat, without making a sound, lay on the floor she grabbed him tightly by his wrist and she began dragging him and I know that she had no idea that I was following after. She took him to a room that had at one time been used as their kitchen but was no longer in regular use.

I was able to follow after without her noticing me and as she went into the room I hid behind the partially open door. I was trying to see through the space that the hinges created between the door and the frame. I was frustrated as I tried to see because she was a great big fat woman and all that I could see was her backside. It was impossible for me to see what was happening but I could tell by the sound she made that she was struggling a bit and I heard her slam a cupboard door. She then left with the words, "I don't think that you'll try that again."

After that woman had gone, I wanted to find my brother. I entered the room and, in a half whisper, called out, *"Pat? Pat where are you?"*

I could hear Pat's voice as he called back weakly, *"Sonny, I'm up here. Help me!"* I then knew exactly where the voice had come from, so I started moving as quickly as I could. First I looked out in the hall to see if anyone was out there. Believing it to be safe, I then slid a wooden chair below the cupboard where Pat had been imprisoned, climbed up, and as I stood on the counter I released him. Using the chair I made my way back to the floor. Pat climbed out, jumped onto the counter and then to the chair.

Freedom was short-lived; however, because just then before Pat even got to the floor that matron was standing over us. We had been caught in the act! For punishment she decided that both of us would spend time in the cupboard. That cupboard was barely large enough to accommodate Pat's body so that matron had to work quite hard to get us both crammed into the tight space and get the doors securely latched again. I do remember that it was a very tight fit for the both of us. There was a strong smell of wood and it was impossible for us to sit up straight. It didn't take long for me to realize how futile it was to make an escape and I had the strong urge to try pushing the door open, but I was afraid to.

This happened before the noon meal and we spent the rest of that day up there. At first we didn't seem to mind our imprisonment too much though, because it wasn't nearly as frightening as when one was alone in the darkness. Even though we couldn't see anything we were able to converse in a whisper as we kept each other company. That only lasted for so long, because we were quite uncomfortable because we really didn't fit up here too well and it was hot, and stuffy. We started to really get hungry. As the time dragged on I started to worry that they were never going to let us out, but I didn't say anything to Pat. I thought, "What if they had forgotten about us?" and "What if they forget and left us up here all night?" And then I thought, "What if they never let us out and we will die up here?" I was quite good at worrying and I unsuccessfully fought the urge to cry. I made no noise while I was crying and Pat, who never seemed to think much beyond the present, just bravely waited in silence.

Fortunately we hadn't been forgotten, but it was quite late in the day when we were finally released. We didn't get anything more to eat before going to bed that evening, so we had no dinner or supper. We crawled into our beds even more hungry than what we usually were. Another result of this incident was that that matron saw to it that Pat and I were never allowed to be together again.

Every child, regardless of age, had a job to do in order to make the institution as self sufficient as possible. I can well recall, with horror, another time in that place when it became my turn to be punished. I don't even remember what it was that I had done wrong, but I think that this time it might have been for something that I was supposed to have done and hadn't. I also presume that it had something to do with my lack of energy. I seemed to be fatigued most of the time and I don't think that my medicines were administered to me as prescribed.

We quickly learned that some of the matrons at the home were to be feared more than others. On one particular day I was unlucky enough to be caught alone, in an area of the building, with the wrong matron. This particular matron was terribly strict and I always had a lot of fear for this person because she always had such a loud and angry voice. She was quite a large and strong person and it seemed as though she was angry all the time. She was so mean that she even intimidated the other matrons. I do remember that because I was quite small for my age this lady was able to easily pick me up but out of fear I did make a strong effort to push away from her. I was using every ounce of strength in me in my struggles to escape from her. I was really afraid because I had watched her horrible treatment of other kids and felt that some how I must escape as soon as possible.

I was extremely frightened and it hurt when she grabbed me and dug her finger nails into my arm as she quite easily restrained me. I remembered that as I was pushing as hard as I could to get away. She then with a terrible amount of force pushed me away from her. Her pushing me away and letting go and me pushing the other way caused me to really go into flight. I don't know if she intended it but my body, for the second time in my short life, went soaring on a violent trip down a flight of stairs. I landed hard about half way down and without stopping, I continued somersaulting the rest of the way to the floor below. She straight away followed me downward and then, I remained lying there and I was also doing the forbidden as I had begun to cry loudly. Standing above me, she in a very angry voice shouted, **"Get up!"** I wasn't fast enough and I didn't give her any indication that I was going to get up. I just continued lying there and crying.

She shouted, **"I'll give you something to cry about!"** Then without hesitation she ran into the kitchen. I was still lying in the same place and I could feel the hurt in my body. I didn't have to see her to know when she had quickly reappeared with a stick of firewood, because I felt the first blow as she started beating me all over. What I remembered most as I was receiving that shellacking is that as I lay squirming there, I covered my face and head with both of my arms and hands. I definitely could feel each solid whack that she administered with her weapon. I had no idea where the next blow was going to land, but I think that if she missed one single part of my body it wasn't because she hadn't tried. There were times as I received a blow that there was a strange sound coming from that part of my body and at other times it sort of knocked the wind out of me. It hurt terribly and she continued to steadily beat on me with that chunk of wood; it seemed to me that she was never going to stop. I also knew that she probably would have stopped if I only could stop crying but it just hurt too much to quit. After far too much time, she finally did stop pounding on me, and then I think it was only because she became exhausted.

I continued to lie there in fear and still expecting the next blow to land, but instead she gave me a powerful kick in my side and she shouted, "Now, **get up!**" I continued to lay there and she shouted even louder, *"Get up!"*

When I, with much pain, struggled to an upright position, I realized that I was unable to walk. I stood for no more than a few seconds and I fell back to the floor. She really startled me when I again felt the pressure of her grip as she roughly grabbed one of my wrists, but this time instead of picking me up she just dragged me across the hardwood floor to the other side of the room, where she shoved me onto a wooden bench.

This was a bench that was designed for kids as a place of punishment where one had to sit straight up with the knees together; arms folded, and required to look straight ahead. What really made it hard for me was that we weren't allowed to lean against the back of the chair. To be caught in anything but that position would automatically provide severe corporal punishment on the offender. I can only remember that it was extremely hard for me to sit properly, but I did. I was there for a long time aching and not daring to move. I was left there all by myself to wonder about what might happen next.

I don't know if it was being thrown down the stairs or the beating that caused my ailment, nor do I care. I knew that something had become seriously wrong with my lower back and it severely affected the use of my left leg. For a long time afterwards, when I would attempt to do any physical activity, the pain in that area was often excruciating.

I also remember the day not much later when my dad finally did come to take Pat and me away from that orphanage. I was now five years old and I was walking by then, but I had more than a spot of bother with it. We had been in that orphanage for less than a year, but it seemed like such a long time to us and it turned out to be far too long for me.

My father couldn't help but notice my disfigured body covered with a lot of bruises and I was limping quite badly and I sort of dragged my left foot as I walked. It was obvious that he was infuriated beyond any words. As Pat and I were in the bedroom getting our things, my dad asked me how I got hurt. I wasn't afraid of anything when my father was around so I explain as well as I could what happened.

I think that my dad may have felt a certain amount of guilt because he wasn't able to provide for us and the fact that Pat and I even had to be sent there in the first place. He was also feeling quite fortunate that he was being allowed to take us from this place because under normal circumstances no one is permitted to leave.

As we were leaving we had to stop at the office where there was a woman sitting behind a desk. I know that my dad was also suffering from an enormous amount of restrained anger, because he knew that the person that he was now confronting was not the same lady who had done this to me. I think that it was quite frustrating for him, because there was nothing physical that he could do for atonement.

I then got to witness the anguish and resentment that my dad felt about what those people had done to me. I was standing beside my dad at the time, and I can still almost hear him angrily shouting at the lady, who was now sitting behind a big wooden desk. I knew that she was not telling the truth when she at first told my dad, "Your son got hurt quite badly because he accidentally fell down the stairs."

My dad then shouted in indignation, *"I don't believe you! You're lying! He told me what happened. "* And then he shouted, *"You don't hit a kid in the back!"* It was frightening for me, because I had never heard my dad shout so loudly.

The lady just sat there and no longer defended her fabrication. She was now quite adamant in her rebuttal, *"Children need to be disciplined!"*

I don't think my dad knew quite how to respond to what that lady had just said. He also knew that he had to be careful because he was able to enlist the help from some politician to make it even possible to come and get us out of that place. Even though my dad was a strong believer in discipline he knew what had happened to me was wrong. He was extremely frustrated and he again thunderously repeated his words, ***"You don't hit a kid in the back!"*** And then he added, *"There is a place designed for that!"* And before we left he was able to repeat those same phrases a couple more times.

Those shouted words were indelibly placed in my mind then, and they were to be repeated in some frightening dreams again and again years later, but that did not put things right for me. It was a great relief for me when my dad, Pat and I finally walked away from that terrible place.

Even today, I strongly believe in discipline and even in the words of Bishop Fulton Sheen, which goes something like, "A child needs to receive recognition every so often with a pat on the back, providing that it is low enough and hard enough." A spanking can be administered with love; but what Pat and I received for punishment, at that home, today would be considered as nothing less than a severe case of child abuse.

It wasn't long after getting out of the orphanage my dad took me to a doctor to determine if something could be done to remedy the impediment I was suffering from in my lower back and left leg. It was painful for me to do even some of the simplest activities. After receiving no satisfaction with the first, he took me to another doctor. With another X-ray and the examinations completed, all that either of those doctors could suggest was to prescribe some pills that I was supposed to take to relieve the pain.

My dad was never satisfied with pain pills as a solution to anything. I think that he found it difficult to deal with the fact that he now had a son with a physical handicap. He certainly felt that I was too young to have these problems, and he wanted something done to put it right and not just treat the symptoms. I even think that in some ways it was far more troublesome for my father than it was for me.

Because of my back, my abnormal life soon became the normal for me. I just got used to it and I dealt with it by making compensations for it. Most of my experiences that I remembered from my early childhood, it seems, were quite traumatic. Those were also the very things that were the most vivid to me. It was not of my choosing to just remember all of those painful episodes in my life. It's just that they leave the strongest of memories in one's mind.

All during my childhood, I can remember being awakened from my sleep by horrible nightmares, and so many times I was forced to relive all of the anguish. Those horrible dreams just wouldn't let me forget some of those incidents. It, furthermore, shows me that pain is extremely powerful, and one can suffer from it for some time after its occurrence. Hopefully there can be some good coming from it and one can also learn something from it. I believe that I became a kinder and more caring person because of it.

For that part of a year, I truly had been ***abandoned in a violent storm*** and I would suffer physically and emotionally for many years to come. The memories could never be erased, but fortunately better days were coming.

- V. On Solid Ground -

THINGS FOR US TOOK a turn for the better because of events that were taking place in another part of the world. In 1940, because of a war that was already raging in Europe, the shipyards in Duluth harbor went into full production and they easily became the largest employer in the area so workers were badly needed. As with so many others in the area, my dad took advantage of the situation to get decent employment.

My dad was then able to afford some better living quarters for his growing family. My mother was carrying another child so my dad felt quite fortunate when he was able to locate a complete house to rent. It was so much roomier and nicer than that old upstairs apartment. There would also be no chance of one of his children taking an untimely expedition down those stairs again.

One of the earliest and most dramatic events that I remember quite well happened when our family was all together on the Labor Day weekend of 1940. It had been an extremely hot, humid and sunny day, as we were returning home from a nice picnic in the country. Air conditioning in cars was unheard of then. We were peacefully traveling along the highway at about sixty miles an hour in the car that our dad had just bought. Pat, Tom and I were riding in the back seat where it was especially warm.

With no other intention then to make things just a little more comfortable for us, my brother Pat reached to wind down the window. Instead of taking hold of the window crank, he mistakenly grabbed onto the handle that opened the door. That was a serious mistake because the back doors on that car opened from the front to the back and quite justifiably they had earned the nick name of suicide doors. When Pat turned that handle, and the door became just slightly ajar, the powerful stream of air moving past our vehicle caught the door, and with an enormous amount of force swung it completely agape. Pat, still hanging onto the handle, had his small body carried outside with lightning speed. He was swung right on around with the door as it was being bent towards the back of the car.

It happened with such swiftness that, in that instant, Pat who had been sitting next to Tom, had suddenly vanished. His body was hurled out and for a short time he was airborne, until he violently alighted on the asphalt road at over sixty miles an hour. I straightaway turned and looked out the back window and shouted to my father. It was frightening to watch while his body was traveling away from us as he was tumbling over and over. It seemed to take forever before he finally came to a stop.

Realizing the urgency of the situation, our dad immediately hit the brakes to slow the car down as he quickly guided it over to the shoulder of the road. Our mother, with the intention of going to the aid of her son, was naturally quite anxious. She jumped out before our dad was able to bring the car to a complete standstill. With her first step, and being quite pregnant, she lost her balance and went helplessly tumbling all the way down a steep bank, where she ultimately ended up in a deep gully.

When our father finally did get the car stopped and the hand brake set, he hurriedly jumped out. I turned and watched as he traveled past the window where I was sitting and he was moving faster than I had ever seen him do before. I then turned back to watch out the back window as I saw my dad rushing towards the place where Pat's body had come to rest.

As my dad was approaching him, Pat was already struggling to get to his feet. He did manage to bring himself up onto one knee, while he weakly called out to our dad, *"Daddy I hurts all over!"* After that he collapsed back onto the road. Dad carefully picked up Pat's limp body, cradled him in his arms, and rushed him back to the car.

Our mother, after struggling up out of that ditch, was completely out of breath as she wearily climbed onto her seat in the car. She was just in time to receive Pat's body as our dad laid his head down on the very limited lap that our mother was able to make as blood was flowing all over her dress and onto the car seat. I was a bit confused as my dad then ran to the back of the car, but it was only to retrieve some towels from the trunk which he quickly threw into the front seat for our mother to use. Our mother then placed one of the towels under Pat's bleeding head.

Our dad then went back to where the damaged rear door had been twisted backwards past the position the hinges would normally allow. He anxiously worked as he tried to bend it back to make it fit again and each time trying to slam it shut. After some violent struggling with it, he was finally was able to get that door to stay in a partial closed position.

I can remember as I had been viewing the events and my eyes followed every move that my dad made. I watched as my dad got back into the car and quickly put the car into first gear and he pressed the accelerator to the floor as the car responded with the rear wheels spinning. He continued with a quick getaway as he reached near top speed in each of its three gears. The damaged door was only partially fitting into place, which allowed a lot of air to leak through the front of it. There was a terribly loud sound that was constantly changing pitch with the speed of the car as the wind rushed in through the uneven openings.

After a short time I was able to comfortably rest my head on the back of the front seat. I had a perfect view of Pat and I could see that his clothes had been badly torn from him in many places. It also looked as though he was bleeding from just about every part of his body, but there was a long cut on his head that seemed to cause the most concern for my mother, as she was using another towel in her continuing effort to stop the bleeding. Pat's eyes were wet from the tears that were constantly coming. I knew that he was hurting, but he never made any sound from his crying.

Our dad had always been quite a fast driver, but his normal driving was nothing compared to now, as he was racing and ignoring stop signs and lights and breaking all of the speed limits to get us to the hospital as quickly as that car could take us. For me it was very exciting and also quite scary as we were going around corners so fast that I was fearful that in one of those turns the car would surely tip over. Fortunately there was not a police car in sight and if there had been I don't think they could have caught us.

Coming to a sudden stop as we arrived at the hospital, our mother with our dad, carrying Pat, hurried to the front entrance and disappeared from our sight. Tom and I had been ordered to remain in the car for what seemed like an eternal wait. I knew that Pat was tough, but now I was so worried that he was going to die. I remember that I cried a lot as we sat in that car.

When would the waiting end? We had arrived there in bright sunshine and now it had become quite dark. I was so thrilled when I saw our dad as he finally emerged from the lighted entrance to hospital, but he was *alone*! My imagination was already at work with the most horrible thoughts. Where was our mother, and did Pat die? It was such a relief when our father did inform us that Pat was alive and that he was going to be all right. He also explained to us that our mother would also be staying there, because she was going to have the sixth addition to our growing family.

Pat remained in the hospital because of his injuries, which were many and quite severe. Our dad told me that the doctors even had to dig out an enormous amount of asphalt and the grit that was imbedded under the skin of many of the cuts that Pat had. He said it took them a long time cleaning out each wound before they could be bandaged. The long cut on the top of his head had to be cleaned and stitched before the skull cast was applied. The doctors said they would keep Pat for a couple of days for observation. Our mother was staying in the hospital, having a baby who would be arriving a little sooner than expected, as a consequence of her tumbling down into that deep ditch.

Just a couple of days later, Tom and I were quite pleased to have both our mother and Pat finally come home from the hospital. I, of course, was excited by the new baby that my mother brought home. That baby was my third brother, Richard Duane, who was born on September 10, 1940. Although he was born a short time before his due date, he was also strong and healthy, so I would still have the dubious distinction of being the runt of the family.

Pat entered the house wearing a strange looking white skull cap, to protect the large deep cut on the top of his head. Tom and I missed Pat, so we were also quite delighted to have him reunited with us.

After wearing that hot, uncomfortable thing for some time, Pat was finally taken back to the hospital to have the skull cast removed. When he came back home from the hospital this time, he had a long narrow scar surrounded by a bald area on the top and slightly toward one side of his head.

It was within a couple of weeks after he had his cast removed when a girl named Jeanie, who lived near us, stood on top of a large rocky ledge waiting for Pat to pass beneath. Just as Pat made his untimely appearance below, Jeanie heaved a large rock down on him. That rock solidly hit its mark and made a deep cut quite similar and about as nasty as the one that Pat had received from his violent encounter with the asphalt road such a short time before. The new wound had created a nearly perfect line of symmetry on top and slightly to the other side of his head. Pat had to be immediately rushed to the hospital again. The next day Pat was brought home costumed in his second skull cast.

As soon as our father became aware of what had caused that second injury to Pat, he felt that he had to seek immediate restitution.

Taking a firm grip of my hand, I was forced to accompany him to the neighborhood grocery store that Jeanie's dad owned. Now I was quite justified in being scared that somehow I would be implicated in all of this. Believing that it would only be justice, our dad was determined that her father was going to at least pay the hospital costs for the injury that his daughter had inflicted on Pat.

Our dad's first words to Jeanie's father were, "Do you have any idea what your daughter Jeanie did to my son?"

Confronted by our dad, Jeanie's father questioned our dad. "Did Pat tell you what he and Buddy Motersbak did to Jeanie?"

Our dad, of course, replied that, "Pat didn't tell me anything, but there can be no excuse for what Jeanie did to him."

Before my dad could say any more Jeanie's dad shouted, *"Now just you wait a minute!"* He then informed my dad that one night in late September Pat and Buddy had forcibly pulled down Jeanie's underpants. "Jeanie came home crying as she told us about it." He then said that he felt that Jeannie did have a good reason for what she had done.

Immediately after receiving that bit of news our dad's interrogation had ended. I was quite relieved when nothing was said about me. Without another word, dad grabbed my hand and quickly rushed me from the store and we took the shortest route for home. Our dad didn't say another word about it, and he felt that Pat had been punished enough for what had happened. But Dad was quite embarrassed by it all. Not one member of our family was ever seen entering that store again.

I had gone to the store with our dad knowing full well what had happened, but out of fear I had no intention of saying anything. I was not completely without fault in that confrontation with Jeanie. I was in on the original plan when Pat, Buddy, and I had contemplated taking Jeanie's pants down. None of us had any idea what a girl looked like without clothes, and I think that we were just letting curiosity take priority over any common sense. I have no doubt that I may have helped encourage the event that took place, but when it came to actually doing it, I left that up to them.

On that particular evening just after the sun was fading from the sky, I stood and watched from a distance as Pat and Buddy did carry out their plan. Jeanie stood there helpless and was crying loudly so it took practically no time at all before the boys let her go and from what I could see they never really got the job done. I was probably just as curious as Pat and Buddy, but I think I was just old enough to realize the consequences of participating in any of the action.

It wasn't until many years later, when I was in high school that our dad could comfortably talk about what Pat had done. He then joked about it and even wondered why it had embarrassed *him* so much. My brother Pat, on the other hand, didn't appear to be bothered by it. It wasn't until many years later that he showed concern, and he expressed a wish that the incident had never happened.

By the time I was ready to start kindergarten, most of my physical problems seemed to be somewhat under control and I got around with just a limp. That very first day at Indian School everything went quite well for me until the school day ended and everyone was sent home. I thought I had started in the right direction but I hadn't gone far when I realized that I had no idea where I was. I just kept wondering about, totally confused and frustrated. I was just trying to locate something that looked familiar but I couldn't. As time passed I knew that I was lost and I became quite scared. Duluth seemed to be such a big city to me. Even though I didn't cry out loud some kind old lady noticed how troubled I was. I told her that I was lost, but I was able to tell her my address. She took my hand and led me to my home and to a dreadfully worried mother. The rest of the year went quite well and I never got lost again.

I continued going to school that year, and I was fortunate to make it all the way through kindergarten without too many more health problems. However, I did spend quite a few of those days at home under my mother's care.

That next June I had just turned six. I enjoyed quite a decent summer, but in the fall of that year my poor health was again becoming the continuing enigma for me from the very first day that I entered the first grade. I started school having severe health problems and I was without the energy to do much of anything. It had been a struggle for me from the beginning of that school year. I was only able to complete some of the first forty-eight days of classes, before I was compelled to give it up entirely. I spent the rest of the school year at home, while I envied my brother Pat as he was going to Kindergarten every day. I did enjoy the wonderful care that my mother provided me and I got to spend a lot of time with Thomas and Richard.

The next year in the fall, I had no choice and I was forced to start the first grade all over again. At the time I didn't mind that at all, because now my brother Patrick would be in the same classroom with me.

I was too young to understand my health problems, but I do remember that I had to regularly take some prescribed medicines and I was also forced to drink a half a glass of dextrose-maltose syrup mixed into my milk every morning and evening. The syrup and the milk didn't mix too well and even though it was very sweet, I really didn't like the flavor. I don't remember what my affliction was, except that it had something to do with my body not assimilating sugars properly, and as a result I was required to consume tremendous amounts of sugar in one form or another.

When my illness was at its worse, it would leave me extremely tired and without enough energy to do what other kids my age would consider to be the simplest tasks. My back was also still a problem with much pain at times. It also seemed that I constantly had to battle infections, which often presented me with some serious difficulty. Even though it improved somewhat, that problem was to remain with me throughout the rest of my life.

We were living in Duluth when the United States started to get involved in that war in Europe. Our father didn't have to go into active service because of his age and the size of his family. He now had four children that had become his responsibility. Instead of going into active service, he continued to work in his war- related occupation, where he daily went to his job in the shipyards in the Duluth harbor.

He also joined the Army National Guard, where he had to spend a certain amount of time training, as he did his patriotic bit in the war effort. On certain nights he also had to put on his uniform and do guard duty at a large warehouse. I thought that he looked quite smart in his full uniform with a nightstick hanging from his belt and marching with his rifle.

It was in Duluth that we acquired a very special dog in a strange sort of way. I don't remember the particular occasion, but our dad was casually driving along in the car with Pat, Tom and me riding with him on that day. Dad stopped the car quite suddenly! At first my brothers and I couldn't see the cause for our dad's urgency. Our dad drove over to the left shoulder of the road and began backing the car up to a certain spot. He got out and we immediately followed his example as we joined him. He pointed and looking down this hill, we were now able to clearly observe two boys who seemed to be enjoying themselves heaving some puppies, as far as they could, out into one of the many fast moving streams that flowed into Lake Superior. Right after splashing down into the water, each puppy bobbed back up to the surface and fought against the current in its struggle to swim back to its launching place to receive another helping of the same treatment.

Just watching what they were doing made me feel so sorry for those little puppies and I immediately felt a strong dislike toward the boys.

In a loud voice our dad questioned the boys, *"What in the world are you guys doing?"*

They stopped long enough to say, "We are trying to drown them."

The next logical question from my dad was, "Why?"

The boys explained that they had a large litter of puppies and that their dad had ordered them to, *"Drown the pups!"*

Our dad asked my brothers and me if we wanted one of the pups, and of course that got all three of us quite excited. We pleaded in unison just how badly we wanted one of those cute little puppies and also, "We'll take good care of him."

Our dad then asked the boys, "Since you're trying to kill them anyway would you mind giving us one of those pups?"

The boys replied that they would be glad to give us one.

Since we could take our pick of one of the pups, and they seemed more than willing to give the one of our choice to us. Our dad selected the one that he thought was the best-looking of those wee babes. Dad told us to get into the car and he then handed the wet and squirming creature to us in the backseat. That turned us into some very happy passengers.

The boys who gave us the pup, seemed to enjoy what they had been doing, and they immediately returned to their assigned task by making flying projectiles of the remaining puppies as we drove away with the one we had rescued. We brought that puppy home and our dad gave him the name Rip. In a short time, that little puppy grew up to be a big beautiful Chesapeake Bay retriever.

As the dog was maturing our father taught Rip to do many tricks and that dog was extremely quick in learning them. As an example of one trick, our dad would say to Rip, "Dead dog," and immediately the dog's body would drop to the floor and go limp all over as he lay there and did a fantastic job of acting as though he was really dead. That dog was so smart that he seemed to almost understand every word that was said to him, and this was just one of several tricks that our dad taught Rip.

One of the neatest things that Rip did, without ever being taught, was to follow right along in the street after the bus that our mother used to take into the city to shop. After reaching her destination, our mother stepped off the bus and Rip was there to greet her. Mother would then go shopping from store to store. Rip would follow her and then he would wait patiently outside each store for her to come out and the two of them would continue on to the next. When our mother had finished her shopping and on the return trip home, Rip would again follow along after that same bus that she was in.

Rip was such a good dog that he earned his place as a permanent and loved member of our family. Our father often had to spend time on guard duty at night and into the early hours of morning. Many times my mother said that she felt complete safety on those nights just having Rip in the house with us.

My brother Richard was not much more than a wee babe at this time and no one had to fear for him as he was playing outside. Rip took on the task of carefully watching over Richard. He made sure that Richard wouldn't wander too far away from the house and also prevent him from going into the street. When he strayed too far away, Rip would bite onto Richard's clothes and tug him back to safety.

When grown-ups walked by, there were always those who would admire and even give a gentle pat on the head of the cute little boy with the curly hair. They would often say some kind words to him. Rip, nervously doing his job of trying to protect Richard, would get nervous and demonstrate to those people that he didn't like what they were doing. He would give every appearance that he meant business by showing his teeth, growling at them, and even the hair on his back stood up. It was effective and it truly did create fear in some of those people so our baby brother was quite safe.

Even though Rip never did bite anyone, some of those people started to complain about the "vicious dog" and they even reported Rip to the police. One of our next door neighbors even got in on the act and cried to the authorities. He developed his dislike for Rip because our dog refused to let his dachshund have free rein in our yard.

In response to all of the complaints that they had received, the police car appeared at our house one day. Two policemen came to the door and talked to our mother for a bit to explain why they were there. Then they had our mother help as they led Rip to the small coal shed at the back of our house and they locked him in.

When my dad came home from work that night, he set Rip free. The next day Rip was in the front of the house on duty with Richard. The police were back and they repeated what they had done the day before, and reprimanded our mother for allowing the dog to be free. As our dad had done before when he came home he let Rip out. Well, finally after going through that the third time, the police lost their patience and they finally had Rip taken away from us.

I know that my mother and I wished that our dad hadn't been so stubborn, because we all really missed Rip so much. I thought that we could have kept the dog in the house and the police would have left Rip alone. It wasn't until many years later that I forgave our dad and I began to think that it was probably right in not wanting to have a dog if he had to be constantly penned up. We were to find out later that Rip was put in the army and he was trained as a guard dog. The very last thing we heard about him was that he had received training and was sent to Europe to do his part in the war.

Another early incident that firmly stuck in my mind was the day that my dad was off work, but it was his payday. I accompanied him as I had so often but this time to get his check at the pay shack in the ship yards. The first thing that I noticed upon entering the small building was that the place was awfully crowded with many men milling about and talking. The place was noisy, smoky and it also had a terribly strong smell of cigarette smoke and kerosene fumes from the heater that they used.

I also could hear one man who was so boisterous that his voice carried above all of the other voices. That man did use a lot of what I considered to be naughty words, but I didn't pay much attention to what that man was saying. My father, who never used "bad words," and didn't like those who did, certainly took notice; and he was clearly offended by them. I was so small and looking up at these huge men caused me to be frightened, but I nevertheless watched, quite fearfully, to all that was taking place.

Without even saying one word, my dad quickly grabbed one of that man's arms and quickly twisted it behind his back. I could see that my dad was hurting that man. Next my dad swung the man around and picked him up, and lifted him above his head. The man made no protest during all of this, but what my dad was doing terrified me as he then shoved the man neatly onto a high shelf. Finally I saw my dad point his finger at that man as he quite placidly said to him, "I don't want to hear another word coming from your filthy mouth." The man just remained quietly on that shelf, at least during the time that we were there.

My father probably wouldn't have reacted that same way if I

hadn't been with him, but I think that he felt he wasn't going to allow that man to be a bad example for me. I also believe that my dad enjoyed showing off his great strength for everyone's benefit. After spending a short time in line, my dad was given his pay, and we walked out. That surely convinced me that when I was with my dad, I needn't fear anyone.

That winter our dad bought Pat and me one pair of skis and one Flexible Flyer sled which meant that we had to take turns. The skis were very simple, with no more then narrow pieces of wood that curved at the ends. They had a leather strap that went through a slot in the middle of the ski which we then buckled over our overshoe.

We had used the sled before but it was the skis that fascinated us most. As soon as we got them, we went into a nearby park and tried them out on a small hill. At first we had difficulty keeping our balance and our trips were usually interrupted by coming to an abrupt end as our body began plowing an enormous amount of snow. We persevered and after we got some experience going down the hill several times, we yearned for more excitement. We added to the enjoyment by building a small ski jump. As we developed more courage, we gradually made that jump higher and higher. I think that we probably would have become much more proficient and enjoyed it a lot more if we each would have had our own pair. The pair of skis and our sled provided us with a lot of outdoor fun that winter.

Of all of my memories of living in Duluth, one of my fondest will always be the times when my mother took me with her to the Bridgeman Russel's Ice Cream Shop. We had our occasional trips all year around, but it was especially nice in the hot summer evenings. My mother always liked chocolate and I developed a love for it quite early too. She and I never had anything else but chocolate sundaes every time we went there. It was our little escape from my dad and brothers, as we ate and talked. My mother and I were the best of buddies. Many times she would take me and hug me tight and say, "I love you so much, I could just squeeze the puddin' out of you."

Our life in Duluth had now settled down to a well structured and safe existence for our whole family. For that year of my life until now, I felt as though we were *on solid ground*. Again as I was about to learn this lesson many times over, nothing should be taken for granted. Our secure existence was to be suddenly and violently interrupted with a tragedy that would be affecting our lives for many years to come.

- VI. Shipwrecked -

On the 13th of May 1942 my dad at the age of 36 reported to work in the ship yards as usual. The weather had turned bad and they were soon experiencing a nasty storm. My father was working on a ladder, when all of a sudden he fell. He landed on the deck and then continued on over the edge and fell into the hold of the large ship they had been working on. My dad's body had so suddenly come to a rest almost forty feet below that rung of the ladder he was on. He landed with all his body weight coming to a sudden stop perpendicular on one large I beam. He had a most terrifying accident.

As soon as the ambulance arrived, my dad's lifeless body was quickly loaded and rushed to St. Mary's Hospital. It was such a bad fall that no one would have been expected to live through it. My dad had damage done to his spine and the posterior portion of his 11th rib had been shattered. He also had numerous other injuries that were really quite serious. My mother was notified straightaway and Pat, Tom, Richard, and I immediately went with her to the hospital. When we got there we had to wait a long time until he was taken to room 295 and became case #49482. Our mother got to see him immediately but none of us boys were allowed to see him that day. At least we were all going home with our mother that day knowing that our dad was still alive.

While my dad was a patient in the hospital, he received a tremendous number of cards and letters. During the one visit that Pat and I were allowed to see him he was proud to show those cards to us. Most of them were from his friends who were the people that worked in the shipyards. The mail was addressed to him and on nearly every piece of correspondence was written to the "Tarzan of the Ship Yards." Almost everyone in the shipyards knew about and admired my dad's great physical strength.

I remember being able to see him only a couple of times when he was in the hospital, but my mother did get to visit him more often. I had a good reason to be happy when he finally came out of that hospital in a wheelchair, on the 24th of May to go home to recover. Sadly, he left the hospital in a wheel chair and was in a terrible amount of pain. The prognosis was not good as it was quite obvious that he would be unable to work anymore for what might be a very long time, if ever.

When he got home he was forced to spend all his time lying in bed and our mother had the terrible task of taking care of a very irritable patient. This was a man that was once able to lift an 883 pound section of rail and now wasn't able to pick up five pounds.

He had to have periodic checks on his condition during this time and. Several times a doctor would come to the house to check my father's progress. On the 14th of October he again had to go back to St. Mary's Hospital as my father needed further care especially for a displaced intervertebral disc. During this time we missed not having him around but I think that it was somewhat of a relief for my mother. He seemed to improve some by the time he was again released on the 6th of November and returned home and it was now that he was able to get around on crutches.

On the 1st of December my father again had to return to the hospital for more care. This time he came out wearing a contraption that was specially made for him to keep the top part of his body from collapsing. The device was made out of canvass which he had to strap around his upper body. There were steel rods that ran up each side and terminating into what appeared to be the top of crutches. He now was able to strap himself in quite tightly with leather straps and buckles and get around quite well with one crutch and a short time later he was able to replace that with a cane. It was on the 10th of December when he got home this time. Even though another appointment was scheduled, he somewhat proudly expressed his decision that he would never return to that hospital again.

Because of that accident it would have a profound affect on my father's way of life later on. It would be our whole family that was to become *shipwrecked* with this disaster, because the consequences were to live for a long time after the event. Many years later it would also indirectly affect everyone in our family in ways that no one could have foretold and created some of the most adverse events.

- VII. Safely Anchored -

I HAD NOT EVEN FINISHED my second year in the first grade along with my brother Patrick, when our family made another move. This time our new home would be an eighty-acre farm that my father had completed the purchase on May 10, 1943 at a cost of $2,250. To obtain that much money our father got a bank loan. He bought the land from Jerry Heindl, but the deed was held by a widower by the name of Frank Goehring.

The farm was situated in Taylor County, Wisconsin. It was a little more than two and one-half miles from the small City of Rib Lake, which was a thriving community of almost a 1,000 people. I remember that when leaving town it was almost a one-mile walk west on the blacktop Highway 102 to where Jim Willet's tavern marked the forty-five degree turn onto a gravel road that went almost south for another mile and then one-half mile east to where our farm was on the left side of the road.

When standing on the road facing north towards our farm, two bachelor brothers with the last name of Vlach lived to the left of us and on the right lived an elderly couple by the name of Resudek.

Going up the driveway about 80 yards one came to the house on the right and a combination garage and wood shed. About another 100 yards was the barn that was to become a large chicken coop. The distance between the house and the barn was interrupted by a small building which in earlier days was a pump house. To the right, left and behind the barn was much of the land that went with the purchased property.

The first thing a person saw upon entering the city was the Rib Lake Lumber Company, which was also the main reason for the community's prosperity. With its large buildings and railroad tracks, it occupied much of the region next to the beautiful lake. They even had their own grocery store where their workers could get credit to buy their necessities. This was a very impressive operation and everything about it seemed to be so enormous to me.

I can remember the time my father took me with him as we made a tour of lumber company and he was continually explaining every little detail to me. The thing that impressed me the most was when we entered this one huge and noisy room and watching a man ride on a large apparatus that had a saw blade that was taller than the man. The fast-turning blade screamed lengthwise through the huge log, creating a rough, long, narrow slab of wood that still had some bark remaining on each edge. Then that machine would carry the man and the still spinning saw blade back to where it started and return to make another cut. This operation was repeated over and over until the log had been completely cut into many slices. On the other side of this room there was another machine just like it operating at the same time. The boards that had been created this way were then sent to another area, and eventually they came out of the mill as smooth, usable boards of different sizes.

I could spend hours watching as each of the railroad cars loaded with the finished wood came rolling down the slope of the overhead tramway tracks. The tracks controlled their direction and there where switches that controlled the proper siding as the load eventually came to a gradual stop quite a distance away. Men working with teams of horses would pull the carloads of lumber as they put together a consist of cars to be taken away as trains by the big, steam-powered locomotives.

After passing under the lumber company's tramway, you would find that most of the businesses were located on both sides of a main street that was no more than two blocks long. This was a very busy area, with a drug store, the Rib Lake Bank, a restaurant, a grocery store, a bakery, the Olsen Hardware Store, a Gambles Hardware Store, the Rib Lake Theatre, an ice cream parlor, the Farmers Feed Company, a two-lane bowling alley, and eleven taverns. Situated among these establishments was also the Rib Lake Herald, a weekly newspaper that every Friday published the latest news about the war but mainly kept people current with all of the local gossip.

Rib Lake was also where, in that fall of 1943, Pat and I immediately started to attend the second grade in the small kindergarten through third grade Ward School in the middle of the city. At first we had to ride with our dad or most of the times walk the whole distance to school which seemed like such a long way. Our father made an appeal to the school board to get the school bus route changed so that it would make a stop nearer to us. His pleas got action and it was sometime in October that the bus did start making a stop each morning so that now we had to only walk about a half mile east from our house to catch the bus. We had to be there early enough to catch it so that frequently we had to wait for what seemed a long time and in the winter it was often a terribly cold wait. That bus took us, on some terribly bad gravel and dirt roads, on the rest of the route and finally ending up at our school. In the winter the bus was noisy, bumpy, and cold but it was far better than walking. At that time the school buses in Wisconsin were painted red on the top third, white on the middle, and the bottom third was blue. It made the buses look quite patriotic during this World War II period of time.

It was only a few months after my father got out of the hospital for the last time, when he bought that farm. He refused to take the advice of his doctor, who told him that it was really too soon after his accident for him to have much of any physical activity. My dad just seemed to think of himself as a sort of superman. He was determined to employ his best efforts at making an investment in something that he thought would have a lot of possibilities and financial rewards. My dad already had a vision formed in his mind as to what his plans were for that farm. His dream would also require a considerable amount of physical effort.

It didn't take my dad long to get started on those plans. The first thing he did was rent almost sixty acres of his land to a man with the last name of Gessert, who in turn used that land partly for crops and partly for grazing some of his livestock. That would furnish a small amount of reliable income each year for purchases that were always needed.

My dad immediately began to completely renovate and make some design changes to the existing barn and again using more borrowed money. He started out by reinforcing the structure of that barn. Then he removed the partitions for the horse stables and the stanchions for the milk cows. On the first floor he had new concrete poured to provide a flat and smooth surface which could be easily kept clean. He completely redid the second floor which had originally been a hay mow. He was remaking that building into quite a fancy two-story chicken coop, with four large rooms; two downstairs and two upstairs.

I understood the reason for the four separate rooms was that if one of the areas got diseased chickens, the other three could be quarantined and taken care of to prevent the ailment from spreading. All four rooms were identical in size, and they each had five windows on the south side that faced toward our house. There were no windows on the other three sides of the building. On the east side of the barn was a small attached one story room which my dad made into what he called a feed room where feed was stored in wooden bunkers for filling the feeders later. From there he constructed a nice stairway to the upstairs which replaced the original hay mow ladders.

The old barn had been replaced by a building that had been carefully designed for just one purpose: to house chickens and produce eggs. Dad put on new siding and he installed all of the newest technology available at that time which included automatic feeders, and water fountains. There were special places for the hens to go to lay eggs, which made it easily accessible for collecting those eggs. When he was finished it would no longer be just an ordinary farm, but what my dad would call his chicken ranch.

    I can remember one of the roles that Pat and I played in preparing this building for its future use. It was a bit frightening, as we had to carefully walk on the sloping feed room roof that was made of moss-covered wood shingles and on that particular day it was wet and slippery. While standing on the edge we would carefully bend over the side as our dad, reaching as far as he could above his head. He would hand us a basket of wood shavings obtained from the lumber company which would provide a cheap insulation above the ceiling of the top floor. We did some sliding about as we then carried each heavy basket into a small opening that positioned us above that top ceiling. We again had to be very careful as we walked across the rafters and dumped our load between them. We carefully stepped from rafter to rafter until we got to the far end and it was quite a relief as the trips gradually got shorter and there were less rafters to cross. It was very hard and tense work for us and I knew that one slip and my foot would have gone right through the ceiling. Pat and I continued by repeating that same procedure many times before we were had finally covered the full length of the attic. I had a terrible fear of my father if anything should go wrong, so I felt quite relieved when the job had been completed without a single mishap.

    Our dad had that building equipped with ventilators, and it even had special timers to control when the lights were turned on or off. To this day I still have never seen a more refined chicken coop. That structure was so nice that I heard my mother once remark that the house for the chickens was nicer than the house that we lived in. Her words were probably no exaggeration.

    The small, six-room house wasn't much to look at; but our dad did have a new roof put on and new siding with a grayish brick design. It had a large living room, a spacious kitchen, and two bedrooms on the first floor. We usually didn't use the two rooms that were upstairs and never in the winter. There was a small porch with no roof that stuck out from the kitchen door in the back. There was a door in the front that led into the living room, but we rarely used it except to use the front screen door to allow air to help cool the house in the summer. In the winter that doorway was sealed up to keep the cold out. The basement occupied less than half of the space under the house and it did have a cement floor and there was only a crawl space under the rest of the house.

The house did have electricity but no central heating, no bathroom and no running water. In the winter heat was provided by a big wood-burning cook stove in the kitchen and what was called a parlor type circulating coal or wood stove in the living room. We did have a small hand pump in the kitchen that supplied us with clean water for washing and cooking.

We washed our faces and hands several times daily in a round pan that sat in a wooden wash basin. When you finished washing, you dumped the pan into the basin and the water ran down through a hole into a five-gallon pail underneath that had to be dumped outside when it got full. This was a job that our dad could easily do or, as it was done most of the time, by Pat and me. We carried that heavy pail by working together on either side of the wire handle that cut into your hands. The worst part was making it down the back steps without tipping it.

There was always plenty of hot water available from the huge reservoir that stuck out of the right side of the wood-burning kitchen stove, which meant that stove had to have a fire burning in all kinds of weather. The kitchen was the warmest and most cozy room in the winter, but during the summer sweat seemed to be an essential part of being there.

We rarely took a bath; but when we did, it was in a big wash tub that was partly filled with pails of hot water from the kitchen stove. Because the tub sat in the middle of the kitchen floor, it provided us with no privacy; so when it was my turn I made a very quick job of it. I had developed a habit when I was in the orphanage of taking a bath just as fast as I possibly could, out of fear of getting caught with no clothes on and not being able to run away. I was also quite self-conscience about my naked body.

The toilet was outside in a very small wooden building with your choice of which of the two holes you wanted to put your most private parts over. It was very hot in the summer and since it lacked any ventilation except for the thin cracks between the boards it created a foul-smelling environment. In the winter the odor was gone but it was quite a frigid thing you sat on and the surface area that your exposed body parts touched never did warm it up much. Those thin cracks between the boards seemed to be quite large when the cold wind was blowing through and even bringing in a bit of snow. Comfort was not even a consideration when this structure was built. It was important for a person to get his job done as efficiently as possible. At first I wondered why two holes; so two people can go in at a time and visit or hold hands while doing their business or was it so one could do part of their job over one hole and finish up over the other?

A provision was made to deal with those emergencies that might arise after we went to bed because one would not want to get out of bed and put on clothes in the middle of the night and go wandering down the path to our little building. Under the bed was what people politely called a chamber pot, but which we simply called a slop jar. It was really a special type of porcelain-coated steel pail with a lid on it. It had a special flared out rim so one could even, for a limited amount of time; rest his posterior somewhat comfortably on it. If one was in dire need of getting rid of liquid or solid waste during the night, you just pulled that "jar" out from under the bed. As a boy, you first removed the lid and then to do your job you would usually just kneel down in front of the jar, or on those more demanding occasions you were bound to sit down on it. When you had finished your mission, it was absolutely essential that you replaced the cover for an obvious reason. It was also extremely important to slide the jar back under the bed. You can imagine the consequences if you came gliding out of bed early some morning and the first thing that your feet should happen to meet is that jar instead of the floor.

Each morning it was a chore requiring two trips as we had to carry that "slop jar" and the one in our parent's bedroom outside to empty the contents. Pat, Tom and I reluctantly took turns with that job. In the summer that wasn't much of a problem, but in the winter when our bedroom was so cold that the contents of that pail would often freeze solid, making the job of emptying it just a bit more difficult in the morning. Then we had to tip the pail over and then dropped it hard onto the snow covered ground which usually broke the iced up contents which fell out in pieces on the ground.

Our dad did have plans to enlarge and modernize the house, but that didn't have as high a priority as that chicken coop. For now all of his attention was focused on turning this farm into a prosperous "chicken ranch," with an unexcelled production of eggs. It wasn't long before he was successfully accomplishing all of that. He even won several awards from the University of Wisconsin for the extraordinarily high egg output that he received from his chickens. It seemed the chickens became our center of attention around our home. Brooder houses, Jamesway feeders, pullets, and candling eggs had become a part of my every day vocabulary. I even knew that coccidiosis was the most dreaded chicken disease at that time.

It was within months after moving there that our farm family began to grow. The chicken coop had eventually become filled with over two thousand laying hens. We had two brooder houses on skids that seemed to be always occupied at full capacity with the baby chicks which later became what we called pullets. We had a pet rooster named King Oscar, a bull calf that we simply called Bully, and one stray black dog for which we never did settle on one name. Because of their reproductive habits and survivability, we had a nameless cat population that was always in the double digits. They seemed to be everywhere and we took care of them and my brothers and I each had our favorites.

I shouldn't forget to mention the two other members of our family. They were the extremely elusive guinea hens and they were the most horrible sounding creatures on our farm. They were a strange sort of funny looking birds with a little bare head and upper neck sticking out of their chubby round bodies. Their bodies were covered with feathers that were black with light colored dots that gave them a sort of bluish look from a distance. To me they looked like something that you would more likely see in the National Geographic magazine with pictures of some far-off place in Africa. We were told that those birds were important to this farm, because they had the task of warding off any chicken hawks. How successful they were in their assigned task, I don't know, but I was often able to observe a hawk going into its circling pattern, but I never saw one completing its descent to capture its intended prey. The guinea hens were also quite a curiosity for any one that came to visit us.

One of the assigned chores that Pat and I had to do was to feed and take good care of the male calf. That calf was really a steer that was intended to provide beef one day. We called him Bully, and as he was growing we became quite fond of him and he developed into sort of a pet. We did our job well and he matured quite fast. It was a miserable day for us when he was taken away and sent to be butchered.

The most essential function for Pat and me in the operation of that "chicken ranch" had required us to spend a lot of our time in the damp partial basement of our house, washing and crating the eggs. This was probably one of the most important jobs on the farm. It had to be done every single day. We took each egg from its wire basket, washed it and held it up to the light to make sure there were no spots of blood inside. We then put it into one side of a wooden crate that held four dozen eggs to each layer. Because there were always so many eggs, this process had to be repeated many times, which made it seem endless.

Working in that basement was a job that we both dreaded and besides it was more than a bit disconcerting when you worked and strange noises emanated from the dark crawl space which harbored creatures that you could only hear but did a lot for your imagination. I found it a bit scary at times and I can remember making noises such as whistling to try and scare away whatever was moving around in there.

One night while we were in bed we were awakened by a terrible noise coming from the basement. It gave us a bit of a scare, but it turned out to be that our father was chasing a muskrat around with a stick until he had it cornered and was able to kill it. The next day our dad ordered Pat and me to carry the rat over to the Resudek's to see if they would want it for the pelt. They didn't so Pat and I took turns as we lugged the creature back home and our dad had us take it to the gravel pit where I thought it should have gone in the first place.

When our dad was going to be away on some extraordinary occasions, Pat and I had to work together to feed the chickens their egg mash and the oyster shells and grit. We also had to fill the automatic water fountains. There was also the huge task of collecting the eggs and hauling the large and heavy partly filled wire baskets to the basement of the house. It took us such a long time and we weren't too good at that. Fortunately our dad usually did it, because he could lift the one hundred pound sacks of feed, and dump them into the automatic feeders. He also knew that job was being done right.

In the fall, the job that was the most work and required the most amount of time from Pat and me was storing all of the wood that was needed for the stoves. It was particularly important to prepare for the winter when we had to feed two stoves with big appetites for fuel. We took turns chopping the wood, from the big woodpile that was located near the pump house that sat between the chicken coop and the house. It was a hard job for us to use the ax to cut the big, round tree trunk pieces into the smaller ones that the stoves could use. It was often that one of us would sink the ax deep into the wood, which left us with the difficult task of trying to remove it, as the ax head seemed to temporarily become part of the wood. We struggled as we kept wiggling it back and forth and finally pulling it free.

After we had built a small mountain of chopped wood, we piled as many pieces as we could onto our red Radio Flyer wagon. Next we hauled each wagon load to the large, unpainted wooden shed that stood near the house. Finally we had to carry arm loads of wood from our wagon and stack it neatly against a wall inside that shed. Then that same process had to be repeated several more times. That job seemed endless; because as soon as we finished chopping one pile of wood, our dad would have another several cords of wood hauled in. We were told that a cord of wood was 128 cubic feet but it was something that was almost impossible to visualize but to us it seemed to be a lot.

The job seemed like it would never end, because it took such an enormous amount of wood to satisfy the appetite of the kitchen stove, which remained in constant use for cooking, baking and heating water as it was constantly taking wood from our pile. Besides the kitchen stove we had to have enough wood during cold weather to feed the living room stove, which also required a steady diet of its share of that wood to keep our house warm.

Even though we had a constant population of about 2,000 laying hens, we only had one, but a very remarkable rooster whom our dad named King Oscar. Whenever our dad was working in the chicken coop, King Oscar would fly up and sit on his shoulder. That rooster would travel around the coop in that manner, as our dad worked or when he was collecting eggs. King Oscar only had that special relationship with our dad and he would never do that with any of my brothers or me.

King Oscar was the most beautiful rooster, with a tall red comb that stood straight up and the most elegantly curved tail feathers. He looked just like what you would only get to see in pictures. I think that King Oscar was well aware that he was a handsome bird, because most of his time was spent strutting around the farmyard just looking so proud.

It seemed to me that our dad was forever culling out the chickens that weren't producing. I hated that job because it could only be done late at night, when the chickens went to roost. Pat and I were expected to furnish our dad with quite a bit of help with catching and bringing him the chickens. We each had a thick wire contraption that was about three feet long with a curved end which we could catch the chicken by hooking it around its leg and dragging it towards you. Picking it up, we carried the chicken upside down by its legs to our dad. When we handed each bird to our dad, he stuck two of his fingers into the proper location to determine if that hen was still generating any eggs. The hens that weren't laying eggs were destined to be butchered before long. Culling 500 chickens took most of the night and we still had another 500 in each of the other three rooms. We were quite relieved when those four nights were over for awhile.

The doomed birds were put into separate cages, and they usually only had to wait until the next day for their inevitable execution to begin. Our dad never chopped off any of the chicken's heads. The method he used was to stick a pointed knife into the chicken's mouth, aiming it upwards so that the blade would penetrate into the brain. Death was instantly and there was no messy blood all over the place. He would kill several of them like that and then he moved onto the next stage of his operation.

He would take two birds at a time from the pile of limp bodies and put them into hot water that was at just the right temperature. From the water he hung the birds on hooks. The hooks were mounted on a board that our dad had nailed up between two large trees. Pat and I worked like machines as we stripped the feathers from those birds. I remember often hearing our dad bragging to others that these two oldest sons of his could completely strip the feathers from two chickens every three minutes.

Occasionally our dad's panel truck was assigned the duties of the tractor that he didn't have. He hitched a wagon to his little truck and pulled it in front of the chicken coop windows. My dad would remove a window from its frame, scrape the manure from under the roosts, and then he forked the manure off of the floor and threw it out that window and into the wagon. Then he repeated the same procedure as he moved on to the next window. After he had filled the wagon, he slowly drove his truck pulling its load of manure out to fertilize the field. It would take at least four loads to complete both floors of that chicken coop.

During these times I always went with my dad, and once we got to the place that he had chosen, it became my job to drive the truck. I had to go very slowly and without any jerking in the lowest gear while my dad, standing on the wagon, forked the manure onto the field. I was only in the second grade and I was so small that I really couldn't see much more than just the sky through the windshield, much less where we were going. It really didn't seem to matter, because I was only expected to hold the steering wheel securely and guide the truck in a straight line. Once we were underway, it was necessary for me to steadily hold my right foot on the block of wood that my dad had temporarily wired to the gas peddle. He shouted to me when it was time to stop. I completely slipped out of sight as I took my foot off the gas peddle and with both feet pushed the clutch all the way to the floorboard and held it there until my dad got inside the truck and pulled the shift lever into neutral. Thankfully I didn't have to worry about the brake as the truck came to an immediate stop when the clutch was depressed.

A tractor would have been much better suited to the job because my dad had to be careful, when driving through the ditches and in the rough fields, to avoid getting the truck stuck. When he did get stuck the job would require a lot more of his precious time while he worked at becoming mobile again. I think that it was probably hard on the truck which was our only means of transportation.

Eventually my dad got a good buy on an old, well-used, gray, kerosene burning Case Model 12-20 tractor with its crosswise mounted engine and large, wide steel wheels in back and much smaller ones in front. That tractor had only three gears; one for reverse and two speeds to go forward. Low gear would move it at 2 ¼ miles per hour and in high gear it had a top speed of 3 miles an hour or as my dad would say it had two speeds forward, "slow and slower."

When I first saw that tractor; it appeared to be so massive and the loud noise it made was quite frightening. In spite of the noise, I would soon learn to appreciate it over the panel truck because I was now able to stand up as I held the steering wheel to keep it going in a straight line. I could now see where I was going and to stop all that I had to do was pull back on the lever which was the hand clutch and I didn't need to bother with the brake. My job became much easier and even somewhat enjoyable and I no longer worried about making a mistake. I felt so big and important when I was "driving" that tractor. Because it moved so slowly I think that the job actually took longer, but we never got stuck again.

The young dog that we had somehow acquired was just a stray black mongrel of a questionable origin, but my brothers and I adopted him as our own. I don't even remember any name that he answered to. We always fed him and played with him, and we had become quite fond of him. He loved being petted and he was undeniably the friendliest dog to be with.

We didn't have that dog very long when one day he did something that was quite unforgivable. He wandered into one of the upstairs rooms in the chicken coop. That dog began making a merry time of it, creating pandemonium among the chickens by chasing them all over the place. As soon as my dad heard the awful squawking noises that were coming from that coop, he grabbed a big stick in one hand and then firmly grabbed onto my arm with his other hand. Without any words, we were suddenly bounding up those stairs in a most determined manner and on into the coop.

As we entered, it was chaos as the dog, with white feathers hanging from his mouth, stopped with his tail wagging as he looked at us for a minute and then darted off as he resumed his chasing the chickens that were squawking and flying all over the place. Some were trying to fly outside as they slammed against the closed windows while others were bounding about on the roasts, feeders, water fountains and nests. It formed a busy scene as the air had become saturated with chickens, straw, dust and feathers which were made quite visible in the sunlight that was brightly shining through the windows. For a while I even lost sight of the dog as I was blinded by the dust that was getting into my eyes.

Closing the door behind him to prevent the dog from escaping, my dad immediately started after him. It seemed that ever since the time in Duluth when my dad dragged me off with him to see Jeanie's dad that whenever there was some sort of crisis my dad would grab me by the wrist and drag me off with him. I suppose that he really brought me along to help him catch the dog, but I never got a chance to do anything. My dad really didn't need me, because it didn't take him any time at all as he darted under the roosts and came out and stood up with a firm hold of that dog. I was there to witness as my dad completely restrained the dog with one hand and then with the other he started beating on him so horribly with that stick.

I remember it quite vividly, as I was watching through my tears, while that dog was yelping loudly from the pain that he was receiving from each one of those hard blows that my dad was now administering so abundantly. As I stood there watching I was scared for the dog and because none of us kids would dare face up to our dad by telling him what he should do. Nevertheless, I heard myself screeching the words to him, **"Daddy, stop! Please!** *You are going to* **kill** *him!"* What I said made no difference as he continued with the whipping and I again, in a last attempt, called to him even louder, **"Please, Daddy stop!"**

I don't know if he even heard me and it probably wouldn't have mattered if he had. He just continued with the beating. It seemed like it was an awfully long time and I was really worried for my dog's life. I felt a lot of relief when my dad finally did stop beating on him. I then watched as my dad angrily dragged that dog to top of the stairs. He opened the door and then with one hand firmly holding the dog by the back of the neck and the other held him by some loose skin near the dog's rump. My dad lifted the limp body and heaved him outward toward the feed room. He threw that dog so hard that its body bounced off only the last two steps on his descent.

My dad turned and without saying a word just started working at cleaning up the mess. He was taking straw and feathers out of the drinking fountains and straightening up the feeders that had been knocked about in all of the commotion.

My curiosity brought me to the doorway and as I looked down to the bottom of the stairs where I had expected to see the dog just lying there dead. I watched in amazement to see that the dog was standing and barely able to limp away from the feed room where he had landed. With his head down and his rump sort of curled downwards and his tail between his legs, he managed to climb over the high door sill to the outside.

I knew that my dad expected me to help him with putting things right and I wasn't going to disappoint him. He then opened one of the windows and I helped him gather up handfuls of the wet straw and throw it out of the window. After we had everything pretty well straightened out, my dad then brought up a bale of straw and we broke the bale and spread the dry straw around. He went after another bale and we did the same until things were looking pretty decent. We then went out of the coop; with my dad heading towards the house.

I waited until my dad had completely disappeared inside the house and when I was sure that he couldn't see me, I went to where the dog was lying. He had only gone a short distance to the back of the coop where he found a place to lie down against the building. His tail started to wag a bit as soon as I sat down beside him. I soothingly talked to him as I was petting his head. I felt so sorry for him and I knew that he must be aching. I told the dog that I understood and as I cried for him I said, "I know that you didn't mean any harm. You just wanted to have some fun didn't you?" The dog was soon wagging its tail in a somewhat feeble manner. I didn't know that what I was doing just then may have been the worst thing I could have done for that dog, because I was sort of validating what the dog had done.

That dog obviously didn't learn a thing from that beating, because it was only several days later, after he had recovered from his beating, he did exactly the same thing again. My dad got a stick as he had the time before and I thought that this time he would surely beat our pet to death. I was pleasantly surprised when our dad went into the chicken house and hit the dog with the stick a few times as he chased the dog outside and closed the door on the coop. The dog ran toward the house where my brothers and I had been playing. My dad then went into the house and within a couple of minutes he emerged carrying his rifle. Just seeing him with the weapon really frightened me.

The dog seemed to sense that he was in trouble. As soon as he saw my dad with the gun, he started slowly in a sort of sideways trot away from us and down the driveway towards the road. His head was lowered and turned to the side and he was looking back as he was moving away. The dog even stopped once and looked back as though he was just waiting for us to call him back and then he turned and continued on down the drive. My brothers and I stood without saying a word. It was so sad and I could feel my dad's determination to forever end his problem with that dog. I also knew that it would do no good to plead with my dad for the dog's life, and I didn't. Horrified, I watched as my dad lifted the rifle, placed the butt against his shoulder, took careful aim, and squeezed the trigger. My whole body jerked as I heard the loud sharp noise from the gun, and at the same instant the dog's whole body went limp as he dropped dead on the spot. It took just a single bullet to do the job.

It happened so quickly, but I found that there wasn't any satisfaction in knowing that the dog probably spent no time suffering. I also knew that I would be missing a dear friend. After that our dad just turned to Pat and me and said, "Take care of him." We understood what he meant as we accepted the sad and dirty job of taking care of the body. We each grabbed one of the dog's rear legs as we started pulling at that lifeless body, with its tongue hanging out and the head dangling along as it was moving in an uncontrollable side to side motion and bouncing on the ground. When we got the dog to the gravel pit, Pat and I pushed its body side ways to the edge and then watched as it tumbled to the bottom. We would become exceptionally familiar with this trip that took us past the chicken coop and out to the gravel pit to a final resting place where all of our dead and unwanted items went.

At first I was mad at my dad and I thought he was so mean and heartless. I knew that I wouldn't dare express any of my anger towards him and it would even cause me to cry about it for a few days afterwards. At times like that, it was my mother who was always there to help me to understand and to console me. I even told her how much I hated my dad. She explained to me that the eggs we got from those chickens were our livelihood and we couldn't tolerate having a dog like that. She also said, "I don't think that it was easy for your dad to do that, but he didn't know what else to do." Even though what she was telling me made sense to my young mind, it didn't ease my anger with my dad. I was still hurting and I felt a real need for her right then.

I later realized that maybe our dad did have some sense of compassion and he must have understood just how badly my brothers and I felt about losing that dog, because he got us another one within a couple of weeks. The new dog that he got for us was a female and a breed of sheep dog with tan and white long, soft hair. We simply gave her the name Poochie. Her life was assured, because she showed no interest at all in the chickens. That dog really had no special talents, but she was friendly and we soon learned to love her too. Actually she was even a nicer dog than the other one.

One night in late October our mother and father left my brothers and me alone with a farm boy that lived about a mile and a half from us. They had hired him to be our baby-sitter. It was a very cold night, and he decided to allow Poochie to come into the house with us. That dog had never been allowed to come into the house before. Naturally, my brothers and I were quite happy to have our excited dog come inside and play with us. We petted and fondled with Poochie as we visited with the baby-sitter until quite late.

My brothers and I were finally sent to bed, and we had no idea that something had gone wrong until very late during the night. I was awakened quite suddenly by my dad's loud, angry voice. I was able to figure out that he was upset about something that the baby-sitter must have done but I couldn't tell what it was. The only part of the conversation that I remember was my dad's loud voice saying, *"You'll **never** baby-sit for us again!"* Then quite hurriedly my dad and the baby-sitter left in the truck.

As soon as I heard the panel truck heading down the driveway, I knew that my dad was taking the baby-sitter home. I also knew that it was now safe for me to get out of bed. I went out to see my mother who was in the kitchen. She knew why I was there because, without a word, she led me straightaway into the living room. I could immediately see what had happened. Lying in the upholstered chair was Poochie who looked very happy to see me. I could see what had caused the problem as Poochie lay there and was quite proud of her litter of squirming little pups. I also saw that the chair she was on looked a mess because it was dirty and there was a lot of blood smeared about that chair. That really scared me because it was still quite vivid in my mind what our dad had done to the other dog for his transgressions. I could tell that my mother was worried too. She said, "Your dad is really upset about what happened here. I don't know what he is going to do about it. I know he was awfully mad about this but I just hope he doesn't take it out on the dog." I obeyed when she told me that I had better get back to bed "before your dad gets home."

That would be the last time that any dog would ever again see the inside of our house, because Poochie ruined an expensive upholstered chair that night when she gave birth to her large litter of puppies. Our dad was angry, because the chair was part of a set that matched the couch that we had. That chair wound up as just another bit of garbage in that infamous gravel pit. That also turned out to be the last time that we would ever have a baby sitter when our parents went somewhere without us. From that time on, whenever they went somewhere without us kids, we were left alone to take care of ourselves.

The next day, in my mind at least, I was to receive more evidence to convince me that my dad really was a terribly mean person. He was without any feelings, because now it seemed to me that he was being dreadfully cruel. I watched in horror as our dad removed each one of Poochie's helpless female puppies, with its eyes still closed. He took them outside and then he raised each squirming pup high above his head and with all of his might he slammed the helpless creature down onto the hard gravel driveway. I could feel it in my body as each of those babies hit the hard gravel, which immediately ended the wee thing's life. He did it all over again until we only had the two male puppies left and he eventually gave those away. Pat and I had the job of putting the tiny dead bodies into our wagon and making another one of those dreaded journeys with some new occupants for our gravel pit.

My brothers and I each owned one pair of shoes. Because Pat was bigger than I, he always wore about one shoe size larger than I. To save money, my parents had planned for me to get Pat's shoes as he outgrew them. Fortunately for me, that wasn't going to happen too often, and I can remember that it only happened twice during my youth. Even those times it was just a very temporary thing until new shoes could be afforded for me. Pat was hard on shoes, so most of the time they would become too worn out to be of any service before the time he had finally outgrown them.

I don't remember ever having very many clothes. I believe that we only had about two of each item, so that we could wear something when our others were being washed. I remember that no matter what we were wearing of our different articles of clothing we would wear it for at least a week or two at a time.

A belt was the one item of clothing that my brothers and I were not allowed to have. I found out at a very young age that our dad had strong feelings about things and only his way was the right way. Dad felt that we shouldn't have a belt during the time we were growing. He felt that suspenders were much better for us, but I hated them. Most of the other kids wore belts and I envied them. Having a nice belt would only be a wish of mine.

Another piece of clothing that I strongly coveted was a white Hudson Bay coat, with the red, black, yellow and green colored stripes around the bottom. I often saw one of the wealthier men in town always wearing one in the winter. From the first time that I saw it, I thought that it was the most beautiful coat that I had ever seen. I promised myself that one day I would be rich enough to buy one.

Some of our clothes were bought from a store or from the Sears catalog, but much of what we wore was handmade by our mother. She had a treadle operated Singer sewing machine, which required no electricity to operate it. She was quite resourceful with it as she busily worked the treadle back and forth with her feet. It seemed that she could do such amazing things with a bare minimum of resources. She saved lots of the white cloth feed sacks that were always so abundantly available from our dad's store and with Rit dye she turned them into many different colors. Without a single commercially made pattern, she was able to make the different articles of clothing that my brothers and I required. We were quite pleased to wear the extremely nice clothes she fashioned out of that sack material.

I remember during our first summer on our farm that our mother created two identical tan shirts and two pairs of tan long pants for Pat and me. It was a time during the Second World War, so we were especially proud to be wearing what looked very much like army dress uniforms. She also made Tom and Richard each a light blue shirt and pair of blue shorts, which made them, look like they were wearing a different kind of uniform. Of course, in the winter we had all the added paraphernalia to put on such as caps, scarves, snow pants, coats, overshoes, mittens, snow pants, and of course it would be unthinkable to consider going outside without wearing long underwear.

We had no store-bought toys, so we fashioned our own. My brothers Pat, Tom, and I were really quite artistic and creative. I believe that it was out of this necessity that we became quite competent at manufacturing so many of our own things. Most of what we made came from the materials that were so plentiful around us which on this farm just happened to be a gigantic supply of tar paper and the enormous amount of wood scraps. We made all kinds of animals, cars, trucks, tractors, and even little houses and barns which provided us with endless hours of play. We wore gun and holster sets that were made out of this tar paper and we were even able to make the belt that was required. I think that one of the real benefits was that our imaginations were being constantly provided with plenty of exercise.

We also built some of our toys from many of the bits of lumber we found lying about that was left over from the remaking of the barn into that chicken coop. We did the necessary cutting with a rusty old saw that the former owners had left behind to be thrown away. To an adult, our toys were probably quite crude, but from our point of view they were some of the neatest creations ever made. As simple as they were, they more than satisfied our needs and kept us happy and busy. We never heard of the word recycle, but we were certainly doing it. I think that we really found more enjoyment from the process of making the toys than actually playing with them. We did get an immeasurable amount of satisfaction and pride out of playing with all of the various things that we had fabricated for ourselves.

We felt fortunate to discover several tins of paint that were stored in the wood shed and garage that had been left behind by the previous owners of the farm. Even though some of that paint was in what we considered the most hideous colors, we made use of it. Our dad probably would never have found a use for any of it, but we couldn't really be certain of that. We never considered asking him for the paint out of fear that he just might say no. Without getting his permission, we felt that it was necessary to conceal the fact that we were using the paint. That paint was just too much of a temptation for our artistic skills to resist using it to add some color to some of our tar paper and wood creations. The former owners were also quite accommodating by provided us with some old brushes which would fulfill the rest of our requirements.

Although we were quite sure that we probably shouldn't have that paint, but we continued to use it anyway. Besides, each time that we pried off the lids, we would only use a small amount from each tin. Another thing, we always had a pretty good sense about when our dad was due to come home. When it was about the right time, one of us was assigned to watch for him and after seeing his black panel truck and the large cloud of dust trailing after, as it had just passed the Vlack farm our time was up. We had to hurry and put the brushes in the turpentine, pound on the lids, and put everything away just so. We had just enough time to get things put right before he would come speeding up our driveway. I would never know if our dad even cared, but we never had any plans of finding out by getting caught. Some of the tins of paint did eventually get emptied and the evidence wound up in the gravel pit. That was a place where I can never recall that our dad went so the evidence was as good as being destroyed.

My dad never liked working for others and he was always searching for schemes to make lots of money. It was soon after we got settled in with the chicken ranch when my dad decided to make another financial investment. Instead of increasing the amount of the loan that he already had, he took out another loan to purchase an established business on the main street of Rib Lake called the Farmers Feed Company. It was a small family owned feed store that had been in the same place for many years. It had a very limited volume of business, serving a small number of farmers in the area. My father believed that the store offered a lot of potential, and he already had ideas for making that business grow.

At the time I remember that it really excited me and made me feel quite proud that my dad was now the owner of an important establishment in town, and that he was also successful at his other business. Without a doubt I was enjoying the most wonderful time of my short life and I felt as though I was on top of the world.

I could tell that our new situation was also making a big difference with my dad. I think that it restored much of the self esteem that he had lost at some time after his accident. It was also obvious that he had become a much happier person, because he seemed to always have money and he treated my mother, my brothers and me more kindly than at any other time that I could remember.

One of the most pleasant memories that I have is about an old man with a wooden leg who sat, most days, with his chair propped up against the outside wall of the feed store. He seemed to be constantly whittling little wooden things. He seemed to specialize in carving wooden whistles, with holes on top for fingering so when you blew into the end; it was capable of producing a full octave of eight different notes. He would gladly make one for any of us kids who only had to ask for one.

Our special treat came while he was busily putting his knife to work; he was able at the same time to tell neat stories to the children.

You could tell that he genuinely liked us. All the kids would sit on the wooden walk in front of him and spend many happy hours listening to all the exciting stories being uttered by his gravelly voice.

That man's wooden leg didn't resemble a leg at all; instead it was just a round piece of wood that started somewhere near the knee. At the top part, it was about as big around as his leg would have been, and it gradually tapered to about the size of a half dollar where it came into contact with the surface he walked on. I believe you could call it a peg leg. He had to be careful when walking on the wooden walkway, because the end could get caught in the larger cracks. To us kids, I assume that the others thought as I did about his wooden leg being the same as a normal leg on any other person.

One day during a break in the story that he was telling, I got bold enough to ask that old man if that one leg of his was really made of wood. I remember that my question seemed to provide encouragement to all of the other kids that were gathered round. In unison they began asking "Yeah, is that leg *really* wood?" The old man immediately responded to satisfy our curiosity. Without saying another word and in order to offer us proof, he surprised all of us when he took his sharp knife and carved a chunk out of "his leg!" The impression it made on me, after seeing the lighter area where he had just removed that piece of his "leg," was one of absolute astonishment. I can recall that it had left me and the others in awe.

I got the impression that my dad didn't like this man, but just seemed to tolerate his being there. I never heard my dad say one word to him and I was afraid to ask why.

Another thing that made my living in Rib Lake so wonderful was that I seemed to have much less problems with my health. For the first time in my life I was able to drink my milk without having that horrid-tasting dextrose-maltose mixed into it any more. Even though I didn't know what it was for, I still was obligated to swallow one pill every morning.

I can remember that my dad often times made remarks that I didn't understand. An example of this is when one of my brothers or I came into the house without taking off our cap. He would say, "How come you're wearing your cap in the house? What do you think you are, Jewish?" The only thing that I understood in those two sentences was that I had better take my cap off or he would make me wish I had. I had no idea what being Jewish was. In fact I didn't even know that I was Catholic but I was to find out quite soon.

It was in Rib Lake that I remember seeing the inside of a Catholic church for the very first time in my life. Until that time I had a very limited concept of what religion was, other than I heard about Catholics, Lutherans, Presbyterians and Methodists. Now I was about to find out that I was a Catholic.

I had just begun the second grade when my dad took my brothers and me to see the Saint John's Catholic Church in town. I remember upon entering that I just stood there in astonishment. I had never seen anything like it in my life. I found it to be so magnificent to see the fancy alter, the lifelike and almost life-size statues of Christ and the saints. I remember seeing the tiers of votive candles and each one gave off a flickering light that was glowing through their pretty red and blue glass. I wanted to ask my dad about them but I didn't; in fact none of us said a word. The church didn't have any lights on but the sun shining through each stained-glass window gave off bright colored rays of light and how illuminating it was. I noticed all of the wood pews and it was obvious to me what they were for. It was also extremely quiet and peaceful as I stood there. I could sense something strange and as we walked out and I was leaving with a sort of eerie feeling inside.

I really didn't know what to think when our dad explained that my brothers and I would be attending church here every Sunday. I also wondered why he hadn't said anything about him and our mother coming here with us. While we were there, we met Father Gengler, the pastor, and we stood there as our dad talked to him about his four boys. It was at this time our dad also got my brothers and I signed up to attend the Saturday morning catechism classes. I didn't like what I had just heard, because it had become quite obvious to me that we would now be coming here on both Saturday and Sunday.

Because of that church visit my brothers and I had to walk the distance of about two and one-half miles each way to attend those classes every Saturday morning in the basement of the church and then take the same route back home again. We had to endure that same round trip the next day as we were obligated to attend the Sunday morning Mass. Our dad was making no exceptions; we *had* to go!

One of the first things that we learned in those Saturday classes was about venial and mortal sins and the bad effect they have on your soul. The worst possible kind of the two was the mortal sin and Missing Sunday Mass was a mortal sin. We soon learned that if you died with a mortal sin on your soul, you were no longer in a state of grace and would go straight to hell where you would burn in the fires for eternity. Eternity became another word to be added to our vocabulary just then. I found it to be so confusing and I wondered why my mother and father should be exempt from those sins. We came to know a God that was very strict and wouldn't hesitate to give punishment if a person was naughty. Everything that I did from now on was going to be governed by a catechism book and the teachings of the Catholic Church. My whole life was being affected as a result of all the new information that I was receiving in those Saturday lessons.

Our dad never once volunteered to drive us to church on the weekends. The walk could sometimes be quite an ordeal, especially in the winter time, with the deep snow and the cold. After some time Pat, Tom and I, in order to decrease the distance, discovered a shorter way by traveling through fields and over and under fences. The trip was still almost two miles each way. There were many times that the trip was almost enough for me to wish that I was not a Catholic and I had never even seen that church.

Another reason that I didn't like going to church was that my mother and dad didn't go with us. I finally did get used to that and I eventually accepted it. There was also a third reason for my contempt which I would never get used to: and that was the fact that in the Mass we were required to kneel at all the appropriate times, and that would cause my lower back to ache terribly. I was always sort of afraid to call attention to myself and do differently, so I just suffered and anxiously waited for the priest's final blessing.

I didn't know whether our dad was checking up on us or if he was truly interested, because each time when we returned home from church, he always asked us so many questions. We had to be able to explain in great detail what we learned in the Saturday catechism classes. On Sundays we had to tell our dad what the gospel was and what it was teaching us. We also had to tell him what the priest's sermon was about in that Mass.

On our way home from church Pat and I would talk about it so that we knew what we would tell dad about the sermon. Occasionally we would have difficulty remembering the homily, but since the priest was so often asking for money for different reasons we would just tell Dad, "He just spent most of the time asking for money, but I can't remember what it was for." He seemed satisfied that it was true, and besides telling a lie was only a venial sin. At the time I didn't like the interrogation, but I think that I might have profited from this. It did make me listen carefully to everything that was said in church especially the gospel because I thought that Dad could check up on that. I also remember that he gave me a whole nickel for being the first one of us to learn the Lord's Prayer by heart.

On Saturday we were taught from the catechism and some prayers to say at certain times. Before going to bed we were taught to say: "*Good night, dear Jesus. Bless all my work and play. Keep me safe through the night until I awake to pray.*" I never failed to say this prayer quietly to myself every night when I went to bed.

We were also taught a prayer to say before meals: "*Bless us o' Lord for these thy gifts which we are about to receive from thy bounty though Jesus Christ our Lord, Amen.*" We told our dad the prayer and I thought that we would be saying it together as a family. He then said, "I'll say my prayer: "*Bless the bread, damn the meat, pass the spuds, and let us eat.*" With that our saying any prayers together before meals had ended forever.

I don't remember ever seeing our dad or mother going to church, but our dad certainly held us accountable for our attendance. I knew that my father belonged to no religion; but I always wondered why my mother didn't go with us, because she was Catholic. I wouldn't get a satisfactory answer to that until a couple of years later.

One of the nicer things about living on that farm was that there were several acres of raspberry bushes. I used to tie a rope around my waist and then take a gallon Karo Syrup tin and loop the wire handle around the rope and let it hang, which would free both of my hands for picking. I remember going out there often, all by myself, and picking that pail full of raspberries. My mother always seemed to be so happy when I returned with my pail filled with raspberries. I would get one of those "I love you so much, I could just squeeze the puddin' out of you" hugs. That was enough encouragement for me to go out and pick even more. During the summer I think that I filled many of those syrup tins. Our whole family enjoyed raspberry shortcake and we could have it often and what wasn't eaten, my mother canned.

Rib Lake is located near the large Chequamegon National Forest, and even most of the farms are separated by all of the many other wooded areas nearby. We soon became quite aware that in any large woodland that had burned down recently, among the shrubs that had begun to grow back, wild blueberries would appear in abundance.

Our father was kept extremely busy with his two places of work, and he had very little time for anything else. Our mother didn't drive and she relied on my dad for transportation; but occasionally there were times we were able to get on without our dad. Blueberry picking was one of those rare occasions. One of the neighbors who owned a truck would volunteer to take our mother, my brothers, and me along with his family to one of those perfect places to pick blueberries. My mother, my brothers and I along with their kids piled into the back of the truck. My brothers and I were always anxious to go along. We enjoyed the trip and having fun with the other children.

It was our mother, two other women, and the one man who did almost all of the picking. My brothers and I would pick blueberries for only a short while. It wasn't like picking raspberries where you could stand and easily pick from the bushes. The blueberries grew near the ground among little bushes and fallen trees. Furthermore, blueberries were so small that it seemed to take forever to collect what seemed a decent amount. My brothers and I just didn't have the patience for that, it bothered my lower back and our mother showed no signs of disappointment that we didn't help. My brothers and I spent most of our time there just playing around with a couple of the other kids who had come along.

When we came home at the end of the day, our mother would have a wash tub more than half full of those tiny and precious wild blueberries. Most of those small berries were canned, to be eaten during the long winter. The pies that she made from those blueberries became my favorite, and for me blueberry pie still remains high on my list of favorite things to eat. I will always miss not being able to enjoy the special taste of those wild blueberries.

Our mother seemed to always be busy in some way. In the summer she planted and took good care of a nice garden, which she had seeded with all kinds of vegetables. That garden provided our family with a large variety of fresh vegetables to eat during the summer and early fall. I really enjoyed eating many of the vegetables raw, right out of the garden. Our mother canned a tremendous amount of blueberries, raspberries, and beets, green beans, peas, tomatoes, onions, turnips, and different kinds of pickles. We were quite fortunate to receive such an excellent diet, of all these good foods during the rest of the year. It saved us a lot of money because we didn't have to buy any canned goods at a store.

All during my youth, whenever I was faced with any problems, I would always be prepared to run away rather than face up to them. I hated confrontation; but if I couldn't avoid it I was immediately prepared to throw rocks. I was to be feared because I could throw very hard and I was quite accurate. I found this to be beneficial when I was having some apparently unsolvable disagreement with my brothers. I could, and on some occasions did, back my three brothers down the gravel road by throwing small rocks at them as they were throwing back at me. I could also throw farther, and I was always able to keep them out of range from hitting me, so I was rarely hit and never with enough force to hurt me. So with three against one they were still no match for me.

We would continue throwing at each other until one of my brothers got hit badly enough in the head to cause blood to flow. That would end our differences and out of concern for the injured one we would all run into the house. Our mother would then have to listen to us all talking at once with several versions of what had caused this. She calmly took care of the wound and she always would tell us that we shouldn't be throwing rocks. We didn't really pay much attention to what she had said, and later on another similar incident would end with almost the same consequences.

The fact that I could throw so hard with accuracy didn't go unnoticed by my dad. One day he surprised us when he brought home some baseball playing equipment: gloves, ball, catcher's mitt and a bat. My brothers and I were completely ignorant of the game but after a brief explanation and the objective of the game he immediately started me out to be the pitcher. In his way of teaching us, he began by taking his stance, with the bat, next to the "plate" that had been marked off on the ground. He told me that I had to throw the ball straight across the "plate" and into the catcher's mitt that my brother Pat was wearing. I did as he told me, but I was very careful not to throw very hard. My dad started out by nicely hitting the ball back for me or Tom to try to catch it or run it down.

After we had done this for awhile, I threw him the ball as I had done so many times before but this time he decided to really swing away. He connected solidly with that ball and without any time to react, I caught that ball in my stomach. The force was enough that in that instant I went down like a sack of feed and just laid there on my back and groaning a bit. At first I couldn't even breathe! He and my brothers stood over me for awhile. Dad did seem to be concerned for a bit as he knelt down beside me. When he felt that I was going to be all right he stood up and showed me no more sympathy, so I finally got up.

Even though I got hurt, I continued to pitch to him, but now I had some fear of being hit again like that. I can remember getting hit only one more time in almost exactly the same way. I eventually did learn to like pitching to my dad, but not until I realized that I could throw well enough to make it extremely hard for him to really make good contact with the ball. I did worry about Pat having to catch what I was throwing. I learned to enjoy throwing and catching the ball, but I never cared very much for the batting part of the game.

My dad even talked about the day when I could possibly become a great pitcher along with Pat being my catcher something like Dizzy and Daffy Dean who were brothers and used to play in the major leagues. He was already anticipating my future with two very different possibilities, one as a medical doctor and the other as a baseball pitcher. I think that I was too young to really think seriously about any occupation just yet. It was sad for us that our dad was always so busy that he would get so little time enough to play with my brothers and me. With him playing with us, we didn't have any arguments or fights and that was nice. My brothers and I really did get a lot of pleasure from the precious little time that we had with our father.

Our dear Irish grandfather, Peter Dufficy, was living in North Dakota at this time; but about once a month he would send a money order to his daughter, who just luckily happened to be my mother. That money order always came with a letter to our mother telling about the latest news and it was this way that she found out he got a new wife. He also ended each letter the same way with, *"With oceans of love, from your dad,"* and he signed it. My brothers and I didn't need to see him to know that we liked him a lot.

This was an especially exciting time for our whole family. My mother would immediately get out the latest Sears, Roebuck catalog with well over a thousand pages of really neat things. My brothers and I would gather around on the couch and look on with her at the many different things that we wished we could have, but our mother could hardly afford to buy any more than what was absolutely needed. I remember one of the things that we kids seemed to always hope for was a farm set made out of a heavy cardboard with the house, barn, silo, fences, animals and even a tractor with wheels that turned. That would remain only a wish, because we just couldn't afford it. The money order that our mother received right before Christmas was a larger amount than the others and it was the one time that each of us kids did get to choose a nice, inexpensive present.

Our mother would have to plan very carefully how she could best spend that limited amount of money on us. She saw to it that each one of us got something that was needed, which was typically clothing. Then she would usually buy one nice, reasonably-priced dress or a pair of shoes for herself.

I continued to have a quite a bit of difficulty at times with activities such as walking and running, because something in the lower part of my back must have been damaged when I was injured in the orphanage. Even though it got somewhat better it still caused me to have a lot of pain on the left side of my lower backside and my left leg. I am also quite sure that is what created all the difficulty for me when kneeling in church. Some days were much worse than others, and on those bad days I just didn't feel like doing much of anything.

My dad explained it to me that I had to accept it as fact that I was destined to have some trouble with my lower back for the rest of my life. There were many times when I was getting dressed in the morning that just putting on my socks would be quite a painful adventure. On some occasions when it was at its worst my brother Pat would, understandably, say that he thought that I was lazy. That hurt but I never complained about it I just accepted it as normal for me. My mother and father were the only ones who really understood.

My affliction seemed to bother my dad more than me. He seemed to show a strong distaste for any kind of physical imperfections in people. I could tell by the way he behaved towards the old man with the wooden leg in front of the store. He treated him with absolute indifference. I observed him being somewhat nasty with another farmer, and I felt that it was just because that man was stooped over and was deformed with a large humpback. I even considered that my dad thought of me in somewhat the same way. I had been flawed, but he also wanted to believe that there was something that could be done to fix it.

My father finally gave up at obtaining any help for me from medical doctors. It was at this time that my dad had heard about something that sounded quite innovative to him and possibly offered the promise of some real help for me and my particular situation. There was a Doctor Peter Peitersen, a chiropractor, who had been practicing his profession in Medford, Wisconsin, which was about sixteen miles south of Rib Lake. My dad had a long conversation with him one day as he explained about me and my problem. That Doctor convinced my father that he may be able to offer me some relief.

The next time we went to Medford my dad left me in the care of Dr. Peitersen for about an hour of treatment. We were both hoping that possibly I would receive the help I needed. Nothing was noticed after that first treatment but my dad continued to take me to that doctor every time we got back to Medford. It was truly amazing, because it was some time after the first two treatments that I appeared to be showing some signs of improvement. It now became about a fortnight regimen of taking the trip to Medford for me to spend that hour with Doctor Peitersen and I continued to show progress.

Within that first year of operation, my dad's business became successful far beyond his dreams. Because he had more than doubled the volume of trade with the regional farmers, he was soon forced to move his whole inventory into a larger and better building. The floor in the first structure had started to sag and it was threatening to collapse under the enormous weight created by all of those piles of hundred pound sacks of feed.

The prosperity of the war years and the large saw mill was enough to keep this small town a thriving community. There was only one empty building available on the main street of the town. That building seemed to be perfectly suited to my dad's needs for size and location. It was situated in the same block and on the same side of the street as his present location, so moving his merchandise required minimal time and work. The new place was a much larger and a far better-constructed building.

Everything seemed to be going so well that within days after his relocation my dad decided to celebrate with a grand opening. He chose the fourth of September and he placed an ad in the Rib Lake Herald advertising the occasion. The event was a success and many of the farmers from miles around came to see the new store and to enjoy the free food and drinks. It was grand and I think that right then our whole family felt like we were on top of the world. I was so proud of my father and my outlook on life was at a peak. I felt that it would last forever; at least I was hoping that it would.

I can remember that from my point of view, the back part of the new store was never very much to look at. To me it seemed to be very little more than numerous mountains of one-hundred-pound sacks of feed, with names like Larro, Gold Medal and North Star. The office was situated in the northwest corner of the store front, with a high counter and the cash register. That was the part that really made the most pleasing impression on me and I cherished the many times I spent there.

Just as soon as we were dismissed from school, I would frequently and impatiently run all the way down to the store which was a distance of about four blocks. It made me feel so grown up and I was so proud of myself to be standing behind the counter. I would even pretend that I was the proprietor. Sometimes when there were customers about, I felt that I was being helpful by visiting with them while they were waiting to see either my dad or the hired man. How could my dad possibly run that business without me?

Fridays were especially enjoyable for me because I was able to help by counting and stacking into neat piles all of the coins that my dad had received by the end of the week. I would then count out all the paper money and have the amounts of each denomination all tallied and written neatly on a sheet of paper. All that my dad had to do was put it all together in a sack and carry it off to the bank. My figures were always correct, because my dad had taught me to always double check everything and just like in school it had to be perfect. At other times I might just watch and visit with my dad and his hired help as they worked.

There was another advantage to going down to the store after school: I didn't have to spend so much time riding that awful school bus. I still had a lot of trouble with my back and the rough ride was a bit painful. It seemed like it took almost forever to get home, because after the bus left the Ward School it had to make a stop at the other school, and we had to wait until the fourth through eighth grade kids were dismissed. When everyone had boarded, we were destined for a long and bumpy ride that seemed to wind all over the countryside. When it finally got to our drop-off, we still had almost a half mile to walk. Even though I was guaranteed a ride home in our dad's panel truck it was a special treat when I got to ride with him on other days.

When we were at the store, there were times that Pat and I did a lot of make believe play. Sometimes we would operate the special Atlas platform scale in the back room. We changed the slotted, circular weights that hung on a steel rod on the right side. Then you had to slide the smaller weights on their metal bars that had been etched with numbers and lines similar to a ruler but represented the pounds and ounces until the arm balanced in mid air which indicated that you had the right weight. We got a lot of practice weighing ourselves and all kinds of other objects that we piled onto that scale. Sometimes we made it into a sort of game by trying to guess the weight of something and then weighing it to see how close we could come to its actual weight. We got pretty good at estimating weights of various items and I think that we weighed just about everything that wasn't attached to the building.

We were really very limited in the amount that we could be of help to our dad in the store though, because it took both Pat and me working together on each end to roll and slide a single one hundred-pound sack of feed. Sometimes our dad would load sacks of feed into the back of his panel truck where Pat and I could feel that we were being helpful by rolling the bottom layer of sacks up towards the front for him.

However, my happiness did get interrupted by an occasional problem that I had with getting infections. A good example of that is the day I somehow got a small cut on the tip of the index finger of my right hand and being right handed it really caused me more than a spot of bother. It started out as nothing more than a small break in the skin, but it received no attention and soon became badly infected and began to hurt terribly. At the time I know that I was hoping that it would get better and go away without any care. I had become too afraid of what I might receive as treatment to let anyone know about it. Finally, after a few days, that finger had really swelled up; and the pain was becoming intolerable. There was a faint red streak going up the finger and into my hand, and it wasn't long before there was a noticeable reddish streak had started up my right arm.

On that morning my dad first found out about the finger, it was because my mother had told him. At the time I sort of felt betrayed by her. When my dad looked at the finger it became quite apparent that he was extremely concerned. Of course, he was also more than a bit upset with me as he scolded me and shouted, **"Why didn't you tell me before now?"** And then he added, "What were you waiting for - someone to drag your dead body to the gravel pit?" And of course, those words really frightened me.

He always expected an answer to his questions. It was the only time in my life that I didn't immediately answer one of his questions. I never did answer either of those questions as the tears were building up in my eyes. When he had finished eating his breakfast, and with obvious urgency he immediately pulled me from my chair saying, "We haven't got all day." And then he ordered, *"Get in the car!"*

I rushed out and I was waiting in the panel truck before he got there. He continued to give me a good talking-to as he sped down our gravel driveway and all the way into town. The only thing that I remember him telling me during the ride was, "Do you know when that red line goes up your arm and past your shoulder to your heart, you will be dead?" I didn't know that and now I was really frightened because I had no idea how long that might take. If that was supposed to be another question, it was the third question in one day that went unanswered and remarkably there was no demand for any answers.

That was the fastest trip we ever made to town. Dad brought the truck to a sudden stop in front of his own store, but he didn't even go up and unlock the door as he was accustomed to doing on other mornings. Instead, he grabbed hold of my left hand and immediately dragged me across the truck seat and out onto the street. He began walking very fast and, still holding my hand, pulled me as I had to run to keep up with him. I didn't even know where we were going. We went diagonally across the street and into the drug store.

The druggist, an old man who wore thick glasses, looked at my injury and directed my dad and me into the back room, where he had all kinds of equipment and what seemed to me like hundreds of bottles and jars of medicines. My father sat on a stool and was holding me as I was just standing there while the druggist started rummaging through some drawers. After a while he turned around, holding some equipment which included a sharp mean-looking knife that had a strange concave curve to the edge side of the blade. At the same time he was making a few disparaging remarks like, "Maybe we should just cut off that finger. You really don't need it do you?" That was my fourth unanswered question in one day. I can tell you that he had me scared and I had already anticipated that whatever he did would be quite painful. He laid his instruments on the table beside us.

I was now standing with my back to my dad as he held me while he sat on the stool. The druggist sat on a stool in front of us and then grabbed my hand and studied it for a while. He then took a firm hold of my finger with one hand, as he immediately started directing that special knife with the other. He proceeded to cut the tip of that infected finger in two directions. He first cut my finger from side to side, parallel with the end of the nail, and then I watched as he cut right through the nail and down the other side, to divide the tip into four parts. That was painful enough but the worst was yet to come.

After that he peeled the finger open, to reveal four bloody wedges, much like you would get when opening an orange. He began scraping inside with a tool that had a short blade that looked almost like a combination knife and a small spoon. It was when he just began to scrape that the pain became so excruciating that I let out one bit of a yelp. The druggist looked at me fiercely; and being afraid of him and my dad, I immediately got quiet. I was now dealing with severe pain and the emotion of fear. I then remained quiet and I didn't cry out loud for pain which was a lesson I had learned so well in the orphanage but I was unable to stop my eyes from watering with tears. I kept still through the rest of the process, even though it all was tormenting me so terribly.

After he had finished all of the digging and scrapping, he washed the finger with something that burned terribly. Then he blew on it which made things much better as it began to feel cool. Next he sprinkled some white powdery stuff into the wound. I had no idea about what it was, but years later I realized that it probably was boric acid crystals. When he was finally finished, he took hold of my finger and tightly wrapped his fingers around it. He seemed to know what he was doing because when he squeezed the finger together very hard and held it that way for some time, the tip of my finger became numb. To my surprise it had actually stopped hurting, but I didn't know why.

The final step was to wrap the finger into a big bundle of white cloth. When the druggist had completed his work on my finger, he told my dad, "I think what I did may have just stopped the infection and maybe saved that boy's life. When he gets home have him soak it in hot water with Epson salts." He seemed a bit pensive and then said, "--- And if it didn't work then prayers are what that boy is going to need." (Another pause) "You may have to bring him back here again in a couple of days. Just keep an eye on it."

I, of course, hoped that he had succeeded in stopping the infection. I knew that I would be quite happy if I never got to see that guy again.

The lunch that my mother made for me had been completely forgotten in our rush to get to town. As soon as we left the drug store, my father took me to the cafe, and he paid to have them put a sandwich and a piece of pie into a sack for me. I took the lunch, and then he told me to get to school as he started heading the opposite way toward his feed store.

I did as I was told and started trotting off to school, but I didn't even get close to the building when the ache and throbbing in that finger really began in earnest. When I got into class, I had more than a spot of bother when I had to write, because the wound was on my right hand. There was the terrible pain, and the huge bandage covering the finger that wouldn't even allow me to feel my pencil. It was also frustrating, because I was always proud of my neat penmanship. Now I thought it was horrible! I always held the pencil firmly and carefully drew my letters, and now I wasn't able to do that.

The procedure that the druggist used was effective and it did stop the infection; but most of all I was ever so grateful that a return visit wasn't required. However, I believe that he managed to damage some nerves in the process, because when I touch something with the tip of that finger it has a strange feeling, compared to my other fingers. Even today I know that it's not quite right, because of that odd feeling.

In the first week of November, my grandfather Peter Dufficy, and his new wife came to visit us. My mother, of course, was really happy to have her dad spend some time with us. I never could understand why our dad just didn't seem to like my mother's dad at all and would ignore him most of the time. It was years later when I began to think that my dad was a bit jealous of him. I had seen this grandfather before but I couldn't recall what he looked like.

This time it would be different and I will remember him well. The first thing that I noticed was that he was so small when compared with my dad. He was also very different from my dad in many other ways. I couldn't help liking him immediately. He was extremely charming, so easy going, and he was joking with my brothers and me almost all of the time. He was also quite proud that he was Irish, and he would immediately let you know it. In fact, I once heard him brag that, "If I wasn't Irish, I'd be ashamed of me self." My brothers and I were thoroughly delighted to have him and his wife visit us. His wife was almost his opposite seeming to be more serious and very quiet. Grandpa Dufficy always had the time for us kids that our dad didn't and he spent a lot of that time with little tricks and just kidding around with us. I felt quite saddened when they finally had to leave.

Everything went the same as usual with us taking a cold lunch to school each day. We did that until on the 26th of November when we could now eat a hot lunch. Thanks to the federal government, it was the first time ever that a hot noon meal would be available to students at school. It only cost our parents 7 cents for the lunch and the government paid 9 cents of the cost. Almost every day we would now have a hot lunch. I remember the first hot lunch that I had was a goulash. Even though it wasn't like what our mother made, it was decent and I ate it.

All four of us boys had to sleep in the same unheated bedroom. The double bed that Pat and I slept in was against the east wall and a narrow isle separated it from the smaller bed that Tom and Richard had to crowd into for the night. The dresser which held all of our clothes was at the end of the isle against the south wall. I can remember when our parents went some place for the evening that we were sent to bed. When my brothers and I were sure mom and dad were gone we would turn on the light and stay up late. We had most of our fun in that bedroom as we would go from one bed across the isle. Then from the other bed we would climb on top of the dresser and cross over to the other bed that way.

On cold mornings, it was not uncommon for my brothers and me to quickly jump out of bed, grab our clothes, and run from the bedroom into the much warmer living room, where we got dressed.

My brothers and I each owned one pair of long, white underwear and I can remember that they got washed only a few times during the whole winter. They were made of cotton, and they had long sleeves and legs with a row of buttons that went down the front from your neck all the way to the crotch. There was a trap door in the rear that had a flap that was the full width of the garment. On each side of the flap was a button to hold it up, so we had to reach around for the button on one side and then to the other side to open or close that flap. When the flap was down, it served a very important purpose as it exposed your naked posterior. During the cold winter even that was more than you wished to bear or bare when you were performing a needed bodily function while seated over one of the holes in that little bitterly cold out house.

One exceedingly cold winter morning, my brother Tom got up ran from the bedroom, and he straightaway started warming up his long underwear by laying them on top of the living room stove. He left them on the stove just little too long, and his underwear caught on fire. The flames were quickly put out, but there were already several holes burned into the underwear by then. He wasn't going to get a new pair, so he still had to wear them the rest of that winter. There were many times before warmer weather of spring that he did freeze his skin where those holes were.

In school, I was always the top student in my class and I received nothing, but straight A's on my report cards. Because our dad would reward us for our grades, my brother Pat would get mad at me about it. He would often say then and for years afterwards, "Sonny, if you're so smart, why did you flunk the first grade?"

And every time my reply would be, "I just wish that some day you will get sick and have to miss a whole year of school and flunk a grade."

I didn't know it at the time that there was any possibility that my wish could possibly come true some day. After all, what was the likelihood that such a desire would really happen, but he did get me upset enough at times that I really did hope for it. It was some time later that our dad started rewarding us for our report cards, according to who showed the most improvement. It was impossible for me to improve on mine so then it was my turn to do a bit of complaining.

Pauly Hohl, a boy who had a voice that was lower in pitch than that of most men, sat just next to me in school. I felt that Pauly was a good friend of mine. But it was especially hard for me when I had to sit next to him in music class, because besides having such a low voice, he was also a monotone. I don't know why the teacher did it, but Pat and I had to sing "Jingle Bells" together with Pauly for one Christmas program. It turned out to be a disaster with our higher voices trying to blend with Pauly's voice. I don't think that it was intended to be humorous, but it did get a lot of laughs. I think that the parents who attended the program thought that it was supposed to be that way but being laughed at hurt my feelings. Pauly always seemed to be such a sad boy. I never saw him laugh, in fact, I don't remember seeing him with a just a bit of a smile on his face.

It happened one day at school when I was in the second grade, while we were having music class. I remember that we were singing the song "Plod Along, Plod Along the Santa Fe Trail," which probably was the only song that was somewhat suited to Pauly's low monotone voice; that is until you got to some very high notes in the verse which went "- - and the Indians watch us ride." Sitting next to Pauly was quite disconcerting as he was droning out those words more than a full octave below the notes that every one else was singing. It was all that I could do to keep from laughing.

On this particular day Pauly and I were sitting in the second row in music class when all of a sudden he gave me a painful jab in the ribs with his elbow. It hurt but it caught my attention and I had to look at him. He was pointing diagonally to my left at a girl in the front row. I looked to where he was pointing and immediately noticed the strange occurrence. Until then I had been unaware of it, but the girl was wetting her pants and the water was running down the chair. I really didn't find anything humorous in that. I then looked back at Pauly and I saw something I had never seen before. Pauly actually had a great big funny grin on his face, which caused me to begin laughing. I turned away and when I again turned to look at Pauly he had just turned straight-faced as though nothing had happened. Seeing his reaction just made the whole event appear all the more humorous and my laughter was now uncontrollable. Even though I tried, I couldn't stop laughing and it had long since caught the teacher's attention.

Just then the music class came to a halt as the teacher made the attempt to find out from me the reason for my behavior and I was helplessly unable to explain. I know that she then had quickly made the assumption that I was laughing at the unfortunate girl and she became really angry with me. She thought that I was insensitive and laughing at the poor girl that had the terrible accident. There was just no way that I could explain that it was Pauly that was making me laugh so. She would also let me know how much it had upset her with a permanent reminder on my very next report card.

My father began to anticipate the perfect grades that I always got in school. Pat and I received report cards every six weeks, or six times a year and this was the fifth reporting period. As soon as we received them, we were expected to take our cards to the feed store to show them to our dad. All the other four reporting periods I had nothing to worry about, and I could always feel quite proud about my card because I never had anything but A's.

I remember the day that I received the report card that followed, within a couple of weeks of that laughing incident in the music class. I was disappointed and more than just a bit afraid because the teacher had given me a "B." I knew it was because of what had happened in music class. I was worried about what my dad would think and especially what he would do to me. I also knew that he would expect me to explain why even though he never accepted any excuses.

My father was quite severe with us and the spanking would mean pulling down our pants, underpants, and bending over a chair as he applied the belt with a lot of force. It was hard enough that just sitting could be uncomfortable the next day. In fact, I was already prepared for receiving a proper spanking with his belt for such a transgression.

As I did every other time, I went to the feed store immediately after school but this time it took me a lot longer to get there. As he was expecting, I handed my report card to my dad. With all of the other boxes filled with A's, I already knew that there was no possibility that my dad might not notice that "B." To me, that "B" even looked much larger than any of the A's, so it just had to get his attention.

I was certain that a spanking was coming. I also knew that he was never concerned about who was around when he administered the punishment so I was also afraid that customers might be in the store and witness my bare skin receiving those lashes and I would be so embarrassed by it all. It seemed that my father rarely said much of anything to us kids except when he was disciplining; and boy.

Boy did he make me understand that he was upset with me after he had just one quick look at my report card. All I was hoping for was that he wouldn't get too angry with me. I could just feel that a hard spanking was coming soon. Fortunately there were no customers in the office at the time since no one interfered when he was disciplining one of his sons.

My dad never said a word about all of the A's I had. I didn't say anything, because I just couldn't explain to him the embarrassing reason for it. I also knew that he wasn't going to accept any excuses anyway. In a very angry voice, he scolded me about the bad grade and the first thing that he shouted to me was, **"Sonny, you should be ashamed of yourself!"** and "There is no excuse for this. You are setting a bad example for your brothers. - - - *and in something like music class?"* I forgot some of the other things he said to show his displeasure but the scolding only got worse. He was talking so loud and he was frightening me with his harsh words, but I was also delighted that, until now at least, I was only getting a scolding. He didn't spank me; he didn't even hit me, but I just knew that it was still coming. I was hurting inside though, because I knew that I had disappointed him so.

All the noise and fuss caught the attention of the hired man and to satisfy his curiosity, he came into the office from the back of the store. As he stood there he soon realized what my dad was angry about and he asked me if he could look at my report card, so I handed it to him. After looking at it, the hired man told me that he thought that I really did very well in school. "That's just about the best report card that I have ever seen." And then he told my father, "Roy, you should be proud that Sonny is doing that good in school."

My dad had intended to have me feel contrite about the "B" and he feared the hired man's words would have the opposite effect.

That last bit that he said was just the right thing to get my dad even more upset, but now he was directing all his anger towards the hired man. In a very loud voice my dad began giving *him* a real talking-to. I don't recall exactly the words my dad said, but I do remember that much of it had something to do with others interfering with the way he disciplined of his children.

It was so frightening for me to watch those two big giants hovering over me, and my dad displaying his intense displeasure because of something that I had done. I finally just walked outside and sat on the chair in front of the store. I also was well aware that the next time I would not be so fortunate. It was quite a relief for me when they were finally interrupted by a customer coming in and needing someone's attention.

Even though the hired man may have saved me from some physical punishment and several days later my father even told me that I was saved that time by the hired man. He also told me, "The next time you won't be so lucky so don't you ever show me a report card like that again." I made up my mind, right then that it was going to be the first and only time that I would ever get a B on my report card.

I enjoyed our simple life on that chicken ranch, with our whole family together in one place, and being able to play and having a lot of space to roam freely all over in the nice, fresh air. My health improved so much that I rarely missed going school anymore. I felt very proud in knowing that my father was someone who was an important person in the community. I was happy most of the time and I never felt better about myself. Living there also had a positive affect on my dad, because he seemed content and he was much nicer toward our mother and us kids than at any other time in our lives. I had anticipated that it could go on like this forever and that is what I really wanted. If only wishes could make it so.

Our happy days in Rib Lake were not going to last, and it all just had to finally come to an end after living there for just a little over two years. To me it seemed as though all at once everything started going wrong for my dad. Even the well on the farm went dry, and our dad started having enough water hauled in to fulfill our needs and that of all the chickens. This was far too expensive and certainly not practical for the size of his operation.

My dad had two unsuccessful attempts made at drilling for a new well which was quite costly. He was about to give up when the third attempt finally succeeded but it seemed to be too late because the cost had been too great to make a new beginning. I could even tell by the way his whole personality was changing that things were not right. I even noticed that the other people in town had started to act differently towards my dad. My mother was some comfort to me during this time, but as always she was unable to effect any change in events.

In the end it was that feed store which would cause most of my dad's financial problems. The only other place in town where the farmers could buy their feed was at the Ralston Purina Feed Company. My father's business in town was a great success, but that triumph was at the expense of his rival. The other feed store had the financial power to put an end to the competition from my father's store. They started a price war to take away the business from my dad's regular customers. The Ralston Company was able to sell feed for a lower price than what my dad could buy from his supplier. He now had less costumers but one couldn't blame the farmers because they have to keep their expenses as low as possible and they couldn't afford the added cost of loyalty.

I was almost nine years old and, in my mind anyway, that Ralston Company had now become our enemy. I remember that I hated even seeing their large checkerboard sign, because I had some idea about what was going on and the part that it played in my father's problems. I really didn't understand much about economics but I couldn't help but notice that during this time the amount of money I counted out on Fridays was becoming less and less with each succeeding week.

My father was running an independent local business, and he wouldn't be able to compete against that giant for very long. With hard work and determination he had built up a business that he was quite proud of and he was even more determined to keep everything that he had gained. It was his pride that was the driving force as he continued to fight by lowering his prices too much and for much longer than he should have. Now, each day that he opened his store, he was losing money. With the store and the farm, the amount that he was now taking in was far less than his expenditures. He had borrowed so heavily to get the farm and then the feed store and now he was using credit to make purchases locally. It didn't take very long before he had become far too deeply in debt with his suppliers.

He had established credit with the bank, other businesses, and individuals in town and now he was even unable to pay those bills. During his time of success he was well respected but now many of the local residents had nothing but disdain for my father. I felt that they even looked upon me in a different way and it hurt.

Everything my dad had acquired to make that farm such a success in the last two years would now have to be sold to pay on debts that he was accumulating because of his other business. In desperation, one of the first things that my dad did, as the ending was becoming more apparent, was to start butchering all of the chickens. Pat and I had developed a skill which was now going to be quite useful, the stripping of feathers from the dead chickens. We did our job well and we would even become more efficient than in the past.

No matter how competent Pat and I were to become, we still had over two thousand chickens, which made our work just seem to go on forever. During that time I would get up each morning and was constantly being subjected to the nauseating stench that was now being inflicted on me by the wet chicken feathers after they had received their hot-water dunking. I absolutely hated everything about the job and I even hated more what it all meant to my family and me. Our dad planned on selling every one of those butchered chickens to help pay some of our present expenses, but it wasn't going to make anywhere near enough money to save anything. Fortunately for Pat and me, the job would end for us by the time we had only a few hundred of those chickens butchered. Our father finally decided to settle some of his financial problems by selling *everything* at an auction.

Even though the farm had always made money for us, it had become too labor-intensive, and my father believed he could operate the feed store and take any money from the auction to help out with that business. He also felt that it was necessary to have a reason, so he gave as an excuse in the ad that he was "unable to give my flock the attention that it deserves" because of the feed store.

This is exactly how the ad appeared in the Rib Lake Herald:

"Another Thorp Sale"
AUCTION SALE
POULTRY AND POULTRY EQUIPMENT
ON THE ROY L. BROWN POULTRY FARM

Located ½ mile West of Rib Lake on State Highway 102 to Jim Willet's Tavern then 1 mile South, then ½ mile East
(Because of my feed store business, I am unable to give my flock the attention it deserves.)

SATURDAY, JUNE 3
SALE STARTS AT 12:30 O'CLOCK

1300 CHICKENS

Consisting of 4 pens of Leghorn Yearling Hens divided as follows: 8 pens containing 175 4AAAA hens each; 1 pen of 175 Key Pen Mating. This flock has recently been culled, are exceptional producers. Inspection of production records invited. This flock is free of any disease. 100 6 week old PULLETS of very best breeding. Here is your chance to get some of the very best started pullets that it is possible to obtain any-where

BROODER HOUSE - BRAND NEW

Size 14x16, mounted on 18 foot skids, 2 ventilating windows on each end. Double wall and double floor construction. Round roof type, Also double roof. Entirely insulated.

BROWERS, brand new 500 Chick Capacity OIL BURNING BROODER Complete with several lengths of pipe and 7 gal. fuel tank

3 5-gal. Galvanized Water Fountains; 5 8-gal. Float type galvanized Water Fountains; 1 Jamesway 10-gal. float type

Fountain; 2 8-gal. double wall Fountains; 3 3-gal. Chick Fountains; 1 Jamesway 3-gal. float type Fountain; 4 1-gal. Fountains; 3 2-gal. Fountains; 2 8-ft. Wooden Feeders mounted on stand.

12 Sections 8-10-12-15 hole NESTS of steel and masonite.
BROODER HOUSE ON SKIDS, 10x12
BROODER HOUSE ON SKIDS, 10x10

16 x12 Brooder House on skids; 12 1-gal. Glass & earthenware Fountains 35 Chick Feeders, gal. and wood, 3 to 4-ft. Long; 9 8-ft. Chicken Feeders 6-ft. Chicken Feeders; 1 4-ft. Chicken Feeder.These feeders all have wire grill tops and are mounted on stands. Part roll of 5-ft. Chicken Netting; 8 steel Fountain Stands; 5 Automatic Electric Water Fountain Heaters

21-hole Wooden Nests with hinges and perches.

Machinery

Case 12-20 Tractor with pulley attachment

In good condition; J. D. 20" Breaking Plow, light tractor type; Steel Wagon; walking cultivator; potato hiller; walking plow; garden seeder; I1 ½ h. p. gas engine; Parmak electric fencer with battery; one high line Electric Fencer; lge galv. Stock tank with pipe outlet; table saw mounted with shaft and pulleys; 120 gal. Steel storage tank with faucet; 2 sec. spring tooth drag; cedar shingles; length of pump rod; 15-gal. steel barrel; coal burning brooder stove; hand corn planter; stump puller; skidd'g tongs; small platform scale; spring scale; pressure grease gun; saw buck; stone boat; wire stretcher; 2 one room oil heaters; 4 tine barley fork; large funnel with strainers; part roll brick siding; numerous steel cans for feed; 4 3 x12x16 planks; 2 shipping crates; wooden feed bin with cover and partitions, capacity 1500 lbs; wooden feed bin with hinged cover, 600 lb. Capacity; 6 galv. Feed pails; 1 new manure fork, 8 tine fork, barn broom, floor scraper, several lengths of garden hose, steel barrel, iron kettle, 12 ft. 1 ¼ Pipe, part rolls 1-inch poultry netting, 100 rods barb wire, 65 pointed cedar fence posts, wheelbarrow, 33-gal. Gas barrel, 3 10-gal. Milk cans, 1 8-gal. milk can, scythes, dog house, 12 gauge single barrel shotgun with box of shells, single barrel .22 with shells.

Coal and Wood heater, Parlor Type Circulating; Iron Baby Bed
Dining Room Set Consisting of buffet, table, and 6 upholstered chairs

FARM FOR SALE (all electrified)

1 area with 15 acres in crops, 5 ready for breaking; 6 room house, with basement, new roof and new siding; garage and wood shed combined, 2 story chicken house, 800 hen capacity, new siding, fully insulated double concrete floor. Good dug well. On school bus route.
Some timber and lots of firewood.

Terms - All sums of $15.00 and under, cash. On larger amounts, ¼ down with the balance, plus recording fee, and 3% carrying charge to be paid in 6 equal monthly installments. No property to be removed until settlement is made.

Roy L. Brown, Owner

Monte Perle Passer, Auct. Thorp Finance Corp., Clerk
P. Jentzsch, Mgr. Medford Br., Laundry Bldg., Phone269

Listen to "Thorp Auction Time" every day between 12:15 and 12:30 on station WIGM and at 11:55 over the Wisconsin network for all. The latest auctions in your vicinity

THORP FINANCE CORPORATION

I remember also, on that particular day, that I was well aware of what was going on and the sadness I felt, as I was watching the auctioneer as he proudly did his job. A lot of people came from all around and everyone seemed to be in a very happy mood just looking for some bargains. It all provided a sort of carnival like atmosphere, as I listened to that auctioneer rattle off words so fast that I couldn't even understand them.

The crowd gathered around and anxiously waited for the auctioneer to shout out the different money figures that didn't even come close to the true value of our possessions. The farm that my father had been so proud of and all of the other possessions we had accumulated in the past two years were being sold away cheaply.

My dad had devoted so much of himself into this farm and the store in town. It had all become his hard fought attempt at achieving recognition and some kind of financial success. I know that my dad must have had difficulty accepting it all, because I didn't even see him around that day on the farm. It was all ending with the most terrible climax to all of his dreams.

At the end of the day, I finally saw our dad as he was taking care of the necessary business of paying the auctioneer and doing all the required paperwork. When everything was over, it would require all of that money just to pay only some of his enormous amount of debts. I think that he felt humiliation and he had become thoroughly demoralized by all that had happened.

To make matters even worse, the injuries that our father had received from his terrible fall in the shipyards were now giving him serious problems with his back. My father still felt that he was able to do that hard physical work in the feed store, carrying all those one-hundred-pound sacks of feed. Even though I think that it was unwise, he quite often carried two sacks at a time. I think that it was too soon after the injury and all of the surgery that he went through. There was no question that my dad was still a very strong man, but it was also obvious that he had clearly outdone himself.

Another reason that he had been able to tolerate working like that was because he wore a special canvass contraption with several leather straps that he tightly buckled around his chest every morning, which sort of held his whole upper body together. That thing had steel rods that went up the sides of it and ended in supports, looking like the top part of crutches, which went under my dad's armpits. Now even wearing that device wasn't providing him with enough of the much needed support anymore.

Even though I had to accept our new situation, this was going to be one move that I really hated to make. Our dog Poochie, the cats, King Oscar and the chickens, the guinea hens, our tar-paper toys, raspberry and blueberry picking, and our nice rural way of living at Rib Lake would be so abruptly left behind. I would miss the time that I spent at the feed store, the one-legged storyteller who sat outside the feed store, counting the money on Fridays, the-wide open spaces for our playground, even the Guinea hens, and above all the feeling of so much pride in me and my dad. I had become so self-assured and I felt good about myself and my abilities. I didn't want to leave behind attending school there and I would dearly miss my friends and especially Danny Vlack and Pauly Hole.

Our old way of life was all being replaced with such insecurity, because none of us had any idea where this next move would be taking us. In fact, at the time I don't think our dad even knew where we would be going next.

That summer we went to live in a small apartment in town for a short time as my dad seemed to have disappeared during this time. I think he was off looking for some other kind of employment. His feed store business still continued to struggle along during that time, but it was now under the bank's management as it was being operated by his previous hired man. He may have made a serious mistake by getting rid of the farm instead of his business in town. As it finally turned out, we were there only about a week before another change in plans was about to take place.

During our short time on our farm, I really did feel well protected and I felt as if it would be lasting forever. I didn't know it then, but during my childhood, I would never come to enjoy living anywhere else as much as I did the little more than two years that we spent there. I felt so secure and *safely anchored* to something that we were happily experiencing, while living on that farm. Our dreams and my father's aspirations were now being washed away from under us. I would be leaving Rib Lake, Wisconsin, with nothing but the fondest of memories.

- VIII. No Safe Harbor -

WE LEFT RIB LAKE with no more than what we could carry with us. It was hard for me to leave behind what few possessions I had accumulated in the last two years. I was also going to miss all of the friends that I had made at the school in Rib Lake. We were now making what was supposed to be only a temporary move as a family. I don't think that even our mother and dad knew where our next permanent home would be.

Our dad loaded the panel truck with my mother in front and my brothers and me in the back and he drove us into Medford. He unloaded everyone and everything we had at the station. We would be traveling to North Dakota to spend the first part of the summer with my grandfather, Peter Dufficy. I was excited about seeing him again and I was looking forward to it, but I also knew that it would be only a visit.

The train started pulling away and our dad wasn't with us and there wasn't even an emotional good bye from him. I had no idea where he was. Our mother told us, "Your dad is looking for a new job and a new place for us to live, so he we will be joining us later." That all confused me because I thought that he still had the feed store to run.

Until now I had only known this grandfather during a couple of short visits, by the letters he wrote, the money orders, and what my mother had told me about him. I had come to like to him, so I was feeling quite good during the trip. The trip seemed long, but we finally got safely to our destination.

It wasn't long after our arrival that I was feeling quite comfortable and I was enjoying our stay with our grandfather. He always had so many different sayings for almost every occasion. One, which I remember him using, was when our mother told him that she and my dad hadn't made a decision where we would be living next. He replied, "Never do anything before you have to, because you might die and you did it for nothing." There were other sayings he was frequently using, but they were so many that it was impossible for me to remember them all.

Our grandfather was living there with his wife who was also quite nice to us. Their house was even smaller than our Rib Lake home and we had one more person staying there so we really were quite crowded. All four of us boys slept in one room, just like in the house we left behind but our mother had to sleep on a couch in their living room. The accommodations were quite similar to the farm but without any of the responsibilities. Within a couple of weeks, I felt as though things couldn't have been nicer. I thought of it as a kind of dream world and wished that it could last forever.

That fantasy came to an unexpected end one day as my brothers and I were playing together and Richard silently wandered away. Richard was still just a wee boy of less than four years and my brothers and I were supposed to be watching over him. It was late morning when he just suddenly disappeared from our sight. We had no idea where he was, but it didn't concern us too much because this sort of thing had happened before and we were always able to find him in a short time. We had no idea about how long he had been gone so we stopped our play as we began to hunt for him.

We had been searching for more than fifteen minutes with no success before we finally got concerned enough to tell our mother.

I could immediately sense her anxiety and the first thing that she asked was how long ago it was since we last saw him. I too began to worry about what might have happened to our little brother. On this particular day I thought how nice it would have been to have our, "Duluth" dog Rip to keep track of him. My imagination was soon creating all kinds of explanations for our not being able to find him and none of my ideas included a whit of optimism. I could even visualize that he might have been kidnapped. I was also afraid of what our dad would do to us if Richard was never found. At a time like this, I felt grateful that our dad wasn't anywhere around. We kept calling for Richard and we looked everywhere, but we just couldn't find him.

As time went on, more and more people heard about what happened and they joined in the search. It wasn't very long before the whole town was emptying its houses with hundreds of people searching for the missing little boy. After several hours of scouring the whole area, it was beginning to seem that we would never see our youngest brother alive again. The light of day would start fading soon.

Finally, as the sun was beginning to set, a man came walking up to my mother carrying a small boy in his arms. He told us that he just happened to find Richard, curled up and asleep, in a deep depression next to the railroad tracks. I could see how troubled and worried my mother had been and the relief that she now felt when her lost son had finally been delivered to her. She was ever so grateful and asked the man how she could thank him. The man just replied, "I am just happy to have been of some help." I was quite relieved too and I think that Pat and I took it more seriously, after that, whenever Richard was put in our care.

Pat and I had only finished the third grade when we made this trip away from Rib Lake, and we were happy to spend most of that summer in North Dakota. In spite of the terrible scare that Richard gave us, we enjoyed the rest of our stay with our grandfather and we all felt disappointment when we had to finally leave there. It would have been easy for me to have stayed with him always, but we had to move on to our next "permanent" home. Even though our mother wasn't with him, she did have some input this time about the new location that our dad chose for us to live.

This time our move would take us quite a distance west, but almost at the same latitude as Rib Lake, to the Granite City of St. Cloud, Minnesota. The city is located on the Mississippi River about sixty miles northwest of Minneapolis. Our dad had already rented the top two floors of a three-story house before our mother, my brothers and I arrived. We were finally united with our dad there and we were a complete family again.

There was no question that our dad was finally being forced to realize that this was the end of any more physical labor for him. I knew that my dad didn't like the changes that he was now compelled to make, because now his choices of occupations were going to be far more limited. I had feelings of trepidation about our move to St. Cloud as we finally joined our father there. I was even a bit afraid to be together again with my father.

Our dad already had a job working downtown in the hardware department of the Montgomery Ward department store. Because he had no car, the one good thing about this job was that he could get to work by walking. It was a position that my dad was never too fond of, and his restless and constant search for something better in a job had already begun. He acted like his work there was lacking in the dignity and monetary compensation that he deserved. During the time that he worked there it would always remain for him as a job that he was less than proud of. His working there was also just the beginning for our dad being employed as a salesman and never knowing true satisfaction in his job.

Our dad still had the feed store in Rib Lake and it continued to operate with the cooperation of the same person who used to be his hired man. The situation with the competition from the other feed store in town continued. Our dad dictated the terms of his battle against them. His pride wouldn't let him admit defeat or accept a smaller clientele. I think that he also believed that one day he would be able to return. He just didn't seem to know enough, that he was in a war that he had no chance of winning.

Things got so bad that finally on the 25th day of November, 1944; my dad was forced to file for bankruptcy. Paul Jentzsch of Medford was made the trustee of that estate after filing his bond in the penal sum of $10,000. Just like the chicken ranch, my dad was now losing the business in town. What had started out so quickly to be such a tremendous success, now even more quickly had concluded with the end to all of his dreams.

I really believed than that if the feed store could have been operating with a profit, our whole family would have moved back to Rib Lake. I had been hoping for that ever since we came to St. Cloud but now I finally realized there was no more hope for that to happen and I was forced to accept our present situation.

The only things my brothers and I salvaged, besides our clothes, from our stay in Rib Lake were a few boxes of calendars with "Farmers Feed Co." advertising on them. The boxes were stored in a closet in an upstairs spare room. Each calendar was constructed of a heavy weight paper that was orange colored on one side. Attached to that paper was a beautiful picture of a mare and her foal and below the picture was some thinner paper with the calendar pages. Just like in Rib Lake, store bought toys were rare, but instead of tar paper we used the white backside of that orange card stock paper to draw and color people, animals and other things which were cut out and played with. These cut out figures provided my brothers and me with a lot of hours of enjoyment as they were brought to life in the stories we made up. I had control over the lives of my creations and I could vicariously live out my own dreams. We had no use for the calendar pages and they were discarded. Even though our dad kept an enormous amount it seemed he would never have any use for those calendars.

We felt that the house in St. Cloud where we were living had almost a perfect location for a family like ours. It sat on a corner lot across the street from a park on one side and across the street on the other side was Lake George, the school playground and the ball park. It was only a block away from where we would attend St. Mary's

School and go to Mass at the church which is now a cathedral. We only had to walk two blocks to be on St. Germain Street which was the main street of downtown. We could get just about anywhere that we wanted with only a short walk. That was always extremely important to my mother, because no car was available and she didn't know how to drive. It had now become important to our dad also, because he no longer had the familiar black panel truck. I don't know what happened to it but, he didn't own any vehicle during this time and we would have to take a bus to go any distance.

Summer vacation was soon over so my brothers and I were going to attend a parochial school for the first time in our lives. It was also a new experience for us to be attending services at St. Mary's Church early every morning. It was nice that we didn't have to walk the two and a half miles like we did in Rib Lake. I still had that horrible pain in my lower back when I had to kneel for any length of time. Now I had to do it *six* days a week! Attending Mass could have been a much more pleasant experience for me if I could just sit when I felt that terrible pain.

Going to daily Mass was really a part of attending the Catholic school. We were always expected to be in a particular section of the church among our own classmates with the nun who would spend the day with us as our teacher. The nuns were quite successful with instilling a fear in me so I was too afraid that the nun would punish me if I would have been bold enough to sit down when we were supposed to kneel. I learned from those sisters that if I was to be a good Catholic I had to respect and obey them. I was supposed to "offer it up" any suffering to God; so I knew that Jesus would be receiving a daily helping of *that* from me.

It was quite a novelty at first for me to learn all of those church songs and sing together with our classmates in a sort of children's choir. I actually enjoyed the sound of those songs that we sang. We had never even seen Catholic sisters before we moved here, and now we would see them Monday through Friday, during the best part of the day as our teachers. Catechism was also something new for us and it was a daily part of our school curriculum. We were quizzed every morning during that special class and our nun intimidated me enough to make me study so I would know all the right answers.

The reason I said that my mother had input in making our move to St. Cloud was because she had several of her relatives living there, and that's where she wanted to go. Knowing our dad and how independent he was, it was quite a surprise that he went along with her desire.

Our mother's cousins Irene, Elvina, and Fritz lived in St. Cloud. Our mother's father and their father were brothers. My brothers, and I became very sociable with them and we visited with them often, especially Irene, her husband, Red, and Irene's mother, Kate. We didn't see as much of Fritz, Irene's brother, and Alvina, Irene's sister. Kate seemed to be quite old, but she was always around and she was an extremely good cook. Irene and my mother were really close to each other and they did many things together. Irene made us feel as though she really liked my brothers and me.

I liked Irene's husband, whom everybody called Red, because he was so much different than our dad. He was a small, thin, red-faced man who smoked cigars almost constantly; but he was so kind and easy going with us kids. He was just so much fun to be with and he could fascinate us with some of his magic tricks and stories. Red also raised rabbits for butchering, and he would occasionally provide us with some rabbit to eat. My dad didn't like rabbit and wouldn't eat it, so my mother would cook it when he wasn't going to be home. My mother and we kids enjoyed those meals with rabbit meat.

I don't remember our dad ever going over to Irene's place. I had the feeling that our dad thought that he was better than Irene and Red, because they did janitorial work for an occupation in the local Paramount Theatre. My brothers and I always felt welcome at their place, and they always had cookies or other treats for us. They even had a nice Springer Spaniel dog that we liked to play with and another reason for going over there so often.

I really liked the idea of my dad working at Wards, because I could go and visit with him occasionally when he wasn't too busy at his job. Because our dad worked at Wards, he was able to buy merchandise at a very nice discount. As a result of that, one day he was able to buy Pat and me a bright red-and-white bicycle.

That bike had a big and heavy 26 inch frame with only one speed. It had what most bikes had then which included fenders, chain guard, coaster brake and big fat tires. It was brand-new and to us it was absolutely beautiful. Our dad always believed in getting things like our shoes a little bigger than the size that actually fit. He believed that we would always grow into them. The bike was no different, because it was intended for grown ups. We were only in the fourth grade and the bike was so big. After experiencing a few spills, we were quite proud of ourselves when in a short time we could finally ride it quite well. Just like the skis and sled, Pat and I mastered it, but we were forced to take turns riding it.

With our dad's encouragement, my brothers and I also developed a keen interest and some knowledge in the sport of baseball. I still had the accurate and hard-throwing arm; and even when we had snowball fights, I have to admit that it was a pleasure to hear, *"We want Sonny on our side!"* Even though I had a great deal of trouble with my back, I was still quite athletic and well coordinated. We also had the baseball equipment that our dad bought for us in Rib Lake. My brothers and I got a lot of practice, because we could play catch at almost any time; and when there were enough other boys around, we could play a game. Once in awhile our dad would find some time to play with us in the school yard that was across the street from our home. We liked that because he took charge and we could play for a long time without any arguments. I always hated it when I had to leave play and go to my doctor's appointment. We also learned to play softball with some of the other kids that lived nearby.

Our dad occasionally took us to see the minor league team, the Saint Cloud Rox, when they were playing one of their home games. It was a wonderful experience for me, and our dad would explain to us every little detail about the game. To me it seemed that he knew everything about baseball. He even showed me how to fill out the score card, which is fairly complicated. Pat, Tom and I would get to share a bottle of pop and maybe even a bag of peanuts. Our dad was good to us whenever we were attending one of these games, and there just seemed to be no more problems in the whole world. It was times like these when I wished that our dad could have spent more time with us.

There was also quite an elaborate ball park about a half block from our home, but it had been specifically designed for softball. It was located on the other side of the school playground, where they had many different teams that regularly came in and played their games each night. Unlike baseball where they only had white or light grey uniforms, the softball teams had really bright colorful uniforms. I got to watch many of the games at night but I never spent a penny to get in. Because an admission fee was charged and I had no money, I would start out by watching the game through a knothole in the high, wooden, dark-green fence, as I waited for my chance and sneak past the ticket takers. Fortunately I was never caught. Occasionally there were games to which children were admitted free.

My favorite team, with their orange and black uniforms, was from Sauk Rapids; and I tried to see them play every time they entertained there. They had a good team and they usually won their games. They had a very colorful character on their team who was also a fantastic pitcher, by the name of Beno Maletti. He could do everything well, except run, but that didn't seem to be necessary for him because he would hit home runs so often. I don't know if Beno was his real name, but he had a big stomach; and his body build reminded me of the pictures that I had seen of Babe Ruth except he might have been a bit fatter.

One night we were given a special treat when a softball team made up of World War II Japanese prisoners was brought in. I remember being so impressed by how quickly they did everything. They easily beat our best home town team. I had hoped that they would get a chance to play against the Sauk Rapids team but I never got to see that.

At times I was still having trouble with a tremendous amount of pain in my lower back, and it also affected the use of my left leg. It was frustrating, because the pain did restrict my movement in some ways and made it extremely difficult for me to do certain things. I would experience a great deal of pain associated with almost any physical activity that I did.

Because of the apparent success with Dr. Peiterson in Medford, Wisconsin, my father arranged for me to have an hour visit almost every week with a special chiropractor in St. Cloud. The chiropractor I went to was recommended by Dr. Peiterson because he felt that I would receive the best treatment from a doctor that got his training at the Lincoln School of Chiropractic in Indianapolis, Indiana. Even though he was trained in the same place, he did some things a bit differently then Dr. Peiterson

I remember lying under his dark blue and the deep red lights and having that doctor cracking my neck and twisting my back, which seemed to be a long way from the problem that I was having. It was a bit frightening and I always dreaded those appointments. I think that I felt so fearful because I could never anticipate exactly when he was going to quickly snap my head from side to side. With each jerk of my head there was a loud crack which also gave me the sensation that he was breaking things. In spite of what I thought of his strange treatment and therapy, it was here that real progress seemed to be made. I think that it was because of the apparent accomplishments that I exhibited in a little more than a year of that, my dad decided that I wouldn't require the services of that doctor anymore.

I have had only minor difficulty with that back problem since then. I knew that my father could hardly stand any physical imperfections in a person. I always had known that he didn't even like how small I was for my age and Patrick, being younger and larger, provided him with a constant reminder of that. Years later, I also thought that the reason that he kept taking me to the doctors was to fix the flaws in me, which he considered to be so unbearable to him. I think that it really bothered me less and I had adapted quite well to it all. My dad may have also suffered some from guilt, because that all happened to me as a result of his own inability to care for us at the time that Pat and I were put in that orphanage. Whatever the reason, I will always be ever so grateful to my dad for seeing to it that I received all of the treatments from those two chiropractors, and I am firmly convinced that they did help me considerably. It was obviously a financial sacrifice for my dad to provide me with that care.

Lake George was the small lake across the street from our house. Sometimes my brothers and I would fish in it with a bamboo pole, using only worms for bait. The fishing was not very good and I never caught more than an occasional bullhead or a sunfish, and rarely would I catch anything that was big enough to eat. I don't remember being taught or the first time that I did it, but I learned to fish in another way as I sometimes used to stand bent over in the water facing towards the shore and as the fish swam between my legs, I would quickly flip them up onto the bank. I really became quite skilled at it and I eventually could accomplish far more that way than I ever did with the fishing pole.

It was early autumn I got to witness an unusual event, watching hunters give their bird dogs practice. Their dogs were trained to swim out and bring wounded ducks back to them. There were two men in a boat who were putting ducks into the water. They had somehow disabled the ducks so that they couldn't fly, which made the ducks appear as though they had been wounded. I remember one of the men telling me that their dogs had to have a soft mouth. The way he explained it to me was that the dogs were trained to hold the birds in their mouths without causing any damage to the fragile bones of the ducks as they carried them back to their owners. I just couldn't help but think that our dog Rip would probably have done a better job than any of those dogs that I was watching. It was times like this that I really missed having him or even old Poochie for a pet.

One evening in late autumn my brothers, some other kids, and I were playing "hide and go seek" in the park across the street from where we lived. Because it was so late in the fall, the fish pond had already been completely drained of any water for the year. The pond was made of concrete, but on the sides it had some rock embedded into the cement. That rock hung a bit over the edge of the pool, concealing the concrete sides that were about two feet deep. I thought that positioning my body tightly against the side under the overhanging rock would make a perfect hiding place. My plan was to just jump into the pond and crouch down where no one would be able to see me. I wasn't aware, however, that workers had put up some steel fence posts and they were connected to each other with just one strand of heavy wire. It was evening and the sun had gone down enough to make that wire invisible to me.

After the person who was "it" started counting, I began running at full speed, with the intention of making a safe landing on the solid floor of the pond, but that wire was just the right height to catch me in the throat, just under my chin. I had built up so much momentum that when I hit the wire, my feet kept on going as my head was being held firmly, under the chin, by the wire. The lower part of my body continued on and my feet went up into the air and that wire wouldn't release me until my head was almost upside down and nearly facing the opposite way. Gravity then took over and slammed my body with the top of my head hitting first on the floor of the pond. The top of my head received my full weight of the blow as I made my landing on the hard concrete at the bottom of that empty pool.

I knew immediately that I was hurt but I didn't know how badly. I just remember that I felt so strange and was somewhat conscious, so I continued lying there for awhile because I found myself completely unable to do anything else just then. I just rolled over and remained there with my left cheek resting on the cold concrete floor. I don't know how long I lay there, but I was quite worried that I had been seriously hurt. After lying that way for several minutes, which to me seemed to be a very long time in my dazed condition. My body kept telling me to stay there and I obeyed for awhile. My mind was sending me a different message that I just had to do something, so finally I very slowly got to my feet. With all the strength that I had in me I forced myself to climb up out of the pool. I remained on my hands and knees on the grass as I was still feeling so peculiar. My head had already begun hurting quite badly. When I knew that I was safely past the wire I got up and sort of staggered slowly towards the house, kind of dumbfounded. I could faintly hear the other kids as their voices seemed to be calling from some far away place, "Hey, Sonny, what's wrong?" I ignored the calls because I was really in no condition to answer as I continued my struggle back to the house.

Usually my dad was away, so he was quite a welcome sight as I entered the kitchen and he showed a lot of concern as he carefully examined my wound and at the same time asked, "What happened?" Without waiting for an answer he immediately placed his handkerchief over the bleeding wound and I held it there as he told me. He then grabbed my hand and we rushed to catch the bus to take us to the hospital. The cut was quite severe, but it was soon cleaned, stitched, and my head was bandaged up. The doctor explained to my father to be sure that he and my mother carefully watch my behavior for a few days and to especially watch my eyes.

Incidentally, I was quite happy that I didn't receive one of those skull caps like Pat got after his accident. I was able to come home that night, but I had severe headaches and it affected my vision for a few days. I felt extremely lucky to have received no permanent brain damage, although I think that my brothers might have questioned that at times.

Lake George was the scene of activity all year round. During the winter, we played on the ice and we got to watch people skating. It seemed that so often we didn't receive some of the nice opportunities that most of the other kids had because we were never able to afford it. Having a pair of ice skates was a strong desire of mine which would never be fulfilled during the time that we lived there. One section of the lake was divided off from the rest to make a hockey rink which was usually reserved for older people and the young men's teams. We got to watch some pretty exciting games.

At one time, I could have made getting those skates a reality, because I saved every bit of my movie money each week. My brothers and I each got seventeen cents: twelve cents was for the movie and five cents for candy or popcorn. There were also other infrequent occasions when we were able to acquire some additional money. I had a bank that was shaped like a world globe, and I put almost every cent that I received into it. Saving all my money had started back in Duluth. I don't know why I had such a hard time letting go of it, nor did I have any idea of what I was going to buy with it. I really didn't know how much money I had, but I do know that it had accumulated into a quite a bit because that bank got awfully full and heavy.

My father seemed to be constantly having one financial crisis after another. One day my dad was in dire need of some money and he completely emptied every penny out of my bank. He told me that he had taken it, and that he would pay me back later. From past experiences, I think that my mother knew that he probably would never be paying me back. The part that I sadly remember the most is my mother crying as she was saying, "But Roy, you didn't even thank him."

I don't think that I cared that much about the money, except now I wouldn't be able to get a half pound box of Fannie Farmer candy as a Christmas present for my mother with some of my savings. I don't think that my mother and I liked anything better than chocolate. After my dad emptied my bank, I started to save all of my money again. I also remember that I made up my mind that my father wasn't going get my money again. To protect my money from being taken by him, I started to give my cousin Irene most of my money each week to save for me. When Mothers' Day came that year I felt quite proud that I had the money to get my mother the box of chocolates.

Our dad was still working at Wards during the Christmas season that December of 1944. I also remember that it was the first time that we ever heard of "Rudolf the Red Nosed Reindeer." We certainly were made well aware of it, because Wards spent a lot of money in advertising it and the store was decorated all over with it. At that time we first heard and read the story about Rudolf the Red Nosed Reindeer and the song with Gene Autry singing it would not come for another five years in 1949.

Occasionally one does something that one regrets and wishes that it had never happened. A good example of that happened one day while my brothers and I were playing together in the spare room upstairs. I got terribly upset about something. I don't recall what it was all about anymore, but I had a pair of scissors in my hand at the time. I lost my temper and I threw them at Tom. The point of the scissors made a terrible gash right above Tom's eye and it was bad enough to require several stitches. It frightened me and I could only think of how close I had come to hitting him in the eye.

My mother was worried about what my dad might do to me, if he knew how the accident had really happened. To protect me, she, my brothers and I agreed to a lie. We had conspired to tell our dad that Tom had fallen and hit his head against a sharp corner of the record cabinet in the living room. The explanation seemed quite plausible and satisfied my father, so the incident was forgotten. That event became a powerful lesson for me and I made up my mind right then, that I had to keep better control of my emotions.

We were to have a good lesson in why it always pays to tell the truth, because that particular lie of ours turned out to be quite prophetic. Some time later when Tom was playing in the living room, he did actually stumble and fall, causing him to hit his head on the corner of that same record cabinet. He received another cut, about the same size, that was less than an eighth of an inch from the scar made by the scissors. I think that it was because that cut looked so much like the previous one that our dad accepted the same, but this time a true story. Tom received a strong scolding from our dad as he again did his duty and rushed Tom off to the hospital to get the needed stitches. I would never know what our dad must have thought about Tom doing that same foolish thing twice.

We almost had a May basket delivered to us in the form of my fourth brother, Warren Michael, who actually arrived on the thirtieth day of April of 1945, just two months short of ten years after I was born. It was a happy event for me, because it provided me with a good excuse to regularly skip school. When my dad was away I could stay home almost whenever I wanted to, and most of the time I found school to be kind of boring anyway. My mother wrote excuses for me that claimed that I was staying home to help take care of my baby brother. The excuses were only partly true, because I did assist my mother, but I think that she could have done just fine without me. I really think that she just enjoyed having me around.

I always got on extremely well with my mother and I think that she did spoil me somewhat. I was always anxious to show my appreciation for the wonderful way that she treated me. I did many things for her, such as surprising her by scrubbing the kitchen floor or doing other house-cleaning chores when she was away. I especially enjoyed all the time we spent together without my brothers being around. I could receive all of her attention then. I know that I was spending a lot more time with my mother than my brothers got to spend with her. The relationship that I had with her became more like that of a brother than a son.

The Second World War finally came to an end in Europe with V.E. Day on May 8th of that year. That night after it had been announced on the radio, there were loud noises and the air was blanketed with band music coming from downtown. My brothers and I weren't allowed to leave the house during that time. It seemed that everyone in the city had gone crazy. Even though they were more than a block away, the noise was so loud that we could still hear the sounds long after we had gone to bed.

I went downtown the next day, and the street and everything else was a mess with small pieces and strips of colored paper covering everything. To most people, the end of the war in Europe came with a hope of better and happier times when we would no longer need those ration stamps, victory gardens, war bonds, all of the other sacrifices, and the sad news about all of the young men who were dying in Europe. Most of all, the war effort could now be concentrated on defeating Japan

That spring our dad got himself a car and quit his job at Wards. He immediately got a job as a traveling salesman which required that he would now be away from home most of the time. At first he came home every weekend but it was only a few weeks after he started that job that he only coming home about once every three weeks or a month. It was as though he was trying to avoid us completely.

When he was away, I used to stay up very late and just spend time visiting with my mother. She would be doing something such as crocheting a rug or some needlework such as decorating a pillow case. As she worked she would tell me stories about when she was young, and she also sang songs that she had learned as a child. An example of one of those old songs went something like:

Little maiden Anne with her pretty little can,
Went to milking when the morning sun was beaming low.
She fell, I know not how -
She stumbled o're the plow.
And the milk went flowing o're the plain-e-o

Then it goes on to tell about the pigs and the other animals that got some extra milk to drink that day. That was a silly little song, but I enjoyed it and her singing.

Another song that I really liked was the Spinning Wheel and I think that it was the alliteration that I really enjoyed:

Mellow the moonlight to shine is beginning
Close by the window young Eileen is spinning
Bent o'er the fire her blind grandmother sitting
Crooning and moaning and drowsily knitting.
Merrily Cheerily noiselessly whirring
Spins the wheel, rings the wheel while the foot's stirring
Sprightly and lightly and merrily ringing
Sounds the sweet voice of the young maiden singing.

The saddest one of all it seemed to me was "My Darling Nellie Gray" which she could never sing without crying. There were so many other songs that she sang to me late at night or on Saturday afternoons. Most of them were of an Irish origin. Some of them I still remember, but sadly there were many more that I completely forgot.

Usually, I slept in a double bed with Pat, but not on the nights when our dad was gone which was almost all of the time now.

When my mother finally went to bed, I would also spend the night in bed with her. That was especially nice when I had one of those frequent nightmares that would cause me to wake up screaming. Sometimes I would dream that someone was coming after me and was going to hurt me. Most of the time I never knew what they were about, but they were always extremely frightening. My mother knew just what to do, and she could always get me calmed down quite quickly.

All during that year my brothers went to the Saturday matinee each week at the Avon Theater. They usually got to see a western movie and the serial that always went with it, but I always stayed at home with my mother and Warren. I enjoyed listening to her stories and songs. She also taught me card games, such as "500" rummy, which we played quite often. We also did a lot of other things, such as working in the kitchen baking a cake or making other things. Warren always took an afternoon nap and I looked forward to those quiet times when my other brothers were away.

I really didn't miss going to those motion pictures too much, though, because Pat did such an excellent job of telling me about that movie and the serial that he had just seen. He seemed to remember everything, and he could relate it to me with the greatest of detail. He had a genius for being so thorough in telling the story that I almost felt as though I had actually gone to that movie. Occasionally I did get to see a movie, but it was at night with my mother when she went. I really fancied her drama and romantic type of movies better than the adventure performances that my brothers always went to see, anyway.

Even though our folks didn't even come to the church to see Pat and me receive our first Holy Communion, we knew how proud they were of their two oldest sons. With such limited funds they were somehow able to afford to buy us each a special dress suit of clothes just for that occasion. Our dad even paid to have our picture taken by a professional photographer and several copies were made to send to all of our relatives. Pat and I stood together, looking quite smart, in our dress suits and ties, and with our hair so neatly combed. While standing we each were solemnly posed holding a prayer book in our hands.

On Sunday mornings when our Dad was home he still quizzed us about what the sermon was about and like we did in Rib Lake, if we couldn't remember we would say that the priest just talked about needing money. It was still a venial sin but now that we had made our first communion we also began going to confession so logic told me that I now had a way of getting rid of that sin which made me feel so much better.

I always hated going to confession every Saturday morning. I can clearly recall going into the confessional and it went something like this: I first made the sign of the cross as I was saying, "In the name of the Father and of the Son and of the Holy Ghost, Amen. Bless me Father for I have sinned. My last confession was two weeks ago. Since then I told lies five times and I said bad words three times. I fought with my brother twice."

I left the very worst and most embarrassing sin until last. I also thought it was a mortal sin and if you died without having confessed a mortal sin you would surely end up in hell to burn forever. I dreaded to even mention it but I would say something like, "I looked at a naughty picture once."

The priest would then ask, "What do you consider a naughty picture?"

I would reply, "I saw a picture of a woman with out all of her clothes on."

The priest then would ask, "Did you enjoy looking at it?"

With my reply, I would already commit another venial sin, "Oh no Father!" I lied, but I could get rid of that as a venial sin at my next confession.

The priest would wait for me to say my Act of Contrition and then usually would tell me, "Say five Our Father's and five Hail Mary's and go and sin no more my child."

Two things bothered me about that last sentence with the instructions from the priest; The first was that I didn't like being called a child and the other was when he said "Go and sin no more" and I knew I would sin again and be back to confess them.

It was about this time that found out why my mother never went to church. Because I asked her why one evening and she told me that she had been excommunicated from the church. She explained that it was like being kicked out of the Church and that it was because she had married a non-Catholic and someone who had been married before and divorced. She told me something about her not being able to receive Holy Communion or the other sacraments. I really didn't understand any of it very well, but I did for many years after blame the Church and their strict rules for what I thought was a terrible injustice. The tragedy of it all is that it kept my mother from something that might have fulfilled some great need in her life. Like confessing sins some of this just did not make much sense to me.

I think that it would have been better if my dad would have continued to work at Wards because after he left that job our family financial situation seemed to get a lot worse. The bills were not getting paid and I could see how worried our mother had become and I began to worry that it wouldn't be long before we would be moving to some other place again.

One day as I was spending my time at home alone with my mother, I went with her as she answered the knock at the door. We were startled by the presence of a man in a suit. He showed us a badge and explained that he was from the FBI. He was inquiring as to the whereabouts of our dad. My mother told him, "He isn't here."

The man asked, "Mrs. Brown, can you tell me where I can find him?"

My mother was telling the truth when she told him, "I have no idea where he is except that he's working as a salesman on a job that takes him all over."

The man seemed content with the answer and left. As a fourth grader I had only a vague idea about what the FBI was and those thoughts were all negative. Why was that man asking for my dad? Had he committed a crime? It all really frightened me and I became concerned about things to come. I asked my mother, "Why does the FBI want to see our dad?"

She only said, "Sonny I don't know but it must have something to do with all the money that your dad owes people. The FBI - It must be serious." I had no choice but to accept her explanation and nothing that was obvious to me resulted from it then.

It was a couple of weeks later that my mother one evening was able to give me the reason for the FBI coming to see us. She said that our dad left no forwarding address when we left Rib Lake. He was trying to prevent the possibility of being harassed by the many people that he was indebted to. The FBI had been sent to locate our father so that some important business dealing with the feed store in Rib Lake could be completed. On the 25th of May, 1945, the bankruptcy proceedings that had been filed on the 28th of November, 1944, were completed, finally bringing an end to his business in Rib Lake. The mortgage had been held by the State Bank of Medford and the real estate was then declared as practically worthless. It was bought by Jerry and Mildred Heindl for the meager sum of $35.

Pat and I finished the fourth grade while we lived in St. Cloud, and we were looking forward to the summer vacation. We had no idea about all the changes that were about to take place in our lives.

As I had already expected we were again going to be moving away from a life style we had just become comfortable with. Most kids looked forward to the beginning of summer and a vacation of fun. To my brothers and me it meant that our happy days together as a family in St. Cloud would be coming to an end. With the move away from that house, I wouldn't see my mother again for a couple of months and I would miss her and the rest of my family.

I was also forced to leave behind most of my possessions, which included the bicycle. I just don't know whatever happened to that bike after we left there, but Pat and I would never see it again. It was months later that I discovered that our dad put our furniture and other possessions into storage. I also found out that he didn't pay the monthly storage fee so most of our furniture and other things would never be seen by us again.

Pat and I finished the fourth grade while we lived in St. Cloud, and in the spring we were looking forward to the summer and vacation. We had no idea about all the changes that would be taking place in our lives. St. Cloud just wasn't going to be the *safe harbor* that we would always be longing for.

- IX Just a Port of Call -

For me, that summer had a unique beginning because our father whom we hadn't seen for a couple of weeks suddenly showed up at the house one evening. He only stopped long enough to pick up my brother Tom and me while he told us nothing about where we would be going. He gave us just enough time to pack some of our clothes and say good bye. I was quite confused because my mother was crying, which to me was not a good omen. He seemed in a terrible hurry and we had only a very short amount of time before Tom and I were in the car and our dad was driving us to some unknown place. As we drove our dad explained that we were on the way to our Uncle Willie's ranch near Wolf Point, Montana.

This was quite a surprise because we had never heard of him before. His plan was for us to stay for just a part of the summer, but I really couldn't be sure that it would be only that temporary. I had sort of figured out the reason that he made these arrangements with Uncle Willie to have Tom and me stay at his place was for financial reasons to give my dad a break. I had figured that getting rid of Tom and me would make it easier for our dad to pay for the care of the rest of the family.

The idea of going to a cattle ranch, being among cowboys, and in the real wild west seemed exciting enough. Would it be like the west I had read about in books? It seemed to be something quite thrilling to me at first; but I had no idea where my mother and my other three brothers were going and that bothered me. I even imagined that I would never see them again. The suddenness of the trip bothered me too. I never knew why our dad chose Tom and me to go there? I would always become quite concerned when I received no good reason for something and this had me bewildered. As our dad continued driving us further west, I was becoming more worried than excited by this trip.

We stopped that night at a hotel in some small town in North Dakota. If we would have started earlier in the day we could have easily made the whole trip without stopping for the night. My introduction to the "real West" was a bit demoralizing. The hotel was old and one could only drink the warm water from a special pitcher that was provided for us because the water from the faucet was too alkali and very dangerous to drink. There were constant reminders of it with the signs all over the place warning everyone not to drink the water from the faucets. My dad told us that many thirsty cattle, horses, and even some people that drank from alkali ponds out on the prairie died from that water. He said that it was just one of the serious problems for the pioneers as they were traveling west in their covered wagons.

Since our dad was raised as a small boy in this state, he was quite familiar with it. Just being here seemed to bring back memories and a strong desire in him to tell Tom and me about numerous incidents in his life out here. Even though everything that he told us seemed to have taken place a long time ago, I had difficulty visualizing what it would be like now. There just seemed to be nothing too appealing about the many things that he was now telling us. I received his words as a kind of premonition of the gruesome place that we must be going to stay for the summer, and it only reinforced my worries.

We arrived at the ranch in the afternoon of the next day, and my concerns had all been without cause. The ranch was quite modern with a brand new house and another older house, which they called a bunk house, and was originally intended for the hired hands. I could tell straightaway that Uncle Willie and his wife were nice, easy-going people. They almost immediately began treating us just like their own children. Tom and I soon got to know their two sons, Harn and Mitts, and also his daughter. Harn was older than we were, but Mitts and the daughter, whose name I forgot, were close to our ages; and the four of us soon became friends and started to enjoy doing things together.

Tom and I got to experience a totally different type of environment than our life in Minnesota, with an enormous amount of wide-open spaces; lots of sand, cactus, cattle, wild horses, rattle snakes; eating wild onions; and the customary ways on a cattle ranch. We adapted quite quickly to it all. Life seemed to be quite simple and devoid of any worries. A good example is that we got a big thrill just standing on the porch of the bunk house and watch the lightning flash across the dark sky on many evenings.

Uncle Willie did have a lot of cattle and they were all branded on the left shoulder with what they called the N hanging C brand which looked like ^N_C. He also owned several horses, and to me that was really neat because I thought that horses were just about the most beautiful animal in the world.

We did get to go for an occasional horseback ride, but not nearly as often as I would have expected. I had imagined that the horse was the cowboys' main form of transportation. In spite of all of those horses, my illusion of the West was destroyed a bit when I found out that most of the cattle herding was done by using jeeps equipped with extra large tires to prevent them from sinking into the sand.

We spent the first six weeks of that summer there. I knew that the stay there was supposed to be only temporary, but we were there long enough to get somewhat settled with that life-style. We began to appreciate everything about ranch life, so when our father came to get us at the end of July, we weren't too anxious to leave. I did miss the rest of our family, especially my mother and I was very anxious to see everyone again. Dad made the trip back to St. Cloud, without making any stops this time.

The trip had been long and tiring and the sun had long since gone down so it was in darkness when we arrived in St. Cloud. As soon as we were within the city, our dad drove directly to a house I had never seen before. He dropped Tom and me, off along with our things. Our dad was acting so furtive and as though he was trying to escape from something. This was next place where we were supposed to stay, and just as suddenly our dad disappeared again. I really don't know what happened, but I believe that our dad was off again on some more of his job hunts. Whatever it was, I was becoming truly confused by it all, and to think that he was unable to take care of his family. I was truly puzzled by it all.

This place was called a welfare home and we received no welcome. I did think how grand it was to be reunited with Pat and Richard. The four of us were anxious to tell each other all kinds of stories about the last two months' experiences that occurred during our separation. I still had no idea where our mother or my youngest brother Warren was.

Our enjoyment almost ended there, because almost immediately I didn't like this home and I was soon hoping that we wouldn't be staying very long. There were three other children living there who were mentally retarded, and they really behaved strangely. We didn't get on too well with them and they were always getting into our things and we were forbidden to do anything about it. Another thing I didn't like about the place was that our mother and Warren weren't there with us. I once got to visit with my mother and Warren briefly, but I never did get to see my father again that summer.

It wasn't too much of a surprise for us when after that couple of weeks, with summer vacation coming to an end, my brothers and I, without any warning, were transported to another welfare home. This time we felt relief to be leaving this last horrible place, but also some anxiety because we had no idea of where we would be staying next. While this was happening, I thought how lucky Warren was, because he would be staying some place else in St. Cloud, with my mother. Whenever we made one of these moves, I always found it to be a bit scary. I think that it was the uncertainty that troubled me most. This move would be no different; I was quite apprehensive about it. This time I was in for the most pleasant surprise, because it didn't take long for my brothers and me to become quite happy with our new home on a farm.

We were first introduced to the most wonderful Irish man and his wife whom we would only refer to as Mr. or Mrs. Shanahan. The wife's sister, Minnie Warehon, also live there. They were elderly people that had grown children of their own and even some grand children. They made us feel comfortable immediately after we got there. Unlike the people who ran the orphanage and the other welfare home, these people were very kind to us and they treated us with some respect. They acted as though they really liked and cared about us. I don't think they could have been any nicer to their own children, and they soon made us feel that we were a welcome part of their family.

Pat and I would begin our fifth grade school year that fall, living at our new home on a small 160-acre farm. Tom and Richard would also be attending the same one room school with us. This farm was located approximately nine miles from Sauk Center, Minnesota, which is about 30 miles west of St. Cloud.

There would be just two things that I felt were missing from my life while staying with these people. The first was that I would never see my mother, father or Warren during the time that we were living there and I really didn't know if I would ever see them again. The second was that even though these people treated us in a more Christian manner than any other place that we stayed, church and organized religion would play no part in our lives there. Even though the kneeling was painful for me, I did miss the music and prayers when attending Mass, at least on Sundays.

I don't think living conditions could have been better for four boys of our ages. Mrs. Shanahan was a very good cook, and we were always given plenty of good food to eat. Best of all, we received fantastic supervision, but not one of us was ever physically disciplined while we were there.

There were a lot of other good reasons for my brothers and me to enjoy our living there. One neat thing about their farm was that there was an enormous amount of natural gray clay in the ground around the house. My brothers and I used to dig it up and mix water into it and mold it into some of the neatest things to play with. When the clay dried, it became extremely hard like concrete. Unlike the store bought clay, once you molded something out of this you could never remold it into anything else. We made animals, people, tractors, cars and many other things to provide many hours of entertainment for ourselves. That clay proved to be much better material for our needs than the tar paper we had in Rib Lake.

Mr. Shanahan was a very dear man who would often speak, out loud in Gaelic, to no one in particular. I don't believe that there was anyone else around who could recognize a single word when he spoke it. Maybe it was better that they couldn't, because he usually did it when he was upset. When he talked to someone in English, his speech had a strong Irish brogue, making it difficult for some to even understand him. I got quite accustomed to the way he talked and soon I had no trouble at all with fully comprehending every word that he said and even began to talk a bit like him during our stay. One would probably say that this man had the gift of the blarney, because he spoke so much.

I loved Mr. Shanahan and I spent a lot of time with him, while he was working. I would often ride on the machinery with him when he was working the horses. How nice, I thought, because it was so quiet without the awful noise like our dad's tractor would make. Mr. Shanahan talked almost constantly, and I could hear every word that he uttered. Even though they couldn't possibly understand, some of his conversation was directed to the horses. He talked to them just as if they were people. Most of the time he was talking to me and he was forever giving me bits of advice, which usually started out with the words, "When you get a little older, laddie, you be sure and - - - -," or "Don't you be about making the same mistake that I did and - - - -." He made me feel as though he really enjoyed having me with him. It seemed so grownup to receive this obvious respect from him.

All of the advice that he was giving me then would never be of any use to me for at least another five years or more. I didn't mind, though, because it was just so much fun to be with him and be given all of his attention. The conversations he had with me always made me feel so grown up and important. I never felt that way since what now seemed to be such a long time ago in Rib Lake.

Mr. Shanahan did not have the use of a tractor, nor would he know how to drive one. He told me that a person could love his horses, but he could have no feelings for a noisy old tractor. He certainly wasn't a prophet, because he had me convinced that tractors would never completely take the place of horses.

He had three horses for doing all of the farm work. No matter how you combined the horses, they would always make a strange-looking team. He had a roan gelding that was appropriately called Roany. With the build of a riding horse, Roany was the most popular of three horses. My brothers and I enjoyed riding him and sometimes we rode two at a time on his back. We also would use this same horse for pulling the buggy.

Mr. Shanahan owned a black mare named Toots. Toots was large and the only true draft horse on the farm that was really bred for farm work. She was the easiest to manage when putting her into the harness or working her. Even though she was so big, a child could have easily and safely handled her.

The third was a bay horse named Mike. He was a stallion that wore a brand on his left rear. He was a western type cow pony and much smaller than Toots. He was just a bit wild, because he had never been completely broke for riding or the harness. Mike was very high spirited, and he would bite and kick to get free of any restraints. Mr. Shanahan was the only one with courage or ability enough to handle Mike. This horse became extremely agitated when anyone else just got near him.

Mr. Shanahan used to pair up either Roany or Mike along with Toots as a team to do the work, such as pulling the loaded wagon, mowing, or raking the hay. Roany worked quite well with Toots as a team. Mr. Shanahan believed that Mike needed some work too, so he would often, with a lot of effort, hitch Mike up as a team with Toots. As soon as he was in the harness, Mike was always raring to go, and he would immediately tug way ahead of Toots. He was really straining as he started out by pulling the whole load and even Toots had to move a little faster. Mike continued this until he began to get tired, he would then settle down and pull along beside Toots. It was quite obvious that Mike never did learn anything from this, because he started out that same way every time.

One day I asked Mr. Shanahan, "Mike does that every time. Don't you think that he will figure it out some day?"

Mr. Shanahan laughed at my question and then he jokingly answered, "*Hell, no, that Mike has too much Irish in him!*" I didn't ask him, but his reply puzzled me a bit at the time and I just couldn't figure out whether he meant that the Irish were awfully stubborn or stupid. Nevertheless, I was happy that Mr. Shanahan taught me how to drive the team, and he gave me a lot of experience handling the horses.

Mr. Shanahan was not always busy at work. There were several times that he took a break to teach me how to do some Irish dancing. Most of what I was learning was really what the Irish call happy feet, where you only move your legs and feet. The rest of the body from the waist up must make no movement of any kind, and your face must show no emotion. He also taught me another kind of dance which included clapping your hands while you did a jig step with one foot and you kept time with the other. He complimented me on how quickly I was learning how to do it, and that encouraged me to do even more. I think that it was from this experience that I came to enjoy not only Irish dancing but all the different forms of dancing that I continued to do.

Mr. Shanahan was usually quite lighthearted, but everyone on the farm knew when he was feeling agitated and he was beginning his day quite badly. He would go outside and walk several times around the house at some time around four or five o'clock in the morning. It would only be a deaf person who wouldn't get awakened from his sleep. Mr. Shanahan would spend a lot of time stomping about the yard and shouting at the top of his voice, making sure that everyone could hear his, *"Misery, misery, misery! All is misery, misery, misery!"* He also said a lot of other things but I can't remember any of those other words because the rest of what he spoke was in Gaelic and at a somewhat lower volume. He would continue to repeat this routine and those same words over and over again. I could never figure out how a person was able to know, so early in the morning, that his day was going to be bad.

I asked Mrs. Shanahan about that strange behavior and she told me that she usually doesn't have any idea what it was that got him so upset. She said that he had started doing that many years ago when they were much younger. Nevertheless, it was a warning sign that he didn't want to be bothered by anyone until much later in the day. It just seemed that he needed this moan every so often.

Mrs. Shanahan's sister was also a permanent resident on the farm. She was a spinster by the name of Minnie Warehon. She told us that a long time ago she once had a lover whom she was going to marry. He had courted her for a long time when one day he got a bad fever and died suddenly, and she made a vow to herself never to marry any other. She also said that she never really met anyone that lived up to what she remembered about her dead suitor. She kept her promise, but it all seemed so sad to me, because she seemed to be such a nice person. I thought that she would have made a wonderful mother.

It was quite difficult for Minnie to move about, and she spent a lot of her time in bed, because she was quite heavy and she had some serious problems with her legs. Walking was especially difficult for her and she made use of a cane to get around. One day I saw that Minnie's legs from below the knees to the ankles were almost black with some horrible-looking sores. Every day Mrs. Shanahan put some kind of salve on Minnie's legs and wrapped them up. I didn't know about those things then, but many years later I came to suspect that she probably had a serious problem with diabetes.

In spite of her condition, Minnie always seemed quite cheerful around us kids. Every morning with bandaged up legs and her sister's help, she would move, very slowly down the stairs. She then was able to maneuver on her own with the help of a cane. She always wore a long dressing gown and a house coat. Her black hair, mixed with a lot of gray, was arranged the same way with a single braid that hung more than ten inches over the back of her gown. She always sat up straight on the same hardwood chair with its back forever positioned in the same place against a wall in the kitchen.

My brothers and I would sit on the floor around her. We would listen carefully so we wouldn't miss a word of the most fascinating stories that she would tell us. Minnie told us stories about the past in that area and some of her tales would border on horror. Most of her stories seemed to be involved with wild and tame animals, along with some very special horse stories. Quite often her stories were for teaching a worthwhile lesson. We would listen for hours, and she always had at least one new story that we had never heard before. Today I wish that I could have had them all written down, because I believe that all together they would have made quite a wonderful book.

I forgot most of the stories that Minnie told us, but there were some that seemed to have left an impression on me and I do remember them. I even told some of those same old stories that she told us to other children after I became an adult. The way those children reacted to them, made it quite apparent that they enjoyed those same stories just as much as I did so many years ago.

A good example of one of Minnie's "horse" stories:

Before World War II horses were beginning to be replaced by tractors. Train loads of horses destined to be slaughtered for glue, hides, and other by-products were being shipped from the plain states of Eastern Montana, North, and South Dakota through Minnesota on their way to Chicago. The steam locomotives required maintenance along the way so they made several stops during the trip. The stops had to have proper facilities for train maintenance and to deal with the horses that died along the way.

At this one particular stop the dead horses were removed from each car load and left lying at the siding. After the train moved on this one very old man always put a harness on this one particular old horse and used him to drag the dead carcass out to a large gravel pit. The dead horse was released to roll and slide down the steep incline to the bottom of the pit. That old man and that same old horse worked as a team hauling them one at a time until all of the dead horses had been disposed of in the gravel pit.

The old man did this every time that the train came through and always put the harness on the same horse for performing the undignified task of dragging the dead bodies. One day when the train arrived with its load of horses this old man went to get his special horse that he had assigned the job to every time. He searched but was unable to find his special horse so he finally gave another horse the task.

With the other horse hitched to a dead carcass, he made the trip to the gravel pit. Just as he was about to release the dead body to be slid down the embankment, he notice that the horse he usually used for the job was lying at the bottom of the pit quite dead.

The Shanahan's farm had seen more prosperous days, but it still required a lot of work. The land was divided into almost equal parts of pasture, corn, oats, and hay. They did have three horses, five milk cows and several cats. Those cows were milked by hand, and my brothers and I soon mastered that skill. Although I would never get as good as Mr. and Mrs. Shanahan, I liked doing the milking. At first it took milking only one cow to make my hands ache terribly, but I thought that I was being helpful.

I remember one late summer morning that we started our day the same as any other. It was sort of gray out and the wind was blowing mildly. We got to the pasture and started out by driving the cows into the barn and locking them in their stanchions before doing the milking. The light through the windows faded and it began to get dreadfully dark in that barn. Mrs. Shanahan lit two lanterns and hung them on hooks so we could see. The wind had been making quite a noise, but suddenly the wind stopped blowing, and it became so mysteriously quiet. Everything seemed so creepy, but we continued on with our work. We had been in the barn for only a short time and we had only about half finished milking the cows, when suddenly, there was another tremendous change in the weather.

It had now become quite obvious that we were already in a bad storm. At first it began with a sudden drop in temperature and the winds began blowing violently and they were causing the barn to give off the most terrifying creaking noises, which kept getting louder. It got so fierce, and we could now easily observe that the barn was actually moving. Being able to see the barn swaying like that was quite frightening. It was really getting colder and I even began to shiver. The lanterns were flickering from the wind, creating an eerie effect on the walls from the moving shadows.

Mr. Shanahan took charge by gesturing and calling out to us orders which we couldn't hear, but everybody immediately responded. We promptly stopped the milking and then we hurriedly opened the stanchions to free the cows and drove them outside. The cows just wanted to stand by the barn. Mr. Shanahan called us to help him drive the cattle away from the barn. When we got back in the barn Mrs. Shanahan covered the partly filled pails of milk with some clean cloth and then she blew out the lanterns.

With that done, we were told to go to the house. As soon as I exited the barn I looked and could not even see the house, so I headed towards the windmill which was situated between the barn and the house. It required a large amount of effort but I made it to the wind mill where the house was now just barely visible. Everyone was running as fast as they could to reach the perceived safety of the house.

Leaning forward, I ran with all the speed that I had in me. From somewhere behind, I could hear Mrs. Shanahan shouting at us, but I couldn't tell what she was saying. I had no idea where anybody else was, and there were many things flying all about. My eyes were watering from all the dust that had blown into them, making it extremely hard for me to see anything. I was so frightened that I wouldn't be able to make it. The howling winds were blowing hard enough that, in two instances, I was quickly picked up off of my feet and I was just as suddenly plummeted back to the ground each time. It seemed to take forever before my struggles finally got me to the house.

Once inside the house, there was calm and the atmosphere was much friendlier. I now felt so much safer, even though I could hardly see anything and the house gave off a constant creaking sound. As we entered the kitchen it was so dark that it was almost as if it were in the middle of the night instead of the early morning. Immediately Mrs. Shanahan lit the mantles of the gas lantern that was on the kitchen table which brought a friendly glow to the room. Then she put a kerosene lantern on the table and lit it too. At first I couldn't understand why because the light it provided was hardly even visible.

After she knew that my brothers and I were safely inside the house, Mrs. Shanahan grabbed the kerosene lantern from the kitchen table. Then she told me to follow her as we almost ran up the stairs and along the hallway with the glow of the lantern to guide us along.

As soon as we entered Minnie's bedroom, Mrs. Shanahan handed me the lantern. Minnie had just been quietly lying there in bed. She had her hands folded over her breasts and to me it looked like she was praying. In her soft voice she told us, "Just leave me alone. I am ready."

Seeming a bit agitated, Mrs. Shanahan asked, *"What are you talking about?"*

Minnie answered, "I'm ready to die now."

Mrs. Shanahan replied, *"Don't be so darn foolish! Nobody is going to be dying.* We are just going to take you downstairs where it will be safer."

Minnie continued to protest and told us to leave her there, but

Mrs. Shanahan wasn't listening to her any more. Mrs. Shanahan had no more patience as she seized the bedding and threw them aside. She grabbed Minnie's legs and pulled them towards her until they hung over the side of the bed. Mrs. Shanahan was quite a large woman but then so was Minnie and I could see that it was quite a struggle as she was helping her, because Minnie wasn't cooperating. Mrs. Shanahan was finally able to bring Minnie into an upright position. As Minnie now sat on the edge of the bed she was still mildly protesting. Mrs. Shanahan held both of Minnie's hands and pulled backwards until Minnie rose from the bed and onto her feet. I slowly led the way along the hallway and down the stairs with the lantern to light the way as Mrs. Shanahan carefully escorted Minnie, who was only in her long nightgown. It seemed to take a very long time but we finally made it down the stairs.

By that time Mr. Shanahan finally arrived in the kitchen. I don't know where he was so long or what he had been doing but I could immediately see an old man that was sort of bent over, and his shoulders moved up and down with his hard breathing. As soon as he caught his breath, he began to tell us about another terrible storm that his family lived through many years before when he was a little boy and how this reminded him of it. He said that their barn was completely destroyed, along with all of the animals that were quite dead as they lay buried underneath a hay mow full of hay. Now it made sense to me why it was so important to him to have all of the cows driven far away from the barn before we came in.

The house was making some of the most horrible sounds, and it made me feel more than just a bit nervous. The noise finally lessened and we felt a small amount of relief and then it had begun raining very hard. I tried to look outside, but I could see no more than just a blur through windows because of the water that was continuously running down the glass panes. The storm was holding us prisoner in that kitchen as we sat listening, waiting, and hoping for it all to end. It was something that I had never experienced, before and I doubt that it was something that anyone would ever get used to. My imagination was out of control and I could just see the house being destroyed and all of us with it.

Usually Minnie could keep our attention with some really neat story, but there were no words being uttered by her now. She just sat in her chair and seemed so far away in thought. I don't know if she was pouting because she didn't want to be there or because she didn't have her usual house coat on over her gown.

After what seemed to be a very long time and things had quieted down, we felt that the storm must have finally ended. Even the rain had stopped as we cautiously wandered outside into the much colder air, expecting to find the most tragic occurrences that the mind could imagine. We just stood there looking at the horrible mess that had been created by that storm. There were tree branches and all sorts of debris scattered about the farm yard.

Mrs. Shanahan walked down the steps of the porch and just stood in front of the house with her hands on both sides of her head as she shouted, *"Oh! Thank God! The barn is still there!"* It was a great relief to see that both of the old barns and the silo were still standing. Mr. Shanahan, Pat and I then started our slow walk as we maneuvered our way through the newly-created obstacle course on our way to the barn.

Since before the turn of the century, the windmill had stood so proudly in the middle of the farm yard with its blades always facing toward the wind and they turned in even the slightest breeze. Now the old, unused windmill, with all its angle iron construction, was lying on the ground in a twisted and mangled-up mess. It made me wonder how the wind could get hold of its steel frame and how other more solid objects were left unhurt. Fortunately, that windmill wasn't any longer needed for its original duty of pumping water. Even so it would be missed, and now it was no longer able to even tell us the direction of the wind.

We passed the barn and into the pasture where we were able to see that all of the animals were safe. The horses were in one part of the pasture and the cows were huddled together in another part. Mrs. Shanahan and Tom joined us as we drove the cows back into the barn so that we could finish the milking. That was something that just could not wait any longer.

With all of the chores done, the milk was brought into the enclosed back porch of the house where the almost new DeLaval Model 12 Cream Separator was that their son had recently bought for them. Mrs. Shanahan poured the pails of milk into the top and then turned the crank as the milk and cream came out and into separate pails. She then carefully poured the milk and the cream into glass jars with lids to seal out anything that might be in the air. None of that milk ever got pasteurized but my brothers and I consumed a lot of milk and the rest was use in cooking. They even made their own butter from the cream.

We went back outside and upon further investigation; it seemed ironic that all of the lightning rods, along with some of the shingles, were torn from the roof of the house. Many trees in the nearby grove had been twisted off and were lying on the ground. To me it seemed quite puzzling how the winds could skip around as it did so much damage and still it had missed the large, three-story house and both of those big barns.

It didn't take long to realize that we were quite fortunate to have received such minor damage compared to others in the vicinity. Information got around the area mostly by the gossip that was spread by people when they met and the party line telephone. It was from the phone that we were able to discover quite rapidly that many of the neighboring farms had suffered far more dearly.

The next day my brothers and I spent most of our time busily helping Mr. Shanahan with cleaning up the yard. We pulled and dragged branches and heaped them into a big pile to be burned later. The broken bulbs from the lightning rods, the torn shingles and other things that wouldn't burn had to be put into barrels. When the barrels were full the rest was put into another pile to be taken care of later. With the exception of the fallen windmill, our hard work finally made all that space between the house and the barn look quite decent.

In the morning of the second day after the storm, out of curiosity, Pat, Tom, Richard and I walked across fields to a farm that was operated by a very large family named Ungar. They owned the largest farm around with several beautiful white buildings. They were considered to be the wealthiest family in the area. We had already heard that the storm had caused a lot of damage to their place.

When we got there, we truly became eye witnesses to nature's tremendous destructive force. What had been their beautiful and huge white barn, with a completely full haymow, had been totally demolished. Only their house remained standing amongst the rubble that had only the day before been their barn and all of their many other buildings.

There were dead cows, calves, and pigs scattered all about that had been dragged out from under their collapsed barn and other buildings. Their bodies were lying there with their enormous round bellies that, we were told, had been expanded by all the gasses that had built up inside of them. Those dead carcasses were already giving off a most putrid stench. It seemed almost miraculous that all of their children, who had been accustomed to playing in the barn during past storms, had stayed in the house on only this one occasion.

I spent a lot of time just watching all the activity that was concentrated around one machine that really caught my attention because it seemed so unique. It made a lot of noise and we were told that this modern invention was called a hay baler. Into one end of the machine sweating men were busily forking the loose hay that had filled their haymow before the storm. A woman had a seat on the side of it and had the boring job of tying the two knots in the twine that each bale required. There were two other men carrying away the bales, of hay, that were being pushed out of the other end of the machine. I was amazed at how much loose hay it took to produce one bale. The bales were being neatly stacked by a man who worked on a nearby wagon. The full load was then hauled into a field, where the bales were unloaded to form another big stack and eventually everything received a protective covering of canvass. The wagon was then brought back to be loaded again.

There was so much activity, and it was very exciting for us. Everywhere you looked there were people busily working at their various tasks to put things back into some kind of order? My brothers and I spent more than two hours observing everything, but there just wasn't anything that we could do to help; so we finally went home, where we excitedly related everything that we had seen to the others who had stayed at home.

One would have thought that the Shanahans' house was in some kind of time warp, because of the lack of the modern conveniences that most people took for granted at this time. There was no electricity or running water.

The radio was one item in their house that one could consider to be somewhat modern. That radio sat on the floor in its beautiful wooden cabinet, a huge thing that stood about four feet tall, with a battery that was bigger than those that were used for starting cars. Mr. Shanahan turned it on about two or three times a month to listen for about one-half hour to one program, and then it was turned off. I didn't miss not having to listen to that radio, because the reception was never good. It certainly was not a nice sort of thing to listen to because of all the static and squealing that it delivered to our ears.

Another somewhat modern item was the party line telephone that hung on the large dining room wall. No matter whom you were talking to, what you heard never resembled the voice very well and sounded so far away that you could hardly hear them. That phone afforded no privacy, because you knew that when you were having a conversation with someone, there were probably ears from several other farms in the area that were listening in, so you had to be mindful of what you said.

One had to be careful about using the phone during bad weather. During bad thunder storms we had literally seen the bright lightning flashes being discharged from the mouthpiece. I could only imagine what would have happened to someone if one was standing near by during that time. When we were in the kitchen we were able to watch through the doorway into the dining room where the phone hung, and in the darkness a supernatural effect was created as each flash of lightening lit up the whole room.

I would have to consider Mrs. Shanahan's gas powered washing machine to be on that short list of rather modern devices, because it was the only internal combustion engine on the farm. I would also consider it to be one of the strangest contraptions. She could only use this wash machine outside in the yard. It was extremely noisy, and the exhaust from its engine was forced out of the end of a flexible metal tube. My brothers and I used to build mounds of dirt to just have them blown away, using the pressure of the gassy air as it was being discharged through that hot tube.

That was the full extent of the modern conveniences. Just like in Rib Lake the water for drinking and washing was furnished by a hand pump near the kitchen sink. We even had the little outhouse and the slop jars under the beds, but unlike Rib Lake there was no electricity anywhere on this farm.

In the winter Mrs. Shanahan washed clothes in a wash tub, using a scrub board and some lye soap that she had made during the last summer. There was a contraption with wringers that clamped onto the tub, and she had to use a hand crank to force the wet clothes between its two rollers as it was extracting much of the water from the clothing. The damp garments were then put into another wash tub with rinse water, and the process of wringing out the clothes was repeated and then the clothes were hung on clotheslines to dry.

After Mrs. Shanahan washed all of our clothes, she ironed them using several flatirons that she placed in a particular order on the hottest part of the wood burning kitchen stove. She had just one handle that clamped onto the top of each flatiron. With that handle she had only to flip the lever and the iron that had cooled from use was released onto the top of the stove to get hot again. With that same handle she could pick up another iron that had been on the stove the longest and continue with the ironing.

As in Rib Lake, our bath water came from the water that was heated up in the big reservoir of the kitchen stove. We took our baths by taking our turns in a big wash tub that was placed in the middle of the kitchen floor. Partly because of habit and partly because I was now becoming extremely self-conscious about my nude body, I really hurried when I took my bath to minimize my naked exposure to others. I also know that I still had that strong fear of getting caught without any clothes on. The unlucky person who had to be last always bathed in the cooler and dirtier water. Fortunately, bathing was an unwelcome event that occurred less than once every two or three weeks.

Also as in Rib Lake, the only toilet we had available to us was in a small house at the end of a path in back of the house, well concealed in the grove of trees. In the summer it always had a terrible aroma inside, so you didn't waste any time. Even though it didn't have the awful stench during the winter, your exposed body became uncomfortably cold so you did it with as much speed as possible. It was amazing that the building was able to withstand the fury of the tornado because so many of the trees that surrounded it were brought down. It is also a wonder that not one of those trees fell on that outhouse.

Our summer vacation had ended in less than a fortnight after we arrived there. We only had to walk a short distance of about one-half mile to the one room country school. I always hated going to a new school, but this time I felt welcome on the first day. Everyone from first through eighth grades had a desk in that same room. Each day my brothers and I carried our lunch, which had been prepared by Mrs. Shanahan. Most often it consisted of little more than a small jar of milk and a peanut butter sandwich on her homemade bread and maybe half of a turnip. When the weather was nice, we ate our lunches outside on the school porch or while sitting on a swing. When we couldn't be outside we ate while sitting in our desks.

There were only fourteen students attending this school at this time, and more than half of them came from just one large family. They were from the same Ungar family that had received so much damage to their farm in late summer. I was so astonished when I found out that they had twenty-one children! I had never heard of any family that was anywhere near that large before.

Our teacher, Miss Gray, was quite young and this was her first year of teaching. This was also the first year that the teacher at this school was paid $30 a month and milk, meat and eggs. I was told that before Miss Gray came along, teachers were paid only $10 a month, but they received room and board by taking turns living at the homes with the families of their students.

After attending the school for only the first couple of weeks, I started experiencing some new feelings within me. I was falling madly in love with Miss Gray. I, of course, wouldn't talk about that to anybody. It made me feel good inside but it continued to remain my innermost secret. I would never tell anyone about my feelings. It was because of her that I took no interest in any of the girls in the school. There were two girls, one in the 5th and the other in the 7th grade that did quite fancy me and they were constantly trying to spend a lot of time around me but I had no interest in either. I would try to brush them off but I didn't dare mention the reason.

I thought that Miss Gray was just the most beautiful and nicest person in the whole world. I believe that I would have done almost anything for her. I considered it a privilege when she would ask me to do any errands for her. Every day I got to spend some of my time helping her with some of the younger children.

Going to school there was really a pleasure, and quite different from anything that we had experienced in our past years of school. My brothers and I did our homework at night with only the light that was provided by a gas light or a kerosene lantern. I think that school was far too easy for me, because I worked far ahead in all of my subjects. I could do all of my school work at night so when I got to school the next day there was nothing that I had to do at my grade level. Even though I was in the fifth grade, I thought it was nice to be able to listen when the two eighth graders were having their class and I think that I learned the most from that.

Miss Gray encouraged us in producing nice art-type activities for the other subjects and it was especially effective in social studies. It was quite a normal day when I got to make pictures, dioramas, and a lot of three-dimensional exhibitions. With Miss Gray's supervision, I also had the enjoyment of making some of the most artistic bulletin board displays. I believe a tremendous amount of learning took place as we did those various exercises, but I know that other areas of the curriculum did suffer. We had no science classes and Miss

Gray seemed to devote an absolute minimum amount of her time with teaching math. I had a lot of time for these projects, because almost all of the real academic work I got done at night. I do believe that she had a lot to do with me continuing to develop my art skills and my desire to eventually become an artist when I grew up.

The school paste came in huge gallon jars which made it quite awkward to use when doing any activity requiring paste. Using a tongue depressor, a glob of the white stuff was scooped from that jar and put onto a square of paper for each student. We could go back to the jar at any time to re-supply ourselves as often as we wanted. We seemed to consume a tremendous amount of that school paste with all those projects we did. Another reason the paste got used up so fast was that it had a bit of a mild wintergreen flavor, and I know that it had become a regular part of almost every student's diet, including mine.

One of our most enjoyable experiences had to be using the four coping saws that the school had. Mrs. Gray taught us older students how to use them. The coping saws were small hand saws with a very narrow thin blade. It was important to move the saw straight up and down as you cut out the design that was drawn on the piece of wood. We soon learned that you could easily cut wood into circles or almost any other shape that you wanted.

The farmers in the area furnished us with several wood crates that were originally used for shipping fruit. After removing the nails from those boxes, we were provided with some wood that was about a 1/8 inch and some that was about a 1/2 inch thick for cutting up with the coping saws. Miss Gray had some patterns for making some neat things that could be traced onto the wood to be cut out. It wasn't long before the patterns became too limiting and just couldn't provide us with enough variety to fulfill our needs. After we cut out our creations, some of them had to be nailed or glued together.

This was another area where my brothers and I were able to put our artistic talents to use and create some very original things. Unlike in Rib Lake we also had some very good choices of colors of paint to decorate our accomplishments. I remember making several nice things such as a pig with moveable ears and legs which we made for the younger kids, but I was especially proud of the wood planter shaped like a swan that I made for Mrs. Shanahan.

I also liked the songs that Miss Gray taught us to sing, such as "Waltzing Matilda." Most of them would now be considered folk songs. My all-time favorite was "My Darling Nellie Gray" which had such sad words, but I felt that the melody was so beautiful. Another thing that made it special is that it would cause me to think about my mother and the way she sang it. I never heard that song after I left there, but that tune has always remained as a very pleasant bit of nostalgia in my mind.

Indelible pencils were quite popular with us that year. They wrote just like ordinary pencils, but the writing looked a little glossier and couldn't be completely erased. If you licked on the point first, it would write in purple for a couple of words and the tip of your tongue and your lips became that same purple also.

Turning to the back of the classroom one could see bookshelves that were built against the two walls in one corner. Those bookcases were only two shelves high, so they were capable of holding no more than 100 books, and that was the complete library for all eight grades. Most of the books were old and well worn. I read most of those books and a few of them more than once. One of my favorites was Black Beauty because I liked the story but I found it to be quite unique because it was about a horse that could think like a person.

In that corner there was also a table with what we called a stereoscope (stereopticon) and a box that contained the special rectangular cards for viewing. Each card had two almost identical, brownish-tinted pictures and a few that contained some very faint colors of pink, yellow, and light blue. To use the contraption, one just had to put the card into a slot on one end of the stereoscope and about 8 to 10 inches from the card you could look through the special lenses at the other end. What you were seeing through the two eyepieces, with clear lenses, had magically changed the two pictures at the other end into one image, but it would appear to be in 3-D (three-dimensional).

There were also some magazine-sized paperback books that almost gave the same effect of viewing in 3-D. The books had pages of what appeared to be some awfully messy pictures composed of red and blue lines. Looking through a pair of special glasses with cardboard frames and having one red lens and the other one blue, the pictures became clear and things seemed to jump out of the page at you.

Our desks were mounted on skids in a set of three to a row, so that the front had a seat but no desk and the back had a desk, but no seat. By arranging two sets of these to make a row, it provided seating for five students. There were just enough sets to make four rows, so I don't know what we would have done if they had more than 20 students.

Since the desks were on skids, we were able to move three desks at one time. When we were having some particular activities such as celebrating holidays, birthday parties, plays or just certain games, we could slide the desks on their skids and line them up against the walls. That would leave a large area in the middle of the room that was only interrupted by the stove that sat in the very center. When we were finished, the reverse procedure was used to get the desks back into their rows again.

The playground had the usual school equipment with three swings and a slide. During recess those were used by the smaller kids as the older ones played games such as "red rover," "tag," "captain may I," or what seemed to be our favorite "pum-pum pull-away." Most of the time recess was just a free-for-all, because we rarely had any supervised activity. We thought we were privileged when Miss Gray would occasionally join our group of kids in a game that we were playing, but usually she spent most of her time with the younger ones.

A good example of our simple forms of entertainment was the use we made with a piece of string and a button. For this you had to take the string and thread it through two of the opposite holes in a button, tying the ends together. We would then put our hands into the loops that were formed on each side of the button and twirl the string. After you had the string twisted up quite well, you then just had to pull the loops outwards and the string would unwind making the button twirl real fast. By moving your hands toward and away from the button, the twirling would continue tightening the string in one direction and then in the other, and create a loud humming noise. We would continue doing that making the button go faster and louder until the string broke. The button would come slamming into one of your hands and it hurt, but we would repeat it over and over again.

An eighth grade boy by the name of Clarence and I were the oldest boys in the school, so we were given the responsibility to perform certain duties. Because Clarence wouldn't be going to school there the next year, the idea was to have him training the next oldest boy, who happened to be me, for taking over the chores for the following year. Each morning Clarence and I carried in several armloads of wood from the shed and stacked it against one wall in a neat pile on the floor in the cloakroom. Then we had to start the fire going in the round, black stove. We had to do this early enough so that the building would be warmed up and ready for use by the teacher when she arrived for the day.

The cloakroom was a narrow sort of hallway that extended the full width of the building as you first entered from the front of the school before going into the classroom. It was used for keeping our lunches on the shelves; hanging our scarves, caps, coats and snow pants on the hooks; and placing our overshoes on the floor directly beneath our other possessions.

Every morning before Clarence and I could start the fire, we had to take the cooled ashes from the previous school day out of the stove, and spread them on the driveway. After we had been starting the fires for several mornings, I decided one day to place some broken pieces of colored glass from old bottles and jars in with the chunks of wood that we put into the stove. During the day, the heat from the wood fire got hot enough to melt the glass and blend all of those colors together. The melted glass would then run down through the grates with the ashes. When we removed the ashes the next day we were always surprised by the aftereffects. I continued each day to put more broken glass in with the wood, and always the next day something quite original came out with the ashes. Sometimes the glass would just turn into nothing more than a mess, but it was worth the delight I had when on those few occasions it would form into the strangest and neatest shapes.

    I was even able to trade one of those "pieces of art" for a two-bladed jack knife from Clarence. My brothers and I got a lot of use out of that knife, playing a game where one takes the knife with the big blade completely extended and the small blade was only half-way out. You would twirl the knife into the air and, depending on which blade, or in some cases both blades went into the ground, determine how many points you got. If the knife fell on its side no points were scored. We didn't have a name for that game then, but I learned many years later that it was called mumblety-peg.

    Bringing in the fresh water every morning was another chore that Clarence and I had to do. After we primed the pump by pouring a small amount of water into it, we then had to hand-pump a pail of water that we brought into the school. We placed it on a table that was against the wall on the north side of the room. Everyone in the school used the same long handled dipper to get their drinks. You just filled the dipper by lowering it into the pail of water, took your drink and replaced the dipper. The end of the handle on the dipper had a sharp curve in it for hooking it over the edge of the pail and the cup part of it went down inside the pail. It certainly wasn't very sanitary, but we never even thought about that and we noticed no ill affects from it.

    The toilets for the school were just tiny buildings much like the one we had on the Rib Lake farm, except there were two of them that sat outside and behind the school. One building had a sign that said "Girls," and the other had a sign that said "Boys." We never called them restrooms and I can tell you that one didn't take time to rest. In the winter time it was so cold that you didn't want to expose your bare bottom for long. In the summer the smell would get you to hurry. You just didn't go into one of those little buildings thinking to get some rest. Speed and not comfort was more the style.

Just like at home, those buildings were so small that even I could stand inside facing any direction, with my arms outstretched, and almost touch both opposite walls at the same time. Inside they had a boxed-in affair of the right height with two holes and just enough width for two people to sit side by side. I don't recall ever seeing the two holes being used at one time, so my imagination provided me some other reasons for having two. I thought that they might have been put there in case of an emergency which I couldn't imagine. Or when it was built they had to do something with the extra space. Maybe two people would go in and hold hands as they did their job or one might do half of his job over one hole and the rest over the other. By the time I was in fifth grade I knew that they had two holes because they could also hold twice as much before they got too full and a new hole needed to be dug. The building had to be relocated over the new hole and dirt was sprinkled over the old one and boy did the flowers grow there!

At the Shanahan's and when we were back in Rib Lake we used toilet paper but at school we had to tear pages from the Sears Roebuck or Montgomery Ward catalogs to use for the same purpose. I don't think that those pages were much more absorbent than wax paper, but that is all that was available. We did learn a trick to make the paper softer by wrinkling it up first but it never did become the nice soft stuff you bought at the store. It seemed to get the job done and those catalogs were getting recycled. The boys had a particular order in which they disposed of the pages from their catalogs. The toys, farm machinery and the tools sections were always saved for the last so that there would always be something neat to look at as we went about our business. Personally, I really didn't much care about that, because I rarely used those little buildings. It would also have been almost impossible to do much reading, because of the poor lighting. There was just one small diamond-shaped opening near the top of the door that was deliberately put there to provide a small bit of light, but the unintentional tiny cracks between most of the boards in the walls provided the most.

One morning during recess Clarence got some of us boys together during the recess period before Miss Gray would ring the bell for school to start. He could have done it himself but I think that he felt our support would be necessary to make him bold enough to carry out his plan to play what he thought was a neat prank on the girls. We listened and his idea sounded like it might be quite funny so we went along with his putting a stink bomb under one corner of the girls' outhouse.

We followed Clarence to the girl's outhouse where he unbuttoned his flannel shirt and removed two sheets of writing paper and the celluloid to carry out his plan. The bomb was simply constructed of old celluloid film, from camera negatives, wrapped inside the two sheets of paper with the ends twisted tightly. Clarence, with our blessing, then set the paper on fire. That eventually got the celluloid smoldering, and it created an enormous amount of black smoke. He then shoved the burning bomb under the back corner of the out house. In just a couple of minutes Clarence opened the door to make sure all was working as expected. The smoke was already coming up through the seat holes and started to fill the building. The smoke alone from that bomb was enough to make your eyes water, but it also produced the most overwhelming odor which the rest of us could already smell.

It was only about 15 minutes after classes began that we were able to see the results of our mischief. Peggy, a third grade girl, raised her hand with her index finger pointing up. Just one finger indicated you had to go to the toilet and if you showed two fingers it meant that you had to go to the toilet but that it would take longer. Miss Gray immediately gave her permission to go. Peggy was gone for a very short time when she came back into the room with tears streaming down her face. She was crying and then started to complain to Miss Gray. In her sniffling voice she said, "I *can't go to the toilet because there is a lot of black smoke it **stinks**!*" That brought Miss Gray immediately to her feet as she started on a run out of the school. All of us kids followed after like a bunch of wee ducks as she rushed towards the rest room to find the problem. She only partially opened the door on the girls out house as a large amount of black smoke made her step back and she immediately slammed the door shut while she gasped for some fresh air.

We boys were all standing together and sort of laughing on the inside. We didn't expect what was going to happen next. She sent Peggy to use the boys out house. It wasn't often, but we could always tell when Miss Gray was upset; and we knew she was really mad at us now. She just turned around facing us boys as she put her hands on her hips, as she tried to look mean at us with half-closed eyes. After just an instant she then heaved up her bosom and in her meanest voice she shouted out just one word, **"Boys!"**

Miss Gray's solution to what had been done was simple and immediate. Even with her long dress, she moved quite fast when she ran back into the school. On her way back we really thought she meant business when she came rushing toward us waving a hammer. To us she even looked angry enough to use it on us and I was afraid that we had gone too far this time. I was quite relieved when she ran on by us on her way to the girl's outhouse. She then used that hammer to remove the sign that said "girls." She then went to the boy's outhouse and replaced their sign with the "Girls" and then put the "Boys" sign on the girl's outhouse. For the rest of the week, she declared that the boys' restroom was now the girls' room. Consequently, the girls' room would be designated for the boys.

It was quite a disappointment for some of the boys, because the smell from that "bomb" lingered and it was extremely offensive to us also. I don't remember that restroom getting much use for the rest of that day. Another thing the boys never thought about was that the girls also had their own interests which were different than the boys'. The four partly-used catalogs that the girls had in their restroom had displayed the pictures an prices of only the dolls, some furniture, and girls' and women's clothes left to look at. To make matters even worse the event happened on a Wednesday and Miss Gray didn't change the signs back until the following Monday.

It really wasn't necessary when Miss Gray got us boys together and made us promise her that we would never to do that again. It did teach us boys a good lesson, though, and without exception we had no intention of ever repeating that mistake.

Quite often my brothers and I played around the old, unpainted machine shed that was located about the distance of a half city block away from the house. We enjoyed climbing all over inside it and even up onto the roof. The shed was quite large and most of the front of it was more than a thirty-foot opening interrupted by only one vertical post in the middle. It had no door, which gave it easier access for the movement of the large farm equipment as it was needed to be brought in or out. There was only about six feet of wall on each side of that huge opening and the building was empty.

While playing out there one early October day I intended to climb onto the roof as I had so many times before. My brothers, Pat and Thomas had climbed up on the inside where they were soon way up on the rafters. I had begun my climb up on the right side of that opening. I was slowly working my way up on the outside with just my left arm inside the shed. I had just put my right hand up on the roof and was ready to swing the rest of my body up when I heard Pat's voice loudly shouting, "Look out!" I stopped where I was. He then shouted out even louder, **"Look out!"** It was his second blood curdling yell that really got my attention. I had no idea what was happening inside and it scared me so my response was immediate when I started to climb back down just as quickly as I could.

I knew that Pat and Tom had climbed up near the ceiling and somehow they managed to dislodge an enormous old log beam from its support inside the machine shed. It came crashing to the dirt floor below. It all happened so suddenly! I had no idea about what they were doing, but at that same time I was still in the process of my downward climb. Since my left arm was still on the inside and completely out of my view, it was impossible for me to see anything that was taking place on the inside of the shed. The beam was really quite large and it frightened me as it landed so close to me and a lot of dust rose up from where it had settled onto the dirt floor just next to me. It hit the ground with a lot of force and I felt relief that it had missed me.

I made my final jump to the ground, but it didn't take me very long to realize that, on its way down, the end of that large beam had landed full force on the thumb of my left hand. I could see that the bone at the end of the thumb had been crushed. I could see that it was just a mass of blood and it resembled something like hamburger, but strangely it hadn't begun hurting just yet. By its ghastly appearance I knew that the thumb had been seriously damaged and that this is not good. I immediately ran toward the house as fast as I could go. The nail was completely off and just dangling from a piece of skin as I was running. I wasn't even near the house when I started to feel pain building up in that thumb.

Before even entering the house I was calling out, **"Mrs. Shanahan! Mrs. Shanahan!"** I ran into the kitchen. Thankfully Mrs. Shanahan was right there to promptly take care of me and knowing that, made me feel better immediately. I was holding my left hand for her to see. In spite of all the pain not one tear came to my eyes.

When she first saw the wound she let out a gasp and cried, **"Oh my God! What have you done, child?"** And then she repeated, **"What have you done?"** The thumb was now beginning to develop feeling and it was starting to hurt terribly.

I answered, "It got smashed by a big log in the machine shed."

I don't know what I would have done if I had know how Mrs. Shanahan would be taking care of it. I pulled the nail away as she disappeared into the pantry. She came back with turpentine and some clean white cloth. With my right hand I held my left wrist and the pain was tremendous now. That horrible pain that I had begun to feel was to be nothing compared to when she began to wash the wound with turpentine. As soon as the turpentine touched the thumb, I can't even express how it had now begun to burn, and it would be impossible to describe that pain. I couldn't help myself as I let out one loud yelp. I then got quiet and grabbed onto the right corner of the collar on the tan jacket that I was wearing and put it into my mouth. I started chewing on it as fast and as hard as I could.

Mrs. Shanahan then took some clean white cloth from some, old, washed feed sack material and she tore it into narrow strips. Even though she was trying to be careful as she started winding one long strip around and around the mutilated thumb the first bits of cloth to touch the wound hurt terribly. I know that if I were an adult I would have received some whiskey to make things more bearable but for a child they had nothing for pain. She then told me that I should go upstairs and lie on the bed with Minnie.

By the time she had finished wrapping the thumb into a very large bundle, I was feeling the most horrible pain and it also felt as though my heart was pounding inside of that thumb. I was given nothing for the pain and I don't think that we even had aspirin in the house. I went upstairs as I was told and Minnie was glad to have me lie down in bed with her. She was so kind and she even held me and that made me feel ever so much better. That also was to be the last time that I can remember that I allowed anyone other than my mother to really hold me. It felt so safe with her and I was ever so grateful. The pain from that thumb was excruciating and it kept throbbing so much, but I made up my mind that I would not shed one tear for it. I just kept gnawing away on that jacket collar.

I chewed the right side of my collar off to where it couldn't be reached any more with my mouth while I was still wearing the jacket. I then started chewing on the left side until I had also chewed off quite a bit of that collar, before I seemed to no longer require that. I suppose that I should consider myself lucky that the log didn't land on my whole hand instead of just the thumb. The weight of that log would have certainly squashed my hand just as easily and I would have been without any left hand.

I was able to put that mangled thumb to some good use later. I mentioned earlier about my feelings for Miss Gray and why I took no fancy to any of the girls at school. There were two girls, one in the eighth grade and the other in the fifth grade who seemed to really like me and I regarded them as sort of pests. I couldn't tell them about how I was really in love with Miss Grey and why I wished they would leave me alone. No utterance was required from me when they would come anywhere near me, I would easily slip off the large bundle of cloth and expose that gruesome-looking thumb. As soon as either of those girls caught sight of it, she would run away. The thumb even looked more than a bit disgusting to me and I would have even liked to be in a different room than it. Actually the end of that thumb at that time had an appearance much like ground meat, and it was several months before a new nail started to grow and it was beginning to look even somewhat decent.

It was quite a few years later before any feeling began to develop in the end of that thumb. It seemed that I couldn't avoid frequently injuring it, because of its inability to react to any stimuli. That thumb is also shorter than the one on my right hand, and the nail looks a bit strange. It's not nearly as strong as my other thumb; and when I'm holding something with my left hand, the thumb tires quite easily and begins to tremble. It still causes me some problems at times. It really made me understand the importance of a thumb for gripping things.

I seemed to have gotten more than my share of distress, but my brothers occasionally experienced injuries too. One good example of that is what happened on another day shortly after my accident while my brothers and I were out in the barn playing. It seemed as though it was Tom's turn to get hurt. Pat was up in the haymow while Tom and I were together down below. We were intending to climb up the ladder and go through the small square opening into the haymow too. Tom had just begun his climb when Pat, without looking, threw down a three tine-pitchfork. He didn't know that Tom was on his way up, and as the fork came down it had enough force to drive one of the tines right through one of Tom's hands.

Tom was always quite tough, and he always seemed to take pain very well. Tom just stood there as that pitch fork was standing up from the top side of that hand. I quickly grabbed the fork handle in order to keep it upright. Pat had quickly climbed down to help. Observing Tom at that moment, a person would never have been able to tell that he was even hurt, because he didn't utter a sound and I thought it was strange that his face didn't show any emotion. He acted as though he would have been quite content to leave the fork the way it was but it would be impossible for him to wear it like that. He did let us know that it really hurt by getting very angry when Pat held his hand and I carefully began pulling the fork tine out. Just like the incident with my thumb, he was not taken to any doctor. It too was cared for by Mrs. Shanahan, with the turpentine wash before covering his hand with cloth and I know how it must have felt from that. I don't think Tom suffered one bit later on because of it. If there was a lesson to be learned from this, it quite simply would seem to be; don't ever climb up anything when Pat is somewhere above.

During our whole stay with the Shanahans, we never once went to town, so we never got to see a movie or be able to enjoy having the occasional luxuries as candy or pop. I think it was for that reason my brothers and I appreciated much lesser things than what other kids our age had. The popcorn that was occasionally made for us was a good example and became such a special treat. The popcorn with lots of butter was put into a covered frying pan and it was pushed back and forth on the hot wood stove until the popping stopped.

I imagine that my brothers may have missed the Saturday afternoon films and the serials at the movie theater. I know that I did miss the occasional times that I went to the movies with my mother and the chocolate sundaes. Sweets weren't really missed too much, because Mrs. Shanahan made up for that somewhat with her cooking, and she did a lot of baking. She could make some of the nicest pastries, cakes, sweet rolls and donuts. We also learned to eat some of the other foods that she and her family liked. There were some foods that I ate but I didn't care for, and one example of that was beef tongue.

For a short time that late summer and fall, my brothers and I were allowed to pick and eat vegetables right out of the huge garden that they had. It was also a pleasant reminder of some of the good times in Rib Lake. I especially enjoyed eating the tomatoes, green beans, turnips and carrots raw. Mrs. Shanahan canned an enormous amount of her garden produce, so that even in the winter we had a lot of canned vegetables and that was another reminder of our days in Rib Lake. That fall we also ate a lot of squash; in fact I liked it and ate so much of it that one day I got extremely sick from it. I couldn't stand eating any squash for many years after that.

They also did their own butchering, which was something I don't think I could ever get used to. In fact, late that fall I got to watch as they butchered a pig and I thought that it was a gruesome sight to be sure. There was always plenty of beef and pork to eat and I really don't think that we could have been fed any better.

When I think back to the days that we spent there, it seems as though it took so little to make us happy. Each day was different from the last as we were constantly having new experiences. My brothers and I were always eager to wake up every morning, and each of us would try to be the first one to get up. We were quite strict in observing "our" rule we made that we were to be served our breakfast food in the order that we came downstairs that morning. I was never a very good sleeper, so I got far more than my share of "firsts" with some ridiculously early times for getting up. We always looked forward to each new day with such excitement, and we were enjoying life. It was so much fun just to be alive.

When we had pancakes, for our breakfast, we always had what Mr. Shanahan called, "bug juice," to put on them. I think we were there for a few weeks before we had any idea what "bug juice" really was. It was nothing more than a clear mixture of hot water that had some white granulated sugar dissolved into it. Mrs. Shanahan put some very small, round bits of burnt pancake into the mixture; which were supposed to make it appear to be genuinely a product of those little "bugs." After all, Mr. Shanahan wouldn't make all that up, now, would he?

In the morning, we did have porridge quite often, especially when it was cold out, but we had cold cereals too. I think that they had a packet of every brand that was available back then, and we had our pick of every one of them. We had Wheaties, Pep, Cheerios, Kix, Rice Crispies and Puffed Wheat. We took turns receiving the small prizes that might be included inside those boxes. No matter what we had, breakfast was always a wonderful and happy time of the day; and besides, we had the rest of that new day to look forward to.

As the fall moved into winter, my brothers and I found that our enjoyment continued. There were some things that were a bit different. One of our most popular games was called Fox and Geese. We started by tracing out in the snow a large circle with several lines crossing through the middle. If one could look at it from above it would have looked like a huge wheel with spokes. There were some variations of the game and sometimes we used the hub for a "safe" base, but only one person could occupy the base at a time. Whoever was "it" had to chase the others until someone was tagged and then that person was "it." It was like a regular game of tag except that when you were running you automatically became "it" if you, even accidentally, went outside any of those lines which would occasionally happen when one was changing directions too fast.

We also accompanied Mr. Shanahan when he went to cut some ice on the pond. My brothers and I were able to pull one large chunk of ice at a time on the sled. We brought it to the house to be placed into the wooden ice box. We only had the luxury of keeping some foods cold in the house during the winter.

After we had spent a nice Thanksgiving holiday there, we started to happily look forward to spending that Christmas with the Shanahans' also. It was in late December when we arrived at school that a surprise greeted us in the form of a new teacher in the school. At first we thought that Miss Gray had gotten sick and she was taking her place temporarily. She was nothing like my favorite young teacher. Instead she was an older woman that was quite large and very mean. Things were not going to be the same without Miss Gray and we were all looking forward to her return.

It was a pleasant surprise when Mrs. Shanahan got my brothers and me together one evening and explained to us that we each could choose one thing that we would like to have from the Sears, Roebuck or Montgomery Ward catalog as a Christmas present from them. Each one of us made our choice, and there was just one stipulation: it had to be in the right price range. I can't remember what each of my other brothers chose, but I was going to receive a new, two-bladed jackknife with a bone handle, because the big blade on my old one got broken.

Other than the cookies and things that our mother baked in past years, my brothers and I usually didn't get very much for Christmas and then it seemed that it was usually just some item of clothing. This was really going to be something special this year. As it was getting closer to Christmas, each one of us was looking forward to receiving that one special thing that we had chosen from the catalog.

My brothers and I had been waiting in great anticipation of having a very special Christmas with these wonderful people. It excited us to think about it, but we were to find out that it was just not meant to be.

We actually left the Shanahan's quite suddenly when without any warning; we were picked up one day and delivered to our folks who were waiting for us in Sauk Center. I really didn't want to leave that farm, but I was extremely happy to see my mother again and to be together as a whole family.

We weren't going to miss the new teacher that replaced Miss Grey. As for my relationship with Miss Gray, that wasn't meant to be, either. My affections had been wasted on the wrong person, because I was to find out a few months after we left there that she got secretly married sometime during that fall and was found out. That broke one of the conditions of her contract. She had been terminated and that new teacher who replaced her was there to stay. So if we had stayed there, I wouldn't have had Miss Gray as my teacher, anyway. My heart was broken and I sort of felt sorry for all the other students at that little school.

After residing there for about four months, I felt that our home with the Shanahans' did provide us with a sense of belonging. We certainly were happy there and we were enjoying the security that we had been seeking. If it had been at all possible, I felt that I could have happily remained there for the rest of my youth. Like in Rib Lake, this was one of the few times in my life when I wished that things would never change. It turned out that this was to be no more than a short *port of call*. It was grand living there but it could never be complete without my mother, father and my youngest brother. It just wasn't going to be the safe harbor that we would always be longing for.

- X. Ominous Dark Clouds -

Events did not happen as my brothers and I had made our plans for them and we never would receive any of those presents that we had our hearts set on, because we were not allowed to spend that hoped-for Christmas with the Shanahans. It was about the middle part of December when we were already making our next move. This time we were being transported by our mother and father to live with them in New Ulm, Minnesota.

The city is situated in the southern part of the state on the Minnesota River, and it was then a very German city. Upon our arrival we were immediately handicapped because speaking German was almost a necessity to get on well with the natives at that time. Soon after arriving there our dad taught us how to say this sentence, "I don't speak German," in German. It was hard for me to believe when I was told that many of the residents were even sympathetic with the Germans during the Second World War.

What I remember most is that I was so tired of all the moving and I just did not want to relocate to some other unknown. My brothers and I enjoyed the time we were at the Shanahans so much that we really didn't even want to go with our own parents. I believe that I could have been quite happy to have lived the rest of my childhood on that farm. I wouldn't immediately know what attending school in New Ulm would be like since we would not be attending school until after the Christmas vacation. I knew that when we openly expressed the way we felt about not wanting to live with our mother and dad, it quite understandably hurt our mother's feelings.

I was hoping that this move would be special with a home of our own and our family all together. Again it was not to be and things didn't start out well for us in New Ulm, because our new home was such a great disappointment, and we were told that we would be moving to a better place soon. I had become quite skeptical, so I took no comfort in expecting that things would get any better. Our living quarters were nothing more than a small, cabin with one bedroom, a living room and a kitchen situated in a group of similar cabins on the outskirts of the city. We knew that we were going to live there for an indefinite amount of time which, to my brothers and me, could mean just about anything.

That cabin was not really designed for winter use or for a large family like ours, so we had to deal with some very crowded conditions. Even though the building had electricity and running water, it was drafty and poorly heated, and I felt that it was not a very nice place. The heating was so bad that the kitchen stove was on constantly and the oven door was left open to provide enough heat to make it somewhat comfortable. Even with that and wearing long underwear, we all wore sweaters.

The only good thing that I could see about living in that cabin was that my brothers and I were back together again with our mother. I think that I had somewhat missed my baby brother, Warren, too. I know that this was one of those times that my brothers and I would have traded the few modern conveniences that we had here for our old way of life at the Shanahans. I actually wished that I was still back on that non-modern farm living with that old Irish family.

Each time that we made a move, it was as though we were abruptly cut off from an old way of living as we were forced to begin a whole new way of life. I could only allow myself to think of the present and dream about the past, because there were so many reasons that this was not the most pleasant time for me.

We did celebrate our Christmas in that cabin, as well as our mother was able to provide for it. She somehow managed to get about a three-and-one-half foot Christmas tree, a set of lights and a few decorations. My brothers and I each got a small present from her but I couldn't afford to get her the box of Fanny Farmer candy that I would have liked to. I remember that my present was a small, red rubber toy tractor with the driver mounted on it. I was quite happy to get it and I knew this was actually more than what she could afford.

Being back with my mother was nice, but even that was somewhat offset by the way that our dad was conducting himself. Dad certainly was not a happy person during this time; in fact, he seemed to be constantly irritated. Our mother explained that it was because of his job situation. When he was upset like that, he took it out on the rest of us in various ways. One thing that was the most obvious was that we didn't seem to have sufficient money to buy enough food. Our mother always did the best she could, but she and we kids were very hungry much of the time.

It was while we were staying in that cabin that I heard my father curse for the first time. He had been gone for more than a week, and it was shortly after he came back home one day that we knew straightaway that he was extremely upset about something. He began talking to our mother and his voice kept getting louder and louder. Even though I don't remember all that he had said it was a frightening surprise when he shouted at my mother, *"Good God, Martha!"*

Those words were certainly effective, because we had never heard him curse like that before. That really made me take notice, and it was frightening to me. I was expecting my dad's wrath to come down on all of us. I only wanted to run away, but I knew that my dad would make me pay dearly if I did. I thought that all kinds of bad things were going to happen; but fortunately for us, it turned out to be no more than some very harsh talking that had only been intended for my mother. I felt a bit better when I realized that he appeared to be only angry with her, and most of that was frustration with his present situation.

I do remember that one particular incident that he was angry about was because our mother was frivolous enough to buy one baby chick for us kids. Our dad referred to it as spending grocery money to get it. It seemed to be sort of a fad that year to give children baby chickens in various pastel colors but they cost much more than the plain ones. We had seen chicks of different colors on display that were being sold in town. My mother bought one of the cheaper chickens which she thought that she would be able to color it herself and save money. She soaked the chicken with dye and then put it in a box on the oven door to dry off. The chicken did dry off but it didn't live very long.

After our short stay of just a couple of weeks in the cabin, we made another move on New Year's Day. This time our new home was a small upstairs apartment but with one small bedroom for Pat and me and another bedroom that was not much bigger than a closet for Tom and Richard to sleep in. Warren slept in his little bed that was in our mother and father's bedroom which really was the middle room between the kitchen and the living room. The kitchen was very small making it impossible for all of us to sit at the table at once and the living room was quite small. We were able to manage with the space in the kitchen because our dad was gone most of the time. The house was located at 115 North Franklin Street which was nearer to the center of the city, and like in St. Cloud it was quite handy for our mother and me to walk downtown to shop.

Our new home was only a block from where "Whoopee John" Wilfert and another block and one-half farther down lived Guy Deleo. Both of these men were leaders of some very popular bands at that time. New Ulm was then calling itself the Polka Capital of the nation. There were several other bands that were located in or near the city, such as Fez Fritsche and his "Goosetown Band."

Our apartment was so much nicer than that cabin, because it was warmer and it had a little more room. We were still a bit crowded and we had to constantly be careful about making too much noise for the people downstairs. If we were a little too loud, the people below us would pound on their ceiling with a broom, and that was an indication that we had to quiet down. We eventually got used to doing things quietly and we also needed fewer reminders. My brothers and I weren't that bad, though, and it wasn't very long before our downstairs neighbors were using their broom only for its intended purpose.

We did begin to enjoy living here, but it never was going to be what we had at the Shanahans'. The family downstairs had a boy that was close to my age and twin boys who were just a little younger than I, so we played together sometimes. There also was a very large family with eight kids that lived across the street, we made friends with them and had fun playing with them too. Their father was a teacher at the Lutheran School, and he was awfully nice to all the kids and I learned to like him a lot.

Soon after we had settled into our new home, we got a chance to find out for ourselves about how true it was that the policemen in New Ulm deserved their reputation for being so stern in carrying out their duties.

One day in January before we had yet begun attending school, Patrick, Thomas, Richard, and I met an older boy. He seemed to be quite interesting to talk to and he was so friendly towards us. He controlled the conversation as we accompanied him to a large vacant lot where we found a lot of pleasure in playing on some construction equipment. We climbed onto the road grader, the bulldozer, the steam roller and all the other equipment, as we made believe that we were really actually operating them. It was wonderful because there was so much equipment we could each have our own.

We had been playing there and enjoying ourselves for more than an hour when we noticed a police car driving across the field and it was coming slowly toward us. At first we didn't think much about it because we felt we weren't doing anything wrong and we certainly weren't hurting anything so we just continued with our play. We watched as the car finally came to a stop near where we were and the red lights started flashing. A policeman got out and he started walking slowly but steadily toward us. It was then that we became frightened, so we climbed down from the machinery.

We followed the example of the older boy and we had just begun running away when the policeman shouted in a very loud and angry sounding voice, **"Stop or I'll shoot!"** He even had taken his gun out, and held it up to make sure that we couldn't miss seeing it. He had us convinced that he would probably use it, so we stopped in our tracks.

We just stood there as he was approaching, and he was already speaking to us. We then stood in front of him and could see that he was quite a large man about the size of my father. He seemed to be awfully angry and he made some remarks in that same threatening voice, *"Just who the f - - - do you think you are? Who told you that you could play on this G - - damn equipment?"* He seemed to be waiting for an answer but none came from us.

We just stood there too terrified to answer his questions. He used a lot of other nasty language while he was talking to us. *"This is expensive equipment and it wasn't made for some little sh - - - to play on."* Then he shouted at us again, **"Who gave you permission to play on this equipment? Answer me, damn it!"**

Our only reply came weakly from the older boy when he said, "No one told us. We were just playing."

Without looking directly at us, the policeman sort of spoke out of the side of his mouth, "Just playing? Well I'll teach you where you should be playing and it isn't here. Just walk over to my car. **You little sh - - s need to be taught a lesson!"** The policeman then followed us back to his police car. He opened the back door of his car and ordered the five of us to get into the back seat with a cage like thing separating us from the front seat. He drove us down town to police headquarters in the City Hall.

As soon as we walked into the station, he pointed out the bench where we were to sit. That bench was designed for just two people so it was quite crowded for all of us on that one bench but we were afraid to do anything but sit there with Tom and Richard doubled up over Pat and me. Then he left us there while he went to talk to another policeman, sitting at a desk, before he departed. I don't know how long we sat there but it did seem to be a very long time. I was worried because I didn't know what they were going to do with us.

Finally the other policeman called us over to his desk where he asked each one of us our names and addresses and I could tell that he was writing all of the information we had given him. He also asked for phone numbers which was no problem for the older boy but we had no phone so my brothers and I had to tell him the number for the people who lived downstairs from us. He then got up, came in front of the desk and commanded us to follow him to another room where we had to stand as he started talking to us about things such as respecting other people's property. As he continued speaking to us, he walked over to a cabinet and took out what looked to me like a great, big whip. My mind was already racing with thoughts of his actually using it on us. We were now becoming quite terrified by this. While holding the whip close to our faces, he asked, *"Do you know what this is?"*

We really didn't know for sure, but it did look a bit like a whip. I did remember about such a whip in one of Minnie Warehon's stories and I also knew that it was a terrible thing to be used on someone. We weakly replied in unison, "A whip?"

He told us, *"You damn right it's a whip,* but it's very special kind of a whip. This is called a cat-o'-nine tails. It can cut right through your clothes and slice the skin right off of your back," making sure that each of us got to see the eight separate ends of it, *"-and it will do it with each of these nine ends."*

If he was trying to scare the daylights out of us, he had succeeded. We continued receiving some more threats like that, and then to our relief he finally said, "If you have to be brought in here again, you will get a chance to feel this." He held up the whip. *"Do you understand?"*

To this we all immediately answered, "Yes."

He then sent us home, after we had promised him that we would never play on that construction equipment again. As we were leaving he called out to us, "I'm going to make *damn* sure that your parents know about this!"

After we left the station, my brothers and I felt relief in thinking that we had just escaped some horrible fate. We couldn't understand it because we knew that we did no harm to that equipment but why were the police so upset with us. The older boy left us and I don't recall ever seeing him again.

As my brothers and I were walking along and discussing what had just happened we were now beginning to dread the very real possibility of receiving a "whipping," from our dad. We had decided that we wouldn't say anything when we got home. Pat, Tom, and I knew that wouldn't be a problem for us but we worried that Richard might say something. We couldn't move on until we had some assurance that Richard wouldn't say anything. "Remember," we told him, "if our dad gives us spankings we will all get spanked, even you."

Richard promised and we continued moving slowly toward home, our conversation dealt with that fear and we were strongly hoping that just maybe our dad wouldn't be home and not find out about any of this. The only reason that we were feeling somewhat hopeful was based on a bunch of suppositions. Suppose our father was gone as he usually was or suppose the people downstairs wouldn't get the call or suppose they may not tell our dad about it. And finally we didn't think that the police would bother coming around and if they did, only our mother would be home. We knew that if it was our mother that found out that she wouldn't get angry with us at all. After hearing our story she would think that we had been punished enough.

As we were approaching the house our worst fear was realized as soon as we saw our dad's car so we already knew that he was home. We went upstairs and quite tentatively walked in the door. It was quite a pleasant surprise when nothing was ever mentioned. We were still worried that Richard would tattle but he kept his word and didn't say anything about what had happened. Fortunately for us, our dad was never notified by the police, or at least he never let us know about it. After that experience, we completely lost all interest in playing on any construction equipment or doing anything that could even possibly be a cause for any irritation to those policemen.

Christmas vacation had to finally come to an end and now I would have to accept, for the fifth time, the stern reality of attending another new school. Changing schools was something that I was never able to get used to. In the past, every time I was forced to attend another school, I always found the first day to be a most frightening experience. I now would be in completely new surroundings and I would have to make new friends.

Experience provided me with some solace in knowing that most of my fears were usually unfounded and that things are never really as bad as they may seem. I also was realistic enough to not expect things to be like it was at the Shanahan's. This time, however, it was going to be quite different, because I had not anticipated that my circumstances were actually going to be worse than anything that I had imagined.

One of my reasons for dreading this school was because it was another Catholic school and from my experience in St. Cloud I knew they are quite strict in dealing with children. It was extremely hard for my brothers and me to adjust to our attending school at Holy Trinity. All of the kids we had become friends with and lived in our neighborhood went either to the Public school, the Lutheran school, or St. Mary's. We hadn't yet met anybody that would be going to the same school that we would be attending. The first day was going to be the same as in the past when I entered the other schools for the first time as I would have to accept going through that terrifying experience again.

This time it was to become even more frightening. For starters, it became immediately apparent to the other students that my brothers and I were poor, because we wore flannel shirts and bib overalls. At Holy Trinity, the girls wore uniforms and all the boys wore white shirts, ties and dress pants so we really stood out from the rest.

When we were among the other students we certainly caught everyone's attention. We were constantly being bullied by the other boys on the playground. They even tried to embarrass us with their attempts to unbutton the sides of our overalls to reveal our underwear. They would tease us by saying, in their sing-song way, such things as, "Farmer Brown went to town with his pants hanging down," and they would laugh at us.

During one such incident I tried to get some relief from the sister in charge of playground that day but all she did was say to me, "God doesn't look at your clothes, He only looks at your soul." I found no consolation from her words and that may be true of God, but I still had to defend myself against the rest of those kids daily. It became obvious that I couldn't turn to anyone in authority for help. I'm sure that they must have known what was going on, but there was very little that the sisters did to discourage it.

The only help that I could rely on came from my brother Pat. I don't know what I would have done without Pat in the same class with me. Those boys who were picking on me soon learned not to bother Pat, because he was bigger than I and very able at defending himself. It took several weeks; but then none of those boys had enough courage to do too much to me, because they weren't about to challenge Pat, whom they all learned would protect me.

Another reason it was so difficult to make any friends at this school is that all of the other kids could speak at least some German, and we couldn't speak any. Because of that we were thought of as being too stupid to associate with them. In the morning before class began, the boys usually played cards. The game they played even had a German name Schafkopf and we weren't familiar with it or the American version called Sheepshead. They only spoke in German while they played so that automatically excluded us.

To make matters even worse, the short, chubby sister who taught our fifth grade class was a very demanding disciplinarian. I don't remember her ever showing any signs of having a sense of humor. She seemed to be so serious about everything. Even the stories she told us had to do with someone doing something bad and how he was severely punished. She wasn't very nice to anybody, and I felt that she could be especially nasty to the boys.

One day I watched as she dealt with one boy who had done something wrong. She spoke to him angrily as she continued to come towards him and he started moving backwards. She had literally backed this particular boy into one corner of the room. I don't know what the boy had done to create so much anger within her. Finally that boy got so frustrated with the sister that he made a fist and it did appear that he was about to strike her. I was watching in fear as she responded by pointing her index finger and shaking it up and down while almost touching his face, and in a very stern voice shouted at him, *"You would dare to strike me, a person of God? You do, and I swear that God will send you to burn, forever in the fires of Hell!"* The boy then finally broke down and cried.

That sister had everyone intimidated by the way she used her position as a nun to maintain strict discipline. She, without exception, did put the fear of God into all of us with stories about the vengeful God who was quick to punish for minor transgressions. I think that there were even times that I felt guilty about something, and I hadn't even done anything. She was very much the opposite of Miss Gray, whom I was already missing so. I was strongly wishing that my dad would have sent us to the public school because anything had to be better than this.

The class was also way ahead of Pat and me academically in the subjects of math and music. This made things quite difficult for us, especially in math. It became obvious straight away that no one was going to help us catch up, so Pat and I had to teach ourselves at home how to add and subtract fractions. As we were struggling with that, in school we were being taught how to multiply and divide fractions.

They also had a music class each day, and all of the other kids had been taught how to read notes. In all of our years my brothers and I never had any exposure to reading music so I really felt left out during this class. This was the one thing that I don't think it would ever be possible for us to catch up with the others and their years of experience, but unlike the math I felt that we could get on all right without it.

During some of the classes, because our dad couldn't afford to buy us each a set of books, Pat and I had to sit in the same desk in order to share the same book. The desk was designed for one so it wasn't very comfortable sitting together like that for a whole class period. I also felt terribly embarrassed and we were sometimes teased for it by the other students.

I remember one example of the type of teasing we got came from a boy by the name of Donald Herbeck, who sat across the isle from Pat and me. He seemed to find a lot of pleasure in teasing us especially during geography class when Pat and I had to sit in the same desk as we were forced to share the one book. On one particular day he was showing off his bright new wrist watch. He pointed and then tapped the face of it as he whispered to us, "Tick, tick, tick, time to take a pee" and then repeated it several times. I really wasn't sure at all what he meant by it, but it was also quite apparent that he was trying to get us upset. I just interpreted this to be some reference to orphanage kids (but how would he have known that Pat and I had really been in one, such a long time ago?) where we always did things together by the ringing of a bell. Anyway, I developed a strong dislike for him and all the teasing.

Donald was a bully and it was because of that incident that Pat finally challenged him to a fight. During the next recess the two decided that they would meet that same night at the bowling alley and settle things. Tom and I accompanied Pat to within about one-half block from their meeting place to be sure that it would be a fair fight. Pat waited for more than one-half hour past the agreed time, and I continued to watch from around the corner. Our antagonist never did show up and we finally went on home. From that time on Donald was far more decent toward us, and he no longer teased Pat or me.

For the first several weeks, it was a dreadful business just getting up each morning and going to school there. We were also back on the same routine that we had in St. Cloud of going to Mass each morning before classes. I still found the kneeling to be a problem for my back. It was during those times I especially wished that my dad had sent us to the public school. I even prayed to God to change things for me.

It seemed that it was taking forever for us to make any friends at Holy Trinity. As time went on, things did begin to improve and the others did begin to accept us. One by one I did eventually develop some acquaintances if not friendships.

After attending that school for a just about a month, John, one of the boys in our class, started telling me about the paper route that he had. He also told me that he was going to quit his route. I became really interested when he told me how much money he was making and he wondered if I would like to take over his route. I also knew that he had asked some other boys before asking me and was refused which caused me to wonder a bit, but I had decided to remain open minded about it and besides I could use some money.

He asked me if I would like to go with him sometime to help deliver his papers and I could see for myself what it was like. I told him that I would let him know for sure tomorrow. I knew that I would have to tell my mother so she wouldn't worry because I hadn't come home right after school. I also knew that she would allow me to go.

The following day with my mother's blessing, I accompanied John on his paper route. I thought that the job was easy enough with only 28 daily customers and it impressed me as an excellent way to make a lot of money. I had decided right then that I wanted a route for myself. John told me that he had to find someone to take his place. As soon as we finished the route that day, I let him know that I would very much like to have his paper route.

As soon as school was out the next day, John had me go with him to the paper office which was downtown in the middle of the block next to an alley. It was nothing more than a garage that had been properly converted for this purpose with a stove and desk. He introduced me to a young man named Wally Ebert, who ran things and would be my boss. Wally talked to me about the job and then he told me that he would give me the route, but only after I had gone around with John for a week to learn the route. As promised, just one week later, I was proud to have my own paper route delivering the Minneapolis Star and Minneapolis Sunday Tribune. I had the responsibility of delivering papers every day of the week and every Saturday I also had to collect the money from each customer.

When I began that route, it had only seventeen daily and fifty-five Sunday customers. I was quite proud of myself when, within less than a year, I had built up that route so that I was delivering to twenty-eight homes every day and each Sunday I had to deliver one hundred fifteen of those huge Tribune papers. Of course, enlarging my route like that meant a lot of extra work, but it also meant making much more money.

That paper route became extremely important to me. It seemed to fulfill some important need within me. I felt I almost had a duty to work and earn money. There were two important additional benefits that went along with the job. Besides earning my regular route money, I had the opportunity to earn additional money and prizes. I would attend every one of the weekly night meetings, where the Minneapolis Star and Tribune provided us with different promotions to get new customers. It was for signing up these new customers that we could earn ourselves some really nice premiums or money. I made sure that I attended each of these meetings and I worked hard at getting new customers. I earned cameras, accessories for my bike and many other wonderful things.

When I arrived at the weekly meeting, Wally would assign each of the carriers a particular area of the city to solicit that night. I went to each of the houses that were not regular customers. It wasn't fun, because I knew that as I approached the next house that I would probably get turned down. It was quite difficult for me, at first, to accept rejection, but I continued on with the hope that the people in next house just might subscribe to at least taking the Sunday paper. After I had worked my region to get new buyers, I had to report back to the paper office by a certain time. I turned in all of the newly-signed customers and made a claim for my premiums.

The second benefit we received for just attending the meeting was that Wally would take all of us out and buy us ice cream sundaes before we went home. It didn't matter if you got new customers or not. This was something that he did for us, using his own money.

We all liked and had a lot of respect for Wally, because he was such a great boss to work for. I felt that he was also my friend and I could talk and joke around with him. I thought it was a bit strange that he wrote right-handed, but he threw a ball and did everything else left-handed. I also could tell that Wally genuinely liked each one of the boys that worked for him.

Another thing that I liked about Wally Ebert was that he was also the first baseman on the New Ulm minor league baseball team. I was greatly impressed by his ability at being such a fantastic player, and I considered it to be a great thrill just to be a part of the crowd when he played. I often went to the baseball games, but I made an extra effort to be there when he was playing.

He had a way of making me feel special and a bit proud to be in the stands during a game that he was in. Every once in awhile, this great player would stretch way over the dugout, and we would talk to each other. I could almost feel the eyes of the other spectators and how they must have thought about me, the lucky boy who was liked by such a man as Wally. I got excited and I would cheer whenever he hit a home run, which he did quite frequently.

Later on when I had enough money I bought myself a Rawlings Trapper baseball glove, which was specially designed for first basemen. I learned to use it well and I could easily catch the hardest hit ball that was anywhere within my reach. Less than one year later, I left that glove on picnic table in the city park for only a few minutes and, sadly for me, someone else became the new owner. It really upset me and I never did get myself another glove until years later when I was in High School.

It wasn't long after I got my paper route; I quickly realized that a bicycle would make my task much easier. I didn't want just any bike and I saw the bicycle I wanted in the Our Own Hardware Store for $72.50, which was an awful lot of money. I thought it was the most beautiful bike that I had ever seen. It was a two tone green Schwinn with a knee-action spring fork in the front, white sidewall tires, luggage carrier, head light built into the front fender, a built-in kick stand and all the other features that one could imagine. It was also the most expensive bike that I could find. I had made up my mind that one day I was going to have that particular bike.

I went into the store and I asked the store manager if he would save that bike for me, while I made payments on it each week. The manager agreed to my terms and he said, "I will personally see to it that this bike will be here for you when you make your last payment." I then gave him the first payment of $3.50 and left the store feeling overjoyed that I now had less than $69 left to pay.

Every Saturday after I finished collecting from my customers, I went to the paper office and paid my bill. Then I went straightaway from there to the hardware store and made as big a payment as I felt I could afford on the bicycle. I also made sure that I got a receipt each time and I saved each one. I wasn't going to leave anything to trust.

Even though my mother knew about my paper route, we never told my dad because we both knew that he would be asking me for money. When he finally did find out that I had the route he was angry with me for not letting him know sooner. He even seemed to be more upset with my mother for keeping it a secret. It was just as my mother and I expected, I was now often compelled to relinquish some of the profits that I made to him. He told me that he would only need the money for " - - - - just a short while" and "Sonny, I will be able to pay you back soon." He assured me that when he received the money that he was owed from his job with an insurance company, I would get every penny back that he borrowed from me. That really troubled me; because he had borrowed money from me before, and he had never paid back any of it. I kept track of every cent that he borrowed from me and now there were times that I wasn't able to pay very much on the weekly payment on the bicycle. I became quite concerned that I would never get that bike paid for.

The amount of time seemed long; but fortunately, after a few months, my father did find a better job with another insurance company. Immediately he seemed to be doing better financially so he no longer required my earnings to help out any more.

By this time, I had all but a small portion of the debt to complete my payments on the bike. My father had figured out how much that it was that I had given him. I also kept close track of how much the amount was, and we came to an agreement on the amount. What he got from me was more than double what was required to pay off the bike. He then gave me just the exact amount that I needed to get the bike, still owing me the rest.

I took the money and as I was going to the store expecting to pay for the bike, I was already imagining myself proudly riding it home. Anxiously, I went into the store to get that brand-new bike that I had waited so patiently for; but I immediately saw that it was no longer there. Still being optimistic about it, I thought that the bike might have been put in the stockroom out of sight. I asked the clerk about it and he told me that he thought the bike had been sold but that I should talk to the manager.

The clerk's words left me quite indignant, so I went to see the manager of the store. This was the person who had told me that he would personally see to it that the bike would be there for me when I had the final payment. When I asked him he explained, "I didn't expect you to be coming to get that bicycle so soon." He told me that he was sorry and he then assured me that they would have another one just like it in only a couple of weeks. I had made an agreement with this man and he didn't keep his word. He had sold my bike. That really upset me, and I was angry with him.

I then let him know just how annoyed I was when I told him, *"We made a deal. I want every penny of my money back! Right now!"*

He didn't want to give me my money back so he began trying to convince me that he would have another bike within a few days and told me that I should wait. I wasn't going to have any part of that, because he had been dishonest with me. It took awhile before I finally convinced him that I wasn't going to give in, and he reluctantly gave me the exact amount that I had already paid on the bike.

I took that money, and I went to the smaller Fasenmeirer's Hardware Store across the alley from that other store, where I knew that they handled Columbia and Monarch bicycles. I decided to buy myself a brand-new, bright red Columbia bicycle, with white trim, from them for only $52.50. The Columbia wasn't nearly as nice as the Schwinn bike, but it had everything that the Schwinn had except the front knee-action spring fork, and it cost me exactly $20 less. That price also included the large wire basket I bought from them to mount on the handlebars and the front hub of the bike, for carrying papers. I gave all of the money that I hadn't spent to my father. Even though it wasn't the bike that I had originally wanted, I was quite proud of it because it was mine and I took good care of it. I felt that it would serve all of my needs for several years and as long as I would need a bike.

My father was gone most of the time selling insurance during the time that we lived in New Ulm. I had very neat handwriting and I had even, throughout my years in grade school, won many penmanship awards. My dad was aware of that, so he enlisted my help in keeping the files of all of his customers up to date. The only thing that being a good student in school and my having nice handwriting was winning for me now was a whole lot of extra work. It took an enormous amount of my time, because that good handwriting was the result of my laboriously drawing my letters as I wrote.

I entered the name of each customer and all of their other information on a file card and I had them filed alphabetically. Dad had a lot of customers and many prospective ones. I had to constantly update all of the necessary information about each one. I also had to keep up to date with another prospect list which seemed endless and it also required constant changing. I spent a large amount of time at the table working on my dad's files. Although I tried hard to be careful and to do a good job, he would get angry with me if I did occasionally make a mistake. If he felt that I had made a very bad error, I would receive a good spanking for it. I would rather have been outside playing with my brothers, because it required so much of my time. It was such an awful chore and also a massive amount of responsibility.

Things seemed to go quite smoothly, at home, when our father was away. I don't think he liked his job very well and he would take his frustration out on us. Sometimes he was gone for more than a week or two at a time, and I would come to actually dread the day or night he would return and we knew all too well when he arrived.

Before our dad departed on some business trip, each time he would assign my brothers and me a list of tasks that we were expected to complete before he came home again. It seemed as though every time each of us would invariably neglect to do one of his assigned jobs. We knew as soon as our dad came home, which was usually late at night, that he would immediately awaken us from our sleep. We would come out of the bedroom in our underwear and stand in front of him in our condition of being half asleep. We never knew why he was getting us up, but his conversation started out in an angry voice with, *"Why didn't you - - - ?"* which was directed at one of us which would also give that person a reminder of what it was that he had forgotten to do. He would never accept any excuse. It was hard for me to understand why he even bothered to ask "why?" He seemed to have an awful good memory for this. He then would proceed on to the next one with the same question but different chore.

As a consequence of our neglect, we were directed into the living room and one by one ordered to bend over a chair. With my posterior pointing into the air, he would give me a severe beating with his belt. I was then sent back to bed crying, with a warning that, *"When I tell you to do something, I expect it to be done!"* Usually Pat and Tom were waiting in line for their spankings too, but that didn't offer me any consolation. We also learned that it was important to cry or the spanking which really did hurt would last longer.

I can remember many times like that when our dad would even get upset with our mother. He would say to her, "Martha, you're worse than the kids," because so many times she would be crying more than we were.

It was that year that Pat somehow had acquired the most astonishing new writing instrument. I had never seen such a thing before. It was called a ball point pen and it was dark orange in color. I was immediately intrigued by it. I was also impatient to find out how it worked. Pat, quite seriously, explained that you had to unscrew one end to separate it from the other. He pointed to a part on the inside of the writing end, and he said that you had to take a match and set that end on fire. This, as he told me, was because you had to heat up the ink to force it flow out. Then you just screwed it back together and wrote with it until it cooled down. Pat was telling me all of this in such a matter-of-fact way that, at first, I almost believed him. He then finally showed me that it was all self-contained and that all you needed to do was nothing except write until it ran out of ink.

I was quite impressed by it, because you never had to refill it like our fountain pens. It was also infinitely better than the tips and pen holders that we had to use in our penmanship classes. Those we had to dip into the ink well that sat in a special hole designed for it in the top right-hand corner of the desk. You were required to dip the pen about two to four times before you completed a sentence, and you were extremely lucky if you didn't get at least a blotch or two per page. If you did get a blob of ink on your assignment, you had to do your work all over from the beginning. I thought that something like that ballpoint pen was a vast improvement over the fountain pens that we had to use and would really be an answer to any student's prayers.

The ink didn't come out too smoothly from those first ballpoint pens, so they skipped a lot when you wrote. Those pens didn't prove to be much good for us in school, because the teachers wouldn't allow them to be used for any of our written assignments yet. I still thought that it was quite an amazing invention and that it had a promising future, in my world at least. I started using them regularly at home and they were invaluable for such things as my paper route. For now it offered a special tool for the future, but it wasn't until three years later when I was in the ninth grade that it would become acceptable to use a ballpoint pen for any schoolwork and that was mainly because of the evolution of the pen itself.

After we had left the Shanahan's and come to live with our parents, I had noticed a change in my mother. It wasn't very often that I got any more of the "I love you so much, that I could just squeeze the puddin' out of you" hugs. She and I were still very close, but she was different and I also noticed that she had been getting physically weaker. The change was hardly noticeable at first. I think that the difference had begun during the time that we were living in the cabin and it continued to worsen into the spring. She seemed to be all right during that summer after I had completed the fifth grade. She and I would even walk downtown, and some of the people on the way said that they thought she was my sister. To most people she still looked quite all right.

The next fall Pat and I started our sixth grade year at Holy Trinity. When the colder weather came, it became quite apparent that my mother was getting noticeably weaker and she began to loose weight. By October there was no doubt that she was unwell. Her physical condition just seemed to keep steadily getting worse. She had been going regularly to her doctor, who was Howard Vogel, but she showed no signs of improvement. She just was not responding to any of her doctor's treatments. She was actually getting much worse.

By late winter things got so difficult for my mother that she got so weak that she could hardly do anything, and she was badly in need of a great deal of assistance. Although he really couldn't afford it, my dad did finally hire a very able woman to come in and provide help for my mother. Assistance came in the form of Mrs. Orth who was quite a hardy German woman. She was also the only policewoman in New Ulm. She not only helped our mother but with her booming voice was easily able to deal with my brothers and me.

As time went on and moved into spring, my mother was becoming thoroughly overcome with some obvious illness and she was now in need of constant help. She had become too debilitated to do anything, and she was now spending almost all of her time in bed.

Dr. Vogel continued treating my mother for what he called a nervous breakdown. My mother was not responding at all to the doctor's treatments or to the prescribed medicines. During that time, she just kept getting worse. She finally became so sick and weak that she wasn't even able to get out of bed and go see the doctor any more.

Things were not good at all and it was obvious that bad times were coming. Those **ominous dark clouds** were followed by the storms that one expects, but the damage was to be far greater than what anyone could have imagined.

My mother with Aunt Eva

My mother and father in Grand Forks, ND

My second picture

Mother during my second picture

In Duluth, MN we each had our own vehicle with Pat, Tom, and Richard in front of me.

My father's tractor with the crosswise mounted engine in Rib Lake - And happy times

Me (left) and Pat - holy communion in the 4th grade

Eighth grade at St. Mary's in Robinsdale, MN

Pat in seventh

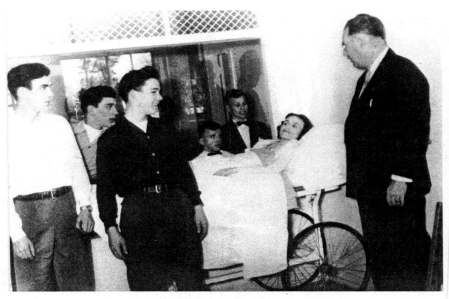

The last picture with our family all together

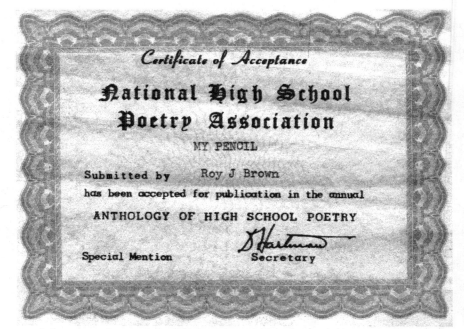

My poem that was published in two books and two magazines.
(Notice the use of my father's first name.)

Graduation! -and next fall to art school

At my father's funeral in 1954 –
Left to right-Thomas, Richard, Patrick, Warren, and me

Mother in apartment sometime after leaving Ah Gwah Ching in 1955

My Pamela from England

4 Years and 8 months after joining the Air Force

- XI. Driven Into the Rocky Shoals -

Pat and I had completed the second half of the fifth grade at Holy Trinity and now we only had a little less than one month to go before we would be finishing the sixth grade, that school year, when my brothers came home from school one afternoon and found the door to our apartment was locked. They had no key, so they couldn't get in. The lady who lived downstairs heard them on the stairs and she called to them. She explained to them that our mother had been taken away to the Loretto Hospital, and that they were supposed to wait for someone to come and get them. She also said that our mother was almost dead when they came and took her away in the ambulance. My brothers did as they were told and just waited there.

I didn't get home until much later, because I had been on my paper route; so I was the last to be informed. My brothers were still there, patiently waiting, and they told me what had happened. They were able to tell me that our mother was in the hospital but they were unable to tell me where Warren was. Since our youngest brother, Warren, was at home when all of this had happened he was already taken away to stay somewhere else. At first we had no idea where he was and it seemed as though no one was going to tell us.

Even though we all knew that our mother was very sick, I think that we all thought (hoped) that eventually she would get well and everything would be put right again. I was bewildered by the horrible news and I became quite alarmed and scared. As so many times before, I began my worrying and my imagination was thinking the worst about the condition of my mother and about what was going to happen next to my brothers and me.

Finally a man arrived with a key to the apartment, and he unlocked the house so that each of us could get some of our clothes. We were each given a paper sack and we were only aloud to carry out as much of our possession as it would hold. He then had Pat, Tom and Richard get into his car to be taken away to another home to stay. Before the man drove away I asked him where Warren was and he wouldn't answer me so it was quite obvious that I was all alone just then.

Before he drove away he handed me a small piece of paper with Mrs. Orth's address at 209 South State Street on it. He told me that I was supposed to go over to her place immediately. The whole situation was quite frightening to me, and even though I asked, he wouldn't tell me where he was taking my brothers. Again I was worried that I may never see any of them again. He had told me where to go, but I was confused by all of this and I didn't know what I should do next. I was quite bewildered as I remained there for quite awhile with my bicycle basket and my bag for delivering papers loaded with my clothes and a few other things. I was just thinking about what I would do next. I finally made up my mind that I wasn't obeying that man's orders to go to the place he had assigned.

Our mother was beginning to understand just how bad her physical condition was and she must have known before she had to be taken to the hospital that certain arrangements had to be made to take care of her oldest son. I didn't know that she had already made some arrangements with Mrs. Orth to take me with her if something should happen. Among all of her children, I guess I would always be considered a sort of the runt of the litter; and I think that my mother thought that I was always in need of special care. My mother was always worrying about me. I think that she didn't want to lose me after she had raised me this far, and while under her care she had come to trust Mrs. Orth.

I think that my mother must have already sensed something ominous about going to another welfare home. As a result of this arrangement I wasn't going to be staying with my other brothers. My brothers already had a place to go to, but my new home was going to be with Mrs. Orth. I really didn't like the thought of not being at the same place with my brothers, but from experience I had learned to accept it as the way things were going to be.

At first I was just going to follow the man's instructions, but something else seemed to be more important to me at that time. After all of my brothers were driven away to their new homes. I did not go to Mrs. Orth's as I was told. Instead, with all the speed that I could summon, I rode my bike to see my mother at the Loretto Hospital.

When I got there, I was disappointed that I was not being allowed to see my mother. The people at the hospital explained to me, "We are taking good care of your mother. She was awfully sick when she was brought here." They also told me, "She is already getting better, and it won't be long before we will be sending her back home."

I thought that I knew better than to believe that. I was angry and I began shouting at them, *"**You are lying to me!** I want to see my mother now! I'm her son, I have a **right** to see her and you can't **stop** me!"* I was wrong, and they were able to quite easily stop me. A large man, about the size of my father, took hold of me and I realized how futile it would be to resist. I surrendered and he quietly escorted me out of the hospital.

I left the hospital and rode my bike, with the load of my possessions, to the address that I was given earlier. When I arrived at Mrs. Orth's place, she welcomed me into her small house and showed me where things were. My assigned sleeping place would be on the couch in the living room

Mrs. Orth was a woman who I think was in her late fifties. She was quite large-boned, with pale blue eyes, and she almost always wore glasses that made her eyes look bigger than they really were. Her hair was dyed black, but it seemed to always have white roots and some reddish tint to it and because of the thinning hair she also wore a partial hair piece that was combed in with her own hair. She was very German, and she spoke the language well and quite often. She talked with a loud voice, and she was quite strict with others and herself. I remember that she had to clear her throat a lot and afterwards she would take the handle and lift the round plate on the top of the wood stove to spit into the stove whether there was a fire or not. She seemed to be quite religious and said the rosary every morning after she awoke. She never got out of bed until she had finished saying her rosary. She always carried it with her to Mass when we went together to her church at St. Mary's on Sunday mornings.

She led a very structured life, and every day was almost the same as the day before. She slept most of the morning and in the afternoon she religiously listened to the same radio programs, such as "Ma Perkins," "Lum and Abner," "Amos and Andy," "The Life of Riley" and a few others. Every night she worked very late, taking care of women prisoners and nursery at the police station in the city hall.

Mrs. Orth had one daughter named Alice, who came to visit us occasionally. She was married and lived with her husband on a farm near Faribault. A few years before I came to live with Mrs. Orth, her only son, Randolph, had died while he was still quite a young man. It seemed that sometimes she was looking to me as the replacement for her son, and she treated me kindly. There were other times that I just couldn't seem to live up to her memory of that almost perfect son, and during those times she was a bit less than kind to me.

Every day I rode my bike down to the hospital right after I finished delivering my papers. Each time I kept pleading with the staff to let me see my mother, and each time my request was denied. I continued doing this until they surprised me one day and I was finally taken to my mother's room at the end of a long hallway. The nurse explained that I would be allowed to spend only a few minutes with my mother.

I hadn't seen my mother for several days now, and as I entered the room I was not prepared for what I saw. I was shocked by how small and thin she looked. She even looked much worse than when I saw her last, and she had become so pale, but she smiled when she saw me. I didn't know what to talk about, but she seemed only interested in my brothers and me. She first asked me how I was doing and how I liked staying at Mrs. Orth's. I told her that I was fine and that every thing was all right. She said, "Sonny, you're the oldest and you have to watch out for your younger brothers."

I didn't tell her that I didn't even know where they were living. Instead I told her that I would visit them often and do the best I could to help them. I could tell that she was having trouble breathing, and when she spoke to me it wasn't much more than a whisper. She must have received a lot of medication because it seemed like she was having a lot of difficulty staying awake. I had been with her for a very short time when a nurse came in and told me that my time was up and I would have to go now. I didn't want to leave because I had been trying so hard to see her, and now I had become concerned that the reason they let me see her was that she was going to die soon.

Within just a few days we were informed that the hospital took X-rays of our mother's lungs. Those X-rays showed without question that our mother was suffering from an advanced stage of tuberculosis. I was also informed that I would not be allowed to visit my mother any more at the hospital. I could sense that it must be really bad.

That news really got me to worrying, because I knew that my mother's mother had died of that terrible disease and she was only 26 years old! Some say that animals destined for slaughter can sense when all is not right. I think that my brothers and I could also sense that some very bad times were coming.

My brothers and I were confused and we felt so helpless, because our dad wasn't anywhere around when all of this happened. I was frustrated and quite angry with him about that. He was still selling insurance and was on a business trip; and when he finally did get back, he came over in the morning to where I was staying. Mrs.

Orth was still in bed, so he didn't want to awaken her. I went out to the car with my dad and as we sat in his car, he asked me a lot of questions about what had happened. By this time I had found out where my brothers were and I was able to provide him with most of the information that he wanted.

He then had me go to the hospital with him, where the first thing my father did was to locate Dr. Vogel and ask him about my mother. When questioned, the doctor assured my dad that my mother did indeed have tuberculosis. My dad further quizzed him about why he didn't know more about my mother's condition before now. The doctor said, "I just can't explain it. I gave Mrs. Brown a Mantoux test and I also gave her two chest X-rays and everything gave negative results."

We then left the doctor to go see my mother. No one tried to prevent me from seeing her as long as I was with my dad, so we went to the special room they had set aside for her. They were purposely isolating her from all the rest of the patients. I think that they were afraid that my mother just might give her dreaded disease to all of the patients and the hospital workers.

During the time we were in the room, I remember my dad asking my mother if Dr. Vogel had ever taken any X-rays of her. My mother replied that he hadn't. My dad then said, "Martha, it's very important. I've got to be sure about this. Is it possible that he might have taken X-rays of you with out your knowing it?"

She answered, "I would have known it if he had taken one of me."

My dad then asked, "Do you know what it's like to get an X-ray?"

My mother said that if Dr. Vogel had taken any X-rays, she would have known it; but she was positive that he didn't. Then she said, "I know what an X-ray is and I know that he never took any X-rays of me."

After we left my mother's room my father, with me still tagging along, went to confront Doctor Vogel again. He talked for quite a long time with the doctor. I could tell that my father was quite agitated, but I really didn't yet understand why. My dad asked

Dr. Vogel, "Why weren't you treating Martha for the tuberculosis, instead of a nervous breakdown?"

He told us, "I gave Mrs. Brown a Mantoux test and it gave a negative reading which meant that she had no tubercular germ. I wanted to be sure, so I also took two chest X-rays, and they didn't show any signs of tuberculosis then."

My dad then asked him, "Didn't that tuberculosis develop awfully fast? How do you explain that it developed so far? According to what Martha told us, she is certain that there never were any X-rays taken of her."

There was some hesitation and then Dr. Vogel answered, "I gave Mrs. Brown two chest X-rays, but she was crying so much. That's probably why she doesn't remember it."

I was beginning to understand what this was all about. When he said that she was crying so much, I didn't believe him because our mother never cried no matter how badly she was ailing. My mother's tuberculosis was too advanced to not have shown up on an X-ray with in the last year.

My father wasn't satisfied with the doctor's answer, but what could he do? The doctor explained that my mother would have to be taken to the state sanitorium at Ah Gwah Ching in northern Minnesota, but right now she was too ill to be moved. "When we feel that it is safe, we will have an ambulance take her there." I was present as my dad and the doctor were speaking, and I had carefully listened to make sense out of the entire conversation.

When we left the hospital and as he drove me back to Mrs. Orth's, my dad told me that the doctor was lying to us. He then explained it, "Tuberculosis takes a long period of time to become as bad as what your mother has." Even though I now understood my father's questioning of the doctor, his words didn't have much impact on me then. As he left, my only concern was that no matter how bad the disease was, I hoped that it still was possible for my mother to get well again.

It was during my dad's visit that I was able to learn the whereabouts of my brother Warren. He had been taken to stay with a family with the last name of Polta. There house was less than a block away from where we lived and we were acquainted with them. I remember they had one child who was a boy of about Pat's age. We thought he was terribly fat and never played with the rest of the kids in the neighborhood.

The Polta's had seen Warren on several occasions and had a desire to have him as there own. As soon as they found out about our plight they volunteered to take him into their home, but they didn't want anyone from our family coming around.

After a short stay in the Loretto Hospital, my mother did improve somewhat. The hospital doctors now believed that it would be safe to transport her up to Ah Gwah Ching, which was the state tuberculosis sanitarium located in Cass County near Walker, Minnesota. I had made arrangements ahead of time with the hospital that I would be making the trip with my mother. They had promised to inform me when she would be leaving the hospital.

They did even better than that by sending the man who owned what had originally been a hearse over to Mrs. Orth's. His vehicle was black and it reminded me a bit of the panel truck that my dad had in Rib Lake, except this had windows in the back. He drove me to the hospital, where my mother was loaded into his ambulance; I crawled into the back with her. I traveled the distance of more than two hundred miles all the way to the sanitorium. My mother lay completely wrapped in blankets and strapped to a special low cot-like affair.

Since there was no place provided for me, I just sat on the floor next to her. We spent a lot of time just looking at and conversing with each other. When we were talking, most of the conversation was about the past and much nicer times. Much of the time, because of the medication, my mother slept.

It was a long trip, and riding in the back of the ambulance was uncomfortable as I was keeping my mother company the whole distance. Even so, when we finally reached our destination, it was far too soon for me. After a short wait while my mother was taken to a room and put into her bed, I was allowed to spend a short amount of time with her. Even though my mother assured me that everything was going to be fine for her, I just did not want to leave and make the return trip back home without her.

So on the 3rd of June 1948 my mother became patient #10919 on floor B3 of Ah Gwah Ching Sanatorium. To me everything seemed so ominous, and in my heart I felt that she would never be leaving this place. She was only 33 years old.

I wanted to stay there with my mother, because this place was such a long way from New Ulm. I was also afraid that if I left, that I would never see her again. The nurses tried to explain to me that it would be impossible for me to stay there, and in my mind I really knew that I couldn't. They also assured me that they would take good care of my mother. They even lied that she would probably be back home when she got well some day soon.

One of the most amazing things about all of this is that my mother always seemed to be so accepting of her terrible affliction. When I rode with her in the ambulance, she only wanted to talk about the happy times when our family was all together. She spoke a lot about my brothers and that I should visit and help them as much as I could. The only thing that my mother said about my dad was that he did care a lot about all of us and that he was doing his best. She always seemed to be at peace and she never questioned "why me?" My mother kept telling me many times that I shouldn't worry about her and that she was going to be all right. She was forever radiating happiness, and one never heard her complain about what was happening to her. She was even smiling as I sadly departed from what would be her new home.

I was a very unhappy lad because I was leaving my mother behind, and I was now facing the long ride back to New Ulm with the driver as company. That driver was a kind person and he seemed to know how disheartened I was about these recent events. He tried to make the trip home as pleasant for me as he possibly could. He spent a lot of the time in conversation with me. He talked about baseball and almost everything else except matters that had anything to do with our family. It did help to take my mind off my problems and he did make the journey a little less depressing. He even allowed me to turn on the siren a few times when he decided to drive a little faster for a short while. During those times, it was kind of fun watching as cars pulled over to the side of the road to let us by. It sort of gave me a feeling of power.

It wasn't until a few months later that I found out the true significance of the conversations that I had witnessed the day our dad talked to my mother and when he had spoken to Dr. Vogel in the hospital. My dad explained it to me that shortly after our mother became a patient in the Ah Gwah Ching Sanitorium, Dr. Crow, the superintendent of the Sanitorium, wrote a letter to our mother's physician in New Ulm. Dr. Crow was then demanding the X-rays that her doctor claimed he had taken of her. Dr. Crow felt it was important to get a dated X-ray, because it would give him valuable information about the development of the disease in my mother. After waiting several weeks for his reply, Dr. Crow sent another letter with the same request. Dr. Vogel finally sent him a return letter, stating that he had taken X-rays but that they had faded so much that they just weren't readable anymore.

My dad also told me that Dr. Crow explained everything to him and he knew better than to believe what Dr. Vogel had said about the X-rays fading. Dr. Crow also said that even with a minimum amount of care, X-rays just don't fade that quickly and in fact they can be kept for several years. Also Dr. Crow knew that if that doctor really had taken X-rays of my mother, he couldn't have missed seeing the signs of tuberculosis. It would have taken far more than a year for my mother or anyone else to have developed that disease to such an advanced stage. He explained that one of my mother's lungs had already been completely destroyed by tuberculosis and the other lung was more than half gone.

As for getting a negative reading on the Mantoux test that the doctor said he had given to our mother, Dr. Crow said that Dr. Vogel may very well have been telling the truth about that. Dr. Crow explained to us how the Mantoux test works. Mantoux tests are supposed to give a negative indication if a person has no tubercular germ. He further explained that the test given to our mother would have had no meaning at all, because you will also get the same negative indication if the person has the germ but that person has no further resistance to it, as in the case with my mother. That is something that Dr. Vogel should have known, but it is possible that he didn't. My father then told me that my mother's doctor was probably lying to cover up his oversight or ignorance.

About three years later, in the New Ulm district court, I would be called as a witness to testify under oath about the conversation our dad had had with that Dr. Vogel, back in the hospital when my mother was his patient. My dad was then the plaintiff in a lawsuit brought against that doctor for malpractice.

Soon after I arrived back home the hospital ordered me in to give me a thorough examination for tuberculosis. They had already started on my brothers. The first thing they did was to give each one of us a Mantoux test, which amounts to no more than receiving a shot in the forearm. After receiving that shot, if the area around where the needle was injected gets red and swells up, it is supposed to indicate that you have the tubercular germ. Our arms did swell up to quite a large size, which meant that all of us had the germ. We had each become what is called a positive tine; but unlike our mother, we still had some resistance to that germ. It is then quite normal to follow this up with an X-ray.

Those Mantoux tests didn't tell them anything that was really useful. They then proceeded with giving my brothers and me X-rays. After reading the X-rays, the results showed that only Patrick gave any positive indication of having tuberculosis. Because of that, on the 5th of July Pat soon after received free transportation to Ah Gwah Ching too. Pat also became a permanent resident as he was labeled patient #10939 on floor E4 of the Ah Gwah Ching Sanatorium. I thought at the time how lucky Pat was to be going up there where he would be with our mother.

It was also fulfilling my wish that I so many times throughout the years had kept saying to him about getting sick and missing a whole year of school, so that he would fail a grade. I was already regretting that I had wished that. I knew that I would also miss him, because we had persevered for so much of our lives together. He would always be my big brother, and he was also my best friend. In spite of all of his teasing, I now would have to get used to not having him with me in the same classroom in school. I have to think that the change may have been good for me, because maybe I had come to depend on him too much. But for now I knew that I would miss him terribly.

The hospital began giving all of us thorough examinations. I was fourteen months older than Pat, but I was much smaller. It was quite understandable that my appearance would have others thinking that I wasn't nearly as healthy as he. It seemed that everyone was just positive that Pat's skinny older brother must have tuberculosis too.

It was during those tests that two different doctors were also showing a lot of concern about the condition of my heart. Except what my mother had already told me about having some heart problem when I was born, I had never been told anything about this by some doctor. I didn't know if it was something else that I should need to worry about. They said that the beats were quite irregular and a valve was leaking. One doctor asked me all types of questions about how I felt and if I ever had trouble with getting tired quite easily or fainting. I gave a negative reply to everything that he asked. Nothing could be done about my heart, and it had nothing to do with tuberculosis, so I was finally sent home.

Less than a week later, I was ordered to go back to the hospital and they started the procedure all over again by giving me two more X-rays. They just wouldn't believe the results from the first ones. They read the new X-rays and the results were the same, but this time the doctor wrote in his report that the X-rays showed that I had extremely heavy lymph. I didn't have any idea what that meant, and they didn't seemed to be concerned about it. A doctor did check my heart again but said nothing. The two doctors had now made the decision to give me a gastric wash.

I reported to the hospital at the appointed time the next morning. The gastric wash really started the day before, because I wasn't allowed to eat after a certain time in the evening. I was forbidden to eat anything the next morning until after I had completed taking the wash. I was quite hungry when I arrived at the hospital and I was forced to stay that way after a long wait. To make things worse I didn't even know what a gastric wash was.

For me, that gastric wash was a ghastly experience, because I was forced to lie down on a bed and then it was essential for me to swallow a small thin orange rubber hose which had to travel all the way down to my stomach. When I was trying to ingest that horrible long thing, I kept gagging up almost as much of the hose as that bit I had just swallowed. I was almost beginning to believe that it was impossible and that the human body just wasn't designed for a snake-like object slithering down into his stomach that way. It seemed to take me forever to eventually get it forced down to its destination. When the end of the hose finally did get down into my belly, the nurses then pumped everything out of my stomach to be analyzed. I wouldn't be finding out the results for a few days, so now it would be something else to worry about. I think that I was becoming quite an expert at worrying about things.

When it was finally all over, the hose was slowly removed. It came up with a lot less effort than when it went down, but now I was really beginning to feel terribly hungry. Within a few days I happily found out that the results of that test were negative too. They now knew that I didn't have tuberculosis, so there would be no need to give me any more tests.

I was wrong, because after a little more than a week, I received another bit of unwanted communication from the hospital. I knew that the people at the Loretto Hospital didn't want me around because they liked having me there, and certainly not after I had been such a terrible patient the last time I was there. One would think that they had more than enough information about me and that they would be finished. That was not to be my fate, however; they again wanted to be sure about the results from that last gastric wash. They were notifying me that they wanted to put me through that whole process again.

With dread, I reported (hungry) to the hospital again as scheduled. At least the second time I knew what it was all about, and they even allowed me to sit on a chair and swallow that awful little orange hose. Another thing about it that may have helped is that my dad just happened to be in town to visit my brothers and me on that day, so he went with me to the hospital. It was so much easier than the first time, I think, that was because I understood what was going on.

It wasn't fair; they never did give that many tests to my brothers. After all the tests that they had given to me, they were still receiving negative indications. After this last test they seemed to be finally convinced that I was probably no carrier of tuberculosis and no real danger to their community. I was finally freed from taking any more tests, except the X-ray that would be required of me each year from that time on.

On that day when our mother was taken to the hospital and my other brothers were taken away from our home, I mentioned that my youngest brother, Warren went to live with the Polta's. We were already acquainted with this family and they appeared to be some very nice people. At first I liked the idea of having Warren sent there, because it was only a short bicycle trip from where I was living, unlike the much longer trip to visit my other brothers.

I would now be able to visit Warren as much as I liked. Eventually, the Poltas' didn't seem to want me coming around at all. I just couldn't understand why at the time, because I know that I behaved well and I brought things for Warren when I went there. I told them that I was going to come and see my brother anyway and that they had no right to stop me. The next time I went there they gave me a schedule of times and days when I would be able to visit my younger brother, which wasn't very often. They really won out in the end, because there were many times that I went over there and I didn't get to see Warren. At times they weren't home or they wouldn't answer the door when I came around.

That summer I also got a job working for the Sister Superior at the Sisters of Christian Charity Convent, which was right across the street from Holy Trinity School. As soon as I finished my paper route, I went to the convent, where I met with my brother Tom. We took care of their gardens in the summer, which kept both of us quite busy as we weeded them every day. They had a large fenced-in yard to mow, and they had several patches of flowers strung out all over the place. During the fall, time was spent raking leaves and in the winter I shoveled the snow off of their many walks and ran some errands.

Tom and I worked hard for the little extra money, which always amounted to something less than two dollars. The real pay, however, was that Tom and I were given our evening meal each day. Those nuns must eat very well, because the meals were always delicious, nourishing and filling. It also meant that I only needed to provide myself with two other meals each day. It also meant that during that time, Tom got at least one decent meal a day.

Because I went to live with Mrs. Orth, the county welfare department would not pay any of the costs for my support. At first it placed a bit of a financial burden on Mrs. Orth. I had the paper route and I worked at the convent, which really didn't earn me enough money to live on. My economic situation got a big boost when Mr. Crystal offered me another job, working nights at his Waneda Cafe, a combination restaurant and bakery.

My job there started each day at 8:30 P.M., which was only about an hour after I got finished with my work at the convent. I never completed all of my chores in the restaurant until about 1 or 2 o'clock in the morning. I always had to scrub the floors, clean up all the equipment until it was spotless, and mop the floors and clean up the equipment after the baker had left. When I was all done, I would usually make myself a big ice cream cone. Sometimes I would make another one to bring to Mrs. Orth on the nights that I knew that she was still at the police station. I was even trusted with a set of keys to the place and my day didn't end until I performed my final responsibility of locking up the main entrance door.

I earned $9 a week there, which was pretty good for a boy of my age in those times. With the three jobs, I had plenty of money to take care of my own food and clothing and all the other things that I needed or wanted. I really didn't need any of Brown County's welfare money.

Having those jobs even provided me with some extra money, so that I was able to give some to my dad when he came around to visit me. I even got into trouble a couple of times with Wally Ebert when I loaned too much money to my dad and I wasn't able to pay my bill at the paper office. I always did my collections from my customers on Friday, as I delivered the evening paper, and during the day on Saturdays. There were two occasions when my dad came to town, and he was in need of money; he drove me around to collect early from some of my customers to get the amount of money that he needed.

The work I did at the restaurant consisted mainly of the endless scrubbing of floors and tables, cleaning restrooms, re-stocking the pop coolers, helping make the ice milk, and running all kinds of errands. When I worked at that restaurant, I did all of my work as conscientiously as I could. I even went out of my way to make my work harder, because I thought it would build up my muscles faster. I believed that I then would soon get strong enough to be able to work on a farm. I think sometimes that it was running me down more than it was building me up, but that did get me through my seventh grade year.

That job at the restaurant created a real problem for me at school, because quite often after staying up so long at night, I would get very tired and have difficulty trying to stay awake during the day. Most of the sisters were well aware of my situation, and they understood quite well. Two of the sisters would even tell me that if I got tired, I could lay my head down on my desk and go to sleep. It seemed to cause no problems with the rest of the students, so I did a lot of sleeping during my seventh grade classes. I was always able to pass their tests, but it certainly affected my grades. I no longer was the straight "A" student that I had been since back in Rib Lake. I was now becoming accustomed to some lower grades in certain subjects.

Staying with Mrs. Orth meant that I was now living in St. Mary's Parish, but I had to ride my bike across town to attend classes at Holy

Trinity School. That meant that all of my classmates lived on the other side of town. Because of that and the jobs that I had, I never did get to know any of the kids from the same parish where I was living. I was also quite shy, so I didn't go out of my way to make any friends and besides what's the use; I had learned to avoid making any close friends because I would be moving to some other place soon. In fact I didn't even try to remember the names of my classmates.

I was now spending most of my free time doing very specialized activities that are best done by an individual. I think that I was also purposely shunning any opportunity to make friends, because by this time of my life it had become apparent that one day I would have to move to some new place. It would be easier to make the change if I didn't have to leave good friends behind. I think that is why I was also beginning to believe that it was just a useless activity to try to remember people's names.

I was earning enough money that I was even able to use some of it for developing some hobbies. One of the first things that I bought when I had the money was a loom on which I started making a lot of beadwork that appeared to be Native American in design. The beadwork was used for such things as decorating belts, arm bands, and even a waistcoat that I had. I even made some things for Mrs. Orth and a couple of her lady friends.

There was another activity that I came to enjoy which started out with the purchase of one rubber mold and some plaster of Paris. I believe that the first one I bought was a mold of a buffalo. I went to the hobby shop and would occasionally purchase another rubber mold to have some variety of objects to form out of that plaster of paris. I used several different colors of a special paint for decorating them. I began making many things for some of the kids at school and even some items for Mrs. Orth and her friends. It seemed that almost all of my spare time was spent in a quiet antisocial existence, so I spent a lot of contented hours alone. I never charged anyone for any of the things I made for them, but I never refused any money that some adults insisted on paying me. My hobbies had now become another source of income.

The most satisfying activity for me was making balsa wood models of cars and planes. I probably spent more free time at this than anything else, cutting, sanding, gluing, gluing and putting on decals. I spent long hours doing all of the fine detail work to make each model as close to perfect as I possibly could. The main problem with this activity was that I earned no money from it.

It was quite by accident one day when I got to see something that was the most astonishing object I had ever seen in my whole life. On the way home from my paper route, I just happened to be passing the appliance store downtown. There was a large crowd that completely filled the store and some people like me were watching through the big front window. On the high counter near the back of the store sat a big wooden box on display. That box was almost a cube, measuring over two feet in all three directions. In the upper left hand corner were constantly moving pictures on a screen that were about five inches wide by about four inches tall and rounded on the sides. This was the first time that I ever saw anything like it and I was completely intoxicated by it.

Some, like me, were able to get no closer than standing outside looking through the window at a distance of more than twenty-five feet. That particular object was causing quite a bit of excitement, even though from my vantage point and with my good eyes, I could just barely make out that a football game was being played.

We were told that the marvelous object that was being demonstrated was called television. I also thought that, unlike movies, it was quite amazing that what we were viewing was taking place at the same time as we were watching it. I think at that time that there were only about three or four hours of programming being transmitted from Minneapolis each day. I never dreamed just how much that it would be affecting people's lives in the years to come.

I was raised to never question the authority of adults, and I always did what I was told. There were some exceptional times that I would defend others against the injustice of adults, but I was completely unable to defend myself. Our dad severely disciplined my brothers and me, and most of our other experiences with adults demanded obedience. I also believed that it was a serious sin for children to disobey their parents. To me it almost seemed as though one of the primary reasons for an adult's existence was to discipline children.

One day I was at a friend's house and we were just having a lazy day of it, as we were sitting on the hallway floor with out backs against the wall reading comic books. My friend's father had died many years before, so he had been living in this nice big house alone with his mother. His mother was gone most of the time working as a nurse at the hospital; but on this particular day she came home from work as my friend and I ignored her and continued to sit and read. His mother asked him to do something, and he treated her request with indifference. I immediately started to worry and I became afraid, because I had it in my mind that a child never challenged the authority of an adult. A second time she told him to do as she asked, and as before he just ignored her and kept on reading. By now I was unable to concentrate on what I was reading anymore. I even whispered to him, "You'd better do what she says."

His reply was, "She'll get tired of asking me." I didn't know if I could believe that. I just kept thinking that his mother would come in at any minute with what I had come to expect which would be a most violent reaction from her for his disobedience. I was afraid for the both of us and I didn't want to be caught up in the middle of it.

I waited for several more minutes and still nothing happened. Finally I heard his mother ask him one more time and she seemed to wait a short time for his reply and he again ignored her and then I heard her strange remark, "Oh, never mind, I'll do it myself." I say strange because this was a completely new and confusing situation for me. Adults are bigger and they run things the way they want. They can beat you up or even kill you, I thought, so this experience left me extremely dumbfounded but left me thinking about it. I think that it did have some affect on my behavior in some of my future confrontations with adults.

Mr. and Mrs. Orth did not live together; but because she was Catholic, she would never consent to a divorce. I thought that they had the most unusual relationship. They had such opposite personalities; she was quite stern, while he was very easy-going. Mr. Valentine Orth, or Val for short, had sort of a pink face, a crooked nose, almost-white thin hair and only one long, crooked tooth left in the front of his mouth. He seemed to be quite old, but he appeared to be a very kind person. I did notice that he would much rather sit and talk than do any work. I got on quite well with him and he could be counted on to tell a nice story about the "good ol' days."

He lived downtown in a poorly furnished, one-room upstairs apartment, which I had been in only once. It had only one room with a hot plate and a bed and one chair. The walls had been decorated with old calendars that portrayed pictures of women with hardly any clothes on. When Mrs. Orth found out that I had been to his apartment, she made me promise that I wouldn't go there again. I don't know why, but the thought did occur to me that she might have known about those pictures on his walls.

Mr. Orth came up to the house once in a while, usually for the purpose of repairing something. On those occasions Mrs. Orth would always feed him a nice meal. There were some rare instances when one of them did something special for the other that would make it obvious to me that they really did still care somewhat for each other. I thought how nice it would be if those two could live together instead of having two different places. It was also a strange way that he and Mrs. Orth communicated without ever speaking directly to each other.

During the time that I was living there, communication worked something like this; Mrs. Orth would say to me, "You can tell him - - - - -. " and I would then repeat it word for word, telling him what she had just said. Then I would turn to Mr. Orth as he would say to me, "You can tell her - - - - -." and I would have to tell her exactly what he had just said. Sometimes he would say to me, "You can tell her - - - -." and before I had time to repeat what he had said, she would say to me, "Never mind! I heard what he said, and you can just tell him - - - - -." And of course I would repeat what she had just said. Sometimes these conversations could go on for a long time, but fortunately most of them didn't.

Mrs. Orth's daughter, Alice, told me that her mother and father hadn't been talking to each other for about the last fifteen years. To this day, I find it inconceivable how they could communicate that way or even got on with each other before I came along. How were they going to be able to manage that task if I was to ever leave them?

Mrs. Orth's extremely small house faced west on a decent sized lot that had plenty of room behind it for the large garden that she had. The house had only three rooms, a small living room, the middle room which she used as her bedroom, and a very small kitchen that was about 16 feet long and only about 7 feet wide, with a big, wood cook stove. You could enter the front door by walking into a small, narrow, open porch that ran along the right side of the house. We typically used the back door, which faced towards the alley, for entering or leaving. Just outside of the back door sat a large wooden barrel with the specific purpose of catching rain water for washing. With some remodeling and some way to heat it, the unfinished attic could probably have been made into a decent-sized bedroom. The house was completely without any basement, which was quite uncommon in Minnesota.

Even though she called it one, it was not really a bathroom, because it really was just a small closet with only a toilet in it so afterwards you could only wash up at the kitchen sink. As in Rib Lake and with the Shanahans', I was again reduced to taking my baths in a wash tub in the kitchen. I rarely took a bath; and when I did, I took it when Mrs. Orth was away and I was sure no one else was around. As in the past, I did it with as much speed as I could. That habit stayed with me, as I didn't want to be caught in my embarrassing nakedness and unable to run away.

When I first moved into her house, I slept quite comfortably on the couch in the living room. It wasn't very long after Mrs. Orth's house had become my permanent residence that Mr. Orth had a friend of his haul some plywood up to the house in his pickup. Mr. Orth and I worked for the better part of a day, fixing up and enclosing the front porch with that plywood. We also had to use some thinner plywood to put over the old front screen door. After we furnished remodeling that porch and added an old second-hand army cot for me to sleep on, I now had my own bed room.

This bedroom of mine was not furnished with any heat, and it only had that single layer of plywood for the walls. Several blankets and a comforter were required to keep me warm during that cold Minnesota winter. It had become mandatory for me to go back to a habit that I had just got over less than a year ago, and that was to sleep with my head always covered. Now it had become a necessity all winter long because, most of the time, the nights got to be freezing cold. Sometimes when the winds were blowing hard, I even had some snow form into small drifts against a wall in my bedroom and a fine dusting of the sparkling white flakes on my comforter. To offer proof that it did get quite cold out there, one night a bottle of Mr. Orth's after shave lotion, that contained some alcohol froze solid.

It had become the standard procedure, as I awoke each morning to quickly jump out of bed and run, shivering, into the heated living room and put on a change of clothes just as quickly as I could. In spite of things such as this, I only considered them to be no more than inconveniences. I could take some comfort in knowing that I had it ever so much nicer than my brothers, Tom and Richard, had at the home they were living in. Actually I really felt sorry for them and wanted to do something about it.

The home that Tom and Richard got sent to was run by a Mrs. Wandersee. She had nothing but the greediest intentions for having my brothers and all of the other county welfare children that were placed in her care. She purposely made her operation quite profitable. It was only a couple of years later that she would brag about the expensive mink coat that she was able to buy as a result of the money she saved by keeping welfare kids.

The food that she rationed out to the poor children in her charge was almost completely provided from one-hundred-pound sacks of farina, buttermilk, day-old bread and coffee. I visited my brothers, and Mrs. Wandersee didn't think to conceal anything from me.

There were several different times I was able to witness firsthand the typical meal that was being dished out to those children: a bowl of gruel made from the farina, and some old white bread. To complete their meal, they got a half-cup of coffee topped off with buttermilk to drink. The children were fed some vegetables from their garden in the summer time only, but during the rest of the year they received none.

The conditions were so bad that this one Indian boy who lived there ended up in the hospital. He had developed the habit of picking up stones and gum off of the sidewalk, and he swallowed them in order to take away the pains of hunger. When I first saw him, I thought that he looked so strange with his very large stomach and hardly any flesh on his arms or legs. At the time I had no idea of why he looked that way, but today I think that his large stomach was the combination of eating the indigestible materials, and parasites. It wasn't very long before Tom and Richard were even beginning to show some signs of malnutrition.

It upset me and I didn't know what I could do about the situation where my brothers were staying, except to tell people about it. I told Mrs. Orth and at first, like everyone else, she had doubts about what I was saying. After I had told her several times, she finally told me that we should talk to Clark Kellet of the Brown County Welfare Department about it. She told me that she thought that he would want to know and have something done about it.

She accompanied me as we went the little more than a block to the Brown County Courthouse to see Mr. Kellet. With her standing beside me, I found enough courage to explain to him what I had observed. I told him what a horrible person that I thought Mrs. Wandersee was and how terribly she treated the kids that lived with her. Mr. Kellet told Mrs. Orth that he had been to Mrs. Wandersee's house on several occasions and he felt that she was doing a fine job with the children. He then talked to me, "You were only there a couple of times and don't you think that you may be mistaken about what you just told me?"

I was quite adamant when I bravely answered, "I was there more than just a couple of times. I'm not mistaken! I *know* what I saw!"

He then just sort of ignored me as he turned to Mrs. Orth and said, "You just can't believe everything that children say. They imagine all kinds of things." I resented being referred to as a child. From that moment on, I didn't like him.

He then told Mrs. Orth that he wanted to talk to me alone, so she left the room and waited for me in the hall. I felt a little less brave as I was now standing there alone. In fact, my stomach was in turmoil, but I was hoping that it didn't show. It was quite obvious that Mr. Kellet was angry with me when he shouted, "You have a lot of guts to come in here and bother me with something that we know isn't true. Isn't that right?"

I answered, "I am telling you what I saw and it's *true*."

That answer got him to start talking in a very loud voice when he said, "Well I happened to know better and every single home where I place foster children is thoroughly inspected. I don't ever want to see you here *ever* again. *Is that understood?*"

After waiting a couple of minutes as I just stood there without an answer, he then shouted at me. ***"Do you understand?"***

His loud voice frightened me a bit but I simply answered with a "Yes"

His last words to me were, "Now *get* out of here! And I don't ever want to see you here again" I turned away and walked out.

I met Mrs. Orth where she was waiting on a bench in the hall and we left that place. On the way home, I told Mrs. Orth what Mr. Kellet said to me. We agreed that we weren't going to get his help to improve conditions for my brothers. I felt better now that I was convinced Mrs. Orth did believe me. Mr. Kellet didn't do too well to convince her of anything because she said, "There must be something that can be done."

I didn't know what I would do next but I told Mrs. Orth about Father Judge and she suggested that I talk to him. Father Paul Judge was a priest, at the Holy Trinity parish and I thought that he was a wonderful man. My impression of him came as a result of seeing him in action when he taught some of our catechism classes at our school. He was such a man that he gave me the impression that he genuinely loved everyone, no matter how old, and that anyone could feel comfortable in approaching him.

It was in that same week that one day at school I again summoned enough courage to get up and without the sister's permission follow Father Judge into the hall after our catechism class. I asked him if I could speak to him privately sometime. There was no hesitation as he said that right now would be a good time. I didn't feel a bit afraid when I immediately started explaining to him what I had seen, about the horrible conditions that my brothers were living under. He really seemed to be listening to every word that I was saying. He told me that he found it hard to believe that such things could still be going on "in this day and age." He then told me what I think might have been one of his favorite sayings when he said that he was going to "search out the truth." When I went back into the classroom, the sister never asked me about what I was doing in the hall but I was already feeling ever so much better.

Father Paul Judge started his investigation the next day, by stopping my brother Tom as he was returning from downtown. Tom was pulling his wagonload of day-old bread from the bakery and a gallon tin of buttermilk from the creamery. This priest was suspicious of the cargo that Tom was carrying, and it supported the information that I had given him about the way the kids were being fed. He spent quite a bit of time questioning Tom about the place where he lived. Tom at first was afraid to talk to Father Judge, and he was reluctant to give the priest any of the information that he was seeking. Tom held his ground, so almost nothing was accomplished on that first meeting.

The next day, in order to avoid being stopped by the priest, Tom came back by a different route that took him more than a block and a half from the church. The priest wasn't going to be deceived that easily as he watched and stopped Tom again under the same circumstances. He stopped Tom a couple more times and logic made him wonder about all the buttermilk and bread that Tom was hauling. How could those children eat all of that unless that's about *all* they had?

Finally, Tom started to say enough to make the priest quite suspicious about their living conditions and realized that what I had told him was probably true. Father Judge was relentless and after a couple more meetings he got Tom to confess about that detestable place and the unspeakable conditions that he, Richard, and the other kids who lived there. Father Judge now had the information that he wanted. He now knew that things weren't right there and that something just had to be done.

He also acknowledged that it would be hard to get anything accomplished through the system, because he was familiar with Clark Kellet, who was in charge of the system that put my brothers in such a place. It had become quite obvious that Mr. Kellet didn't seem to want to know or even care about what was happening as long as things ran smoothly and easily for him. Father Judge called me out of class one day and he assured me that he was determined to get something done to get some changes made at the Wandersee's quite soon. It really made me feel better to know that.

I don't exactly know how he did it, but after some time he finally did achieve some results for all of his efforts. The first thing that he did was to take some parish money to buy food and give the food directly to Mrs. Wandersee which was to be given to the children. He knew that help had to be given only as food and clothes and not more money. Straight away the children did benefit some from this aid.

I do know that after some threats of an investigation using the children as witnesses and the evidence of that Indian boy, Father Judge was able to get some more permanent changes made. Mrs. Wandersee was forced to modify the management of her home for the benefit of the children. Things had improved somewhat, but never as much as they really should have.

One result of my meddling was not good for me. I wasn't wanted around that foster home any more and Mrs. Wandersee made it difficult for me to visit my brothers. They were ordered inside when I came round. I was not one of Clark Kellet's favorite people and I did as he told me and stayed away from that building that housed the Brown County offices.

As Christmas drew near that winter, I was happily surprised one day to receive so many of the nicest gifts from the city of New Ulm and the Police Department. I suppose the fact that Mrs. Orth was working there might have had something to do with it. I got far more than what I thought any boy would ever want or deserve and certainly much more than at any other Christmas in my life. Among the presents that I received was, what I thought, the neatest Shakespeare steel rod and reel, accompanied with a nice metal tackle box that was filled with all kinds of fishing lures. I was also given a neat mechanical pinball machine, two balsa wood models, lots of candy, and all sorts of other things. This was quite a new experience for me and I was overwhelmed by it all. As nice as all of that was I think I would have gladly given it all up if I could be living with the rest of my family together.

My relationship with the police had become quite opposite of the day that my brothers and I had been taken in for playing on the construction equipment about two years before. All of the policemen got to know me quite well, because I frequently went down to the City Hall. Mrs. Orth got off work at about the same time as I; so many times I walked her home after I got finished at the restaurant, when it was so dark in the early morning. Before leaving the café, I always made us each a nice big ice cream cone. In fact, one night just before locking up Mrs. Orth and her daughter Alice had come down to the restaurant and pounded on the door. I let them in and I made the three of us the biggest ice cream cones I had ever made.

Mrs. Orth worked late almost every night at the station because she was the only policewoman in town. It wasn't until then that I found out that occasionally women might get arrested too. I was still a bit too naïve to know what they might have done and Mrs. Orth told me that I really wouldn't want to know.

It was getting towards spring when I got extremely sick with my tonsils becoming severely infected. My glands swelled up and I had a terrible fever. I was sent to the doctor and during the time he was examining me he noticed something that I was getting quite used to. Like every other doctor, he had also showed a lot of concern about the condition of my heart. I seemed to have quieted his fears when I told him that's the way it always was. He then gave me a prescription to take care of the infection. After my glands returned to a normal size, he had me put into the hospital to have my tonsils taken out.

It wasn't long after I got to the hospital that I felt quite embarrassed as I had to put a gown on that didn't even have a back to it. I tied it in the back but it was still hard to keep it from opening and revealing my posterior. I was taken to the operating room and I can remember as I was lying on my back that there were a bunch of bright lights shining into my face. A cloth covering had been put over my nose and mouth, and a nurse ordered me to start counting backwards from 100. She held a bottle of chloroform, and she started pouring the liquid from an eye dropper, drop by drop, onto the cloth mask that I was wearing. I started counting, as she had told me and the last number that I remembered saying was 92. Everything went black, and I don't remember anything else.

When I awakened, I was lying in a bed in another room with no knowledge of how I got there. I also remember that I still had the same gown on and that it barely covered me and that they might have seen some of my nakedness. In another bed in that same room with me, there was a little boy who was less than two years of age. Like me, he had just had his tonsils removed. I found it to be absolutely disgusting that he was able to immediately eat his ice cream, seemingly without any pain. I was hurting so badly that it even hurt too much for me to swallow water. They had some ice cream brought in for me, which just sat there as it melted down into a warm liquid and I was still unable to eat or drink anything.

I slept that night in the hospital, and I returned home the next morning. I was still very sick, so I spent most of my time just lying on the couch in the living room. I didn't eat anything that day or even the day after. On the third day after I got home, a lady friend of Mrs. Orth's came over to visit with her. That lady brought with her a cold bottle of Coca Cola. She surprised me when she opened it and gave it to me. I had never drunk a cola drink before, but I found it to be quite soothing to my throat, and I managed to drink the whole bottle. I'm not at all sure just how much the coke had to do with it, but it was soon afterwards that my throat had become noticeably better. It was shortly after that when I became able to eat some much-needed food again.

I found out where my youngest brother, Warren, was living and I went to visit him and I tried to visit him about every other day. Because of the way they treated me, it also became quite obvious that the Polta's didn't like it when I came around.

Warren was only three years old at the time our mother had been taken away. This cute little boy easily stole the hearts of everyone wherever he was seen. We had known the Polta family where he was staying almost since the time that we had moved there, and they seemed to love Warren. I was to find out later that it didn't take the Poltas very long before they made strong overtures to Mr. Kellet that they wanted to adopt my youngest brother. For a short time they were taking care of Warren without monetary assistance from the County Welfare Department, but that was due to change.

The Poltas first tried to initiate an adoption legally through the welfare department in New Ulm, which would require at least our dad's authorization. Since the county was also financing some of the costs of our mother's stay at the state sanatorium, they felt that in her condition she could be easily dealt with later. They contacted my dad, and he informed them that he wouldn't ever consider an adoption under any circumstances.

After receiving my dad's answer, the Poltas then went as far as consorting with my old nemesis, Clark Kellet, of the Brown County Welfare Department. Mr. Kellet agreed to assist them in getting this adoption completed. It was in the county's best interest, because it would also be one less child that the county would have to provide for. Supposedly his response to them was that he would "do whatever it takes to get it done, legally or otherwise."

The proceedings to successfully adopt my brother had begun in December. It wasn't until in March, however, that Mr. Kellet with the assistance of the county attorney, George D. Erickson, took action by having a warrant put out for my father's arrest.

It was near the first of April that my father drove into town to see my brothers and me, and the city police arrested him. I don't know the exact day, because he was in jail for a couple of days before Mrs. Orth found out and told me. She had accidentally stumbled upon the information while she was on duty at the city hall. Because of the embarrassment, I don't think that my dad wanted me or any of my brothers to find out.

My dad had been turned over to the county sheriff and he was immediately confined to the Brown County Jail at 15 South Washington Street which was behind the county courthouse where Clark Kellet had his office. The reason given for this detention was a charge brought against my dad, originating from Clark Kellet of the County Welfare Department, with the crime of "deserting your children."

With my mother in the sanatorium and my dad in jail, Mr. Kellet and the Poltas', felt that they were now ready to put their plan into effect to get complete custody of Warren. If my father didn't consent, he was now facing the real possibility of being sent to the state prison in St. Cloud, Minnesota. Mr. Kellet could bargain my dad's freedom in exchange for his signature on the proper documents. It would then be easy for the welfare department to get my brother turned over to the Poltas for adoption.

To me it seemed as though no one was in any hurry, because my dad spent more than three weeks in their county jail. He was quite surprised when I showed up one day at the jail and, because he asked I told him how I found out. From then on I became his daily visitor and I could tell that he liked it. He made it quite clear to me that he didn't want any of my brothers to know anything about this. I did keep that and all of the other things that we talked about in jail as our secret for many years. My dad must have been quite lonely, because with the exception of an attorney, I was his only visitor each day and it wasn't long before it became obvious to me that he looked forward to my visits.

As time went on, I really did become worried that they were never going to let my dad go free. I could clearly observe my father's anger about all of this, and he tried to make things clear to me so I would know what was going on. He explained to me that Clark Kellet had told him that he could be released if he would just sign some papers to allow the adoption of Warren to take place. I did have some trouble understanding all of this, but now I had become worried that my brother was going to be taken away from us. This was also another secret that I was not supposed to let my brothers know.

My dad believed that what Mr. Kellet and the Poltas were doing was illegal. He also was very angry, because he couldn't do anything about his situation and he felt so helpless and out of control, being in that jail. He told me that he felt that he did the best he could to provide for my brothers and me. In my mind I had some doubts about that and some of the other things that he was telling me but he was my father.

The jailers must not have worried too much about my dad, though, because they didn't even lock him in his cell. He was completely free to roam about as he liked, but he had to stay in the building during the day. They did make sure that he was securely locked up in his cell each night at about 5 o'clock.

I visited my dad right after I got finished with my paper route each day. Because he liked them, I would usually get ice cream drumsticks for us to eat together. I couldn't stay long, because I had to go to work at the convent, but I would come back for another short time before I went to work at the cafe. On Saturday and Sunday, I spent a lot of time with my dad in that jail with conversation, checkers or a game of cards. I usually could expect to be sent on numerous errands for him which I didn't mind because I could get anywhere in the city quite quickly on my bike. There were even times that I visited him after visiting hours and I had to stand outside, beneath where his cell window was, and he could talk to me through the bars.

The first time on a Saturday that I got there at the usual time after I had finished my paper route, I found out that the hours were different than on the week days and the jail was closed. I had brought my dad an ice cream drumstick and I had intended to visit inside with him. The only way that I could think of to get the ice cream up to my dad was to lean my bike against the building. Then I climbed up and stood on the seat in order to be able to reach high enough to hand it to him as he reached out through the bars. It didn't seem that security had a very high priority then.

I don't know the exact number of days that he spent in that jail, but my father was finally taken to court on the twenty-first of April for his hearing. It was fortunate for my dad that he was always sort of a pack rat and he was always reluctant to throw anything away. This is one of his traits I think that I acquired from him, and it would come in handy for me in the future. I think that it can sometimes be quite beneficial. His attorney had my dad's trunk taken from his apartment in Minneapolis and sent down to New Ulm. This trunk contained all of his important papers and records and all the receipts of where most of his money had been spent.

It just so happened during that year my dad's job required that he travel a lot and so he put a lot of mileage on the car he had. As a result that car demanded a lot of repairs that were quite costly and he had saved the receipts for everything. He was able to prove to the judge that he was doing about the best that he could with the income he received and still keep that car in a serviceable condition.

Our father's attorney, R. T. Rodenberg, advised my dad to plead guilty to a felony charge. Later I felt that his attorney wasn't working in my dad's best interest at all. I considered that he had been conspiring with Clark Kellet to get my father sentenced to prison so that my father could have been blackmailed into Warren's adoption for his freedom. I strongly believed that the burden of proof should have been up to the prosecution. After pleading guilty of the charge of desertion, our dad was sentenced by the district Judge A. B. Gislason to be committed to the state prison in St. Cloud.

Impressed by the evidence that my dad was able to provide as proof of his finances, the judge surprised everyone when he made his final decision. He ruled for a stay of execution of the sentence, but he also included three conditions that must be met. Our dad was released after he provided his signature to the document that he would abide by the requirements as stated: First, he must not take intoxicating liquors of any kind (No problem with this one, because my dad never did drink anything with alcohol and actually had a strong contempt for it.) Second, and this would be the hardest part for him, he must contribute at least $100, and more if possible, each month to the support of his family. And third, he must conduct himself in all respects as a decent and law-abiding citizen. If he lived up to these conditions, then this sentence would ultimately be suspended.

It was quite obvious that Judge Gislason was an honest man and wasn't a part of any conspiracy against my father. I was delighted that the original sentence brought against our dad wasn't carried out and that Clark Kellet wouldn't be able to coerce our dad with another offer for his immunity. I was also glad that I would never be able to find out if our dad would have given up Warren to obtain his freedom.

Because of all that my father had told me, he really did have me quite concerned about the real possibility of loosing Warren. I now felt sure that there was no chance of Warren ever being adopted and that he would remain a part of our family. I felt so strongly against the adoption, even though I knew that the Poltas would have given Warren a good home and that in some ways he really might be better off with them. He certainly would have had an easier life than my brothers and I. As it turned out, before he reached his twelfth birthday, Warren would live in 24 different places that he would call home.

Since the Poltas' would be unable to make Warren a part of their family, they soon lost interest in providing a home for him. In less than a year after he had moved in with them, Warren would be moving away to live with another family. Sadly for me, I found out that his next home was much too far away for me to visit him. In fact, I never even got to see him for almost a year.

My dad was able to keep his job in truck sales at Baston-Barrington Chevrolet in Minneapolis. As a result of what happened to him, it had cost him financially, because he had been out of work for more than three weeks. He was quite fortunate just to retain his employment at the Chevrolet dealer.

In my mind I felt that a great wrong had been done to my dad. I thought that they had made a mistake, so why wasn't Brown County held liable for what they did? I believed that the whole matter was so wrong and unfair and it was all because of the vindictive nature of one man, Clark Kellet. There never was any compensation made to my dad for this injustice. That and the experience with the police two years earlier left me at the age of 14 with a less than favorable impression of our country's legal system. I, also admit that I was being strongly influenced by hearing so much from my dad's point of view.

I can't swear to the accuracy of everything that I say here about some of those things that happened in court and with the Poltas. I am telling this just as my father related it to me and the rest of the information was obtained from the archives at the Minnesota Historical Society Building in Minneapolis. My dad was always quite an honest man, so I can't help but believe what he told me was the truth. I have also in my possession the actual transcript of that hearing, which verified much of what he had told me about the outcome of that trial.

It was only a couple of months after that trial that my dad came to visit me again and I was to receive some more bad news. He showed me a terrible-looking sore on the calf of his leg that he said started out as just a small cut that he received when he accidentally scraped his leg with the bottom corner of the door of his car. That infected sore continued to get worse, but of course I didn't realize any significance in that. My dad then explained to me that the reason that it wasn't healing was that he had sugar diabetes. He also told me that he was very sick and that he had to take shots of insulin for it. I felt saddened and sorry for him. Now I had to accept the reality of it, that both of my parents were quite unwell.

That summer I tried working on two different farms. The first place that I went, the farmer immediately put me on the chore of stacking hay bales in his hay mow. I tried, but some of the bales were almost as heavy as I, and it was really more than I could handle. I went to work at another farm, and the results were almost the same. After trying my best at those two places, I left after they each said I was too small and just not strong enough. I went back to my old job at the Waneda Cafe.

Later that summer I decided to go to the Brown County Fair and spend a little money that I had saved just for that purpose. I went there with my friends who lived across the street from where we used to live. Their father, who was a school teacher at the Lutheran School, drove all nine of us to the fair. We were tightly packed together in his small and overloaded Willis Overland car that he had.

Going to a fair and having money to spend just for the fun of it was a new experience for me. During my time at the fair, I got to do all the usual things such as going on some of the rides, drinking pop, eating a hot dog, watching the arcade games, and just looking at all sorts of the new and colorful trappings that happened to come within my view. I enjoyed the large amount of time that I spent in the barns looking at the cattle, pigs, horses and sheep. Just thinking about what happened in Rib Lake gave me no desire to look at the chickens or anything with feathers for that matter.

It was while I was looking around that my eyes were drawn towards a booth that had caught my attention because of a very loud and excited woman's voice. I stopped to watch the woman on a makeshift stage that had been set up on a trailer. She was holding up a jar of something, that she professed to be a product that had just recently been developed and that had never been shown to the public before. She also claimed that we were privileged to be the first to see the only product available to be able to make the claim that it could actually prevent the loss of hair and even promote the growth of new hair. She even said that it would be impossible to have truly healthy hair without her product. The way that she presented herself created quite a spectacle and it was attracting quite a bit of an audience. My curiosity just wouldn't allow my feet to move from the spot, as many people were now gathering around me. Before I realized it, I was suddenly standing alone in the middle of a large crowd and the friends that I had come with were no longer in sight.

I was completely surrounded by other people: but that lady must have taken notice of my thick, uncombed hair, because out of all of those people, she called me to come up there with her in front of that whole gathering. At first I considered walking away but she was quite persuasive. Being as shy as I was, I really don't understand why I didn't leave. Instead I just walked up there as she had requested.

She had me climb onto a tall stool and sit, so that I was clearly within the view of everyone watching. Now that I was up there, I was beginning to really feel quite embarrassed about it, because I knew that hundreds of eyes were focused on me. She began her demonstration by taking a glob of thick, creamy stuff from the jar that she had been holding during her talk. She then rubbed it together in her hands. Next she began using both hands as she started thoroughly mixing it into my hair. As she continued working in her mixture, she then commenced tugging and pulling quite hard on my hair with enough force that my head was being jerked from side to side and up and down. She said that all this was necessary just to wake up the scalp. All the while she was continuing to excitedly talk to the crowd about this wonderful hair cream and how to apply it. When it seemed to me that she was finally finished, she began the drudgery of dragging a comb through my thick messed-up hair.

After my hair was neatly combed, she continued with her well-prepared speech about the benefits of her new product. Then she explained that she had an excellent bargain offer at a remarkable introductory price that she was making available to only those who had viewed this special demonstration. She then explained to everyone how necessary it was to keep healthy hair, and if you believed what she had said then having healthy hair could only be achieved by using her product. I thought that she was really quite convincing.

Interrupting her speech, she then turned away from the crowd and began speaking only to me. She still spoke in a voice loud enough that everyone could hear when she asked me, "Which would you rather have, this nice new dollar bill or some of this marvelous preparation that I have in this jar?"

My answer even surprised me when I said, "I would like to have both."

She then asked, "Would you please tell all of us why?"

I answered, "I would like to have a jar of your hair cream because I want to keep my hair and I would also like to have the dollar to spend at the fair."

Laughingly she said, "Now that is a very wise answer." She then asked me to turn toward the crowd and I obeyed. She then turned to the crowd and asked, "Now isn't he just about the most handsome young man you've ever seen?" I really felt embarrassed to be talked about this way and she never used my name.

Then I was pleasantly surprised as the lady announced, "I am going to give this young man this dollar *and* this" as she handed me the jar the hair cream. "It was awfully nice of him to come up here to assist me. Now don't you think that he deserves a hand for helping me?" It was embarrassing for me as many of the people actually did clap. I also felt quite lucky, especially about getting the dollar.

As some of the people lined up to make their purchases, I just climbed down from the stool and disappeared into the crowd with my neatly buttered locks, a jar of her product, and an extra dollar. Although I did bring that jar home with me, I remember that I never used one bit of that particular product that she had given me. I put it somewhere after I got home and then forgot all about it. Actually, I didn't use any product in my hair except soap when I washed it. As a matter of fact, I never even bothered to comb my hair.

One thing I did like about living at Mrs. Orth's was that on the nights that I didn't have to work and during the days when I didn't have school, I would often go to work in the reception area of the Gedsted's Funeral Home. It was only a short walk down the alley from where I was living. I liked that job, even though I didn't receive a penny for it, because all I had to do was answer the phone and record the information. Occasionally there was some food left over from a party that I could have. The rest of the time I was on my own. I could read, work puzzles, draw pictures or do almost anything that I wanted.

To me the main attraction was a typewriter which, for me, was payment enough for doing the job. I had the Gedsteds' permission to use it and I did use it a lot especially for writing letters to my mother and to Pat in the sanatorium. Using that typewriter could completely occupy my time while I was there. I really thought that it was so neat to be able to write and send letters that were typed, even though I had no typing skills. I just poked about using one finger on each hand so it even took me much longer than if I had used a pen or a pencil and written it out. With experience I became familiar with the location of the letters and eventually my speed improved as I got more practice. With all that practice I got I was finally able to type a bit faster than I could write.

That funeral home was one of the largest houses in New Ulm at that time and it was constructed of brick. The building was quite unique, because it had a tower that I thought was so elegant, and to me it seemed to give the house a somewhat castle-like appearance. The owners, who were quite wealthy, lived on the second floor. They went on many trips, so they were rarely at home: therefore the need for someone to watch the place. Up on the third floor lived a nice young man who was the undertaker with his beautiful wife. The funeral part of this mansion occupied the whole first floor.

It was on the first floor that I spent all of my time in the quiet and friendly lobby. I never cared to roam about that first floor at all because there seemed to always be a dead body on display in another room which always made me feel quite uncomfortable just to look at it. It really was my job to answer the telephone calls as they came in. If the call was intended for the owners, I would write down a message for them to pick up later. If someone was calling for the undertaker and needed to talk to him at once, I left the phone off the receiver and I ran directly up the stairs to his apartment.

One evening while I was working at the funeral home and I was all alone, I answered a call from someone that said it was urgent for him to speak to the undertaker. The only way to get to his apartment on that third floor was to go up the dark, spiral staircase in the tower.

That tower didn't have any lighting, so with that and with more than a small bit of my fantasizing, I found climbing those stairs to be somewhat frightening. Usually when I answered a call requiring the undertaker, I would run as fast as I could, going round and round up the two flights of stairs in the tower. I would knock on the door and anxiously await the friendly light to shine on me when he opened the door and I would give him the message. Going back down was never a problem, because the undertaker would always accompany me on the return trip.

This one time, however, he told me to tell the caller that he would call him back later. That really disappointed me, because now I would have to come down those dark tower stairs all by myself. As soon as he closed his apartment door, the tower became frightfully dark. I immediately turned around and rushed down the winding steps as fast as I could go. I was hurrying so fast and concentrating so hard on just getting out of that unfriendly tower, that I didn't notice when I ran right on past the first floor, causing me to quickly open an unfamiliar door into their dark, damp and musty-smelly basement. That was really frightening to me and I immediately pulled the door shut. I went flying back up those stairs to the proper floor and back to the congenial, well-lit reception area.

A few years before, when Pat realized that I was afraid of the dark, he explained to me, "You shouldn't be afraid of the dark, because other people can't see you either." The logic of those words did help me some. I had become somewhat less afraid of the dark, but being alone and the atmosphere in that funeral home just provided my imagination with too many frightening thoughts. I ended my tour of duty at about midnight, when in almost total darkness I had to face the short walk down the alley, into our backyard and into the back door of the empty, unlit house. Mrs. Orth hadn't come home from work yet. I found that trip home to be bit frightening right up to the time that I turned on the first light in the house.

When Pat got released from the sanatorium in the spring, he lived for a while with our dad in an apartment in Minneapolis. One day our dad brought Pat to stay with me for a few days, and we were really enjoying our time together. One night I took Pat with me to spend a typical evening in the funeral home. I gave him a complete tour of the place, and I made sure that he got to see all three of the dead bodies that had been prepared for display that night.

I then showed Pat the typewriter, and he got just as excited about using it as when I first got to use it several months before. I spent a little time explaining how to use that typewriter, such as loading the paper, capitalizing, tab settings, etc. I then left him alone to type while I did some reading. Immediately, he began very slowly typing away, and I had trouble believing that I had ever typed like that when I began. I stayed nearby so I could be available to help him when he asked for it.

I always admired the way that Pat appeared to be completely fearless, and he gave me the impression that he wasn't afraid of anything. After he had been pounding away on the typewriter for quite some time, he had to go to the toilet. He didn't know where it was, so I had to show him. I led him into another room, down a narrow row that was lined with caskets on both sides. We then went down a short hall, turned the corner, and finally ended up in the bathroom.

I had decided to play a trick on him by doing something that I thought would give him a scare. Just as soon as he started relieving himself of some bodily fluids, I quickly ran back to the reception area, shutting off all of the lights as I went. I finally thought that I would have the satisfaction of seeing Pat get a bit scared; but after he had felt his way back to where I was, I think he was madder at me than frightened.

I had been living with Mrs. Orth through the summer of 1949. She had provided me with a decent place to live. I felt that she had also treated me in quite a civil manner. Therefore, I was not looking forward to another change of address. I had come to hate even the thought of ever moving again. If, however, the move would involve being reunited with my brothers, that could provide me with some optimism. Everything wasn't great at Mrs. Orth's and I really didn't fancy the lonely kind of existence that I had come to accept and

I would never really get used to it. I also wasn't looking forward to another year like my last, working my three jobs and attending eighth grade at Holy Trinity.

Without much warning, my stay at Mrs. Orth's was to end quite abruptly. It was near the end of summer vacation that my dad suddenly arrived to pick me up. I had to quickly pack up all of my things and say good bye to Mrs. Orth. It was the first time that I had ever seen this strong woman cry. She even told me if things didn't turn out right that I should come back and I would always have a home with her.

It seemed so long ago that my mother was taken to the hospital in the spring of 1948. For my brothers and me, our ship had been *driven into rocky shoals*, but still our family was able to survive. The damage couldn't be avoided some of it was beyond repair, but it must be dealt with. There always remains the hope that the future is going to become better.

- XII. Another Port of Call -

My father was enjoying one of his more prosperous times as a salesman for the Baston-Barrington Chevrolet dealer in Minneapolis in charge of country truck sales. He had a salary of only $50 a week but quite often he was able to earn much more than that because when sales were good the commission could be much more than his salary. Everything seemed to be going quite well for him, and he felt that he had become financially able to adequately provide for us. That would also mean another move for me.

Without much warning, my stay at Mrs. Orth's was to end quite abruptly. It was near the end of summer vacation that my dad came and picked me up and I had to say good bye to Mrs. Orth. It was also kind of sad, because it was the first time that I saw this strong lady with tears in her eyes and I would miss her.

All of my brothers and I were making another one of our frequent moves. Our new address became a place near Crystal Village, Minnesota, located about five miles from Robinsdale, which is a suburb of Minneapolis. My dad had assured us that this move was going to be quite special. He told us that he wanted us to live together as one family in one home. I had welcomed the idea of being reunited with my brothers. My dad had made financial arrangements with this couple that we only would know as Mr. and Mrs. Jewett, who were in their late 50's, to care for us. My dad, my brothers and I were to occupy the second floor of their house, which included two bedrooms and a bath. Pat, Tom, Richard and I slept crowded together in one bedroom on a double bed and a cot. When our dad was around, he and Warren slept in the other bedroom.

Things were not as nice as I was expecting, because I never did care much for the place, the arrangements, or the couple who owned it. Mr. Jewitt seemed to be so weak and let his domineering and spiteful wife have her way about everything. It seem that she was so frequently punishing my brothers and me by making us spend a lot of our time sitting in different corners of their dining room for the least little thing that met with her disapproval.

Mrs. Jewitt did cook our meals each day for us, and the food was quite decent. Her one specialty seemed to be blood sausage, which quite frequently was a main part of the meal. It took a bit of time for me to develop a taste for it. I found it to be quite amazing what one will eat if the only alternative is to go hungry. My brothers and I were required to take turns doing the dishes after meals.

Wherever my brothers and I stayed, we made very few demands for such things as our living quarters or the food that we ate. During our whole lives very little consideration had been given for either doctors or dental requirements. The only time I went to a doctor was when I was in dire need of it and I had never been to a dentist. It was a big change for me, then, when for the first time in my life I started brushing my teeth before I went to bed each night, although I still never combed my hair.

Pat, Richard and I traveled the five miles on foot every school day to St. Mary's Catholic School in Robinsdale. Unlike my 5th grade teacher in New Ulm, I remember that I had an exceptionally kind and caring 8th grade teacher there, by the name of Sister Mary Joseph. Pat and I would once again be going to school at the same place, but he would now be one year behind me in the 7th grade.

Once in awhile, when we were having a bit of really nasty weather, Sister Mary Joseph would give me a job cleaning the sinks, toilets and latrines in the boy's restroom. After I completed the work, she would give me three dimes so my two brothers and I could ride the bus that would make a stop about one-half mile from our home. We would rather walk and save the money for other things, such as books, wood models, or almost anything else. Whenever I got my hands on any money, it had become important for me to purchase something that I would be able to have in my possession for some time afterwards. In my mind just having things were important and meant that I wasn't poor.

It was this year that my brothers and I developed the habit of listening to certain radio programs everyday. As soon as we got home from school each day we would gather around the radio and listen carefully to our special programs. They always provided our imaginations with the exciting and continuing episodes which we tried not to miss. Some of our favorites were "Superman," "Straight Arrow" and "Bobby Benson and the 'B' bar 'B' Riders." The only thing that would occasionally prevent us from our daily escape from reality was when we were being punished for some minor transgression against Mrs. Jewitt.

None of the students who went to St. Mary's lived way out where we were. Because of this I never made close friends with any of them and why should I even remember any names. Because they didn't have enough room for one more student at the 5th grade at St. Mary's, my brother Tom was forced to attend the public school in Crystal Village. It was also much closer to where we lived, so he didn't have to spend nearly as much of his day walking. As it turned out my brothers and I had a good reason to be happy about that, because Tom's school friends lived in the same vicinity that we were living in.

The Jewitts' didn't have a television, but one of Tom's friends would invite Tom and the rest of my brothers and me over in the evenings to watch TV. It was a real treat for us as we sat on the floor in the darkness and ate popcorn. We got to see some entertaining programs such as "The Lone Ranger," "Jack Benny" and "Milton Berle."

We also were exposed to an overabundance of the ridiculous wrestling. We got to see matches with such characters as Gorgeous George strutting around the ring, bragging that he used Georgie pins and not bobby pins in his long, blonde tresses. We could tell that all the wrestling was not real, but it was a bit entertaining. My brothers and I really appreciated these opportunities and we were always very well behaved, because we wanted to be invited back to their homes to enjoy many more evenings of television.

At St. Mary's we met Father Brown for the first time where he was teaching some of the catechism classes. It was just a coincidence that his last name was also Brown, but he was not related to us. He was a small man, and I thought he was quite young for a priest. When he said Mass, I remember that he always gave a sermon that made sense to me; and he wasn't constantly asking for more money as the older pastor did.

Pat and I thought that he was one of the neatest persons, because he was also quite athletic. Father Brown was very quick, and all the boys enjoyed playing basketball with him. It looked a bit strange to see this priest rushing around and playing with us when sometimes he was still wearing his long, black robe. To free his legs, he had unbuttoned the bottom of it and sort of tied that part around his waist. Father Brown always found the time to kid around with us and everybody, especially the older boys, thought the world of this man.

On some very exceptional schooldays Father Brown would occasionally load up his station wagon far beyond its capacity with Pat, some of the other eighth grade boys and me. Then he would drive us into Minneapolis to attend a special presentation by the Minneapolis Symphony Orchestra.

That first time that we made this trip, it was exhilarating and also quite scary for me. I had become used to, what I thought was my father's fast driving, but even his driving was nothing compared to when Father Brown was behind the wheel. This priest drove as he played basketball, which was awfully fast with quick turns. He was constantly weaving in and out of the traffic on the crowded streets of Minneapolis. His driving also kept the silver rosary constantly in motion, swinging back and forth as it dangled from one of the matching chrome knobs in his black Plymouth station wagon,. To get through traffic, I remember that there were times that he would even drive for short distances on the sidewalk. The way he drove, Father Brown must certainly have kept God and all of his angels busy watching over him and his excited passengers.

When we got to our destination, I remember that Antal Doroti was the conductor of the orchestra and we were privileged to attend one of the special concerts designed just for children that he had several times throughout the year. I enjoyed the programs that we attended very much, because before each piece of music was played, this conductor would spend time explaining about the composer and the story behind the music. With all of us eighth grade boys that Father Brown had with him, there was never any discipline problems.

The return ride was just as exciting as the trip in, but the other boys and I wished he would drive a bit slower; not out of fear but because we weren't that anxious to get back to school so soon. I looked forward to the time that we would get to attend another one of these performances. I was grateful that Father Brown cared enough to bring a bit of culture into our lives and also a break from the regular school routine.

Each day Pat, Richard and I had to walk the whole distance of five miles from home to the school. As in Rib Lake we did find a short cut through some fields that probably shortened the trip by about one-half mile. I still had my bicycle and Pat had one too; but our dad insisted, if one had to walk, all three us had to walk. Pat and I could have taken turns giving Richard a ride but we weren't aloud to do that.

There were times, when the weather was really nasty with bitter cold, that Pat, Richard and I would on some of those occasions get a ride to school from a man who sometimes drove by at just the right time in the morning. He would stop and we would climb into the back of his dump truck. It was a very frigid ride as he sped along with a lot of sub-zero wind that was attacking from all directions as it was swirling around us in the back of his truck. We were well compensated for that, because the trip didn't last nearly as long as if we were doing our usual walk.

There were several times when, in our effort to speed up our trip to school or back home, that we would run alongside and then grab onto a freight train that was going our way at the right time. We always continued our ride until the very last moment and then we would jump off at our desired location. Because quite often the train would pick up a lot of speed since we started our ride, our departure usually sent us tumbling down a bank. We sometimes received minor injuries as we made our non too-graceful landing. We would then agree that it was foolish to take such a chance and we would never do that again. Nevertheless, we still did it again whenever the opportunity presented itself.

In my short life I had come to believe that balls were always a perfect sphere in shape. I was to discover differently when I saw, for the first time, a ball that had pointed ends and someone explained to me that it was called a football. In the evening high school boys played what I thought was the most ridiculous game with this funny ball and a game that was also called football. This game was played every fall after the baseball season was over. The players wore shiny, colorful helmets that kept their ears warm in the cool fall air, a lot of padding on the shoulders that gave them a sort of gorilla-like appearance, and funny looking-pants that had padding and left the bottom part of their legs naked.

I thought it was strange that even though they called it football, they rarely used their foot on that ball. When I bothered to watch one of the games, I noticed that most of the time they really weren't even playing. They did a lot of standing around, and I firmly believed that there was no way that they would ever get tired enough for taking all of those time-outs.

When watching the game, one observes the two teams of men lined up so that they face each other. A signal is given, and someone who is bent over in the most ridiculous position passes the ball between his legs to a person waiting behind him. That person either passes the ball to someone else or runs like hell, trying to avoid being pulled to the ground by a player on the opposing side. At the same time that is taking place, the two lines of players who seem to be mad at each other and go crashing into one another as they try to push the opposite man out of the way. Then most of the players just stand around as the action centers on the ball and those closest to it. Just when it seems as though they are beginning to do something, someone in a striped black-and-white shirt, called a referee, blows a whistle. All the action stops! Next, one of the two teams gets into a small circle, and they bend over and whisper to each other. Then they get back into their lines and they repeat the same routine all over again. None of it made any sense to me. I found it to be quite a boring game, so I just couldn't bring myself to waste any more of my time watching it and I certainly would resist any attempts to force me to be a participant.

It was that fall that our dad got Pat, Tom and me enrolled in the boxing program at Robinsdale. Our dad had done some boxing when he was young and he thought it would be good for us. Our dad rarely missed driving us to our weekly training sessions throughout that school year. We took it seriously and developed quickly in our new sport and did become quite proficient at it. Patrick would always be quite a bit bigger and stronger than I. Even Tom, I knew, was going to be stronger one day. Those two brothers of mine quickly became quite extraordinary as fighters in that sport.

In the beginning I didn't like the idea of boxing and trying to hurt someone, so at first I resisted it. However, the more that I was exposed to it the more I was caught up in the excitement of it. I also did believe that the exercise was good for me. In that first year I too achieved a very high level of mastery. Being small for my age was a severe disadvantage in that program, but my speed provided me with a great deal of effectiveness. They used age and weight for matching up the fights, so I usually had to fight someone that was bigger than I. Because of Pat's size, I was never matched up with him.

My brothers and I did take our boxing quite zealously, which meant spending a great deal of time training at home. We got a pretty good workout when we would often run the whole five miles from home to school and then the same distance back again. I know that no adult would have designed a training program as severe as the one that we imposed on ourselves. Every day we did our routine of exercises, jumping rope, a lot of running and bicycling. We spent much time driving our fists into the heavy punching bag our dad bought us. We also practiced by fighting with each other, using the new boxing gloves that our dad bought for us. We worked ourselves into extremely fine physical condition.

We had such well-developed stomach muscles that we were capable of tightening up and making them so hard that we could take the hardest punch from each other's bare fist without any pain. We thought nothing of jumping into each other's stomach. One of us would lie with his back on the floor while the others could take turns jumping. We got onto the bed and then jumped as we came to a landing with both feet on the stomach of the one who was lying on the floor. Pat, Tom and I that did that quite often, but we never got hurt at it.

Our lives didn't completely revolve around boxing. We also enjoyed nature and the outdoors. In fact my favorite magazines then were Popular Mechanics and Field and Stream. This also led my brothers and me one day in the early spring, after going through a long and very cold winter, to make plans to take a bit of a weekend trip, just for the fun of it. We made ourselves some sandwiches, bought a big bottle of Dad's Root Beer, and we started off on our journey. Pat and I pedaled our bicycles as we carried Tom and Richard with us. The day was nice and sunny, with a temperature somewhere around thirty-five degrees, which after a steady diet of frigid weather we would consider that to be quite warm.

We had no destination in mind. Our only plan was to find a nice place to spend some time and have our pop and sandwiches. I guess it could be called a sort of picnic. We were already living in a sort of rural area so we just started out in the direction away from the city to see where it would take us. We made good time on our bikes and we finally came upon a nice, wooded place that we all seemed to fancy.

We knew that our journey had taken us more than fifteen miles away from our home, but that really didn't concern us because we thought it would be no problem making the return trip. The place that we had chosen to spend the next few hours playing in, included some snow covered rolling hills, a nice grove of trees and a good-sized pond that was still completely covered with ice and a dusting of snow.

It was sunny out, and I think the temperature did get up to a high of about forty-five degrees that day. But it felt much warmer in the sun, so we had taken our coats off. In the open areas where the sun could shine, the snow was melting. It was good for making snowballs, and we threw them at one another. We did a lot of running around in the sun and managed to keep quite warm by just staying so active. After a while, we decided to take our shirts off and even take the top part of our long underwear off, which compelled us to wrap the sleeves and tie them around our waists. We spent a lot of time running around in the open areas, enjoying the warm sun on our bare skin and breathing the fresh air.

It was while I had been running like this that I eventually decided to make a quick crossing on the partially snow-covered ice on the pond. I hadn't reached the middle yet when quite suddenly I began to lose my footing as the ice was getting a bit spongy and slippery underneath me. This threatening activity caused my feet to go right out from under me, and I was brought violently into a sitting position. I immediately got back on my feet, as my next warning came when water started to seep up onto the ice. I could easily see that I still had the other half of the pond to cross.

I proceeded to carefully and slowly walk over what must have been the deepest part, when quite suddenly I broke through the ice. As soon as the lower part of my body sank down into that icy cold water it was a terrible and sudden shock to me. In fact, it took my breath away and I was completely unable to call out for help. My feet didn't touch bottom so I had no idea how deep it might be so I now I had become really frightened. I grabbed onto the ice around the hole that had just been created by my body so that I was barely able to keep my head and hands above water.

I felt completely helpless as my mind was immediately filled with images of slipping deep into that icy water and drowning. Was my life going to end in this way? My mind was racing as I thought of a lot of things such as the thought that I would never see my mother again. I then started to call out for my brothers to help me. In terror my hands were clawing for something solid to grasp, but it wasn't there. I tried to climb back on top of the ice, but it was no use, as it just kept breaking and sinking down in front of me. My hands sank out of sight with each broken piece of ice, and I quickly grappled for the next piece in front of it. I was in a half lying position as I kept on doing this for what seemed such a long time. During my struggles I kept shouting to my brothers for help.

Finally my brothers heard my cries of desperation and took notice of my plight. They could see that I was in serious trouble. They immediately ran to get some long branches that would enable them to reach out to me, with the intention of pulling me to safety. In my struggles I hadn't even realized that I had been moving forward very slowly. By the time that my brothers got to me, their help was no longer needed; because I did finally make it near enough to the edge of the pond that my feet were finally able to feel the soft, muddy bottom. It was with great relief when I was now able to stand up and walk onto some dry solid land.

That ordeal had left me completely exhausted and very wet. I immediately realized that my troubles weren't over yet, as my whole body was now having violent tremors and my teeth were chattering from being so cold. I didn't know anything about it then, but I think that I was suffering from what they would call hypothermia today. I was able to sense the danger I was in, but my brothers would come to my rescue again. They each took off some of their own clothing to give to me. Fortunately I hadn't been wearing my shirt and coat, making that at least some clothing of mine that wasn't completely soaked. I took off all my clothes that I was wearing when I got dunked into the pond. I then took certain articles of their clothing, which may have been a strange looking combination; but I was now able to completely cover myself.

We worked quickly to gather up some branches so that we could build a nice lean-to that would provide shelter for me on three sides. Then we draped my wet clothes over the branches to dry out and at the same time to create a wind break. Since their dry clothes didn't give me the proper combination so that I could run around with my brothers, I lay inside the shelter that we had just completed. That lean-to did provide me with some necessary protection from the chilling wind. I used my brothers' coats like blankets, while they continued to play. They kept up like that for more than another hour, so that I could recover a bit and my clothes would be given some time to dry. I finally stopped shivering and even got a bit comfortable. When my brothers stopped playing, we ate our lunch together.

It was shortly after we had finished eating, that we felt it was time to go home; but my clothes were still quite wet. To give them more time to dry, my brothers decided they would just keep running around for a while longer. They did that for about another hour, but then we had run out of any more options. The sun was getting low in the sky and the temperature was dropping. We had to start back if we were to have any chance of getting home before it got dark. My clothes had actually dried out very little. My long underwear, pants, and socks had frozen and became stiff. I was able to wear Pat's dry underwear and my dry shirt, coat, mittens and cap. Without any socks on and wearing wet shoes I knew that my wet feet were going to get cold. Modesty had forced me to wear what had been wet pants, but now as the weather had dropped below freezing they had become quite stiff and cold but I put them on. They felt as if they were made of cardboard because they resisted my movement which was forcing them to bend. We started the long journey back home on our two bikes. The faster we rode the more the wind would chill my body, so I was terribly uncomfortable and shivering.

The ride back seemed to take so much longer than the trip up. It was work and climbing the hills with my brother Richard as a passenger made it almost impossible at times. My feet, hands and legs were so cold that it seemed almost unbearable. With each seemingly endless crank on the pedals of the bike, my body was telling me to give up. I just had to keep moving, because I was wearing a frozen pair of pants that had become so stiff that they behaved as if they had been starched far too heavily. It was becoming a long and horrible experience for me. To make matters even worse, we had to go the last few miles in total darkness. The lights on our bikes provided much too little light to really get a good view of the road ahead but we felt it was important to be visible to cars that were on the same road. Lights in the buildings that we passed looked so inviting, but we were forced to continue on.

The warmth of our home was so welcome when we did finally arrive safely. Mrs. Jewett was a bit angry and would except no excuse for being so late. She and her husband had already eaten their supper. She was nice enough to feed us baloney sandwiches and milk before we had to go to bed.

At the time we moved to Crystal Village and during the first half of that school year, our dad had been working as a car salesman in Minneapolis. He was home each night and he drove to work every morning. Things changed as the year went on, because he started changing jobs again. Each new job seemed to require that he had to spend more time traveling. We started seeing less and less of him.

It got so that by early spring we hardly ever saw our dad, except when he took us to our weekly boxing and when he went to my graduation. The seemingly prosperous time that our dad was enjoying at the beginning of the school year had all but vanished, leaving him in some sort of a financial crisis again.

As the end of that school year came near I knew that my father's financial condition had become quite difficult for him. He started to treat my brothers and me differently and he was no longer coming around to take us to boxing. He was now gone most of the time. It seemed as though this happened every time that he changed jobs. He was getting farther in debt and he was behind on paying his bills. I also knew that he hadn't paid anything for the last three months to the people that we were staying with. Mrs. Jewett spent a lot of time complaining to us and it hurt when she called our dad names and there was nothing we could do about it. They told us that at first they believed his excuses, but not any more.

My brothers and I were all able to complete our respective grades at school that year. On the second of June, 1950, I attended my eighth grade graduation from Sacred Heart School. The school had a very formal ceremony and we even received fancy diplomas. I did feel quite proud of myself as my brothers and dad watched on, but I really wished that my mother could have been there. Even though I was so much younger, I now had more formal education than either my mother or father. After the ceremony my father disappeared again and I wouldn't see him again for several weeks.

I again didn't completely understand all that was happening, and it seemed as though no one wanted us to know. We were given no explanation, when we had finished school that year. Why couldn't my dad, at least, have told me what was going on? It happened one day that my brothers and I were simply driven off to St. Joseph's Orphanage on 1458 Randolf Avenue in St. Paul, Minnesota. I was feeling as though no one wanted us. As had happened before, during a crisis our father was just nowhere around. It was extremely frustrating for me, because I had no idea of where or why our dad had disappeared. I was very angry about everything and I felt as though he was deserting us once again.

As soon as we came in sight of the large brick orphanage, I began to have strong feelings of trepidation at just seeing the place with its high chain-link fence around the play area for containing its inmates. Right then my mind was taken back to another orphanage and some of my most gruesome experiences that I had been trying to forget. Would we be receiving the same type of treatment that Pat and I experienced in that other home for children? It also worried me, because I could imagine my brothers and me spending the rest of our youth in a place like that. The worst part of all of this was that there wasn't any way of knowing how long we would be staying at this place, which I was already imagining as my prison. As soon as we got out of the car I had the strongest desire within me to run away as soon as I got the chance. I probably would have too, except that I didn't want to be separated from my brothers again.

When my brothers and I walked into this home we didn't have much, and almost everything that we did own we carried with us. We each had a paper sack full of our things and I carried my four tube radio separately. We were greeted nice enough by one of the nuns, but then it was almost immediately after we entered the building that all of our belongings were taken away from us. Among my treasures was a Sears's radio, a hunting knife with a mother-of-pearl handle that I bought when I lived in New Ulm, and a few other possessions that I treasured. I had no idea where my bicycle was or if, like the one we had in St. Cloud, I would ever see it again. The sisters even took the wristwatch that Mrs. Orth sent to me as a present last Christmas. It was explained to us that to be fair to all of the other children, no one was allowed to have more possessions than anyone else. I was satisfied with the logic of that, but I didn't like it. If we were ever to leave would I get any of my belongings back?

The orphanage was run by Catholic sisters and every eventful part of the day was begun with the ring of a bell. Everyone moved in unison and they even rang the bell at the same time every morning and again in the evening, when we were expected to kneel down beside our beds and say prayers. The home didn't seem to have very much, but we were treated kindly and they fed us decently. The one thing that was constantly on my mind and worried me so much was the uncertainty of not having any idea how long we would be staying there. Even though we were treated well, I still felt anxious for the day that we would be leaving this place. The nuns certainly treated us much better than the way Pat and I were taken care of in that other orphanage and it didn't take long to figure out which ones were nice and the ones that were quite strict but most of them were kind to us. I still couldn't help feeling that I had my freedom taken away from me. No matter how nice they might be to us, it would never be the same as a "home."

I may have found some solace in the fact that I can remember seeing other children who, I think, had it much worse then my brothers and me. There was one boy while we were there who should have been celebrating his seventh birthday, but he spent most of that day feeling angry and crying almost all the time.

When I see someone that is feeling hurt, I always become concerned and want to help. That boy explained his sadness to me this way; he said that now no one would want to have him. He said that people only wanted the very young children. Both of his parents had been killed in a car accident, and he had been waiting patiently at this home for more than two years. He just wanted someone to take him from this place as a new member of their family. Now he felt that it was hopeless, because he had the impression that he was now just too old to ever expect being adopted. I understood his depression, but I couldn't do more than console him. I wasn't even able to help myself.

Another boy who was living there told us how one day he had climbed over the high fence that surrounded the orphanage. He had made his escape! He ran away, but within a few days the police brought him back. He was then put under constant supervision and he was never to be left alone again. He said that for him the home had now really become his prison.

After we had only spent three weekends there, my brothers and I were taken away from that orphanage. Again nothing was explained to us about what was happening. I alone was sent on a Greyhound bus to New Ulm to live again with Mrs. Orth. As so many times before, I just had no choice but to accept these new circumstances. I had no idea where my brothers were taken, and all I could do was worry that they were going to be all right. When would I see them again, if ever?

As soon as I arrived at Mrs. Orth's, I felt welcome and she seemed to be happy to have me back. Even Mr. Crystal, who owned the cafe, seemed glad to see me again; and without hesitation he let me know that I could have my old job back. I think that my father saw this as a threat to him having supervision over me. I didn't want to work on a farm but my father wanted me too whether I liked it or not. I was obedient and tried to work at a couple of different farms first but it seemed that I was just not strong enough. I then went back to work at the Waneda Cafe and Bakery

I felt very lonely, living there and being separated from my brothers once again. I again had to be contented with no knowledge of how long that I would be staying here. My dad came to visit me one day, and I was overjoyed to see that he also brought my bicycle with him. I had thought that I would never see it again.

The one thing in my life of real consequence that happened during that summer was that I bought myself a puppy from a friend. The dog was half Cocker Spaniel and the other half was Springer Spaniel. He eventually turned out to be the size of a Cocker Spaniel, but he had long, soft, black-and-white hair. That dog soon became my best friend and constant companion, going almost everywhere with me. He was extremely affectionate as a puppy. As he was growing, it soon became obvious that he was also quite intelligent, and I started to teach him some tricks. Even though he didn't resemble him in appearance, I think that I named him Rip in memory of the dog that I loved and was taken from us so many years before in Duluth.

It seemed so long ago since the spring of 1948 when my mother was taken to the hospital. For my brothers and me, the last year was spent in just **another port of call**. It all came to an end once again with the members of our family being separated and transported to different unknown destinations. The events must be dealt with as they happen, but there is always hope that the future is going to be better.

- XIII. Reaching a Safe Harbor -

As so many times before, my brothers and I were going to be making another one of our dreaded moves. I was sincerely hoping that this would be the last for several years. I had been spending quite a decent but lonely summer at Mrs. Orth's when one day my dad suddenly arrived telling me to pack up everything that I owned and load it into his pickup.

He had come unannounced and it surprised me, but I didn't question him and did as I was told and loaded everything that I had except my dog, Rip. I was afraid to tell my dad about him, and I really didn't know what I should do with him. Mrs. Orth was at work, so we stopped at the city hall to let her know that I was leaving. I didn't even mention Rip; I just couldn't tell her that I had left the dog behind. I felt that she would take good care of him. She seemed to have grown quite fond of Rip, and maybe she would like him for her own dog. I could tell that she hated to see me go, because as we were saying good bye, I got to see her cry again for only the second time since I had known her.

My dad seemed to always be in a hurry; but before we left

New Ulm this time, I convinced him to make one more stop at the restaurant so I could say good bye to my dear friend and employer, Mr. Crystal. As soon as he saw me, he made it quite obvious that he was glad to see me and he grabbed my arm and purposely whispered in my ear so that my dad couldn't hear. I could barely hear as he said, "If things don't work out, you are always welcome to come back here, and I will give you a very nice place to live." I really liked this man and I knew that it was a kind and genuine offer. I even thought that I would probably be better off going to live with him. I don't know why, but I had an ominous feeling right then that I would never be returning and never see this man again.

As we drove away my dad wanted to know what Mr. Crystal said to me, and I just told him, "He said that I could have my old job back if I ever came back to New Ulm." My dad seemed satisfied with my answer and I felt satisfied that I really didn't lie to him. I just didn't tell him everything.

Only a few days before the start of the new school year, I was reunited with my brothers once again. It was quite a reunion and we were really happy to see each other again. We were all anxious to tell about our experiences and hear about the others' during that summer. We just took our turns and within a few days it was almost as if we had never been separated.

This time we were going to live together with our father in Goodview, which is a small city in the southeast corner of Minnesota, situated about five miles from Winona, a larger border city on the Mississippi, and just across the river from Wisconsin. My brothers and I had never been this far south before, so it didn't take us long to notice that the weather was a bit milder than what we were accustomed to.

My father had bought a beautiful, small, two-story stucco house on a corner lot, with a large weeping willow and a nice goldfish pond in the yard. We thought it was an ideal location for a family like ours, because the place was quite private. We only had one neighbor living to the south of us. Across the road on the west side was nothing but woods that climbed up a very steep hill. Across the road on the north side was a large, unused field of lowlands leading into a sort of small lake that had been formed from the backwaters of the Mississippi River. East of the house was a large garden area that we were able to put to good use. The garden also shaped a part of the shoreline of that lake.

If I had only known that I would be staying for only that summer at Mrs. Orth's, I know that I would never have got that dog. Because I was afraid to say anything to my dad about the dog, I could now only pine for him. Even though I was reunited with my brothers I had become quit attached to the little dog and I missed him terribly.

Mrs. Orth wrote a letter to inform my dad about the dog that I had bought that summer. She asked him what she was supposed to do about the dog. I had no knowledge that she had written that letter and just assumed my father knew nothing about the dog.

Only a couple of weeks after we moved there, I had just come home from school one day when my dad produced the most wonderful surprise for me. He had furtively returned to New Ulm and brought Rip back in the pickup with him. At that moment when I saw my dog, I felt that it was the happiest time of my life. Rip acted as though he had missed me just as much as I had missed him. To me he was the most beautiful sight as he came rushing towards me with his long, drooping ears flopping,

Occasionally there were the times that my dad could show some kindness and understanding, because he quickly learned to like my dog. He even bought all of the food that I daily fed to him. He also gave me a quite a bit of advice, which I heeded, on how to care for and train Rip.

It was obvious that dad was quite happy during this time, and he seemed to be going through another one of his few times of prosperity. He was now working for the International truck dealer in Winona. I had become quite cynical and was already wondering about how long it was going to last. I had no choice so for now I would try to enjoy my present situation.

He even hired a housekeeper to come in each day, to clean and straighten up the house a bit. She also cooked the evening meal for us and washed the dishes. The downstairs bedroom was provided for her so she could stay overnight if she needed to.

The first housekeeper lasted no more than a couple of days and then we got a new one who stayed for almost a month. That housekeeper had to leave because our dad found out that she got cigarettes for Pat, Tom, and me with money that we gave her. As I had come to expect, no more housekeepers were hired after the third one finished her short term. At the time I wasn't completely sure if it was because of my dad's finances or because of my brothers and me. Later on I knew that it was only a matter of economics. My brothers and I were now expected to take care of everything for ourselves. Actually, we didn't do an awfully bad a job of it.

After going to eight different grade schools, the diploma that I received from St. Mary's implied that I was now ready for high school. I really thought that I was prepared to enter a regular high school and that I would be finished with Catholic schools, but I hadn't anticipated what my dad had in mind for me.

My dad made the decision that the high school that I would now be entering had to be a private boys' school in Winona. I was being forced to spend that ninth grade year attending Cotter High School. I thought it was quite a unique parochial school because instead of the sisters, I now had Catholic brothers for my teachers. Before then I hadn't even known that there was a male counterpart to the nuns. These teaching brothers expected a lot out of their students, and they always maintained strict discipline, which wasn't terribly different from most of my past encounters with the nuns.

Upon entering, a student was only given two choices from which he was obliged to choose; he must either enroll for academic or vocational classes. This would determine what subjects he would be taking. Since I was to be academic, my classes included courses such as Latin and algebra.

I can't explain why, but it seemed that I had become worse with my shyness. I didn't even try to make any friends there, so I never did enjoy the time that I spent at that school. My dad gave me money to buy myself a hot lunch each day, but I never ate even one lunch in their cafeteria at the school during that whole school year. I went without lunch and instead spent the money on things such as books, model cars and planes, and an occasional 78 rpm phonograph record. I was quite proud of the splendid library of paperback books that I was accumulating during that year.

My brothers went to a St. Joseph's Catholic grade school. I missed not having them with me, especially my brother Pat. Since I went without eating any meals at my school, I spent the noon recess either visiting my brothers at the grade school or walking downtown to visit for about one-half hour with the man who ran the basement hobby shop. Without question, that was to be the loneliest school year in my entire life.

Since I didn't make friends with any of the students, I think I may have been in need of having someone for a friend. There was one kind brother who taught my Latin class at Cotter High who made my school experience a little less unpleasant. He was quite congenial with me, and we often became preoccupied in a lot of nice discussions about religion after school. He also realized that I had some artistic talent; and with just a little encouragement from him, I willingly made some large murals of almost five feet wide and three feet high. The murals were large enough to cover the space that was normally taken up by *two* bulletin boards. I think that it was also one way for him to get out of putting up the dreaded bulletin boards that he felt so obligated to have. I enjoyed doing that kind of art work. These pictures that I made were always on some religious topic. I also used some of my talent that year in making their homecoming parade banners and several posters advertising different events throughout the year.

When we first moved there, our dad was an International truck salesman in Winona. As time went on, he left that position and got another job as an insurance salesman. He even had my brothers and me go from house to house, delivering handbills throughout the city of Winona. After we had pretty much blanketed the city he even drove us to the surrounding smaller towns where we placed advertising inside the front doors of their houses. I think that I hated this job as much as the job of pulling the feathers from the chickens in Rib Lake.

It was while we were in one of the smaller towns and I was going from house to house delivering hand bills and I returned to the car to get some more. I hated doing it so much that In order to delay having to go back out again I decided to distract my dad from what I was supposed to do. I just quite bluntly asked him why I wasn't given a first name. It surprised him that I should ask and he wanted to know how I knew that. I told him that our mother told me when we lived in St. Cloud. He then told me almost the same thing that my mother told me about not wanting me to have his name and that they couldn't decide on another name that they both might like. They had intended to get it done later and time passed and they never did. He then asked, "Have you told any of the others?"

I answered, "I never told anybody."

He then said, "Well don't. Not even Pat."

With his new employment, the time that he spent at home was becoming less frequent. On one of those times that he did come home when we hadn't expected him and there was plenty of evidence that there had been some cigarette smoking in the house. He questioned the housekeeper about the smoking and she told him that it wasn't she who had been smoking. That meant, of course, that it could only have been my brothers and me. Eventually, the housekeeper admitted her part in it and that she had even bought some cigarettes for us. Hearing that really got our dad upset. So that turned out to be the reason that our dad terminated her employment and she became the last of the housekeepers. Smoking of any kind was something that our dad just hated, and he only thought of it as a very filthy habit.

My brothers and I often did things that we shouldn't, but we would always be quite honest when we were questioned about it. No matter how much we feared our father Pat, Tom and I readily admitted what we had done when he asked us about the smoking, besides the basement where we did our smoking reeked with the smell.

Our dad had been to an office party the night before, and he just happened to have received two cigars from a fellow worker who had become a new parent. Since our dad didn't smoke, he never had any plans to smoke them. Now he felt that he would put them to some good use. His plan called for adapting those two cigars as a treatment for my two brothers and me so that we would get sick and never have the desire to smoke again. Before we went to bed that night, our dad told us that the first two of us to get up in the morning would each receive a cigar to smoke.

Usually I was one of the first to get up; but for some unknown reason, I got up a little late that particular morning or maybe it was because Pat and Tom were overanxious to get the cigars. By the time I got downstairs, our dad along with Pat and Tom were already up, and I had missed the opening ceremonies. When I finally entered the kitchen, there was our dad sitting on one side of the table. He had his elbows on the table with his chin resting in his hands, carefully watching everything on the other side of the table. He was making sure that Pat and Tom, who were seated on the other side, knew that he was aware of their every move. Those two brothers of mine each had a cigar, and at first they were just calmly smoking away.

I didn't even like the smell of cigars, so I wasn't really disappointed that I wasn't going to get one of those stinky things to smoke. Our dad was seeing to it that as my brothers drew in on each puff of their cigar, that they were inhaling every bit of smoke deep into their lungs each time. Now I was really glad that I had missed being a part of this activity, because when I tried once to inhale on just a cigarette I didn't like it or the dizzy feeling I experienced.

When I first began watching them, Pat and Tom were acting quite arrogant about it. They behaved as though they were really enjoying themselves. After they had smoked for a while I noticed that their expressions were gradually changing from the pretended joy into an absolute show of distain. My two brothers kept on smoking and inhaling until the cigars were finally burning down to a short nub.

When it was all over, I could see that our dad was really satisfied that both of them had become quite sick, especially Tom. When Tom left the table there wasn't a door in the house wide enough for him to pass through without bumping both sides. I thought that I could see some satisfaction on my dad's face, and I believe that he thought that if you got really sick enough when smoking, you would never want to do it again. That treatment obviously didn't have the desired effect, because the three of us still continued to do some smoking in secrecy and when our dad wasn't around.

Quite often we would challenge ourselves with a climb up the steep hill across the road on the west side our house. It was one day during one of these climbs that Pat and I had what we thought was a grand idea. We couldn't help but notice the bunch of huge high-power-line poles lying on the ground. They had been replaced with new ones. Pat and I thought that it would be so neat to use them to build ourselves a raft, since the lake was so close to our home. We began the mammoth task of cutting up one of those poles. The job took us almost all day, because we only had one small, old hand saw. First I would saw back and forth until I got tired and then Pat took over. We just kept taking turns like that until we had cut it all the way through. It was awfully hard work, because those poles were composed of some pretty solid wood and they were about 18 inches in diameter.

It took us several hours, but Pat and I persevered and we did finally finish the chore of getting two poles cut, with each being about eight feet in length. With that done, we now were faced with the job of getting those heavy logs down the steep hill. Since it was all downhill, we hadn't anticipated that it would be much of a job to get them to their destination. We were wrong in our thinking that the hard part was over, because even though the hill was steep, the poles wouldn't just go rolling down that hill as we had expected. To make a poll roll, we had to push it and sometimes even turn it around to get it over rocks and around all the bushes and trees. It was a struggle every foot of the way, and it took all our combined strength to keep it going in the right direction. After we finally got the first one to the bottom of the hill, we then had to climb back up and go through that same strenuous procedure all over again.

When we had finally finished getting both logs down the hill, we did get to a relatively easy part. We had the logs positioned next to the road. After we made sure that there was no traffic in sight, together we were able to roll one log down the smooth asphalt road and across a bridge. We had the distance of almost a city block to go, but there was a gentle slope that helped us, as we had to hurry just as fast as we could move. We still had to work hard to guide the logs in a straight path down the center of the road. We had to hope that there would be no traffic coming during the time we were blocking the road with one log and fortunately no vehicles were in sight during the time we rolled the two logs.

Once we had rolled it across the bridge and onto the other side, we then turned the log 45 degrees and pushed it off the road and watched as it rolled down the very steep bank. It finally came to rest at the bottom where we still had quite a struggle as we moved it around to be perpendicular to the shoreline. Now we just had to return to the other log and go through the same procedure all over again with it.

The next step was to position the logs together on the bank, each with one end pointing toward the water and parallel to each other. We then aligned them so that we had about a three foot space between them and the ends were directly across from each other. We then put a board at right angles to the logs at each end. Finally, we took some long spikes and drove them through the board and into the log. Our only hope was that after we had nailed them together it would prevent those logs from separating and going off in different directions. We lastly took some regular smaller logs that had been stripped of their bark and we tied them in the middle to create some extra buoyancy and security. By this time it was really getting dark, so we were forced to finish the job with Tom holding the flashlight. When we finally had our crude raft finished, we had no idea whether it would even float or how deep the water would be where we were going to be taking it.

It was a backbreaking job that Pat and I had as we struggled for some time to slide that heavy craft inch by inch until the one end began to float. After that it was so much easier to get the remaining part of the raft into the water. We didn't have too much confidence in our hastily constructed craft, so we told our younger brothers to watch the flashlight and listen for us, in case we needed help, because neither of us could swim. I really don't know what they could have done if we would have had any problems.

With our raft launched, Pat jumped onto one end and I got on the other as we sort of straddled the two main logs. The logs in the middle must have been too green and they just seemed to sink. Because we only had one board at each end, the rest of the area between the two logs was now just water. We took turns propelling the raft by sinking a long pole into the muddy bottom of the lake and pushing. We continued to push farther out into the darkness as we were gaining more confidence. Maneuvering the raft was quite unwieldy, compared to a boat. We soon discovered that we really had no reason for any skepticism, because that raft proved to be quite seaworthy and it could have easily carried twice our load. Both of us felt quite proud of what we had accomplished that day.

Our experience with that first raft encouraged me to build other rafts even though Pat seemed to have lost interest. I made rafts of different sizes for going out on that lake with my dog, Rip. I was really a loner back then, and I had become content with that. I enjoyed many sunny days floating lazily on that lake. It was so peaceful when my dog and I were able to spend time on those rafts. I even built two nice docks, one on each side of the lake, to secure the rafts. It became quite nice because it made it possible to board or come ashore without getting wet.

One day while my dog and I were just lazily spending some time drifting along on one of my rafts, a muskrat happened to swim by. Rip spotted it and he was off like a shot as he jumped into the water and gave chase. The rat quite obviously knew that he was being pursued, because he immediately started to swim much faster. Remembering the tales that I had heard about how raccoons can climb upon a dog's head and push it under the water and drown the dog when he's trying to swim made me fear for my dog's life.

I shouted his name as loud as I could and then I called again, *"Here Rip. Here Rip. Rip, come here!"* But he continued on and acted as though he didn't even hear me. This was the first time ever that he did not respond to my calls for him. Rip was able to swim at about the same speed as the rat. I was quite happy that he wasn't gaining on the rat, in fact; I would have been quite satisfied if he never caught up to it. The raft was big and heavy which made it impossible for me to keep pace with them as they were putting more distance between them and me.

Rip continued following the rat as it went up onto a narrow strip of land. In that instant, I was feeling a bit better about it, because I believed that Rip's chances on land would be better than in the water. Rip, still in close pursuit, finally caught up to that rat. I was now becoming quite afraid for my dog because, when Rip was soak and wet, I could see that he really wasn't much larger than the rat.

From my location on the raft, I was watching as the rat stopped and turned to face my dog. That rat looked quite fearsome as he sort of reared up and was showing his long, brownish front teeth. Rip stopped with the rat only about two feet away and squarely in front of him. I could tell that he was breathing hard the way his sides were heaving in and out. He seemed to be undecided about what he would do next as he faced the rat.

I was wishing that he would just turn away and let the rat go. I thought to myself "you dumb dog!" because he now started to wag his tail. I thought that I might be able to get his attention now, so I called to him, "**Rip – Here Rip!**" and again he ignored me. He didn't even turn to look at me. Suddenly, Rip lunged forward and everything began to happen so fast that it was hard for me to follow exactly what was happening as the dog and rat were now locked in a mortal combat. The most terrible fight had developed between them. I could tell that several times the rat's teeth found their mark and Rip was getting hurt. Not long after their fight had begun, I caught sight of blood running from somewhere under Rip's chin. That scared me and I was now afraid that the rat was winning.

I shouted, "**Here Rip!**" I called Rip's name over and over again as loudly as I could, trying to call him off; but it was of no use and he continued his assault. I was terrified for my dog's safety as I was crying and shouting at the same time. The tears flowing from my eyes made everything within my view look a bit blurry. I was poling the heavy raft just as hard as I could toward the conflict. It was terrible to hear the combination of yelping and growling sounds coming from Rip.

With every ounce of effort in me, I finally got the raft close enough to shore where I hoped it would be safe to jump into the water. I was still holding the pole tightly as I intended to use it as a weapon. I plunged in and began sinking into the muddy bottom and the water continued up to just below my neck. The water and the soft bottom were resisting my efforts as I struggled in the direction of the two combatants. I started to move faster as the water became shallower, and I finally got on solid ground. By the time I got there I was quite exhausted but I had the pole ready for striking. I was too late to offer any assistance because, even after he had received such a horrible beating, Rip finally sunk his teeth deep into the rat's throat which seemed to have brought the fight to an end.

By the time I got to him, Rip was standing proudly over his victim and wagging his tail. Without a doubt he was proud of what he had just done. The rat then jerked a little, and Rip swiftly grabbed the rat by the throat again. He held the rat in his mouth and he made a low growling sound as he was biting down hard and shaking it from side to side for a short time, and then he dropped the rat again. Rip had made sure that there wasn't going to be any more movement from that lifeless body.

I wiped my tears on the sleeve of my flannel shirt and immediately proceeded to examine Rip's bleeding wounds. I knew that Rip wanted my praise for what he had accomplished, and I did compliment him; but I was more worried about those terrible-looking cuts. His worst injury appeared to be a severe cut in the area of his throat, from which he did recover and showed no after-effects. I then sat down on the grass as I hugged and petted my very special dog.

Occasionally, I might just spend some lazy time with my dog as I fished off one of the rafts. It was fun to watch Rip as he would get so excited with every fish that I was landing. The way he was jumping around and wagging his tail, you'd think that it was something really special that he had done. He seemed to keep his enthusiasm, as he behaved the same way whether it was the first or the fiftieth fish that I caught. In one morning I could easily have caught more than one hundred fish, mainly bullheads and sunfish. I cleaned a large amount of fish that fall, but they were really good and my brothers and I fried them in cracker crumbs and ate a lot of good free food.

I really trained Rip well and, with the exception of school, he went almost everywhere with me. Rip even at times rode with me in one pocket of the saddlebags on my bike if I had to travel a very long distance. One of the most useful tricks that I taught him was when we would walk along together and without even a glance towards him, I would say, "*Stay, Rip - Stay!*" And he would sit right there and would not move until I called to him. I never did find out how long that he would stay after leaving him, but from experience I know that it was more than an hour. When I left home on my bicycle and I didn't want him to follow, I just had to say, "*Stay home, Rip!*" and he stayed near our house until I returned hours later. I was so proud of my dog and we were truly the best of friends.

I also felt a lot of pride because I knew that Rip would respond to my commands over those given by anyone else. In fact, one time my dad decided he would test Rip by using a package of raw hamburger that he had just opened. My dad stood quite a distance from me as he called Rip over to him and Rip responded; but just as he got close enough to have a good smell of the hamburger, I called his name. He immediately turned around and came running as fast as he could back to me. It convinced my dad that Rip was truly my dog.

Many times after it got dark, my brothers and I would cross the lake on one of the rafts. When we got to the other side, we would tie the raft to one of those nice docks that I had constructed. From there, it was just a short walk to the nearby outdoor movie theater, which we would sneak into. We would go to one of the stalls in the very back row and turn the volume up on the speaker and watch. We would all lie on the ground because it was comfortable but mainly to make it difficult for anyone to see us and possibly chase us away. Lying on the ground like that, Rip would lie motionless as my pillow, during the entire length of the movie.

Even though Pat and I were together quite a bit during our youth, we used to fight far too much with each other. It seemed as though we were quite frequently getting angry with each other. Anyone who had seen us fighting must have thought that we were going to kill each other. There was no question that Pat was much stronger than I, but he never got the better of me nor me of him. What I didn't have in strength I made up for by being quicker than he. I think that most of the time during our fighting the reason for it had already left us, because usually it happened over such small matters. I was also quite certain that if someone else had interfered in our fight, we would have stopped fighting each other right then and fought against the intruder. Even though we got quite vicious at times, neither of us got too badly hurt.

What started out as a nice, warm, sunshiny day almost turned into tragedy when I took my youngest brother, Warren, along on the raft with Rip and me. We were planning on doing some fishing for bullheads and sunfish. Because he had requested it, I gave Warren the pole to propel the raft. He did it just as he had seen me do so many times, and we were moving along quite nicely but quite a bit more slowly than if I were doing it. Suddenly the pole got stuck in the mud at the bottom of the lake and Warren was unable to pull it out. Warren held on tightly and wouldn't let go of the pole, and the raft just kept on going, right out from under his feet. Even though Warren was only four years old, I believe that he had a pretty good grasp of the situation that he was in, and he was becoming quite desperate to be rescued. He called to me and I could see that he was scared.

There Warren was, hanging onto that pole in the middle of the water, as the raft was slowly moving away. At first I had become delighted that he continued to hold so tightly to that pole. I knew that he couldn't swim, and I was quite afraid for him. I could imagine him slowly tipping over with the pole or might be unable to hang on until I was able to get to him. Either way, he would end up going into the water and drowning. It all was quite frightening and I was very much afraid for him and, I suppose, for myself too.

I yelled to him, *"Just keep hanging on, for God's sake! It won't take long. I will get back to you pretty soon."* I started frantically using my cupped hands to reverse the raft's momentum away from brother. I felt so helpless as I Paddled as hard as I could with only my cupped hands to use as oars in a desperate attempt to get to him. That was enough to cause the raft to progress in the right direction but at an almost unbearably slow pace.

I knew that Warren somewhat understood his situation and he was crying and at the same time screaming at me to save him. I continued to maneuver that heavy log raft in that manner towards where Warren was perched and could do nothing but wait. I called to him again, *"I'm almost there! Hang on! Just a little bit longer!"* Even though it wasn't going to really be "soon," I was doing the best I could.

I spent a large amount of time and about all of the energy that was in me, but I finally did get that raft back to Warren. I was able to rescue him and the pole that he had become so intimate with. I was exhausted but I was also relieved and it sort of made me feel great to know that I had rescued him and maybe even saved his life. I know that at the time it must have been quite a frightening event for Warren. Occasionally he still explains in great detail about this "encounter with death," and how I tried to drown him.

Another time that Warren and I experienced an unwanted adventure which could also have had tragic consequences for both of us was one of the times that I was giving him a ride on the handle bars of my bicycle. I had just turned in from the road onto our driveway, which sloped quite steeply down toward the garage and if you made a turn to the left, you were heading toward the house.

I had intended to just scare Warren a little by shouting, *"I'm going to run into the garage!"* It was my plan to drive us toward the garage and then at the very last moment to turn sharply toward the house. I didn't think that I was taking much of a risk, because I knew exactly how much distance was needed to make the turn and using its coaster brakes to bring the bike to my planned halt just short of the house. We were traveling quite fast at the time, but as it turned out I frightened Warren far more than I planned. I was able to scare him enough all right and I believe that he must have thought we were really going to crash. I can only think that he was so frightened that he completely lost control when he unwisely tried to stop us by sticking his foot into the front spokes of my bicycle.

That bike had never before stopped so quickly and I never even got a chance to use the brakes. We did crash, but I had just completed the quick turn to the left on the concrete, which prevented what could have been a very serious accident! My body had been unable to stop at the same time as the bike, so as the rear of the bike lifted off the ground and started swinging around I went rocketing into flight. I passed Warren as I came to a headfirst landing on the ground. Warren still had his foot caught between the front fork and the spokes of the bike as it was now facing in the opposite direction. Warren was lying on the edge of the lawn. He was unable to free his foot from the bike. He must have thought that he would have to wear that bike on his foot forever, because he was making a horrible amount of loud noise with his bawling.

Warren's wailing cries got Tom's immediate attention. At that instant I was unable to help Warren as I was also lying hurt on the ground. Tom came running over to us and shouted at Warren, "Shut up!" He then hit the crying Warren and yelled at him again to shut up. Warren finally did as Tom had told him, and after much effort Tom was able to get Warren's foot separated from the bike by bending some of the spokes of the wheel. Warren and I recovered from our injuries well enough, but my bike wouldn't recover unless I was somehow able to acquire enough money to buy a new wheel.

For a boy of only four, Warren seemed to be in the middle of a lot of strange happenings. Probably the most outlandish of all was what happened one time when he was taking a bath with my brother Pat. Warren was trying to make bubbles in the water by farting. This time he just tried too hard and he produced a turd that came floating to the top of the water. That brought an immediate response from Pat as he began shouting angrily at Warren. I, hearing the noise, came running into the bathroom. When I saw what had happened and heard Pat's complaining, I just couldn't help but laugh. My laughing was more than enough to get Pat even more upset and he became extremely angry with me.

With our father's encouragement, Pat, Tom and I did continue with our boxing program that we had started in Robinsdale. We went to Winona for our lessons and training once every week in the evening. We still had the heavy punching bag and we got a lot of conditioning with that. We also practiced by having fights with each other, jumped rope a lot, and did our other training at home. We would move the dining room table to create a large enough space to fight. Then we set up our own bouts with three rounds lasting three minutes each. Boxing was one sport that Pat, Tom and I did become quite accomplished in.

I think that each one of my brothers and I found a different way to cope with all of the different problems that we were forced to deal with in our lives. I never really wrote much about the things that my brother Richard did. There just isn't much that one could say about him, because he was extremely successful at becoming anonymous. He became quite proficient at making those around him completely unaware of his presence. He was just a bit different and he stayed mainly in the house, quietly occupied with his reading.

My brothers and I even began to think that Richard was hard of hearing because when he was reading, he was completely unaware of anything around him, as though he couldn't hear anything. At times like this you would get no answer from Richard when you called to him. For example, if I would call out loudly, *"Richard!"* I would get no response. If I called again even louder, **"Richard!"** he would continue reading as though he hadn't heard me. The only way to get him to recognize me was to call his name loudly and at the same time shake him.

He would then appear to be surprised as he looked up at me and responded with, "Yeah, what do you want?"

I then would start talking to him, expecting some sort of reply and it wouldn't come. His eyes had already drifted back into the book he was reading and he was lost again in a whole different world. From these experiences I realized that it was necessary to take away whatever it was that he was reading in order to talk to him. It was only then that I could expect him to participate in any dialog.

Eventually I found out the reason for his inability to hear. He really didn't hear, because he was able to concentrate so well that he could exclude everything going on around him. It was Richard's way of dealing with life by just shutting out all of the unpleasant reality around him and going into a much nicer world in some book or a daydream of his own creation. It was many years later that I was to find out that he was really quite intelligent, with extremely acute hearing.

I think that my escape must have been the same as it was when I was living with Mrs. Orth. I did a lot of daydreaming and thinking back to better times. I still found a lot of enjoyment in making balsa wood models. The only difference was that I was developing more interest in war planes. I began to do a lot of reading about planes, and it became sort of a hobby for me as I had to know about each one's specifications. I also dreamed of the day that I would be able to pilot my own plane.

I spent an enormous amount of time sanding, shaping and painting. I also made some cars that were powered by carbon dioxide cartridges. They would go very fast, but they were almost impossible to control as they would take off like a rocket. I would have done a lot more model building than what I did, but than it would have really required me to be even far more creative to obtain the money that was required. Money was always a problem, but some of the needed funds I got from my dad and he wasn't ever aware of it, because it was intended for buying my lunch at school.

This was the year that the song "Mockingbird Hill," was released and it became very popular. I bought the recording of it on a 78 rpm record, and I enjoyed it so much that for some time I kept playing it over and over. I had the original version of that song and it was that same version that was being condemned by many of the churches in the area and even the Catholic Church, because of some of the song's lyrics in the chorus. I didn't know about that until I heard about it on a news broadcast on the radio after I had already bought the record, but I still enjoyed it when my dad wasn't around.

I knew that I didn't have to worry about any of those churches, but I knew that I didn't dare let my dad hear or even know that I had that recording. He got very upset the year before after he heard the song, "I Saw Mommy Kissing Santa Claus." He thought those lyrics were so horrible, because of the misunderstanding that it might give to children. We were never allowed to go to a movie until our dad saw that Parents' Magazine had it rated as all right for children or was approved by the Catholic Church's Legion of Decency. He was very strict about things like that, but I think it also showed his concern for us.

My father at this time had a lady friend who lived in the Minneapolis area and was a widow by the name of Lillian Skoine. It was much later that I found out the important role she played in helping my dad get the needed financing for the house. She and my father seemed to enjoy each other's company and he brought her to the house to meet my brothers and me. Mrs. Skoine, as we called her, seemed like a decent sort, and my brothers and I liked her immediately. It helped that she also showed a genuine liking for us.

My dad and Mrs. Skoine seemed to have a very nice relationship. My brothers and I did not think that there might be any sort of a problem with this friendship that they had. We would never suspect my dad of doing anything wrong, because he was married to our mother. We also knew how conscientious he was about things like that. I think that one big reason that we liked his relationship with this woman was that whenever Mrs. Skoine was around, my dad was in the best of moods and he treated us kindly so it had to be a situation that was good for our father. In fact, when she was present, our dad acted as though he was quite proud of his five sons. Maybe we were more than a bit naive, but then again maybe it was for the best.

My mother had now been in the sanatorium for almost three years now. She by this time had one of her lungs completely collapsed and the other lung was less than 50% effective. During this time her best weight was only about 68 pounds and there really seemed to be no chance that she could recover enough so she would ever be able to leave that place. Her confinement at the sanatorium was only to keep her alive as long as possible with really no chance of ever returning to a life on the outside.

My father and Mrs. Skoine seemed to have developed a mutual enjoyment for square dancing at this time. They took lessons, and they went to a lot of these dances together. They would often take my brothers and me to these dances with them. During these times, our dad tried with very little success to get my brothers and me started into this square dancing.

Richard seemed to be the only one of us boys who genuinely enjoyed it and participated in the dancing. I was always very shy, so I didn't do very much of it. I did learn how and I did a bit of dancing with some of the single older women at those dances. I never really got interested in that kind of dancing until more than a year later, in a different place.

Some of the things that my brothers and I did were the result of our dad's influence. He would tell us about something he did as a boy and we thought it would be neat to experience some of the things that he did when he was young. A good example of that is the time he told us that when he was about our age, he borrowed his dad's car and drove it for quite a distance without him ever knowing it.

One day Pat and I decided that we were going to do that very same thing with our dad's 1947 Nash. We knew we could do it because we had studied how our dad shifted gears and used the clutch and the brake. Pat had made up his mind that he was going to do the driving and I would ride with him. I believe that my main function in this was to go along and provide Pat with enough courage to do it. I think I also trusted that Pat had a lot more ability than he may actually have had. Without even considering the consequences, he and I got into the car. He was going to do the driving and I was going along for some support. He put the car in gear and backed it out of the garage just like our dad would have done, with no problem. We then started down the road for about a distance of two miles with no problem. We turned off the road, parked, and we just sat and talked for a bit. It was now time to think about what might happen if our dad did awake while we were gone. Then we turned around and Pat drove back home and put the car back into the garage and with no problem.

Our dad had been asleep when we left, but he had awakened right after we had driven away, so now there was a problem. He didn't like what we had done, even though we reminded him of what he told us he had done when he was a boy. He said that he wasn't accepting that as an excuse. I really believe that he did, though, because he truly surprised us when he didn't take off his belt and give us a beating. He just gave us a good scolding, telling us that he doesn't ever want us to even consider doing that again and we did promise we would never do it again.

Living there was nothing like Rib Lake or the Shanahans'. For me there was the good and the bad of living there. I was lonely very much of the time, but I did have my brothers with me. I also got to spend a lot of time together with my best friend, Rip. I don't think that I could have ever learned to enjoy going to that private school in Winona.

The whole time that we spent in Goodview was our family's attempt at **reaching a safe harbor**. It did provide our family with a nice place to call home for a little less than one year. That spring, as too many times before, my brothers and I were going to be separated once again. I would now be going to one place and my brothers would be sent to some other places. I was also leaving my little friend, Rip, behind and not knowing if I would ever see him again. I still had the hope that one day my brothers and I would again be living together as a family. At that time I had no idea where I would be going next. I could only imagine and hope that I would be somewhat happy with my new home and what my future had in store for me.

- XIV. Adrift on the High Seas -

AGAIN I REALLY DON'T understand all of what happened, but our dad was having financial problems again. It seemed that he was always changing jobs and in the end things just never worked out as he planned. The short time that we spent in Goodview was just enough for my brothers and me to get used to a somewhat "normal" life like other kids.

In the spring of that year our dad put the house up for sale, and after school was out for the summer my brothers and I would have to move again to some unknown place to start over. Our stay in Goodview was so short; but just like always it was such a disappointment when I realized that we were going to be moving again. I had become so frustrated with all of this moving from place to place and never staying anywhere very long. For me the only good that would be coming out of this move was that I would not be going back to Cotter High School next year. I wasn't going to miss that at all.

That summer I went to work on a farm again but with a far better chance of succeeding than in the past. By now I was weighing in at about 90 pounds, but I had become quite strong for my size. My new home was about one mile from where my brother Pat was living and working. It was also only one mile from Fremont, Minnesota, a very small town with a general store, creamery, a no-longer-used old brick elementary school, town hall, and a few houses and a total population of about fourteen people at that time.

A few miles from Fremont was Lewiston, a city with a population of about 800, where I would be attending high school for my sophomore year. I now had a home with a very nice farm family, Gerald and Grace Simon and their three children, Audrey, Yvonne and Jerry. Throughout the school year I got paid $7 a week, plus room and board. In the summer months I was paid $100 a month, plus room and board.

This was a dairy farm, so the days were long and hard. Without exception, the cows had to be milked twice a day every day even on Sundays. That summer I worked hard every day of the week, except I always got time off every Sunday morning to go to church and I had a few hours in the afternoon to do as I pleased. When I figured out how many hours of work I averaged each week during the summer, it is no exaggeration to say that it was more than 100 hours. I was their hired man, so I had to be available to do any work that they wanted done. I learned my jobs well and did a lot of those jobs that were the type of work that no one else would want to do. Another thing most of my work was done while I was alone so I had a lot of time to think. When I was working at some of their more nasty jobs, it had become my dream that one day I would be employed in some occupation where I wouldn't have to work on Sundays and maybe even have the whole weekend free.

It was in late summer and less than a week before school would begin, when I was pleasantly surprised to see my little friend again. My father brought my dog, Rip, out to the farm. He got permission from the Simons for me to keep him there. There was one problem with this because Rip was a breed of bird dog so it was only natural that their chickens would provide him with some sport. The chickens were a part of the Simon's livelihood and they were there to stay, so something had to be done with my dog. During the day my dog was to be tied up to a stanchion in the barn. Another problem for me was the fact that when I was home I spent almost all of my time working so I had almost no time for my dog.

When I had to leave for the first day of school, I told Rip to stay home and I went down the driveway and caught the bus. The year was starting out with school only lasting for a half-day, so I arrived back home at noon. As soon as I got off the bus, Rip saw me start up the driveway and came running so fast toward me that sometimes his back legs were going faster than his front, giving the appearance of him running almost sideways. He was so glad to see me. I picked him up and held him as he licked my face with that rough tongue of his.

The next day, I got done with chores and ate breakfast but it was getting late. Without thinking, I hurriedly ran to catch the bus. I forgot about Rip being tied up in the barn and I was in quite a hurry so I didn't tell him to stay home and I'm not sure it would have made any difference anyway. I spent a full day at school and then in the late afternoon the bus dropped me off at the end of the driveway.

Like the day before I was looking forward to an excited greeting from my dog. I started up the driveway and was disappointed because there was no Rip coming to meet me, which made me wonder where he was. I called out "Rip" several times as loudly as I could, with no reply. I ran to the barn and looked and calling out for him. I quickly searched some of the other buildings as I continued calling for him. He didn't answer my calls, so I knew that he must not hear me. Why couldn't he? Where could he have gone? I started to worry, but I also knew that my first obligation was to the people whom I was working for.

I felt very anxious as I ran into the house and asked Mrs. Simon if she knew where Rip was. She told me that she hadn't seen him since early in the morning. After I had quickly changed into my work clothes, I ran outside and called for my dog some more, but I still received no response. I continued to look and call as I was doing my chores. I went in and ate supper, and afterwards I came back out to do my chores and help with the milking. All during that time I wished that I could be looking for my dog.

I was impatient to get done with the chores and the milking so I could go looking for my dog. As soon as we were finished at about 8:30, I got on my bicycle to begin my search for Rip. I rode my bike down the driveway and onto the gravel road in the dark. My bike had a light but it was only marginally effective as it illuminated a small bit of road in front of me. I thought that Rip would probably go in the direction that the school bus had taken me away that morning. As I peddled along on my bike, I quite frequently called out Rip's name as loudly as I could. I know that I was crying and already hurting inside, because I was missing my dog and my best friend so much. I also realized the futility of ever finding him.

I was still crying as I came to Fremont and made a left turn to go north down that road, every so often calling my dog's name. I turned around and went back to Fremont and continued on south of the town, frequently calling out "Rip!" as loud as I was able. I kept riding for almost three hours without any success.

I was so sad, but I was also quite angry, because in the back of my mind I thought that maybe these people didn't want my dog on their farm. They might have purposely got rid of him. Maybe the dog got in the way and Mr. Simon drove over him with the tractor. I was thinking all kinds of bad thoughts. Why didn't these people try to help me find him? They didn't even show one bit of interest in my loss. I finally gave up, rode back home, went to bed and cried myself to sleep.

The next day after the evening chores, I again peddled my bike and I and turned east this time. As I did the night before, I continued the search for my dog on my bicycle as I kept calling out his name. I again rode in different directions until late into the night. I continued doing this each night for the rest of the week and I finally had to admit to myself that my dog was probably gone forever.

I spent several nights after that, crying myself to sleep. I also said a lot of prayers, during this time, asking God for help in finding my Rip; but this time it seemed the only answer I would receive was "No!" I was aching for my dog and I was angry because he was just something else that I loved that had been taken away from me. I became so suspicious that the people that I was living with. I would always have this doubt in my mind that the Simon's purposely got rid of my dog, but I honestly would never know. At that time, I really didn't trust anybody.

When I arrived at the Simon's I had really become no more than their hired man. When I went to school, I got up early each morning at around 5 o'clock and I did chores and helped with the milking. When I got home from school, I did chores again until about 8:30 in the evening, when the milking was done. During the summer and on weekends, I worked all day, starting at around 5:30 in the morning, and I didn't get finished until around 8:30 at night. During the school year I averaged at least 63 hours of work each week. There were many times that the day would end much later, culling chickens until after midnight, working late on the tractor during spring planting, or doing the unforeseen jobs that would occasionally come up.

My first year there was my sophomore year at Lewiston High School. It was so much different from my freshman year at Cotter High in Winona. Lewiston High was a public school, the classes were much easier and in fact I thought it was too easy. The teachers weren't nearly so demanding and in fact I thought that it was too easy and I really wasn't learning much. The whole school seemed to have a much more relaxed atmosphere. The students seemed to be a lot more amiable, so it was much easier to develop friendships. I found that I was even able to begin developing a few new friendships. Unlike at Cotter High, I knew that there was no need for me to be lonely at this school.

I was still quite self-conscious, but it was during that school year that I made friends with John Milde, a classmate. He had quite an important effect on me, and it was going to change my life considerably for my remaining years in high school. He influenced me to take enough interest in myself to begin combing my hair every day for the first time in my life. He even showed me what to do. For some reason, I had developed a feeling that I was not very good to look at, and until then I think that I never combed my hair because I wouldn't even look at myself in a mirror. With just a bit of prodding from John, I started to become concerned about my appearance and how I dressed. With some of the money that I made, I also started to buy some nicer clothes for myself.

Another thing about John is that he was at least one-half inch shorter than my-five-foot-eight inch height. I was surprised when he told me that he was going out for basketball, and I tried to tell him that guys like us were just too short for that sport. He ignored me and went to basketball practice every day after school and, of course, I had to go home to do my chores each day. By the time that the basketball season was over that year, John had already grown to be a couple of inches taller than I. I was quite jealous of him because I hadn't grown an inch, and I was so disappointed that I remained the same height.

It was then that I began to realize that I was probably finished growing. Mrs. Orth was wrong: I was not going to be the tall, dark and handsome man she said I would be. By the next year John ended up to be six feet four inches tall and I still hadn't grown any. I would always wish that I was taller, and I would always feel self-conscious about my height and quite defensive about it. In fact, if someone taller than I made any comment about my small stature, I would usually snap back with, "They sell manure by the height of the pile."

I can look back now and know that my own, badly lacking, self-esteem did improve somewhat because of John's help, but it definitely was not what it should have been. Patrick was in the freshman class, and he seemed to be a lot more outgoing than I and much happier. He was also a couple of inches taller than I, which was a problem for me, because I always was disappointed that I wasn't bigger than I was. I wished I could be more like him in the way he looked and the way he acted. I had become very jealous of him.

I always ate a good breakfast in the morning before school and I always had a good evening meal. When I went to school, it was a different matter. When we had our lunchtime at school, instead of eating in the cafeteria I got into the habit of going to a small store that was only two blocks from the school and buying something to eat. Usually I ate snack foods, like a pint of ice cream, Hostess Cupcakes, etc. I still had my love for chocolate that I had developed when I was very young. In fact, I think that chocolate had become an addiction for me. At least two or three a week, at noon I would buy a six-ounce tin of Hershey's syrup and drink it. I know that if the Simons had known about this, they would have been quite upset with me. I really don't think that they could have done anything about it. My noon time meal had become a nutritional disaster.

Saturday was the hardest and longest day of the week for me. I worked very hard for at least 15 hours each Saturday. During the winter months, I was almost always completely alone as I did the work I had been assigned. Every Saturday after we finished milking and had eaten a breakfast, it seemed that I spent most of the day cleaning manure out of the young-stock pens, where the calves are raised.

Week after week, those Saturdays seemed to be always filled with the same tedious routine. I would drive the tractor with the manure spreader alongside of the barn. I had to align the spreader with the window of the pen that I was cleaning. I then went in the barn, climbed into the pen, removed the window, and started to fork the heavy straw mixed with waste into the manure spreader. After I had filled the spreader, I took the tractor and hauled my load out to the field and spread it about. That routine was repeated several times during the day as I carried out several loads. The job was quite boring but I got used to it. When I finished that, I still had all of my evening chores to do. It seemed to me that Saturdays lasted longer than any other day. I was always anxious for the evening to come.

The next day was Sunday, and there was a typical routine about it too. We started chores at about 5:30 in the morning just like any other day. After we finished the milking, we went to the house and ate breakfast. Then we put on our good clothes for church. At about 10 o'clock we went to Mass at the church in Lewiston. We then came home and ate a big dinner. I now had about five hours to spend on whatever I wanted to do before it was time for the evening chores.

The Catholic Church in Lewiston had a big hall, and that fall they started giving square dance lessons once a week. After the milking, the Simons would take me with them to go there on those particular evenings. They always had a lot of food to eat and then we would dance until late into the evening. I was becoming less self-conscious, and I was beginning to enjoy these nights and the dancing with the different girls of my own age.

The Simons' daughter, Audrey, was one year behind me in high school, and she always came along too. She was an extremely bright and very pretty girl, and after a short time I did quite fancy her. We really got on quite well with each other, so I always had a nice dance partner for the evening. I still had some difficulty with my feelings for her. I developed the impression that her mother and father thought that I wasn't quite good enough for her, because of my position as their hired man.

Later on, I started going out with the Simons as though I was a part of their family. We went to many evening social events, such as the card parties and several other kinds of parties, which the farm families prepared for in the Fremont Town Hall. We even had lunches followed by "500" card tournaments. Sometimes we would have waffles and whipped cream or box lunches to bid on, followed by the dances that were held there. Later that winter we were given some square dancing lessons too. I still felt quite happy to have Audrey available at any time as my dance partner there too.

Going out with girls and dancing became a very important part of my entertainment that year. This was certainly a big change in my life, and I was enjoying it. I also started going to the dances every Friday night in Wyatville, which is another very small town similar to Fremont and a few miles from Lewiston. It had one major difference, which was the tavern with a nice ballroom attached to it. Mr. Simon would drive me to the dance and I was able to always able to find some other friend with a car who would bring me home at about midnight. I was disappointed that Audrey wasn't allowed to go along on these nights.

Because I didn't bring a date with me, I got to dance and meet many different young ladies. The ladies sat on chairs around the outside of the dance floor and I learned to ask, "Would care to dance?" Almost without exception I had myself a dance partner and possible future friend. It was there that I got a lot of practice doing the old-time dances, such as waltzes, polkas, fox trots and schottisches. I think the dancing for me became a good escape from my extremely tedious and lonely life as a hired man on the farm.

Early that spring Mr. Simon surprised me when he asked me how I would like to raise a pig to show at the fair. I really got excited about that so, of course, with my affirmative answer, he informed me that I could take my pick out of any of the litters of pigs. I was allowed to then separate that pig from the others and it became my responsibility to take care of all of its needs by myself. I thought it would be a nice challenge to choose a barrow that was the runt from a large litter. A barrow starts out life as a male pig, but he is then castrated when he's very young to be marketed later for its pork. I also made sure that the pig I selected had a nice shape and good black-and-white Hampshire coloring. Mr. Simon even provided me with a special pen with a concrete floor in the barn so I could raise him apart from all the rest of his littermates.

I began my project using information that I read about in some farming magazine. One particular article suggested using automatic feeders and making all of the food available for the pig. Their study claimed that a pig was the most intelligent animal on any farm and has the ability to balance its own diet if the proper food is available. I was quite excited to give it a try, so I followed the instructions. I provided him with an unlimited amount of the suggested feeds in an automatic feeder. He could eat, cafeteria style, as much and whatever he wanted and whenever he felt like it.

The success of putting that theory into practice became quite obvious in a very short time. That pig soon became much larger and far better developed than the rest of the litter that he was taken from. He developed an almost perfect lean shape and size.

It wasn't very much longer when Mr. Simon and I really believed that I was raising myself a sure winner for the county fair in late summer. I felt that I had reason to be really proud of that pig. I was confident that he would do well, and I was anxiously waiting the time that I would get to show him at the fair. I made the bad mistake of letting him become my pet. He became such a pet, that when I let him out of his pen, he would follow me and made an effort to copy everything that I did.

It seems that it so often happened in my short life that things just didn't turn out as they were originally planned. I never even got the chance to show that barrow I was so proud of. No pigs were allowed to be shown at the county fair that year, because there had been a large outbreak of hog cholera that summer. The county extension agent sent me a letter explaining everything, along with a well-appreciated check for $7. I would have gladly given up the check to have a chance to show my pig.

I really got quite attached to that pig, and the worst part is that I would have to get rid of him soon. It was, therefore, quite a sad day for me later on when he had to go to market with the rest of the hogs.

My dad during that time was a salesman in Minneapolis, selling Dodge cars and trucks. He was an excellent salesman and he earned his place as a member of the Dodge 400 club, which included only their top salesmen in the whole United States. As a reward for his sales success, he was able to win some very nice prizes for my brothers and me. He got me a nice Royal portable typewriter, which I was really grateful for, and I made very good use of it. Like at the funeral home in New Ulm I could again *type* my letters to my mother. I joked with my dad that he got me a typewriter because they didn't have stethoscopes. He often made sure that I knew that he was still expecting me to be a doctor some day. Pat was given a nice wrist watch; Richard, with his fine ear for music, got an accordion; and our dad got a nice clock radio for Tom and Warren to share.

I got through my first year there as a sophomore at Lewiston High School without too many problems. That following summer

Pat and I were determined to get ourselves a car. We really couldn't each afford one, so we decided we'd go together and share the cost of buying and paying for the maintenance of having a car. Being a car salesman made it easy for our dad to get a good buy on a nice inexpensive car for us. He found us a two tone green 1942 Dodge that was a trade in for a new car. It was a four-door with a 1947 six-cylinder engine in it. The price made it affordable for us, so Pat and I gave our dad the money for it and only six days after my birthday, we became proud owners of a car. At the time I thought that I had just received the grandest of all birthday presents. You could say that, for the United States anyway, we had a prewar car with a postwar engine. I felt that it was about the most beautiful car.

Throughout the years Pat and I had become quite used to sharing. We now had to devise some equitable scheme for sharing the car. We finally resolved that conflict by deciding to alternate the weekdays that we would each have the car in our possession to drive. One would have it on Monday, Wednesday, and Friday one week and then only have it on Tuesday and Thursday on the next. The one who had it on Tuesday and Thursday would then take possession on Saturday and keep it through Monday of the following week.

Having the newer engine in that car also gave it much more power than what the original motor possessed. Our dad made it quite obvious that he was concerned that Pat or I might drive the car too fast. To solve that problem, dad had a governor installed on the carburetor to limit the top speed to only 50 miles per hour. Our dad even had a seal put on the governor so one would know if it had been tampered with. Pat and I didn't like it and at that time, I thought of that governor as something that demonstrated to me that our dad didn't trust us. Most of the time having that governor wasn't any problem but when you needed to pass a really slow moving vehicle it seemed to be an obstruction to pass safely. I later realized that it was our dad's way to handle his sincere concern for our safety.

We had purchased our car on the third of July, and everything was proceeding according to our plans. However, only eight days later, on the twelfth of July, when it was my turn to drive the car, our plans for the day turned into tragedy. For the first time since I started to work for the Simons, I arranged to get a weekday morning off work so I could go into Winona to get my driver's license. Pat also made similar arrangements with his boss.

Pat drove the car over to where I was working and I drove the car from there to Lewiston where we purchased a dimmer switch to replace the bad one in the car. With me as the driver we proceeded on to Winona. We had no more than entered the city when Pat asked me to let him drive. I at first protested but he continued to beg me to let him drive the car during the time that we were in the city. He insisted that he had a lot more experience than I with driving in city traffic. I finally gave in and handed him the keys, which I would dearly regret later.

I always did feel uncomfortable when I rode with Pat behind the wheel, because he always drove so aggressively. After receiving the keys he immediately began cruising so confidently about the streets of Winona. I noticed the speedometer and saw that he was usually going faster than the posted speed limit, but I reasoned that I didn't want to get him upset by saying something and possibly cause him to drive even faster. He hadn't been driving very long when he failed to notice a stop sign and drove right through it and with a lot of speed plowed into the side of another car.

As I remember it, I had the dimmer switch, we bought earlier, in my lap and with a screwdriver I was changing the terminals around so it would work properly in our car. I was busy with that when all of a sudden Pat shouted, "Holy Christ!" Immediately, I looked up as my body was being thrown with so much force that my head completely mangled the steel-framed rearview mirror, turning it into something almost unrecognizable. Because our car hit the other one at an angle I was being thrown forward and towards the left side of the car. My head came smashing with a tremendous force into the partitioned windshield on the driver's side.

I don't even remember getting out of the car. When I next became aware of anything, I was walking around on the sidewalk in sort of a daze. My forehead, nose and legs had been cut up quite badly.

There was blood squirting out of my head with each beat of my heart, and that blood was now running down my face and beginning to cover the front of my jacket. People seemed to be coming from all directions as they started gathering around me. I became terrified, and all I could think about was that I needed to run away. Flight was the only clear thought in my head and I was just ready to run, but I was stopped right there.

Luckily for me a nurse, who lived in that same block, shouted some orders to three men who grabbed hold of me as I was trying to flee. I struggled to free myself but it was no use; I was being forced to the ground. The men held me so that I had to lie on my back on the grassy boulevard as I was trying frantically to see where Pat was.

I finally gave up my struggle to get away as I became quite calm and just lay there. As I was looking up, I was able to see a ring of people standing above and staring down at me. I was now able to see Pat, and from the expression on his face it appeared that he was worried. At that moment I wanted to talk to him and say that it was all right, but I didn't. It wasn't long before all of the faces vanished, because blood was getting into my eyes and I had to close them.

That nurse seemed quite anxious, and while we waited for the ambulance, she was now frantically putting layers of gauze on my forehead in an attempt to put a stop to the blood that was continuing to gush out of my forehead. Even though I couldn't see, I was still quite aware that a lot of people were there, because I could hear their voices. Their conversations seemed to be mainly about the damaged cars and me. I knew that I must have been hurt quite badly but I couldn't understand why I wasn't feeling any pain.

To me it seemed like I had lain there an awfully long time waiting for an ambulance to come. The nurse was having some success in trying to stop the blood by the time I heard the siren from the ambulance as it drew near. Coming to a sudden halt next to the curb, I was immediately put onto a stretcher and quickly slid into the back of the waiting vehicle. The hospital must have been only a few blocks away, because it didn't take us long to get there. I remember that during this time I was wondering where Pat was.

After arriving at the hospital, I was pulled from the ambulance as I was still lying on the stretcher on which I had been securely bound to with straps. I so terribly wanted to get up and run away from all of this. I still tried to see things in spite of the blood. I was able to partially open my right eye, but all that was visible, as I was being rushed down a hall, were the lights on ceiling of the hallway.

We finally came to a stop in some well lit room and straightaway a nurse began to wash all the blood from my face and out of my hair. When she was finished, she put a dry covering of gauze over my head wound, and the bleeding had been stopped completely. It was so much nicer to be able to see out of both eyes and I could now see clearly as another nurse came in and the two of them began examining me to see if there were any other injuries. Because my slacks had holes cut into them and a lot of blood in the area around my knees the nurses worked the slacks up until they were able to examine the cuts in my knees.

Not knowing the extent of my head injury, I asked the nurse, "Can't you just put a bandage over the cut on my head and let me go home?"

She answered, "A doctor will have to see you first."

Up to this point nobody had really done anything for me except washing the blood away, and I was beginning to wonder when they were going to take care of my injuries. It seemed like a long wait before a doctor finally came in and immediately began to examine my wounds. I think that he must have been trying to decide where he should start but he never said a word.

Because there was no skin remaining on the left side of my forehead to stitch, the doctor had to take the skin from near my hairline and the skin above my eyebrow and pull them together over the bare flesh until they met. With some help from a nurse he used some steel clips to hold the pieces of skin where they met. He then stretched the skin together some more until he was able with two more metal clips to completely cover what had been exposed flesh. The one good thing that I can say about this is that I still wasn't suffering from any pain.

With that finished, the doctor then removed a tiny bit of bone from way up inside of one of my nostrils with something that resembled chrome-plated needle-nosed pliers. Removing that piece of bone from my nose was the only part of the whole process that really hurt for a bit and it made my eyes water. He set my nose straight and he proceeded to bandage it up well, with not much more than my eyes and lower face visible to others. My slacks with the holes cut into them had been rolled up and the bleeding about my knees continued. The doctor had one of the nurses wash the blood from my knees. The doctor, after examining those cuts, decided not to do anything about them except have the nurse bandage them.

It would have been impossible for the doctor to take all the hundreds of tiny fragments of glass out of my head, so he just left them alone. Until now the doctor only talked *about* me to the nurses, but now he explained to me why all those little shards wouldn't need to be taken out. He said that with time they would eventually work their way out by themselves. Later I was to find out that he was right but removing those small bits would continue for a couple of years after. It seemed to be about the same each time as I would be picking at what seemed like an ordinary pimple on the left side of my forehead, but in reality was just another one of those tiny pieces of glass that had worked its way to the surface.

I got out of the hospital in the early afternoon and I was driven back to the Simon's farm by my brother's boss, Mr. Loftus. By now I was feeling some ache in my legs where they had been cut and bruised and I also had a severe headache. I was also angry with Pat and about the fact that if he had driven more carefully this all could have been avoided. The ride seemed to take a long time but that was just fine by me because the way that I was feeling I felt dread at having to go to work after what I had gone through.

After arriving at the farm, I went into the house and was straight away stopped by Mrs. Simon as she asked me all kinds of questions about the accident and how I felt. Even though I felt terrible I lied when I said that I felt fine and that everything was ok. She said,

"Maybe you should go into the living room and just lie down on the couch for awhile."

I replied, "I'll be all right" and went upstairs to change into my work clothes. I then went out to the barn and climbed up about a 45-degree slope provided by the bale elevator into the haymow. Every one was asking me questions about my accident and I spent some time telling about it. I took my place at stacking hay bales as they were sent up to us on the elevator. In the heat I began to sweat and I wished that I could take the bandages off. After a few hours of that, and probably because of the heat of more than one hundred degrees in the haymow, not eating anything since breakfast, and losing all of that blood, I started to feel very strange, light-headed, and it was even affecting my vision.

It was now about 8 p.m., and we were going to finish the last two loads before we went in to supper. I couldn't wait anymore I finally told Mr. Simon, "I don't feel very good. I'm getting sort of dizzy."

He replied to that with, "I think that you had better go to the house. We can finish the rest of this." As I was walking towards the elevator, he then said, "I thought that you were kinda crazy to be out here in the first place."

The reason I was out there, was that I was afraid that if I wasn't, I would probably lose my job. I climbed onto the elevator that had been bringing the bales up. I did all right climbing slowly down from paddle to paddle on the part that was still inside of the barn, but I soon began to crawl through the opening that brought me outside. I had been sweating a lot, so when I hit that much cooler air of about eighty degrees, it was quite a shock and I began to shiver. My body then started to tremble all over and I had only enough strength to just barely catch myself as I nearly went tumbling over the side. I hung on with everything that was in me and continued ever so carefully crawling and sliding on down until I was able to stand safely on the ground and I just stood there for awhile. The next load of bales had come in, but everyone just waited for me until I had completely got out of the way.

I felt so strange and very weak and it was a struggle just to stay on my feet as I staggered slowly towards the house. I entered where Mrs. Simon was in the kitchen preparing our supper. From my appearance she was able to recognize that all was not well with me. She asked, "Are you going to be all right?"

I replied, "I think so but could you give me some aspirins?"

She brought me two aspirins and a glass of water which I took and drank the whole glass of water. Then she told me, "You go wash up now and wait in the living room. Supper will be ready soon." I washed up and went into the living room as she had commanded me. I remember sitting on the couch and that was all.

I must have been awfully tired, because that was the last thing I knew until I woke up the next morning in time to help with the chores. When the chores were done I was anxious for breakfast, because I had become so hungry that it hurt. After I ate I felt better, but I still wasn't quite right. It took me a couple more days before I really felt well and I regained all of my strength, but I didn't miss any more time from work. The bandages were quite uncomfortable in those hot days and later on it began to itch underneath but I was afraid to scratch.

My brother Pat at this time was living with and working for a farmer named Bernie Loftus. I didn't like the guy, because he treated me terribly with his very negative sarcastic remarks. He was extremely opinionated besides being quite unforgiving and critical of others. His humor consisted of a lot of "put-downs" and trying to make others feel inferior. Mr. Loftus seemed to be having quite a negative affect on Pat, as I observed my brother change into a completely different person from what I had known him to be in the past. Pat even started to talk and act like his boss, and he also appeared to become so unfeeling towards others. Like Bernie, Pat also seemed to enjoy using jokes to put down other people. I never criticized him about it, but I started to avoid being around him. This is when we each started going our separate ways and to develop friendships with different students.

I really wasn't too surprised then when Pat demonstrated that he didn't have much empathy about what had happened to me in the car accident. I remember one day when my brothers and I were traveling together with our dad on a trip to see our mother in Ah Gwah Ching Sanitorium. I was acting a bit upset about what had happened in the accident, when Pat said to me, "What are you complaining about? The insurance paid for everything." I thought to myself that my complaining was quite legitimate, because the insurance didn't pay for the pain, inconvenience or any of the scars.

Even our dad took my side on that one and thought the remark he made was terribly cruel. He even asked Pat, "How much do you think the insurance paid Sonny for the scars that he will have for the rest of his life?" I also thought that with a little more careful driving, that accident should never have happened. He had been charged for speeding, failure to yield the right of way, driving through a stop sign, and having no driver's license. All of that could easily have been avoided.

Another thing that the old Pat wouldn't have done was to sell that car for junk, and take the whole $50 that he received for himself. He would have thought the same as I that half of that money should have been given to me, since I was a co-owner of the car and paid half when we bought it. I never did bother him about it, because he was now becoming unapproachable by me; and I just thought that he should have known better.

Because of the blood I had lost and the cuts on my legs, it was less then two weeks after that accident that I got a serious infection in both of my knees. From all my past experiences, I guess that I should have expected the infection. Like so many times before, I didn't tell anyone until my knee joints became almost too painful to move. One of my legs got so bad that I could not even slightly bend it at the knee.

It became necessary to be driven all the way to the doctor in Rushford at the appointed times every day for a couple of weeks to receive treatments from the doctor there. This was quite a bother for the people I stayed with, and also because I could only get around with much difficulty and it limited me to only certain kinds of work that I could do and the efficiency that I could do it. I tried my best but it had become impossible to even do some of my regular chores and I felt terribly guilty about it.

I rode with Mrs. Simon each day, and I found those rides on the winding gravel roads to be quite exciting. I was a terrified passenger and I was always grateful when we reached our destination, because Mrs. Simon drove quite fast and the back end of that Nash would slide out as we rounded each turn. One time as we were going around one of those turns in the road, the car slid around until we were facing the opposite direction. All that she said was, "Oops, I must have been going a little too fast there," and we continued on home. That incident seemed to have a very small effect on her future driving habits. It was certainly a strong motivation for me to have my legs put right though. I remember how relieved I was when I no longer had to go every day and then finally not at all.

During my sophomore year I noticed that I was developing a sort of thin mustache, and I didn't like the looks of it. By spring quite a bit of facial hair was becoming visible and was changing my appearance; and by the time that summer had arrived, I had to buy myself a razor and begin shaving. I didn't like it, because it hurt as I scraped through the foam to get a smooth face. By the time school started that year, it had already become necessary for me to shave every day, but my shaving experience wasn't quite as bad after my dad bought a new Norelco Electric razor and gave me his old one.

Later in the fall of that same year, I accidentally got a small cut in the palm of my left hand. We had been playing basketball on the court behind the school and somehow another boy scratched me with his fingernail. Still having the problem that I have always been plagued with throughout my life, I got infection and it spread throughout the entire palm of that hand. Foolishly, as so many times in the past, I could tell that it got infected. I kept hoping that it would go away and even though it began to hurt I kept putting up with it. It was only a few days before my hand had swelled up enormously and had begun to hurt terribly, and eventually I could stand the pain no longer. It became impossible to do anything with it as it became quite obvious that I had a lot of difficulty doing the jobs which required the use of both of my hands. Mr. Simon told me that I had better go to the doctor. By now it was hurting so badly I would have done anything to relieve the pain. I finally felt compelled to ask Mr. Simon to take me to the doctor in Lewiston.

After he examined my hand, that doctor told me that he believed that I might have waited far too long before coming to him and he may not be able to save the hand. That scared me and he told me that he would do his best; but ultimately to get rid of the infection he would probably have to cut into the whole palm of that hand, which would affect the cords that controlled the fingers. When he finished examining the hand, he said that he was afraid that my waiting may very well, cause me to end up with a completely stiff and useless hand.

He seemed quite serious about what he was saying, and his words frightened me. He then said, "Should I try to get rid of the infection for you? Or maybe you would like it if we could do it the easy way and cut off the hand, because in the end that is just what might *have* to be done." His remark reminded me of the druggist in Rib Lake, and I didn't think *his* remark was funny either.

He first told me that it might be best if I didn't watch as he worked. He said he had another man come in just the week before with something less, and he had fainted. I told him, "I need to watch what you are doing."

He said, "Suit yourself." and with that, he took my hand and with a sharp knife he made a long cut in the palm between the index and the middle finger. Immediately the cut he made began to burst with a tremendous amount of pus mixed with blood. It hurt terribly as he pressed on both sides of the cut to get as much as possible squeezed out and more came oozing out. The next part of his treatment I wasn't expecting as he took out what appeared to be a pair of tongs which he inserted the flat ends into the open wound that he had made. He started to spread the handles apart which were stretching the skin to open the cut wider. I can tell you that I wasn't quite prepared for anything like the hurt I felt then. I can't even describe the pain as he was stretching apart that tough skin in the palm of my hand.

He said that this was necessary and it would give him a window to the inside of that portion of my hand but to me it felt more like he was making a huge door. Then while he continued to hold the cut open, he began scraping at it and this proved to be the most painful part. He scraped and cleaned out some more of that puss-looking stuff. After flushing the open wound with a strong concentrated spray of water, he placed a dressing over the cut and completely wrapped my hand with gauze to form a thick, useless bundle. Next he gave me a prescription for antibiotics and pain pills. Finally he handed me a small sheet of paper with another appointment scheduled for the same day of the next week.

After I got home, it didn't take any coaxing to get me to follow his instructions. I spent several long hours in the evenings, soaking that hand in hot water with the dissolved Epsom salts. Within a couple of days I was able to tell that the some healing had begun because didn't think that it was hurting so much. I really was hoping that the hand would get well enough that I wouldn't need that second visit to that doctor.

During that time I pretty much lost the use of my left hand. It just happened to be during an extremely demanding time of the year, because the fall plowing had to be done. I had an awful lot of plowing to do, but I only had the use of my right hand which would make it quite hard to operate the tractor and the machinery.

Just a couple of months before, Mr. Simon had traded in my favorite tractor, which was his old Minneapolis Moline Z for a brand new and much larger Oliver Super 88. Trading in the Minneapolis Moline turned out to be fortunate for me, because his new tractor, which he now had me drive, had a wide track front end instead of the more typical tricycle-type row-crop front end. This made that tractor easier to control with one hand, because I could align the front right wheel in the dead furrow. I could almost let go of the steering wheel, because the tractor would then almost guide itself. I don't know how I could have done the job without it, because my left hand was wrapped in a big bundle and just rested uselessly in my lap, so I was only able to use my right hand. When I got to the end of the row I had to start steering the tractor and then let go of the steering wheel with my right hand as I sort of held the wheel in place with the upper part my leg. Then I would quickly reach behind me to pull the trip rope to raise the plow as I was able to steer the tractor's right front wheel around and back into the next dead furrow. I then straightened out the wheels as the front wheel was aligned in that dead furrow and then I had to pull on the trip rope to lower the plow.

The next week I was dreadfully anticipating the second visit and all of the pain that went with it. I didn't want to go, but I knew that I had no choice because I knew that my hand hadn't been put right yet. My fears were well founded, and that doctor didn't disappoint me; because when I went back to him, he did the same thing all over again with those tongs of his. It was exactly the same extremely painful treatment that I was subjected to before. It took time but the results were good and I was certainly grateful when I was able to gain the full use of that hand again. I was also thankful that I didn't have to go for a third visit nor did he have to do quite the amount of cutting that he said might be needed

It was in the fall of my junior year at school that I began to somewhat accept my way of life on the farm and I decided to take a more active interest in farming. I was beginning to think that possibly there was a future for me in farming. I realized that it would be a lot more pleasant life as a farmer instead of a hired man.

I signed up for an ag. (agriculture) class that year to become more knowledgeable in farming as a profession. Gordon Jacobsen, the ag. teacher, encouraged me to join the F.F.A. (Future Farmers of America) organization. I joined and took advantage of all of their facilities. I now had access to the centrifuge in the ag. lab room to perform monthly butterfat tests on milk samples that I had taken from each of Mr. Simon's cows. Together with some help from Audrey, I kept records of the quantity and quality of what each of the cows produced. I even made soil tests on the farm to determine fertilizer requirements. I participated in some cattle-judging and shearing contests. I also took seventh place out of more than 100 boys that year in the tri-county soil-judging contest.

My father was against all of this interest that I was showing in farming and he told me that I was being unrealistic. He said that I was just too small for that type of occupation. He may have been right about my size because I now only weighed a little more than 120 pounds and it looked as though I had finished growing, but I was quite strong for my size. It was obvious that he still had his own plans for my future as a doctor and an agenda for getting there.

It was on Sunday, the fourteenth of December of 1952, that my dad came to pick me up to go with him to Minneapolis because of a court trial that I had to appear in. He told my boss that I might be staying with him for more than a week. I really liked that, because I would get out of school and all that farm work during that time. I also thought that it would really be exciting to be called as a witness in court. The actual trial was to begin the next morning in the Ninth District Court in New Ulm, Minnesota.

My father had brought a lawsuit against my mother's former doctor in New Ulm on a charge of malpractice. My father, mother and my brother Patrick were also named as the plaintiffs with a claim for $125,000 against Doctor Vogel who had treated her.

On the first day of the trial a jury was impaneled and it was decided that all three actions be consolidated into one. I attended the full week of the proceedings, and some of it was quite interesting. There was also much of it that I didn't understand too well, while an awful lot of it was just very boring. I had to be there because I was to be called at some time as a witness. I also think that my father wanted someone just to be with him during that time.

I also heard the reading from Dr. Crow's deposition at the Ah Gwah Ching Sanatorium that left me feeling quite hopeless about ever seeing the time when our family would be together again. The doctor's sworn testimony explained how my mother never weighed more than 67 pounds. He said that every morning since she arrived at the sanatorium over four years ago, he had been expecting to find my mother's name on the list of those who had died sometime during the night. He said that he did not expect the day would ever come when our mother would be able to leave the sanatorium.

There was also some further information given in a deposition on the second day by Dr. M. M. Williams, who was replacing Dr. Crow as superintendent, and he just confirmed what Dr. Crow had written.

Late on the third day of the trial, I was finally called as a witness to testify about the conversation my dad had with Dr. Vogel back in the Loretto Hospital in summer of 1948. I answered the questions presented by my dad's attorney and then I was cross examined by Dr. Vogel's attorney. I was so worried that the doctor's attorney might trick me into saying the wrong thing, but I just told the truth and afterwards my dad's attorney told me that I did fine. That was very important to me.

My brother Pat was also called to the stand to just make a statement that he had been a patient for about a year at the Ah Gwah Ching Sanatorium. The news of the trial appeared each day on the front page of the local New Ulm Journal.

On the last day of the trial after all of the testimony had been heard, Dr. Vogel's attorney, S. P. Gislason, made a motion for dismissal. Judge Erickson had decided not to allow the jury to be involved in making the decision and that he was going to move on the defendant's motion to dismiss the case. The judge could see that the case would have gone against Dr. Vogel if it was allowed to go to the jury. The judge and Dr. Vogel lived in the same town and knew each other quite well. Everything finally culminated for us when Judge Erickson finally arrived at an obviously biased decision against my dad.

I was with my dad when his attorney, Tom Moore, told him that he wasn't surprised at all by the results and that he had pretty much expected this. He also stated that it was obvious that the judge was biased, but he explained that it was necessary to try the case in the doctor's hometown first.

I know that the trial was extremely hard on my dad, but it was also a discouraging ordeal for me. I thought that it was all a farce and it made me angry. I had just witnessed another pathetic example of the legal system in our country and I didn't like it.

My dad's attorney immediately filed for an appeal to the Minnesota Supreme Court. We were told that it could take more than a year or two for our case to come before that court. That would probably be close to six or seven years after the incident took place. Why must it take so much time before one can expect to achieve some form of justice? I had quite a lesson on the way that our judicial system worked. I didn't think much of it and I came away from it all very angry and a feeling of hopelessness.

When I found out in 1948 how that doctor had been treating my mother and the significance of not discovering the tuberculosis earlier, it made me extremely angry with him. Four years later, after I heard all of the testimony during that trial, I became even more upset with him, and I developed a strong hatred for that doctor. It seemed that I couldn't help but place all of the blame on that doctor for what happened to my mother, and I really wanted to get even with him. That hate lasted for so many years, but I have long since forgiven him. I did finally come to believe that what he had done was not malicious or may not have even been negligent but was just a matter of the incompetence of a small town general practitioner. The fact that he lied and wouldn't admit that he really hadn't taken any X-rays, I find unconscionable. I also realize that the world is full of people like him and that integrity is just not a part of their character. There must have been many people in New Ulm that felt that he was a good doctor because years later they even named a stadium after him.

During Christmas vacation of that year, our dad picked up my brothers and me and we made a trip to see our mother in the sanatorium. In the past we got to see our mother as she lay in a gurney in a hallway. They now had built a special place so that our dad, Pat, Tom and I could be in the same room with our mother. Richard and Warren were on the other side of a glass separating their room from our mother's.

Quite opposite to what I thought, I also found out that the room for the children was to protect the patient and not the children who were in it. That room was vented at the top so that our mother could hear Richard and Warren when they were speaking. We had a nice black and white picture taken, with our whole family surrounding our mother as she laid on her gurney. At that time I don't think that any of us realized that this was going to be the last picture taken with all of us together.

The headlines in the New Ulm Journal on the twentieth of January of 1953 read, "Eisenhower Inaugurated." The front page of that same newspaper on the twenty-fourth of January, 1953, had a Notice of Taxation of Costs and Bill of Costs and Disbursements filed with no objection from the plaintiff who was my dad. Instead of collecting some financial compensation that he was seeking for the obvious malpractice by Doctor Vogel in treating my mother, my dad was being forced to pay out money. Because of that trial in district court in New Ulm, this also appeared in another part of that paper: "Roy L. Brown was ordered to pay $24.70 for Martha Brown's claim, $19.75 for Patrick Brown's claim, and $131.95 for Roy L. Brown's claim."

That really made me angry because I felt that it was more than just a bit unfair and why should they punish my father. It was because of that decision that I had completely lost all faith in the legal system. I felt that the trial had been a travesty of justice. My attitude towards life had changed and I became angry with the whole world. It was also sad to see my dad being beaten that way and that hurt. I even lost all interest in farming. When my dad brought me back to the farm I was a very angry person. I would now be taking out my anger on others and some of them would be the very people that I really began to care for.

That winter, with the same arrangements as before, Mr. Simon drove me out every Friday night to the dances in Wyatville. The only reason I wanted to go was because I loved to dance. When the dances were over, I would catch a ride from some person who would be kind enough to drive me home and I would be up early the next morning to do chores.

I made all kinds of friends there, and some of them, as it turned out, were not good for me. I now had a lot of anger and a completely changed attitude about dancing which now became of less importance to me. I had never tasted any hard liquor before, so when it was offered to me, I was curious enough to try it. It was a completely new experience for me, and I wasn't able to handle it too well.

It all got started on one of those Friday evenings in January at that dance. I joined some of the other guys out by the cars in the parking lot. At first all I did was become a part of their conversation. As we were talking, someone in the group offered me a drink from a bottle that he was drinking from. I had tasted beer before, but I didn't care too much for it because I thought it was too bitter. And when I lived in Rib Lake, my mother gave me some wine to drink and I enjoyed it, but it was nothing like this. I remember that the first drink that he gave me from that bottle was peppermint schnapps. It tasted good to me and I was surprised by how sweet it was; it almost tasted like candy. Afterwards, I got to try someone else's sloe gin. It also tasted good to me, so I drank a quite a bit of that too. At first those drinks didn't seem to affect me and the way they tasted, I didn't think that they could.

I was so naive. I continued to take one drink and then another. I kept on drinking, and at first it was beginning to put me into a happy mood. It was after midnight and I persisted with drinking more and I was starting to get sick. I just realized that *I was drunk!* My stomach didn't seem to accept the drinks too well, because I began to throw up. I vomited a couple more times and then I felt as though my stomach needed to get rid of more and I continued to heave but nothing would come out. At that time I wasn't thinking that it was fun anymore, and then everything went blank as I passed out.

I had no idea when or who, but someone put me in his car and drove me home. After he had driven up the driveway, the driver woke me up and with his help I was able to get out of the car and then he drove away. I was able to stand but my legs protested as I started to walk. It required a great amount of effort as I was making my way slowly towards the house. I didn't turn on any lights as I entered in total darkness but habit directed me through the kitchen, part of the living room and on to the stairs. I know that I must have made a lot of noise with my stumbling, because it was a struggle for me to climb the stairs to my bedroom.

When I got to my room, I didn't even undress. I just crawled into bed and lay down, and I started to have another new experience when I got dizzy. The whole room was spinning around. I couldn't stand it anymore so I got down on the floor and rested my back against the bed. I was still sitting; sound asleep, in that position when Mr. Simon called me at 5:30 that morning to do the chores.

I awoke with his first call, but I had probably the worst headache I had ever experience in my entire life. I quickly changed into my work clothes and went down to the kitchen. I knew that Mrs. Simon was suspicious that something was wrong when I asked her for some aspirins. I took the aspirins and I went out and did my chores as usual, and later I did my regular Saturday work. The horrible way that I was feeling all day made me think that I would never want to stay out late or ever again take a drink that had any alcohol in it.

Before I left the house that next Friday, Mrs. Simon told me that she didn't think that I should go. Mr. Simon said, "She's right, you know." I insisted, and Mr. Simon didn't object any and drove me to the dance as he had so many times before. The regrets from the previous Friday seemed to have been forgotten, because I stayed out late again and did some more drinking. I got drunk again and the evening ended almost the same way as the Friday before. This was now developing into a new way of life for me. Every Friday night became almost a carbon copy of the previous one. I met with the same guys and we did a lot of drinking in the parking lot and in some of the cars. I wasn't going to Wyatville for just the dancing anymore; in fact, some of those Fridays I didn't dance at all.

These drinking buddies of mine and I had created a strong demand for quite a bit of liquor. We were all under the legal age, but we discovered a good source for anything that we wanted. We drove to Winona, which was only about 15 miles from Wyatville, and then we crossed the Mississippi River into Wisconsin. From there we turned right and it was only a couple of miles downriver to a place called the Wine Pool. It was located right next to the highway, all by itself, so it was out of the view of any town police or any other authorities. The store seemed to be quite prosperous, and they had a large supply of any kind of alcoholic drink that one could imagine. Considering the numerous visits that we made there, I think that it is quite amazing that not once did we run into any kind of problem.

The person who worked at the Wine Pool did check some people for their age. It didn't take long, however, to realize that I was the one who seemed to have the most success going into the Wine Pool and buying the liquor. I ended up going into the place many nights and making purchases for all of us, without anyone ever asking my age or checking me for identification. My friends had started to depend on me, and I felt that I just couldn't let them down. There was an added incentive for the person who made the purchases, because the other guys paid for all of the liquor. I never had to contribute a cent.

It turned out to be quite an enigma, because, at the time, I couldn't even understand why I was behaving in this manner. I was now doing something that I knew that I shouldn't, and I was also quite aware that it could not be good for me. It seemed that out of habit it had now become the easiest way for me to enjoy myself and forget about anything that was troubling me for that short while. I think that this new behavior had become my escape from an unpleasant reality during that time. The worst part about it is that I was getting used to it and it had now become comfortable as my way of life. I had become a person that was harboring a terrible amount of anger and resentment, but I was only taking it out on myself. My feelings seemed to have had its true origins sometime in December after that horrible court trial in New Ulm.

It was also on one of those Friday nights in January that some of those same "friends" and I went to a small town in Wisconsin. I don't even remember the name of the place, but we had already tipped a few drinks of hard liquor before we got there. We went into one of their taverns; and since no one asked us for identification, we sat there for the evening. Since we weren't bothering anyone we were allowed to keep ordering more drinks.

After sitting there for some time and consuming more than I obviously should have, I began to feel a bit dizzy and I knew that I was starting to get awfully sick. I didn't want to muss up my new coat, so I took it off and laid it over the back of the chair where I had just been sitting. In my shirt sleeves, I walked outside in the below-zero temperatures but I was quite impervious to it all. I knew that I'd gone just a short way when I had to stop and I started to vomit. I continued like that until I felt as though I had emptied myself of everything that was inside me. Then, doubled over, I still kept on heaving and my stomach was aching and there was nothing coming up any more. It was quite similar to my first night's experience with hard liquor at Wyatville. After my bout with that, I was feeling terrible and confused. The cold air felt good but strangely I didn't feel cold. I started wandering about for a while, with no idea where I was going. I didn't have any idea where I was nor did I care. I just kept walking until I started feeling tired and I wanted to sit down. In my half dazed condition I just let myself fall back into the soft snow, and then everything went blank.

I don't recall another thing until I awoke sometime early in the morning. At first, I was startled by my strange surroundings and I new straight away that something was wrong. Everything seemed so odd to me, when suddenly I realized why. I had been lying on a bunk that was chained to the wall in a jail cell. I could also feel the presence of someone that had been standing outside the cell, watching me. I looked up and I saw a man in a police uniform and his first words were, "How do you feel, kid?"

I gave my honest reply, "Rotten." Then I asked, "How did I wind up in here? What did I do? Where are my friends?"

He answered, "First of all, I was ordered to stay the night here to watch over your sleeping ass. You were carried in and your friends didn't stick around. I'm not sure where they are now, but I think they all went home. One of them did mention that he worked in Winona and said something about coming back later in the morning to get you."

I asked, "How did I get here and where are my friends?"

He then told me, "You don't realize how lucky you are."

I had no idea what he was talking about so I just asked, "Why do you say that?"

I listened, "Almost everybody in town was out looking for your drunken body. There were a lot of people who were out there searching for a long time." I had a quick thought about the time that my brother Richard got lost and people had to search for him. He continued, "Then Bill, who is a neighbor friend of mine, came half-carrying and half-dragging you in here. Bill told me that as he was on his search for you he just happened to be walking along side of the highway and he slipped on some ice and fell. He went sliding down a steep hill where he accidentally came to a stop right next to where you were lying, not far from the main road out there. You were sound asleep in a snow bank."

I then asked, "Do I have to stay here?"

My jailer replied, "Hell, no! In fact you aren't even locked in. We are just taking care of you, because it seems that you do a pretty lousy job of it yourself. Actually, you can go at any time." And then after a short pause he said, "Stay here awhile and you'll be getting some breakfast."

I really didn't have any choice about staying there because I had no transportation. I asked for and I was given two aspirins for my terrible headache. True to his word, I did get to eat a nice breakfast with eggs, bacon, and toast and I thanked him. I sat and ate from a tray that I held in my lap.

My friend LeRoy who worked at a factory in Winona and didn't work on the weekends did come back at a little after 8 o'clock to take me home. He also brought my new coat with him so I put it on and we started for home. By the time we arrived at the farm where I lived, it was much too late for doing my regular morning chores.

Without saying a word to anyone, I went into the house, changed my clothes. I then came out and I was glad that no one said a word to me. I just got the tractor and pulled the manure spreader up next to the window in the barn and started to clean out the young stock pens. I spent the rest of the day cleaning pens and then did my nightly chores. I was miserable all day because I was tired and still had the most terrible headache.

I knew that Mr. Simon didn't like what I had done, but he surprised me when he didn't give me the scolding that I was expecting. He asked me, "Did you have a good time last night?"

I answered, "It was a horrible night."

He only replied to that with, "What you are doing is not good for you and you are known by the friends you keep." Mr. Simon meant well and he was really a wonderful and understanding person. He seemed to always have good advice for me but I was never listening. I think that he was trying to find some way to help me through my problems. I knew that I wasn't being fair to him and his family, but I guess that I wasn't ready just yet to make any change in the way I was living.

In the spring I wanted to go to the Junior-Senior Prom and I had a friend by the name of Tom Cunningham who said he would like to have my date and me come with him and his date. With the transportation problem solved there should be no reason that I couldn't invite someone and go. I really wanted to invite the Simon's daughter Audrey. I thought after the way I had been behaving, I felt that it would have served me right if her parents would not allow it. After waiting until it was almost too late, I did get up enough courage to invite Audrey to go to the prom with me, and she accepted immediately. Even though she accepted I had serious doubts that her parents would allow it. I felt that I was quite fortunate then when I realized that her folks would permit her to go with me.

I was quite excited when I got Audrey a nice flower corsage to wear, and she dressed up in a beautiful long, yellow formal dress. She really looked lovely and I could only think about how lucky I was. My dad took me to a men's clothing store in Winona where I picked out a sports coat, dress slacks, shoes, and tie which I would wear just for that occasion. I had no car, but my friend Tom with his date picked us up and we double-dated with them.

The four of us first went out to a fancy restaurant to have a nice supper there. I never did this sort of thing before. Ordering the food was different from anything I had ever done before. We first ordered our meal, and the waitress asked me if I wanted French, Italian or a thousand island dressing on my salad. I had never used dressing on any food before, but I decided to order the thousand island dressing only because the name sounded good. When I got the salad I was surprised to see this almost pink stuff spread all over the lettuce, so I tasted it. I didn't know quite what to make of it but it really tasted quite good so I ate it. It wasn't until much later the rest of the meal was brought in and I was brought this steak that was larger than I had ever seen or eaten before and a huge baked potato with lots of butter. I also had my favorite vegetable which is green beans. The meal was very good, and the four of us really enjoyed ourselves. After I got the bill for Audrey and me, I knew why I wouldn't be eating like that very often. However, everything was going so well that I wouldn't have wished it to be any different.

The four of us went from there to the dance, which was nothing like the old-time waltzes and polkas I danced at Wyatville. We had a nice time, dancing mostly some very slow dances where you really get close to your partner. The whole evening was very nice, and we got quite intimate with each other. From there we went to Whitewater State Park where Audrey and I lay on the ground with a blanket where we spent our time doing very little else but cuddling. It was probably the nicest evening that I can remember in my entire life. The only bad part of it was that we didn't get home until after 2 o'clock in the morning and I knew that we all would be tired during the following day.

It was in that same spring of my junior year that I was asked by our local 4-H leader to represent the boys in the county good-grooming contest. I was still quite shy but after some coaxing, I finally gave in to her request. I dressed myself in the same clothes that I had already bought for the prom. After the judging was completed, I was surprised to discover that the judges had chosen me to win the first-place position against all the other boys who had been sent from their clubs in the county. After that win, I now had the responsibility to represent our Fremont Green Clovers 4-H Club in the tri-county contest.

That same spring was the beginning of probably one of the hardest times in my life for me. I believe that I was rebelling but I really used no reasoning in all of this. Even though it had its beginnings sometime last winter, and I really wasn't enjoying this I just didn't seem to know how to turn things around. During that time, I had developed a feeling of anger with the whole world. I took my anger out on anyone who was around at the time. I presume that there was also some jealousy, because all the other students in school seemed to have a much nicer life living with their own families. Other boys whom I knew were not being used as just a hired man. I was dissatisfied with the kind of life that had been forced upon me. Everything just seemed to be so unfair to me.

Early in the summer of 1953, the tri-county good grooming competition was held for the three members who had won in each of their own counties. I prepared myself in the same manner as before and I was feeling a bit strange, because it seemed so vain and I was showing nothing but myself. The judges chose me as the first-place winner again, so now I would be representing the three counties in the contest at the Minnesota State Fair.

All of the clothing, shirt, tie, sport coat, slacks and shoes that I wore had been carefully selected by me, with no assistance from anyone. I really felt quite proud of that fact. Besides dressing up smartly, I had to do something about my typical hired-man's hands. I used peroxide to solve that problem by letting it boil out the grime that was imbedded in my finger nails and into every little line and crease in the palms of my hands.

I continued the drinking and fighting that I had started during that winter at the Wyatville dances. But in addition to that, I met up with a bunch of older guys who were no longer going to school, and once in a while I had a night out with them. There were the four of us:

one was 19, two were 20, and I had just turned 18. It didn't take long to discover that I was the only one of us who was able to purchase the liquor without ever being asked for any proof of my age. Instead of only staying out late on Friday nights and maybe an occasional Saturday night, it had now become about every other night.

My normal workday was from 5:30 A.M. to 8:30 P.M. weekdays; of course, that included being in school for part of that time. I still found time to go out often with these guys, at night until early in the morning. We had quite a wild time of it; but to get enough sleep, I was now doing that in school. Some of the teachers seemed to be frustrated and even got angry with me when I would doze off in their classes. In fact, the sleeping had now become a routine in certain classes. The teachers didn't seem to know what they could do about it because, even though I knew that I could have done better, I was always able to pass their tests.

Mr. Gessner, the principal, talked to me about what I was doing. He told me, "You know that you are going to need a good education and you just can't continue like this. Roy, you should be the top student in every class that you take." During this time I wasn't receptive to advice from anyone. I didn't seem to want to take responsibility for anything in my life and in my mind I felt that the only one that I was really hurting was myself. I was just unable to imagine that there may be other people that cared about me.

The weekends had become the hardest part of my life because of the work all day Saturday and part of the day on Sunday. On Saturday's I didn't have the relief that was afforded me by sleeping at some time during the day and on Sunday I didn't want to waste any of my meager amount of free time lying around in sleep.

Wherever we went, it seemed that my friends and I would frequently get picked up by the local police for drinking and just being quarrelsome. Then we would be given a place to sleep for the night in some jail. We constantly managed to get ourselves into a lot of fights. I was becoming used to doing that, and because I was getting used to it, it developed into a somewhat comfortable way of living. I had this big scar on my forehead from the car accident of the year before, and I had a very low self esteem and this feeling that I was ugly anyway. I didn't care if someone hit me in the face.

It was those times when I was put into jail for the night, that I had come to take it for granted that I would always be released the next morning. Each time it would be the same as I was then able to return home, with whoever had the car. It also meant that each time I would arrive at the Simon's farm far too late to do my assigned share of the morning chores. Mr. Simon wasn't getting full value for what he was paying me.

I think that another reason for my rebellious ways was that after I had spent about 18 months with the Simons, I was beginning to realize that these people had begun to like me. I was also beginning to like them too much. They even were treating me in some ways as one of their own, and I felt a lot of resentment for this. With all the moving around that I did when I was younger, I learned that it was far better not to make any really good friends. I could remember the names of friends I had when I was in first, second, and third grades in school but no one beyond that. I didn't want to get too close to these people either, because I didn't want to go through the hurt when it was inevitable that I would have to leave them some day. Some of the feelings I had I really didn't understand, but my time with them had turned out to be too long. I was now forcing them to make me go away.

One unforeseen problem that developed while I was living there had to do with their daughter, Audrey. I was beginning to fancy her far too much. Outside of my mother, she was the only real love, or maybe it was no more than a form of infatuation, in my life since Miss Gray, my fifth grade schoolteacher. Audrey was a very bright lass, and she was just a grade behind me in school. I also think that she may have developed some feelings for me. We seemed to enjoy doing so many things together. This was something else that just seemed too good, and that being only the hired man that I had no right to feel this way. I felt that for my own good I must give it up.

I know that the Simons tried to be decent with me, but I also knew that they were becoming quite annoyed with me but they just didn't know what to do about it. I could understand what I was doing and that I wasn't being a very nice person to anyone so it was quite selfish of me to think that my behavior was only affecting me.

One of my final acts of protest was that I even quit going to church on Sundays. In an effort to help me, Mr. Simon even had Father McShane, the parish priest, come out and interrupts my work to have a talk with me one Saturday morning. I wasn't taking anybody's advice and it was to be no different with him. I was extremely rude towards him and I showed no respect for what he represented. He even warned me that I was committing a serious sin by not going to Mass on Sundays. He gave me some warnings about how I must change my ways or suffer severe consequences because I am answerable to God. He made it sound as though God would punish me if I didn't change my ways.

After I told him my negative thoughts about *his* Mass and *his* God he seemed to have finally realized any further talking to me was hopeless and he wished me well before he left. I believe that this priest was very irritated with me as he got into his car and drove away.

I was a terribly mixed-up teenager, and it really didn't make any sense as to why I was doing these horrible things. I think that I could have stayed with the Simons if I would have changed my behavior but I just didn't seem to want to. The Simons finally had more than enough of this unacceptable behavior that spring, and it just had to end soon. I knew that I was also a bad influence on their three children.

I understood all too well when Mr. Simon asked me to find another place to live. I didn't even raise one question because I knew the "why." I didn't try to make excuses for myself or ask for another chance. I just accepted it as the way it had to be. I also knew I didn't have to worry about getting another job because there were always other farmers looking for hard-working guys like me who would work the long hours demanded of a hired man and for such low wages.

As soon as I had completed my junior year and summer vacation was beginning, I contacted another farmer who seemed to need a hired hand. He hired me and I immediately left the Simons and went to work for this farmer. He was a big, muscular guy by the name of Jerry Corcoran. He and his wife was a much younger couple than the Simons with two small pre-school children. He expected a lot of work out of me. I didn't disappoint him, at least not at first. He was quite nice to me, and his wife was a good cook. What more could I want? I now had another job that I thought would at least take me through the summer and another school year but I wasn't even thinking a day beyond the present.

The Corcoran's' farm was probably the worst location on this earth for me. They just happened to live just across the road from one of my partying friends. Fortunately, he was another 4-H member and not one of my drinking buddies. My friend's name was Clifford Pierce, and he had already graduated last spring from Lewiston High. His situation was quite a bit different from mine, because he was the son of the farm owner instead of just a hired man. Clifford could go out whenever he wanted to, because he didn't have to work the next day if he wasn't feeling like it. Living so near to him made it much easier than ever to arrange our nights of fun. Cliff had a nice, almost-new Chevrolet that he always let me drive when we went somewhere. We certainly did spend a lot of very long nights together on the town. I was already heading down another road to disaster.

I did do some good things that summer, and a good example of that took place one Sunday during that summer. There was a tri-county 4-H picnic and fun day at a very nice park called The Arches that was located not far from Winona. The members, who were farm boys and girls of different ages from all of the 4-H clubs in three counties, were attending. We had foot races, games and many other activities. It was a lot of good, clean fun; and we also had a lot good food to eat. I entered the foot race that was for boys and girls of all ages. I was quite proud of myself for so easily winning first place. It left no doubt in anybody's mind; I was the fastest runner there! That good feeling I got from this and any successes that I had never seemed to last beyond that day.

Each 4-H club had its own softball team. We had several games going on at one time, and we were all competing until there was a final playoff against the two undefeated teams. Our team, the Fremont Green Clovers, was one of the teams, so we had to play against the other winning team. It was very satisfying for me that we were able to defeat the other team in a very close game. Each of our players received a big felt patch declaring us the 4-H softball champs. Like the foot race it was another affirmation that wouldn't mean much.

During that summer I did make one big change for the better. I completely quit going out nights just to have drinking parties and get into fights. It was during that time that I had spent time in eight different jails and a couple of them more than once. I had made up my mind that I wasn't going to spend any more nights being locked behind bars. It really wasn't too hard for me to stop the drinking, because I never did enjoy getting drunk. Another thing: my friend Clifford, his brother and all of his friends were not drinkers.

I did, however, continue the going out far too often at night. Clifford was always ready for a night out, and I was always eager to accompany him as he was quite happily occupied in the back seat of his car with some pretty girl. Whenever we went some place, he furnished the car and without exception I was the driver. We were having a tremendous amount of fun, which always involved meeting and taking out some girls. We never went any farther than going to movies, restaurants, dance halls and some necking in the car, but the problem was that we never got home until early in the morning. This wasn't a problem for Clifford, but I had obligations to my boss and it just couldn't last long for me.

It was while I was living at Jerry Corcoran's, that I was going to spend three days, together with Clifford Pierce, of course, at the Minnesota State Fair in Minneapolis. Clifford was going to the fair to exhibit some his fine Montedale sheep. Incidentally, these were the same Pierces who developed that new breed of sheep called Montedales. Most 4-H members would be attending the fair to exhibit some farm animals or something that they had made; but my exhibit was quite unique because I was going to be showing just myself as a contestant for the good-grooming award. I think that it was the first year that they ever had something like this.

Our sleeping quarters were provided for us in a large boys' dormitory for the two nights that we would be there. During our stay at the fair, Clifford and I were intent on enjoying our nights in the big city of Minneapolis. We were among the few 4-H members who were lucky enough to have a car. Having that car made it so easy for us to get dates from some of the girls who had gone to the fair from several of the other 4-H clubs. I think that a lot of the thrill was just the conquest of getting girls to go out with us.

The first night we were there, Cliff and I persuaded two girls, from a 4-H club near St. Charles, whom we had just met to come along with us for a joyful evening in Minneapolis. Without any hesitation, they enthusiastically joined us. We first spent a lot of time just driving around the city and seeing the sights. We then went to a fancy restaurant to have a real nice evening meal. After that we were to experience something quite amazing that none of us had witnessed before. We went to see a 3-D movie, which we had only heard about, but none of us had ever been exposed to the real thing. It was something that had only recently become popular. It also got me to reminisce a bit about a much nicer time with the more simple 3-D stuff we had on the back table in that one room school when I was in fifth grade and my brothers and I were together at the Shanahan's

The first thing that made you aware that there was going to be something different about this movie was that upon entering the theater, each person was handed a special pair of glasses to wear. The glasses had cardboard frames, with one red lens and the other blue and after the movie they were meant to be thrown away. As I was watching the movie, it seemed that I was constantly ducking as different objects appeared to be jumping out of the screen at us. Even though the glasses were a bit of a nuisance to wear, we did enjoy the show. Afterwards, we were all in agreement that the 3-D was excellent entertainment. We were definitely committed to seeing other 3-D movies. The next night the four of us went out again and enjoyed another evening together.

My father just happened to be working at the fair that year, as a salesman for Brede Truck Body & Equipment Co. They were having a special very impressive demonstration of their "No Spin" differential for trucks and trying to influence new buyers. The next day I went to see my dad at his booth and, of course, I was proud to have Cliff and some of our other 4-H friends meet him too. My dad always did well at making a good first impression on others that he was a very successful person. As I expected, all of my friends thought that I had a really neat dad. I think that was also one reason that he was such a good salesman; he could sell himself.

After my friends and I agreed to meet later at a certain time and place, they left. My dad and I were now able to spend some time alone together. I got to observe him in action as he dealt with his prospective customers. My dad always impressed me with how comfortable he seemed and what a smooth talker he was with those who showed any interest in any of the products his company was marketing. He certainly had a gift for selling. I often wished that I wasn't so shy and that I possessed just a wee bit of his talent. I'm not so sure that I would have limited that skill to just selling.

Later that afternoon while I was visiting him, my father offered to buy me something for my supper at a nearby stand. I certainly wasn't going to turn down free food. I believe that he was eager to order something for me that he liked, but he knew that I had never heard of it before. It was touted as a new type of food from Italy, and it was now available at the fair that year. That new food had the funny-sounding name of pizza pie. I had heard of it about three years before in a song that Dean Martin sang that had the phrase, "When the moon hits your eyes like a big pizza pie, that's amore." Pizza pie had no meaning to me then. After trying it, I really didn't know if I really liked it or not, but I ate it anyway. Although I got to savor its spicy taste, it didn't make too much of an impression on me and I wouldn't be eating it again for another two years. I always liked to try new things, so the State Fair that year did turn out to be quite a special experience for me.

I thought that it was quite amazing that I got to try out two new products that I had never experienced before that summer: pizza pie and 3-D movies. When I look back at it, I can see that I would have been a poor judge of what it is that people want and what will sell. It now seems sort of strange that I was extremely impressed by the 3-D movies, which never really caught on and soon died out. The pizza pie didn't do anything for me just then, but it later was to become one of the most popular foods for almost everyone in the country and I would learn to enjoy this food.

I was enjoying myself at the fair, but on the third day, I had to face up to the reason that I was there. I now had to show up for the Good-Grooming Contest, which my club had the right to expect me to do well. I cleaned up and dressed myself in the best way that I knew how. During the contest, I had to parade about in front of all the judges, which did make me feel just a wee bit foolish. It all made me almost think of myself as some sort of thing to look at, instead of being a person. It reminded me that I wasn't much different than the various farm animals when they are judged and win their ribbons. Nevertheless, I went through all of the required procedures as well as I was able. Everything had to be done just so as I had to walk out. I had to stand in front of the judges, then turn slowly and make a complete circle and then stop and show them the palms and the backs of my hands. I had to turn around again in front of them, and finally walk back to my place.

When the judges were deliberating and finally came to a decision, I was pleasantly surprised again when it was announced that I was one of the first place winners for the boys. I was presented with a blue ribbon from the Robinson School of Beauty Culture in Minneapolis, and I also received a nice hair brush from them and several other prizes. When I got that ribbon I thought how vain and how similar it was to what the livestock parade around with. Even though I had a somewhat competitive nature and I enjoyed winning I was also realistic enough to know that this success was going to be short lived and within a couple of days it would all be meaningless.

Clifford's Montedales also did extremely well in the sheep judging. For now at least, we both could come home feeling quite proud of ourselves and our accomplishments and that we did well in representing our 4-H Club, the Fremont Green Clovers, from the very small town of Fremont, Minnesota.

After we got back home, we picked up where we had left off with our routine of meeting young ladies, double dating and staying out until the early morning. We did this about every other night, and it was beginning to have some affect on my work. I had lived with the Corcoran's for more than two months and it seemed as though I didn't even care about the consequences of what I was doing. And like when I was at the Simon's he wasn't getting full value for what he was paying me. So I wasn't at all surprised when Jerry, my boss, told me one day that he couldn't afford to keep me anymore. It was now up to me to find myself another place to live.

It didn't take any time at all to get a new job, because I was a hard worker and I still had a good reputation. My next move would be less than two miles away from the Corcoran farm. The very next day I would be working for a guy named Donny Randal. He and his wife had known me somewhat from the events we attended at the town hall in Fremont. They were kind people, and they were quite decent and patient with me, as I realized the futility of some of my bad habits. I quit going out so often in the evenings and started developing a nice relationship with my new boss. That short move made it enough of an inconvenience to meet with Clifford Pierce and our old relationship ended. Mr. Randal could rely on me to do a good job and always be available but it was also quite lonely for me.

I got there just about the right time for harvesting the oats. I drove his big old truck, and Donny drove the tractor pulling the big combine. Without stopping, we would unload the hopper of the combine into the truck. In order to do this, I had to sit on the right side of the truck, with my left foot gently controlling the gas pedal while I reached way over to hold onto the steering wheel with my left hand. I had to guide, ever so carefully, that truck with its right fender within a couple of inches of the huge, turning John Deere

"G" tractor tire. When I finally had three hopper loads from the combine, I drove the truck home and unloaded it. When I got to the elevator, I had to shovel off the load as quickly as possible so Donny wouldn't have to wait long as I returned to the field to receive the next hopper load from the combine. I also had my regular daily chores of feeding and milking the cows, besides a lot of field work on the tractor. I did all the jobs that were required of me quite well.

Donny Randel had a beautiful American Saddle Breed race horse, which gave me one good reason for getting some real pleasure from my stay at his farm. Besides being an excellent show horse, he was also very fast. That horse, with his low pasterns, gave a nice easy ride, so I enjoyed riding him very much.

It had been a couple of years since the horse had the experience of a person riding him, so it took a lot of my time as I patiently worked with him, until he would accept someone on his back again. The next thing that I had to do was to teach that horse to respond to my commands. Because he hadn't been ridden for such a long time, he had become very temperamental. I also had to break him of the bad habit that he had of always making a sharp turn off the road and going into an abandoned schoolhouse driveway that was about a quarter of a mile down the road from where we lived.

I was just beginning to believe that he was getting used to me, and everything was going well as I rode him around the farm and mostly in the grassy pasture. When I felt that he was ready I decided to take him for a ride down the gravel road. Everything was going fine as he was easily galloping along, when suddenly at the driveway of the old schoolhouse he made a sharp turn to the left. I hadn't known about that little trick of his, and I was unprepared. I turned hard on the reins to get the horse to go straight ahead, but it was no use. The results were disastrous, and we both ended up in the ditch, but I stayed with him. The next time when I walked him past that driveway, there was no problem. It was when I tried to gallop past that things didn't go right. It took several more attempts before I eventually got him trained so that turning into the school was no longer a problem.

The horse was very high-spirited, and he constantly needed to be shown who was boss. I also had to teach that horse how to cross bridges without fear. It seemed as though the change in the sound of his hooves would spook him and he would suddenly stop, rear up and fight against making the crossing. It took some work before I was able to break him of that problem. My lessons for him started out by stopping right before the bridge. I then got off, turned him around, and then I held the reins and pushed against his chest as I kept repeating quite firmly over and over the word *"back!"* I had forced him to go backwards across the bridge. I surely wasn't going to do that each time we went for a ride, but I had to do that several times before I was able to next lead him across forwards. We kept practicing going back and forth on that bridge until he seemed quite comfortable and it was no longer a problem.

One Sunday afternoon during the time that I was off work, I was just enjoying my ride on the horse. I had ridden about two miles to the Fremont Store. I visited for a while with the men who were there. I then decided to ride the horse over to where this friend of mine worked, which was about nine miles from where I lived. When I got there, I found out that he was off work too. During my visit with him, we made some plans to spend that afternoon together, just riding in his car and going to St. Charles to do some cruising.

Our plans did not include the horse; so obviously, I had to ride him back home first. I started for home as fast as the horse would go. I had no intention of riding the whole distance that way, but I had wanted my friend in the car to follow along to see how fast the horse was. He drove along side of me for a short distance, and he shouted to me that his speedometer was reading over forty-five miles an hour. My friend shouted back to me that he'd be meeting me at my place as he drove off. He was fast moving out of sight in the large cloud of dust that was trailing after him.

I had only ridden the horse a short way at a full gallop when the sailor hat, which I was wearing, blew off. I turned the horse around to go back and retrieve it. I then jumped to the ground, picked up my hat, and stuffed it into my back pocket. I had been riding bareback, so while holding the reins in my left hand I had to grab hold of the horse's mane with the same hand and throw my right leg up over the horse's back.

Just as I was throwing my right leg up, something spooked the horse, and he was off as though he was leaving the gate. Since I was still holding those reins in my left hand, I immediately reached over with my right hand, so I could hold tightly onto the reins with both of my hands. I had made up my mind that I was not going to let go, because it would have been a very long walk home and I was determined that I was not going to spend the afternoon walking that distance. I got my 128 pounds dragged for a while on that rough gravel road. The weight of me kept the horse's head turned so I was not trampled, although the hooves did appear larger than life as they were pounding the gravel and missing my face by only inches.

After a short distance, and probably because of my weight and his head being turned, the horse finally came to a stop and I still tightly holding the reigns got to my feet. I had been wearing an almost new pair of my Lee Riders, which now had a part of the left side torn into shreds. The upper part of my left leg had been scraped badly from dragging in the gravel, and there were already several lines of blood that had started to trickle out.

After that experience I learned an important lesson to make certain that when I was mounting that horse, I had to hold tightly onto the reins and pull the horse's head as far back as I possibly could. That didn't solve all of my problems when I was mounting him, because that horse was skittish and he was always moving. Now I had to swing up as he was going around in a circle, but that was somewhat manageable. I climbed back onto the horse and came on home to meet with my friend, who was there waiting for me. Because of the problem I always had with infections I washed my left leg with alcohol before I changed into another pair of jeans. We went to town and enjoyed our afternoon together. We even picked up a couple of girls that were our age and seemed interested in us.

When I first moved to Randals' I did quite well until school commenced that fall and I started making some new friends. I also began going out once in a while during the week again with some of my old drinking buddies. It was on one of those nights that some friends of mine and I got stopped by a policeman in Winona, because we had illegally purchased some alcoholic beverages. We had several bottles of it in our possession and we were giving that policeman every indication that we had already sampled far too much of it. The policeman had the four of us get out of the car and just stand as he called for a backup. When the other police car arrived our liquor was immediately confiscated. They then had two of us get into the back of one car as the other two got into the other. The car we had come to town in was left abandoned on the street next to the curb. We were then rushed off to the city jail.

After spending the night in their jail, we weren't released as usual. The police told us they were going to call our families to come in and pick us up. I protested that I wasn't living with any parents. They just weren't listening to me and demanded the name and place of the people that I lived with, which meant my boss. I finally told them, and they called Donny Randal and told him that they wanted him to come in so that they could talk to him about me. My friends had their parents come in, and after a short visit with the police and making promises that I knew that they wouldn't keep, they went home.

All my friends were gone and I was now alone. My boss and his wife drove all the way to Winona and came down to the city hall to bring me home. I was very nasty to them, and I quite arrogantly told them, "I don't need *you* here! You're not my parents! I got myself into this and I can get myself out of it and I don't need any help from you." They didn't know what else to do, so they left.

The police did something else that I wasn't expecting. They told me that since no one was taking me home that they weren't going to release me. That worried me because I didn't know what they would charge me with and how long they intended to keep me. I just accepted it and sat in my cell waiting the rest of the morning with nothing to do. They fed me a regular jail dinner of mashed potatoes that were covered with a lot of chicken gizzards in thick gravy and a slice of bread and butter. It was a meal that I never had before and it didn't taste too bad. I actually thought it was quite decent and far better than only the bread and water that I'd always heard that prisoners got.

I think that they finally gave up with me, because I had no intention of calling my boss again to come for me and there was no way they could coerce me. It was quite late that afternoon when a policeman finally opened my cell door and told me, "Well kid, you're free and you can go home now." That did me a lot of good; home was more than 20 miles away and I had no transportation. They were kind enough to permit me to call a friend to come and get me, but he told me that he couldn't until some time after 8 o'clock when he had finished chores. I called another friend and I was lucky that he was home and could come straightaway and drive me back home, where I would have to face my boss again. Both of the calls were long distance and I was surprised that they didn't ask me to pay for them.

That fall I started my senior year at Lewiston High School as I had the two previous years, except I was still going out and having my long, wild nights. I had only attended school for about two weeks, when one day I went downtown before school that morning to get some stamps to mail two letters. For me, at least, it was also important to get myself some chocolate to eat in school.

I was on my way back to school, when a 1939 Chevrolet pulled up beside me and I heard my name being called. I was surprised as I looked into the windows that it was some my student friends. I approached the car and one of the guys said to me, "We are going to skip school today. How would you like to come along?"

I had never done that nor even thought to do something like skipping school before. I answered them with, "Maybe some other day."

The driver called out, "It'll be a lot more fun than school." And I would have to agree with that.

I was about to continue on my walk back to school, when the guy in the back seat shouted; *"Chicken if you don't!"*

My reply to that was, *"No one calls me chicken!"* And I immediately grabbed the handle and opened the back door as that guy slid over to make room for me. As soon as I was inside the driver spun the tires as if he was in real hurry and I was being rushed to some unknown destination.

The guy who drove the car enjoyed driving so much that we spent the whole morning just traveling all over on gravel roads in that area. The rest of us found that to be a bit boring, so we convinced him to drive us into Winona and park the car. We then began walking the streets, enjoying our freedom and fooling around in the different stores.

We had already planned our departure so that we would arrive at the school at just the right time for me to catch the bus and ride home as if nothing had happened. It seemed that no one ever noticed that my friends and I hadn't been in school. This happened to be on a Thursday, which made it much easier for us to skip school again on the next day. The logic was that since tomorrow was Friday the school would have more time to forget that we had been gone and just maybe we wouldn't need a signed excuse to get back.

The next morning after completing my chores and eating breakfast, I got on the school bus as I usually did every school day. As soon as I arrived at school, I got off of the bus and walked downtown to meet with my friends for another day of playing hooky. The day started out much like the previous one, and in the afternoon we ended up back in Winona just fooling around again. I didn't enjoy it all that much, but it did beat spending the day attending classes that I felt were quite monotonous.

We were walking along, enjoying the day, when two Winona policemen approached and blocked our path. One policeman immediately started talking to us, "We saw you here yesterday and we figured that you were probably high school students. We really got suspicious when we saw you here again today." That same policeman then asked, "Where are you guys from?"

In unison we answered, "Lewiston."

The policeman asked, "What are you guys doing here?"

One of the boys answered, "Just looking around."

The policeman than said, "You can do your looking around somewhere else, but right now I want you to get in your car and get back to your school. What's your principal's name?" We told him and he said, "I'm going to call Mr. Gessner to make sure that you get back safely, understand?" With our affirmative replay we began to walk towards the car and the policeman called to us, "You make sure that you report to your principal when you get back, because we will be checking up on you."

We left Winona and drove right back to our school. I remembered my experience in New Ulm and I was against telling the principal and I told the others, "Let's just wait for the buses to line up and then get on as if we had come from the school."

As much as I tried, I couldn't talk the others out of it so without wasting any more time, I followed along. The first thing we did after entering the building was to naively follow the policemen's instructions. I proceeded with my friends to search out the principal. We found out that he was occupied with teaching a class, so we went to that classroom and knocked on the door. Mr. Gessner came out into the hall and closed the door behind him. I knew that something wasn't quite right when he had such a quizzical look on his face and he was almost whispering when he asked, "What's wrong?"

Speaking softly, one of my friends told him a small part of what had happened to us in Winona. Then that same boy asked, "Didn't the police call you here?"

They were amazed that the principal didn't know a thing about any of this. It was just like New Ulm and I wasn't surprised at all. Those policemen had lied to us!

The principal then asked us, "Why should the police have called me?

One of the boys answered, "We really didn't do anything wrong."

Mr. Gessner then said, "Before any of you will be allowed to come back to school, you must come back accompanied with your parents. I want to speak to both of your parents." He also said that he would like to spend more time with us, but just now he had to finish teaching his class. Then he ordered us, "Wait in the assembly room, because I want to find out just what happened in Winona and I want to talk to each of you again before you go home."

At first I followed his instructions and I went to the assembly room with my friends. I sat with them but I then began to think over the whole situation and I started to get angry. I thought to myself that there was nothing Mr. Gessner had to say to me, because I was on my own. I was making my own living, and I wasn't living anywhere near my parents. After reasoning it out like that, I felt there was just no way that I would allow someone else like my boss to come in to take care of my problems. I had been supporting myself, and I didn't need anyone representing my parents. I told the others, "I'm not staying here for any of this. I'm leaving now!" And I angrily walked out. I also had reasoned that I got myself into this mess and I would have to accept the responsibility of somehow taking care of it myself in my own way.

Without thinking I left the school building and started to walk towards the downtown. I started to think about it and couldn't understand what I would do there because I had no transportation. I then turned around and went back to the school and hid in the basement until it was time to board the buses. Then at what I thought was the right moment, I ran and jumped on my bus just as it was ready to leave.

I rode home, and the bus dropped me off as it had the day before as though nothing had happened. I changed my clothes, did my chores and said nothing to anyone. Things were still quite normal the next day which was Saturday. I did my chores and all the other work that was expected of me.

Sunday started out in quite the usual way. I did my chores and afterwards I had the rest of the day off. My friend came over and we went to St. Charles.

That principal and my boss, Donny Randal, just happened to go to the same church, so they saw each other that Sunday. It was just my bad luck that they started talking to each other after church service. During their conversation, my boss found out from Mr. Gessner about my skipping two days of school.

When I got home that same afternoon, Donny was really upset with me. He angrily told me, *"I want you to go out and tell your friend right now that you will be leaving here now and that you need a way to haul all of your things!"*

I immediately ran out and was able to stop my friend before he left. I told him to wait for me and he did. I then went back into the house and Donny was able to finish talking to me as he said, "I want you to go upstairs and pack up everything and take it out to your friends car and I don't care where you go from there. I want you out of here and you can just find yourself some place else to live."

I only replied to that with, "ok." I accepted that and made no attempt at trying to get him to reconsider. Without saying another word to Donny, I went upstairs to my room and did what he had told me to do. I packed up everything that I owned, which wasn't very much besides my clothes, and carried them out to the car. When I came back down Donny gave me a check which I could cash later for my back wages. I then loaded all of my things into the back seat of my friend's car and I was again off to some other place to stay.

I really had nowhere to go and I really didn't know what I would be doing next. My friend invited me to stay temporarily where he lived. My options were quite limited so I accepted his invitation. He had quit school and worked full time working as a hired hand like me, and he shared his bed with me that night. In the day time my friend let me use his car for driving around during the time that he had to work. I had my back pay so I was able to pay to eat out each day. I had considered myself expelled from school. I was really concerned that I had no means to support myself, but for now I would only deal with my present situation.

I continued to live that way throughout that week, and on Wednesday of the second week I was driving around town and happened to run into my brother Patrick in downtown Lewiston. Pat informed me that Mr. Gessner wanted to see me. At first I wasn't going to bother; but then after some thought, I decided to go to the high school to see what the principal wanted.

I went to the principal's office, not knowing what he would have to say to me. I was surprised when the first thing that the principal told me was that he was sorry because of what had happened to me. He said that if he had only known, he would never have told Mr. Randal about what I had done. Mr. Gessner also explained to me that was one of the reasons that he wanted to talk to my friends and me in the assembly room, during that last period in school on that Friday. He told me that he knew about my situation being quite different from that of the other boys and he wanted to talk to me apart from the others. He also told me that the main reason that he told Mr. Randal on Sunday was that when he didn't get to see me on that Friday, he said he was concerned that I might never come back to school again. He wanted me to know that he would like to see me finish my senior year in Lewiston.

It was a real surprise when Mr. Gessner then explained to me how he had found me another job on a farm that was just outside of Lewiston. He even told me that they would be willing to pay me $10 a week plus, room and board, which was more than the $7 that I had become used to receiving. He finally told me that I would be with a very nice family, and I could continue attending and be able to graduate from Lewiston High School.

I then realized for the first time since going to school there that this principal really was a decent sort. He was a kind man and I would never forget him for his undeserved kindness towards me. I thanked him and told him that I thought that it was better that I left the area. I must get away from my old friends and start over somewhere else.

In many ways the last two years had been a good experience for me, but the last few months had become so tragically unsettled for me. Because of the bad choices that I made, I was destined to be directed through a lot of hurt and a great deal of discontentment. I would miss all of my old friends in the Lewiston area, especially Tom Cunningham, John Rownan, John Milde and most of all, Audrey

Simon. I didn't know if I would ever see any of them again.

I was feeling like I had been left ***adrift on the high seas*** and I lacked the skills to deal with it. I was feeling as though I was being driven towards some unwanted destination. There I was again, an angry person with nothing but so many mixed-up and half formed ideas. I knew that I had to change my behavior, but would I be able to turn my life around and give it some useful purpose. I also knew that it was only I that could make that difference and I would have to decide and then take charge.

- XV. Taking Over Command -

Throughout my life I have always made decisions that I knew would leave me hurting inside for some time, but I *usually* did what I thought was best for me at the present time for dealing with my future. I had determined that this was one of those times, because I certainly knew that I could do better. Departing from those whom I was developing strong feelings for and the few *good* friends that I had made in that region was not going to be easy.

I had already made my decision to leave the very area around Lewiston that I knew best. It was the same place where I had experienced some of my best times and also some of the worst times of my life. I had no idea where I would be going, and at the time I didn't even know if I would finish high school and graduate. My mind was so full of so many mixed up ideas and anger, but I was old enough and smart enough to know that I just had to make some changes.

Several times as a young boy I mentioned that I always hated having to move from place to place. I had no choice then; but the last three moves, within the period of four months, I had forced upon myself. I couldn't place any of the blame with my father anymore. I have to accept full responsibility for my fate from now on. I also knew that my next home would only be a temporary move for less than a year, because I only planned to stay long enough to finish high school. I didn't know what was ahead for me in moving to some new place again, but I was now 18 years old, and it was about time that I took full control of my life.

After more than two weeks of bumming around and half-heartedly searching for some new place to work, I finally got serious and found employment on another farm. My new home was going to be living with Bill Lafky, his wife, and young son. In that same day I moved my things which amounted to no more than my clothes, some phonograph records, and some books. After a minimum of instructions, I started with my assigned chores that same night. These people were immediately quite nice towards me.

I was now beginning to think seriously about my future. I had already made a strong commitment to quit my wasteful night life and stop all of the fooling around. I figured that by now I must have driven all of the wickedness out of my system. I felt that I was now ready to settle down and be the good hired man that I had been in the past and also go back to school. I didn't even have a full year left and I thought if I wanted it badly enough, nothing could stop me from completing my senior year of high school and graduating.

I was on my own and I had no family that was making any demands on me to finish school; the compelling force had to come entirely from within. There was one foremost thought in my mind that had become the motivation for me to complete high school. Several years ago I heard an aunt of ours, in a conversation with my father; tell him that not one of his boys would ever make it through high school. I was now going to prove that she was wrong, no matter what it took.

After I finished breakfast that first day with the Lafkys', Bill Lafky drove me to the Rushford High School to register. I began classes straightaway that morning. It was always a horrible experience at best, but for the eleventh time I was again entering a new school in the very Norwegian town of Rushford, Minnesota. I didn't know anyone when I started going there, and I remember feeling so lonely and Lewiston seemed so nice to me just then. I was really regretting what I had done to have the Simons turn me out.

I was going to spend the remaining part of the school year attending classes there. Another thing that made it a bit difficult for me was that I would be starting there about five weeks after the normal starting date, so I had a lot of catching up to do. To make matters even worse, not one of my new classes resembled any of the ones that I had started attending earlier at Lewiston High.

From the beginning, this school appeared to be quite a bit different from the more carefree ways of Lewiston High. The whole atmosphere seemed to be so much more serious. I was an outsider, and at the beginning I didn't get on too well with some of the other students. I didn't feel welcome there, and I realized that it wasn't entirely their fault, because I didn't put much effort into making new friends. I also think that I was still carrying around quite a large chip on my shoulder. I know that I still had a tremendous amount of the anger and jealousy that I retained from the year before.

I remember I had been in their school only a few weeks when an incident occurred that should never have happened one day in one of our English classes. It took place during the second half of the period while Mrs. Hatleli, our English teacher, was sitting in the back of the room, correcting papers. All of her students including me were supposed to be reading a Shakespeare's "Hamlet" assignment.

For some reason, John Jertsen, a classmate, and I had some difficulty getting on with each other from the very first day that I had entered this school. We were also taking all the same classes and, as much as I would try, it was impossible for us to completely avoid each other. On this particular day he was sitting in his assigned seat which was the desk just behind mine, and he had for some time been verbally teasing me. I was reminded of the saying as a young child about "Sticks and stones may break my bones but names will never hurt me." It had gone beyond the name calling and was getting a bit physical.

I don't know what had started it this time, but suddenly John reached over and began messing up my neatly-combed hair. He clearly knew how much that was upsetting me, because he began blowing down the back of my neck. He started whispering such things as: "Cool down. Don't lose that Irish temper." He continued repeating it and other things in an obvious attempt to irritate me. Even two of the girl students who were witnessing it didn't like what they saw. Each of them was quietly whispering across the isle, telling John to stop what he was doing.

He just ignored them as he still continued with this harassment for some time, until I finally decided that I was going to take no more. Perhaps I did finally lose my Irish temper, because in the middle of one of his vocal provocations, I swiftly swung my arm all the way around as hard and fast as I could. It had happened so quickly that I caught the unprepared John on the cheek with a powerful blow from the back of my hand. That produced just one loud crack in an otherwise very quiet classroom. Everyone heard it! I immediately felt a strong sense of fear at how the school could really make me regret what I had just done.

That immediately brought Mrs. Hatleli to her feet as she hurried to the front of the room and stopped in the aisle next our desks. I didn't know how she knew that the disturbance involved John and me, unless she had been watching it as it was happening. She couldn't see John's red cheek, because it was on the side away from her. Without saying a word, she just stood over us for some time. John and I just sat quietly and waited for what she would do or say next. I could feel the tension building before she finally asked, *"John, what happened?"* When she got no reply from him, she asked John the same question again. Getting no answer this time she turned to me and asked, *"Roy, do you want to tell me what happened?"* I, of course, didn't say anything either.

Every student in the room was anxiously waiting to see what would happen next. The whole room was hushed again for a long time, during which all kinds of thoughts started racing through my mind. I thought that now I had really done it. I was now expecting to be punished in some way, and I was even anticipating that I might be sent to the principal, Mr. Hans Sonsteng, who I knew didn't like me from the first day I entered his school. How could I expect to be treated fairly? I knew that if Mr. Sonsteng was told what I had done, he would expel me for sure, and I wouldn't be able to graduate. I was afraid of the expected consequences, but I also realized that whatever happened because of it, I probably deserved it.

It was welcomed and a pleasant surprise, then, when finally Mrs. Hatleli, in a very stern and loud voice declared, *"When I see that someone has a hit coming, I say hit him again and I'll hit him one too!"*

For the first time since coming to that school, I felt that there was one person who was on my side even if it was for just this one time. It was such a relief to realize that I wasn't alone and that I may have a friend and that the principal wouldn't be getting involved. Because of this I was developing a tremendous amount of respect for this woman.

As it turned out I was later thankful for what I had done because everything seemed to change for the better from then on. A lot of it, no doubt, had much to do with my change of attitude. It wasn't very long after that episode that John and I became very good friends. He, Jerry Larson, and I even did many of our projects in the agriculture class together. Our senior class even chose to dedicate the school yearbook, which was also the twenty-fourth issue of The Valley Legend to Mrs. Cyrus Hatleli. She would have certainly got my vote on that.

Our senior class was very small; in fact, the agriculture class that I was in had only four of us boys in it. It was during the time that I was in the ag. (agriculture) class, that I entered a tri-county soil-judging contest. I was quite proud of myself when I learned that I had won third place in that event as I was competing against more than 200 other F.F.A. boys.

Harold Swanson, our ag teacher, spent a lot of time that year teaching the four of us how to arc weld using their newly-purchased

Forney Arc Welder. I learned well, and I put my newly-learned skill to use when I designed and built a very nice trailer with an adjustable hitch. That experience was also put to valuable service on one of the jobs that I got the following summer.

All high school classes I had taken in the past, with the exception of agriculture, were academic classes. When I entered Rushford High, I decided to do something different that year and take a shop class under Val Jean Christenson which I really enjoyed. It seemed that everyone in his class started out by making a knife out of a wood file by grinding it and properly tempering it. After we put a nice, sharp edge on it, we made a handle out of wood. When I had the knife finished, I was free to do some other small projects.

With all those other projects finished and the school year over half-finished, I decided I wanted to do something that would be more challenging. I got the approval of Mr. Christenson to build a very nice, solid-walnut cabinet from some plans that I had drawn up. I then obtained the necessary wood which proved to be quite expensive. I was particularly proud of it when I finished, because I had designed it myself and the style has been able to fit in with most other furniture of almost any period of time. That cabinet has followed me around with almost every move I made since then, and I still have it.

Several students and some of the teachers discovered in a strange way that I was possessed with some artistic talent. I used to doodle and draw pictures in class whenever I became bored. Then as I left the class each time, I would just throw my scribbling into the litter basket and go to my next class. There happened to be some of the students who saw what I had been doing. They then started digging out some of the things that I had been throwing away. My hastily-drawn pictures got shown to others, and my talent for art was judged by those scribbles that I had been tossing away.

The teacher in charge and some of the students asked me if I would work on the annual staff as the artist. I was reluctant at first, because I didn't think that I would be good enough for that. I finally gave in to their request and I did end up doing all of the art work for the high school annual for 1954.

Since the day that I started attending Rushford High, I was determined that I couldn't continue living the way that I had for the previous nine months. I knew that I might not be able to graduate in the spring if I didn't quit all of those night-time escapades. Without any doubt, I had made up my mind to attend the Minneapolis School of Art after I finished high school. It was imperative that I receive a diploma. To accomplish my goal, I decided not to go out at night anymore. There would be no more drinking parties with my friends, not one date, and I wasn't going to do anything that would cost money. I stayed at home each night and saved every penny that I was earning. I was aware that it would be quite expensive to attend that school and, at the very least, my intention would be to have more than enough money accumulated for my tuition.

My dad had always, since I was a small boy, still had this dream of me becoming a doctor one day. I also knew that anything less than that was going to be a great disappointment to him, but I just could not fancy me being a doctor. Even though I had mentioned to him about my strong desire to go to art school, my dad was quite opposed to it. He really didn't think much of anybody who could make a living by drawing pictures, and he believed that he could get me to think differently about it.

In an obvious last desperate attempt to have me change my mind about art school, my dad one day in early November stopped at the farm and took me to Minneapolis to stay with him for four days. I spent three of those days working with his doctor and friend, Dr. Smidel. That doctor even had me wear one of his white smocks to make it more convincing when he introduced me to some of his patients as an intern doctor. My dad must have believed that if I saw what life was like for a doctor, that it just might get me interested in becoming one. I had a hard time convincing my dad that I had other interests and that I never had any desire in becoming a doctor at all.

I think that my dad thought that being an artist was just a kind of frivolous way of life and wasn't as honorable a profession as being a doctor. He also made it clear to me another reason for deciding my occupation was that he believed that success was measured by wealth and doctors were quite well off financially and that seemed to be so important to him. It was only after I threatened to join one of the military services after graduation if I couldn't go to art school that my dad finally gave in. He was beginning to recognize that he would no longer be able to control my life.

After finally accepting my determination to be a commercial artist, he and I spent quite a bit of time discussing it. We had it all planned out. Together we decided that I would attend art school and that, in order to reduce my living expenses, I was going to live in an apartment in Minneapolis with my dad. I would also get myself a job, working evenings, so I could earn the rest of the money that would be required for me to live on.

My dad and I had earlier agreed that I was going to save all the money that I earned during my senior year. During the summer I would make the rest of the money that I would need so that I could start school with at least a sufficient amount to pay the tuition for my first semester and possibly a little extra.

As winter was slowly moving towards spring, our English class was given an assignment to write a poem. I didn't want to be bothered with it for what I thought were two good reasons: one, I didn't have much time for myself after I did all of my chores on the farm and two, I felt that a poem required a sharing of oneself and I was a private person.

I was hoping that the teacher would be satisfied with my not doing it and respond by just lowering my grade. The day before the poem was due to be handed in I decided to talk to, Mrs. Hatleli about it. I respected and had come to feel quite comfortable with her so I wondered if there was a way out of writing the poem. I asked her, "If I don't write the poem, could you just give me a cut in my grade instead?"

She told me, "I'll give you a cut in grade all right. I'll give you a failing grade." She assured me that would be enough to prevent me from graduating. She also tried to convince me that she believed that I was quite capable of producing something worthwhile and that she was only expecting me to put my best effort into it. Mrs. Hatleli had given us a couple of weeks for the assignment, which was certainly plenty of time. Because the deadline was the next day, I was now feeling quite desperate. Because of the way I felt towards her, I was left with no other alternative but to write the poem.

I can't describe the anxiety that I felt from just the thought of writing a poem and having it due in the next day. I had always been a very private person and my writing that poem would be sharing a little part of myself with others, which I was finding extremely hard to even consider. I still hadn't decided on what I was going to do. Now I felt as though I was being tested to see just how important it was to me to graduate.

That night after I finished my chores, I went up to my bedroom as usual. I was greeted by a lamb that I saved from certain death, because the mother would not accept this twin. I was bottle-feeding it warm milk, and the lamb spent each night in bed sleeping under the blankets with me. I treated that lamb very much as though it was a human baby.

I straight away undressed and went to bed. I was just lying there on my stomach with my left arm around the lamb and in my right hand I was holding my pencil as it just hovered above the blank page in my spiral-bound note book. I was trying to think about something neat that I could write about for that poem. My first thoughts were to write about me and my taking care of that lamb, which I thought would be a sort of special and pretty easy subject to write about. What I was trying to do and what I was able to do couldn't seem to come together this time. My mind just couldn't seem to envision anything of the sort.

As things turned out, it wasn't the lamb and me that I was going to be writing about in that poem. The more I tried, the more that I seemed to be unable to get that lamb and me together in my thoughts for this assignment.

Quite suddenly, while I was lying there thinking and just staring at that pencil occasionally, it came to me. I had decided that I would make that pencil the main subject in my poem. I would write about that pencil's importance to me as a tool for creating my works of art. I guess there are times when one gets an inspiration; because once I had decided on the theme for that poem, it took me no more than about ten minutes to write it. Because it did take me such a small amount of time to write, I felt that I was sort of cheating on the assignment because the teacher had told me to just do my best but it was for such a small amount of time that I had done my best. However, right now it seemed to be more important for me to just finish it so I could have it ready to hand in tomorrow.

The next day, after just making the deadline, I handed in the poem that I completed the night before. I had simply given it the title "My Pencil." I was quite shy anyway and also a bit ashamed to hand it in, because it wasn't very long and I had spent so little time on it. I took my paper and stuck it somewhere in the middle of the stack of the other student's poems. I also remember what Mrs. Hatleli had said about "best effort," and I believed that I hadn't really put my best effort into it, at least not very long. I didn't think that my poem could possibly be very good and I felt that it may even appear a bit silly to someone else.

The following day, after she had finished reading everybody's poems, Mrs. Hatleli returned the graded assignments to the students. She made me feel quite proud when she informed me, in front of the rest of the class, that she thought that my poem was exceptionally well written. Because I valued her opinion so much, what she said about it gave me a wonderful feeling inside. She then handed the poem back to me, so that I could correct some punctuation errors, which she had clearly marked.

The next day I had completed the rewrite, so I returned the corrected poem in my neatest handwriting to her. After she first received my approval, she sent it in to the National High School Poetry Association in California.

That poem read:

My Pencil

My pictures it sees first hand
Of settlers and Indians of the frontier land;
Of days of old and lands untold;
Of horses at a hearty gait,
With me it does collaborate.
Always looks so straight and arrogant,
Sometimes my head can, but it can't.
Does what I want usually,
But then again with much obstinacy
For me to part, would break my heart.
My Pencil

It was a few weeks later, after I had forgotten all about it that I received a nice certificate of acceptance from the National High School Poetry Association. A little more than a month later I was quite surprised when I received a package in the mail. I opened it to find that it was a copy of the book from the annual <u>Anthology of High School Poetry</u>. The table of contents told me the page to find my poem that had been published along with the poems from other high school students from around the United States. Shortly before summer vacation I received another book <u>Songs of American Youth</u> and the poem was in it. Two magazines during the summer asked for and got my permission to publish the poem. I have to admit that all of this changed my attitude about the poem, and I was now quite pleased that I had been forced to write it. I came to realize that I was my most severe critic and not always the best judge of my efforts. I now felt quite proud of what I had done. I was now a published author! I must also acknowledge my gratitude to Mrs. Hatleli for the special part she played in this, because the poem would never have been written without her stern encouragement.

The time had come for the Junior-Senior Prom, but it also became victim to my austerity measures to raise the money to attend art school in the fall. I had made up my mind I wouldn't be going this year. So it was a surprise and a coincidence that my dad and Mrs. Skoine came down to visit me on that particular night. I told them about the prom and my dad just ignored me, but Mrs. Skoine made a big fuss about it and praised me. My dad thought that I should go to the Prom even though I didn't have a date. He ordered me to dress up in my best clothes and I did what he told me to do. It was the first time that I dressed in those clothes since I wore them for the good grooming contest last summer. Mrs. Skoine, and I rode along as my dad drove us to the front of the High School in Rushford. The door was open and the lights were dimly lighting the dance floor. I walked to the entrance, looked in and I could see all of the students sitting at tables on both sides. I then turned around and went back to the car and told my dad that every one was paired up as boy and girl and I just couldn't go in alone.

I think that my dad was beginning to give up trying to influence me to do his will anymore, because he didn't try to change my mind about this as I had expected. I told my dad that I would rather spend my time with him and Mrs. Skoine at the dance in Winona. He drove us to the dance and I did some dancing but I enjoyed spending most of the evening just visiting with them. All of that school year I spent so much of my time being alone in the evenings and nothing else to do but the chores and going to bed.

I still had the essential paperwork to send in to be accepted into art school that fall. There were instructions with one of the forms that I had to fill it out and then have my high school principal finish it and sign it. I never even considered that there would be any problem when I presented the form to my principal, Mr. Hans Sonsteng. Even though I knew that he didn't like me, I was surprised when he said that he had no intention of putting his name on that form for me. I don't remember his exact words to me anymore, but he was making some disparaging remarks that included something about his belief that I was going to be nothing more than just a farmer. I thought that was a strange remark for him to make in such a rural area as this. It was hard for me to believe what I had just heard and it made me feel so dejected and I was never able to deal with rejection too well.

I could not understand the reason this man really didn't like me. I don't think I had done anything to him that would cause him to have such an attitude about me. I could feel, ever since I entered school there, that there was more than just a personality conflict between the two of us. During my life I was going to discover that there are many different kinds of prejudices, but this was one that made no sense to me. I thought that I was just going to have to accept it because I believed that it would be a futile effort on my part to make him change his mind. It's wrong that a man like him should have that kind of power. With his refusal, I was getting quite concerned and I was now becoming worried that saving my money was going to be all in vain and that attending art school would only be an unattainable dream for me. I now hoped that there would be some other way to accomplish what was needed.

After eight grade schools and three high schools, I finally graduated from Rushford High School on the third of June, 1954. I was the first of my dad's boys to graduate, and only my dad and Mrs. Skoine were there to observe that. I had wished that all of my brothers could have been there to see me. The one person that I really missed the most was my mother. I know that she would have been very proud of me and I know that she would have given me one of those "I could just squeeze the puddin' out of you" hugs which I hadn't received since so many years ago in New Ulm.

Now I had to face the dreaded long, hot days of summer with hard work on the farm, to earn some more money to save just in case something happened which would make it possible for me to go to art school in the fall. I was having difficulty accepting it as a fact, that one man could prevent my dream from becoming a reality.

After graduation and summer had begun I was forced to pack up my few possessions and move to another farm, where I would be able to have a full-time job. Because the Lafkys didn't have a very large farm, they would be unable to have enough work for me to be employed there full time during the summer.

The next farm that I moved to was south of Utica, a small town about five miles west of Lewiston. The farm was owned by the Nesbit family that was known for raising Ayrshires a breed of cattle that originally came from Scotland and were quite unique when compared to the usual Holsteins that are on most of the area dairy farms. Because they didn't have a very large farm either, I was often loaned out to work for other farmers. How different this summer was to be, compared to the last two. I worked on different farms as I had to deal with farmers that each had their own way of doing things. Even the tractors and equipment I had to use were quite different on each of the farms. I also completely avoided my friends and didn't go out once in the evenings for fun. The most important thing for me was to work hard that summer, and continue to save all of the money that I earned for art school.

During the time that I was living there, I use some of the small amount of spare time to complete all six of the pictures that were required of each student wishing to be admitted to the Minneapolis School of Art. I was obligated to send the school a picture of a family member, some animal, the house I was living in, a piece of furniture, a nature scene, and one other picture of my choosing. "My Pencil" was again put to good use for this. I think that deep-down I was holding on to the belief that I still might be able to attend the art school, even though the principal had refused to fill out one of the required forms.

The next time my dad came down to visit me that summer; I explained to him what had happened between the principal and me and about the principal's refusal to sign the art school form. My dad had me get into his car immediately, and he drove us in to Rushford. He had that look of determination that I had seen many times before. He was going to allow no one to get in his way until he accomplished his objective. We went straightaway to the school to see Mr. Sonsteng, the principal, but we discovered that only the custodians were working there. After finding out his address we went to see the principal at his home, but no one was there.

A neighbor of his told us that he and his family had gone away on vacation. It was getting late in the evening and I was becoming despondent and beginning to think that just maybe it was hopeless after all.

Since the principal wasn't available, my dad decided to drive me to the superintendent's home, which wasn't far from the school. I wasn't really expecting to achieve any success, because that superintendent, C. R. Lewis, couldn't possibly have known me. I went to his front door, showed him the form, and asked him if he would complete it for me. He read it and said, "So you want to go to art school? I'll be glad to sign it." He didn't even hesitate for a moment to fill out and sign that form for me and then he wished me well. This man was truly a decent sort. Except for the money, I now had everything I needed to enter art school.

It was when I thought about it later, that I really felt some relief that my father wasn't able to locate that principal. I don't know what he might have done to him, and I didn't want dad to get into trouble because of me. I knew that when my father was on a mission, he would tolerate no obstacles and he could get quite physical.

The 10th of September was the date that I was expecting to arrive at The Minneapolis School of Art and my dad was going to see that I got there on time. On that day my dad would be picking me up at the farm where I was working and from there go to Minneapolis to live in his apartment with him, and I would be there in time to enter the art school.

It was my dad's plan to start his trip on the day before, pick up my brother Richard at his home in Wisconsin and take him to the preparatory seminary in Bellevue, Illinois. Then early the next day he would continue north to where I was living, have me ride with him, and arrive in Minneapolis some time in the afternoon on the tenth. He would take me to the art school where I could get registered and then look for a job near by.

Our dad's doctor was opposed to his taking any trip, but he also realized that he couldn't prevent him from doing it. Since our dad was going anyway the doctor recommended that he take short drives with frequent rests. Our dad ignored the doctor's advice as he drove to the farm in Wisconsin where Richard was living.

It was on the ninth of September when my dad picked up, my brother, Richard as planned and started on the long trip to the seminary. Richard had completed grade school that spring and was the top student in his eighth grade graduating class. He expressed a strong desire, with our dad's encouragement, to one day become a priest.

On that same day I awoke early, did my chores and had a normal day of work with the constant thought about my future in Minneapolis. I was quite anxious about the move and I had all of my things packed to go. In the evening as I was about to go to bed when I was interrupted by Pat and Tom coming up to my room and shocking me with the horrible news that our dad was dead. Instead of going to Minneapolis tomorrow I would be taking a trip tonight to my Aunt Dorothy's place near Hager City, Wisconsin.

My dad was driving his big Packard somewhere in Wisconsin with Richard as his passenger. I can only relate all that Richard told me what he was experiencing during this time. Our dad had been driving along quite fast, as usual, and he was eating pieces of an orange that Richard had peeled for him. Suddenly, our dad slowed the car down to about forty miles an hour. Richard said that our dad turned to him as he quite calmly announced, "Richard, this is it." Richard said that he next heard a strange gurgling sound which seemed to be coming from our dad's stomach. It happened very quickly as our dad stiffened up a little, and he was dead. Richard had to bring the car to a stop and immediately get some help. It was good to know that our dad's last bit of life was apparently without much pain and he seemed to accept it. He seemed to be at peace with himself before he died.

Richard did finally get to go to the seminary as he had planned, because there were funds that had been provided for him by the Church. He only spent eighteen months there and then, for reasons that only he knows, he quit. That would also be the end of his formal public education with the equivalent of only a year and one-half of high school.

My dream of going to The Minneapolis School of Art ended then and I never did get to go to art school as I had planned. I knew that it would be impossible to finance the high cost of that school on my own. I was saddened and quite disappointed, because I had so much anticipated fulfilling my dream of possibly becoming a great artist some day. I realized that it was just something else that I had to accept, as I did so with many events in my life, for which I had no control. It all meant that I would be forced to change my plans. The money that I had saved for art school was spent on funeral arrangements and for me to live on for a short time to stay at my Aunt Dorothy's place.

When I first heard about our father's dying, I had a lot of difficulty believing it. He seemed so big and he appeared to be so healthy when I last saw him. He seemed to be in better shape than he had been for many years. In fact, he looked especially robust then, because he even had lost a quite a bit of weight. My brother's boss, Bernie Loftus, had difficulty believing it, and according to Pat his reaction was, "Dead? Hell, he ain't dead; he could fight a bear with a twig!"

It left me with an awful lot of guilt about the part that I might have played in causing or at least speeding up my dad's death. He had called me from Minneapolis just two days before he died. We talked long-distance for a much longer time than we usually did, and near the beginning of our conversation he sadly said to me, "Sonny, I'm awfully sick." I thought with those words that he was referring to his diabetes, which I was quite aware of. I became apparent that I didn't treat what he had said as seriously as I should have. Our conversation did seem a bit strange to me, because he was sounding so sad, at a time when I thought that he should really be happy for Richard and me.

He finally got to what I thought was the real purpose of the call, and he asked me if I had the money that I would need for my tuition to the art school. I told him that I didn't, and after that he really sounded like he was very disappointed with me. With almost no expression, he repeated those words a second time, "Sonny, I'm awfully sick," and I just ignored it again. It had been my intention to surprise him when he came to pick me up. I wanted him to be happy and proud of me, when he saw that I had far more than enough money for school. I never got to show him that I not only had the needed money, but quite a bit extra. I thought at that time and for many years after, that his disappointment with me might have been part of the cause for his early death so I felt a lot of guilt about it.

The death certificate stated the official cause of our dad's death was arteriosclerosis or hardening of the arteries, causing a massive heart attack. The doctor told us that our dad's arteries had closed up on him like that of an eighty-year-old man though our dad was only forty-eight years old.

The doctor also let us know that our dad might still be alive if he had just taken a glass of wine, a bottle of beer, or a shot of whiskey each day; but our dad just did not believe in drinking. In fact, he even changed doctors once when the first doctor had even suggested the drinks. Our dad kept a very rigid lifestyle and the only thing he drank was enormous quantities of water. He also bragged that he never spent a penny on cigarettes.

Our dad had been given instructions by that same doctor not to take that trip. The doctor was quite adamant when he suggested that if our dad just had to take that trip, he should do it by spending at least two hours resting for every one hour that he spent driving. Of course, our dad didn't follow his doctor's advice with that either.

My brothers and I chose to have our dad's funeral at the small Catholic Church in rural Big River, Wisconsin. There isn't any town there, just the white, wood-framed church situated on a hill, with a nice graveyard behind it. It wasn't far from where our Aunt Dorothy, or Mrs. Ferdinand Denzer, lived at the time. Dorothy was one of our father's younger twin sisters, and she was very kind to our dad during the last two years of his life. At the time, she was the only one of his brothers or sisters who volunteered to come to his aid. Aunt Dorothy even provided a home for about two years for my three youngest brothers, Thomas, Richard and Warren, to live there even when our dad was unable to make the payments to her in the monthly amount that he had promised.

Together, my brothers and I picked out the oversized casket that was needed to bury our dad in, with a design that we could agree on and within reason for cost. We also were planning ahead, so that our mother could be buried next to him when she died. We chose to get four lots right next to each other, for our mom, dad, and we would have two extra ones.

Our mother, quite naturally, couldn't be at the funeral. All of my dad's brothers and sisters who were still alive attended his funeral. Most of them stayed in a hotel in Hager City or Elsworth. There were also some who stayed at my Aunt Dorothy's house, with her family on their farm. It was really a crowd that was far too large for their little house. There were even some, like me, who stayed for some time after.

Our dad's brother Sherman, who had received all of the formal education at the sacrifice of the rest of his family more than thirty years before, had become a high school principal. My dad had always held a lot of resentment towards him which whether justified or not did influence my ill feelings about him. On this solemn day my brothers and Dorothy's kids and I were forced to listen as he just had to recite a couple of poems, which he had committed to memory. There was no escape; he stood in the doorway of the bedroom where my brothers, our cousins and I became his captive audience. I think that he felt it would be appropriate for the occasion. My brothers and I just didn't understand any significance in them at the time, nor do I recall one word of them or even what they were about. Sherman as I remembered him, seemed always extremely arrogant and a bit obtuse when speaking to us kids anyway, making it quite hard to understand him at times. He also acted as though he was better than his brothers and sisters. He certainly wasn't our favorite uncle.

We attended the funeral Mass at the little church in Big River, and then we had a ceremony at the gravesite behind the church. My brothers and I cried and we were quite saddened as they lowered our dad's body into the grave. I think it was so hard for us, because we were so young, and that our dad wasn't very old. We weren't aware that he had been in the process of dying for any length of time, and I don't know if one can really prepare for such a thing but it did seem to happen quite suddenly.

I think at the time that I was feeling almost every kind of emotion. I was angry, because I even selfishly felt that it was just another time that he deserted us and that he was not going to be around again when he was needed. I even remember thinking that I would miss him, and I did a bit of reminiscing about some of the good times that we had had together with him. I felt an awful lot of guilt about our last telephone conversation. I was feeling some relief too, because I now had none of his expectations to live up to. He made me feel so often that because of the choices I was making that I was just another one of those great disappointments to him.

My dad did not have a very satisfying life on this earth, and it was certainly filled with a tremendous amount of tragedy and disillusionment. He was always optimistic enough to think that things were going to improve. He always believed that his next job was going to be the right one, and it was going to be much better than the last one he had, so he constantly continued on his search. I don't think that he ever truly adapted to performing the non physical work that he had been forced to do as a result of his fall in the ship yards.

I just have to think that my dad was going to be better off now and that he no longer had to look for that something better. He has now truly found a peace that he never seemed to have been able to enjoy in life. I also must think like a proper Irishman and that "death *is* a promotion." I do believe that our father lived his life the best he knew how. Although he may have been lacking in some skills, I think that he did as well as he could.

My father's death did put another detour in my life's path, so my plans for my future would have to be altered. I realized that I would never be able to afford to go to that art school now. Although going to college some day was still in my plans, I would have to go about doing things differently in order to afford the costs. So it was just then that I decided that I would go into military service in order to take advantage of the G.I. Bill to help pay for my college education when I get out.

The case that had been initiated by my father against Dr. Vogel would never appear before the Minnesota Supreme Court because of my father's death before it was scheduled to be heard. All of the charges that were brought against that doctor would later be dropped at the request made by my mother. She had always considered it just a form of revenge and it could never put things right so she wanted no part of it.

A short time after our dad's funeral, I went to Minneapolis to take the tests and the physical examination to join the Air Force. I wasn't worried about giving the needed background information or taking any of the written tests, but I was extremely concerned about passing the physical. I had pretty much got used to the strange remarks about my heart whenever doctors examined me in the past. I would always reply to them, "That is just the way it is. It has always been like that."

I had, as long as I can remember, an enlarged heart with a severe murmur; and I also heard one doctor refer to it as an arrhythmic heart. The pulse rate, even at rest, was always extremely fast also. I did get a bit of a scare when the examining doctor questioned me at length about my heart and whether I ever had rheumatic fever sometime in my life. Even though it made me think about it, I wasn't going to mention that my half-brother Bobby had severe health problems resulting from rheumatic fever. As a result of that physical, I was finally going back home to Dorothy's without knowing if I had been accepted into the Air Force.

I had made the decision to join the Air Force instead of one of the other branches of service, because I always had a keen interest in airplanes. I was always intrigued with the idea of traveling from place to place with the speed that was only possible by air. I also thought that I would have more opportunities to get a job that would be similar to some civilian occupation that would be available to me after I got out of the service. I also had it in my mind to join one of the other services if I wasn't accepted, but getting the benefits of the G I Bill was still the most important thing to me.

It was during the time that I was staying at Dorothy's that I decided to get myself a driver's license, since she had allowed me to drive her car whenever I wanted. I drove into the city of Elsworth, Wisconsin, and went to the police station and told the policeman that I wanted to apply for a driver's license. I only had to wait for a few minutes for the secretary to type it up. The Policeman gave me a prepared license with my name on it. It seemed strange to me that all I had to do was sign it.

I asked the policeman, who I then found out was the chief of police, if I didn't have to take some kind of a driver's test first. His answer to my question was, "Hell no. I already know how you drive." So I got that Wisconsin driver's license without ever taking any test. I used that license to get another license in Nebraska, and that would lead me to getting licenses in three other states without ever taking a written or driving test.

I told my brother Tom about my experience with getting my license, and I told him that I didn't see how that policeman would have known how I drove. He told me that I probably never recognized when he might be around because he drove a green Mercury instead of the usual marked "Police" car.

I would have to wait for more than a month and a half before I finally received notice that I had been accepted into the Air Force. During that time, my Aunt Dorothy was kind enough to let me stay there, but I was quickly running out of money. I was also informed that I should report to Minneapolis to receive my orders to be sent from there to a basic training camp in California on the first of November.

During the last year I had started **taking over command** of my life and I had a destination clearly in mind, but I had no control over the events that might prevent me from charting that course. It was a big decision for me to make, but the character traits that I always seemed to possess in abundance were hope for the future and enough drive to do something to direct my destiny in what ever direction I was being led. I was now looking forward to the future and the hope of setting some goals and improving things for myself.

- XVI. Detour into the Skies -

It was on a very cold and snowy, first of November, when a lady friend of Dorothy's drove me to Minneapolis. Last September, after signing up, I was anxious to go, but now as I was actually leaving, I felt more than just a bit of anxiety. I would be traveling by railroad all the way to San Francisco, California to begin a new way of life for the four year duration that I had signed for with the United States Air Force.

At first the trip had been quite uneventful. It had been a very long and lonely trip, but that was to change. As I was looking out of the windows sometime after the train had entered the state of Colorado, I got my first sight of mountains like nothing that I had ever seen before. We made a stop in Denver and another young man was waiting at the depot and got on our train. This new passenger was heading to the same destination as I, because he had also joined the Air Force. Usually I wasn't very sociable when first meeting with strangers, but for some reason, I quickly got to know this person.

I was to soon learn that this tall man was a Blackfoot American Indian who lived near Browning Montana. His name was Frank Still

Smoking and, straight away, I liked him and I felt that his feelings for me were the same. It didn't take me any time at all before I began to feel as though I had known him for a long time as we comfortably visited with each other. We quickly became friends and the long trip was already becoming much nicer for the both of us.

Frank and I really had two good reasons to enjoy our journey out there, because each of us was now traveling with a friend and the railroad or someone had made a big mistake that was beneficial to us. We were given first class accommodations in everything, even our meals. We had a roomette to sleep in instead of the bunks. Not too often, but once in awhile, there are those rare occasions when, things really go better than what one had planed on.

The railroad furnished us with some of the best meals that I had ever eaten in my life, but there was one dinner that I will always remember. Frank and I ordered the leg of lamb, which with the rest of the meal was out of this world. I had never had so much good meat that I was expected to eat at one meal. Neither Frank nor I was able to eat all the food that had been put in front of us. We were fortunate to experience such a wonderful time during the whole trip, courtesy of the Great Northern Railroad.

It was still dark, when the train arrived, very early that morning of the second day of my trip, at the station in San Francisco. Frank and I knew that we may have to wait for a long time before someone would come and get us. Parks Air Force Base, where we were heading, was located on the other side of Oakland, so we had to wait for some transportation. The weather was damp and kind of hazy and, although nothing like Minneapolis, we were surprised at how cold that morning was. This is not what we were expecting in "sunny" California. Everything just seemed so dark and gloomy, which seemed to affect the way we felt.

I think that the weather was having the most adverse affect on Frank, when he commented about the nice meals we had on the train and he compared that to how they always gave a condemned man a good meal. He had already begun talking about how homesick he was and how he missed his mother, father and the horses that they raised. After we had been waiting there for a couple of hours three other guys who seemed quite friendly arrived at the same station. They saw us and asked us where we were going and it was just our luck that they had signed up for the Air Force. They now joined us in our long wait. Having all five of us visiting and joking around together did seem to help raise Frank's spirits somewhat.

We were finally picked up by a dark blue Air Force bus and driven to our new home at the Air Training Command at Parks Air Force Base. That was going to be our new home, and we were going to be spending the next three months there. It was called basic training although by the time I completed my stay there I could have given our stay some more appropriate names.

Frank and I had arrived at the base in total ignorance of what was to follow. First of all, November in California was a constant reminder that I wasn't back home in Minnesota or he in Montana. One couldn't help but notice things such as palm trees, the warmer weather, and lack of moisture.

When the bus dropped us off we were taken as a group, still wearing civilian clothes, towards our barracks. Approaching us from the opposite direction was a group of uniformed airmen in formation and as they passed us one of them called out to in a sing song way, "You'll be sorry."

Frank heard it as though those words were being directed to him alone. Later that same evening when we were in the barracks Frank asked me, "Did you hear what he said? You'll be sorry." I, of course, had to admit that I had. It appeared to me as though his spirit had been broken from that moment on.

I tried to console Frank when I told him, "That guy who said that was just trying to be funny. It really didn't mean anything." I didn't know what else to say and I could see that no matter what I said it wasn't having much affect on him. He had become so depressed.

In the Air Force a group that is made up of between forty-five to fifty men is called a flight. Frank and I were put together with a group of forty-six other men that came from every part of the United States. Some of them talked differently and, even though it was supposed to be English, it was hard for me to understand some of them.

There were others who, I thought, acted strangely like the young guy from Mississippi that claimed that he had never owned a pair of shoes before in his life. He was so proud of the ones that were issued to him, that he even wore his brogans when he went to bed at night. However, it was Frank that was worrying me, because it seemed that he continued to be so depressed, so I tried my best to cheer him up.

Our basic training had now started for real, on the fourth of November. Within a couple of days, after we got to the base, Frank and I made friends with another guy by the name of Jose' LosBanjos. Jose' had just arrived a couple of days before from his home in the Philippines. The three of us really became the best of buddies and during our small amount of free time we went everywhere and did almost everything together. We talked about it and we made the decision that we were going to help each other make the best of our stay here. We were determined to get some enjoyment out of this way of life. I still had a strong feeling that Frank would remain the weak link in this agreement and that it would be a real challenge for Jose and me to keep Frank in good spirits.

We were going to receive $72 a month and we were given the rank of airman basic. On that first day some guy with two stripes started barking a lot of commands at us and began marching us all about the base in our civilian clothes. Then we each were given an eight digit Air Force I.D. (identification) number which I would remember for the rest of my life. We each received one half of our first month's pay.

We were marched to the base commissary where we were issued our clothing. That clothing consisted of; five pairs of one piece fatigues, two sets of dress blues, with slacks, shirts, ties, a hat, Ike jacket and a parade jacket, five sets of khaki shirts and pants, a fatigue jacket, a cap, two pairs of brogans (high top shoes), one pair of dress shoes, several pairs of black socks, six tee shirts, six pairs of boxer shorts, and even some towels. Finally we were each given a white duffle bag, which would require more than a bit of a struggle if it was to hold all of our newly acquired possessions.

We were then marched back to the barracks and told to put on a pair of fatigues and brogans. It seems that I was luckier than many others, because everything that was issued to me really fit quite well. I could wear everything that was given to me, with only one exception. I refused to wear their boxer style shorts, so I would have to buy my own jockey type underwear at the B.X. (Base Exchange).

Our next trip took us to another building to pick up our bedding consisting of two sheets, pillow, pillow case, two blue wool blankets, and a foot locker. We stuffed everything inside of the foot locker and took them back to the barracks.

From there we were marched over to a small store to purchase our necessities, such as cigarettes, soap, tooth brush and paste, shaving needs, deodorant, shampoo, and hair dressing. We also bought stationary, envelopes, stamps, pens, and pencils so that our war stories could be sent back home.

We were marched over to our barracks, to be furnished with our sleeping quarters. We each claimed a cot, deciding whether one wanted to sleep on the top or the bottom (I always chose a bottom bunk). We were instructed the only way to make the bed and how everything else must be arranged. We were now able to put everything, which we had just received, away.

I knew that I wasn't going to like our next little journey which would take us to the base barber shop where we would receive our first hair cut. We at least didn't have to pay for it, but I felt that it should have been free because it took only about four minutes for the complete cut. When I walked in my hair was a neatly combed 10 inches long. I came out like all the others, shaved almost to the scalp and I wouldn't need a comb for some time.

All of the barracks were identical large two story wood frame buildings and neatly lined in rows. Each one of the barracks had three main rooms on each floor. The large room at each end was for a bedroom, lined with two rows of bunk beds stacked two high for sleeping. Against the wall at the head of your bunk, was a metal locker with just enough room to hang your clothes in. All of your remaining possessions were kept neatly in a foot locker at the foot of your bed which you kept padlocked.

Separating the two rooms for sleeping was another large room that was furnished with a television and some chairs. The T.V. spent most its time as just a decoration, because we rarely were given any chance to watch it. For some illogical reason that center room was called a day room, but it only got some use at night and then it was for a mandatory meeting where all of the residents received a lecture that was considered important.

Everything had to be fastidiously clean and tidy with everything arranged just so, because we were subject to their incessant unannounced white glove inspections. Our shoes had to be polished to such a shine that when you looked at them you were able to see your face reflecting back. Our uniforms had to be worn cleaned, pressed, and in just a certain way. When your bunk was made, the blankets had to be tucked in so tight that it would enable a quarter to bounce up a certain distance when it was dropped onto your bed. We had to scrub, wax, and polish their maroon tile floors so that in the dark, if you would shine a flashlight towards it, the beam had to reflect brightly onto the ceiling.

Three times a day, we waited in long lines, at the big mess halls, to receive food that was completely lacking in imagination and sometimes it appeared to be unappealing to both your eyes and your taste. You didn't have any choice, so you ate it because you were hungry.

If the food wasn't enough to complain about, you soon learned the meaning of "R.H.I.P— privileges, because now you had to call everyone "sir," that was one rating above you. Since you were of the lowest rank, which included an awful lot of other people, you seemed to be addressing everyone as "sir." If, heaven forbid, you should happen make some kind of a mistake, of any kind, the answer that was expected from you was to come to attention and say, "No excuse, sir!' It didn't matter if there might have been some good reason for the error.

Probably one of the activities that I disliked the most about basic training was constantly being herded about, in the hottest part of the day, in our uniform of the day which was usually our one piece fatigues.

We were always marching in cadence, from place to place and looking forward, with great anticipation, to an occasional smoke break. They made sure that things were just bad enough that those breaks became a real special treat. At least that treat wasn't very expensive because, cigarettes cost us only $1 a carton at the B.X. When we got our break, the T.I. (Technical Instructor) would tell us that the smoking lamp was lit and almost everyone, including myself, would light up. When we finished smoking we were required to field strip the cigarette which meant that we had to tear paper from it and let the tobacco fall. We then would wad up the paper along with the filter and put it into our pockets.

Those few who didn't smoke were inflicted with the privilege of taking in breaths of everyone else's cigarette smoke. If you weren't a smoker when you went into the service, you more than likely would soon become one. Conversing and smoking were the only two things that you were allowed to do during those frequent but brief intermissions.

There were some, of the men, who found it to their benefit having this military routine and they seemed to enjoy it all. Frank and I really never fully adapted too well to the living conditions on this base. Along with Jose, the three of us stayed together constantly or, at least, as much as we were permitted. Frank could play the harmonica quite well. In the evenings Jose and I would sit with him as he would play it, but he would always play such sad songs. He could even make that instrument sound as though it was crying. There were many times that he was feeling really down and he would even cry. During some of those times, Jose and I felt so inadequate in trying to cheer him up, but we continued trying.

Frank had never been away from his family or his home before so, I think, that he was suffering a lot from homesickness. I think that it was so much easier for me because, the life that I had become used to as a boy sort of prepared me for dealing with this type of existence. I was never bothered very much with getting homesick, although I did miss my freedom. Frank and I were both quite sad at times and we would try to support each other, but I spent much more time trying to console him. I was to find out later, that things really were to be much more difficult for Frank than anything I might have suffered.

Early on in our training, we spent a lot of time being marched to our classrooms to receive training on various subjects. I remember one of those times when we were being shown what they called "training" movies on sex and related diseases. Frank and I were so naive and we certainly were deficient in knowledge of matters dealing with that sort of thing.

One of the movies, that we were shown, was about homosexuals and neither Frank nor I had ever before heard about such things. We did as we were told and like all of the others we just paid attention, but we couldn't believe it, much less understand it. I remember as we were watching one particular film on homosexuals and as if on cue, we both turned to each other and we asked, at the same time, "How do they do it?" And then we both had to laugh about that. So much of what we were being shown gave our imaginations some exercise, but it seemed to be so preposterous to us. I guess in some ways we were just too immature and lacking in experience to really deal with it all.

On November 15, 1954 after being on base for only 11 days, I was notified by my T. I. that I had to report to the base hospital. I, of course, wanted to know why. It seemed as though "why" is a word that you are not supposed to use in the service, at least not in basic training, because the T. I. said that I was just supposed to go and that I didn't need to know why. I went as I had been ordered, but it bothered me that I still didn't know a reason.

I got to the hospital at the appointed time and, of course, I asked that question and the receptionist wouldn't give me an answer either, instead he just told me to have a seat and wait. I finally ended up spending a lot of time in the waiting room without any reading material so all that was left to me was to worry. I still wasn't given any explanation as to why I was there and the longer I sat the more it was beginning to bother me.

Finally, I was sent in to see a doctor who immediately began by having me sit down and putting a stethoscope to my chest. He was obviously checking my heart murmur, because he began questioning me about it. I thought that I had completed that entire bit, during the physical examination that they gave me in Minneapolis. After the doctor checked me, he started to ask me the very same questions that I was asked back at the Recruiting Center. I also had the same answers to give him. He wanted to know if I ever had rheumatic fever and I told him that I didn't. He asked me again and after receiving another negative response from me, it seemed as though he still didn't believe me and I thought that he would finally just give up and send me back to my flight.

I wasn't going to be that lucky. He then had me sent, of all places, to a psychiatrist who questioned me further. I knew that I wasn't being sent to him because they thought I had some mental problem, but I supposed that they thought that he would be able to tell, with a different line of questioning, if I had been telling them the truth. The psychiatrist kept asking me a lot of questions. I noticed that he repeated several of the same questions, but he phrased them in different ways. He even asked me many questions, which I didn't expect, about my mother and father. He even asked me about my brothers and if they had any physical problems. He even asked me if I liked going to school. Afterwards, he had more questions about my heart and especially about having rheumatic fever. After his interrogation, it appeared to me that he still didn't seem to be satisfied with the answers that I gave him. It eventually seemed to me that he had just given up or maybe he just ran out of questions. Without any further explanation he finally sent me to yet another doctor.

The third doctor I had to see started out by taking my pulse and listening to my heart. I was now beginning to worry that all of this may lead to my discharge from the Air Force. I always knew that my heart sounded funny, but I felt all of this was needless because it seemed that my heart was doing what it was supposed to and it had been serving me quite well. That doctor then had me jump around on one leg and then he listened to my heart again. He had me sit awhile and he checked my heart again. He questioned me about my heart and about the possibility of having rheumatic fever at some time in my life. He also asked me if I had occasional spells of dizziness. I was getting rather tired of all the questioning and I gave him the same answers that I told to the other two doctors. I finally emphatically stated, "I know for sure that I never had rheumatic fever." After some more checks and just a few more questions, he did finally quit and I thought I was done.

I was wrong because that last doctor had me sent to another room, where a nurse told me that I was going to be given an electrocardiogram. I had to lie down on a bed with the top part of my fatigues and my t-shirt off. I even had to take my shoes and socks off. The nurse put some gel on different parts of my body, including my head, chest, hands, and even on my feet. Then he put shiny metal things with wires attached to them on the places that he had put the gel. The wires went to some sort of an apparatus with meters and lights. He turned it on and strip of paper that was a little more than an inch wide started to come out of one end with jagged lines that were suppose to be the shape of my heart's beating.

When they were finished with the tests, they had the printout of my heart. Then several two an on-half inch pieces were cut from different intervals along that long strip of paper and taped onto another sheet of paper with some information under each bit. Near the top of the form was written "Sinus Arrhythmia" which had no meaning to me. That whole sheet was put into a folder after it had been shown to me. As the nurse was explaining it to me, my eyes had wandered to the bottom of the second sheet and I could clearly read that it had something there about having some restriction. I asked about the restriction. The nurse explained to me that I would be strictly limited as to the type of work I would be allowed to do while in the Air Force. He claimed, "The tests that you had been given indicate that your heart shows that it had been damage too severely."

He said that I was "restricted to ground duty." My worst fears were over because that means even though I would be given a ground job, they at least won't be discharging me from the service. I was, however, extremely disappointed, because I didn't like the fact that, I was in the Air Force and, I wouldn't be able to have a job that would require working on or even traveling by airplane.

Later on, our flight spent a few days being given all sorts of other academic tests, to determine our aptitudes and abilities. This was done so they could place us into the proper kind of training to learn some Air Force occupation. At the time I felt quite strongly about getting into the field of photography. I could see where photography was related to my strong interest in art. They had no openings in that field however, so I was given a list and an explanation about some of the other occupations that I could choose from, which was almost everything. Many of the jobs they had available were in the kinds of work that I knew nothing about. After looking over all of the possibilities, I finally decided that radio and radar might be interesting, so that is what I picked.

Within the first two weeks after arriving there, we had to be given our shots. They had shots for just about everything imaginable so there were a lot of them. One of the things about a place like the Armed Services is that they are always handling such large numbers of people, and as a result the personnel who work at processing all these people become quite expert at their occupation.

A very good example of that is when we were receiving those injections. The speed at which they could parade a line of men through their gauntlet was astounding. The men nurses who gave the shots were so good and so efficient, that they could take a syringe in each hand, take aim, and simultaneously sink both of them accurately into the bull's-eye, which was their victims shoulder. They were able to do this with the precision of a fine machine, and the only indication that they had done something to you was the two mighty sore arms afterwards.

After giving shots to the person in front of you, each of these men picked up one of these evil looking weapons in each hand. As you were proceeding through the line one of these nurses stood on each side of you while you were to become the fortunate recipient of four shots, all at one time!

When I went into the Air Force, I had just recently come off of the farm, as a hired hand. As a result, I was quite well developed physically, and especially the muscles in my arms, so they were extremely hard. Like all the other airmen, I was moving along in the line until it got to be my turn to get shots. No pretty nurses to be caring for us, these nurses were men! As had been done with everyone else in front of me, there was one man standing on each side of me anxiously waiting to make sure that I got those four shots.

They each rubbed alcohol, simultaneously, on both of my shoulders and they gave me instructions to relax my arms. I relaxed as they had advised me, but they weren't satisfied that I was, because my shoulders were still hard. Again, they impatiently reminded me to relax. I tried as much as I could to do as I was told. I then told them that I was just as relaxed as I can possibly be. With that, they gave me my shots. With the precision, of what was expected of them, the four needles entered both of my arms at about the same time.

Things were not quite right though, because one of the needles broke off in my right arm. The line came to a halt while I stood there patiently. Blood had begun running down my arm, as they were trying to remove the remaining piece of the needle. The broken end was flush with the skin surface, so they were unable to get a grip on it. As I waited one of the nurses went to get something. I along with the others behind me continued to wait until that nurse finally returned with what looked like a silver colored pliers which he called a forceps. Even though the broken needle was hardly visible, he pushed jaws of the forceps down hard on both sides it and then squeezing the handles together he removed the offending piece along with a small amount of my flesh. I now had a nasty gash which was bandaged to stop the bleeding. The delay, while they were extracting the remains of that needle, was enough time to make my arms really begin to ache terribly. To make matters even worse, after they finally got the piece out, I had to have that same shot given to me again.

When they had finally finished their torture my arms by this time hurt so much, that pain had rendered them almost immobile. I tried, but I was completely unable to get my arms into the sleeves and pull the top part of my one piece fatigues over my shoulders. It was quite obvious that the two nurses weren't going to offer me any help as they were already attacking their next victims. Thankfully a sergeant, who had been sitting at the desk, had observed everything that had been occurring in front of him and he took pity on me. I thought that he was awfully kind to leave his desk and assist me at getting the rest of my clothes on.

A few days later one of the squad leaders decided that he was going to bully me around a bit. I wasn't in his squad and I refused to let him push me around, so what started as pushing each other around turned into a fight. He was much bigger than I but he really turned out to be no match and I quite easily beat him up quite badly. He begged me to release him after I had his back bent across a foot locker. I don't remember anymore what it was that caused the fight except that, in his anger and embarrassment, the squad leader reported me to the T. I.

The T. I. immediately sought me out and ordered me to get a pail, some soap, and a scrub brush. He then assigned me the job of scrubbing one set of the stairs as my punishment. I was supposed to scrub, as he had said, *"Until those stairs are so clean that they turn completely white!"* The stairs had been painted a dark gray, so I knew that I would have to scrub for a long time. Knowing that I had been given an impossible assignment, I thanked him and I started straightaway working on my penalty.

As soon as my friend, Jose, saw what I had to do, he went to the T. I., on my behalf. He went in to argue my case with him, that he thought that I had been wronged. Jose said, "I saw everything that happened and it was the squad leader that had started that fight with Roi so he shouldn't be punished for it"

After Jose had completed his complaining to the T. I., that T. I. decided that he would punish Jose for, as he called it, "questioning my authority." For his punishment, Jose had to scrub the other set of stairs with the same conditions that were given me. Without any further complaining Jose got his bucket, soap, and brush and went about his nasty job. We worked at that job, during our off duty hours, for several days after.

Finally one day the T. I., when in one of his kinder moods, told Jose and me that we could quit. We certainly did get the stairs spotlessly clean, but not one of those steps ever became significantly less gray. I don't think that it was any coincidence that Jose and I were the only ones from our flight that had been assigned K. P. during both of the holidays of Christmas and New Year's Day. It was quite obvious why but neither one of us felt it would do any good to complain.

They seemed to be saving the best, of the basic training for us, as a kind of Christmas present. We were unfortunate to be spending almost the whole week before Christmas on bivouac, where you are required to sleep out in a tent and do other nasty things to simulate combat conditions. It may not have been planned that way, but as some of the activities turned out for us, they would have stirred the imagination of the Marquis DeSade.

That first evening we were given what they called a "night problem," for which they dramatically told us the importance of our mission and then we were given our instructions. I was on the team that had to crawl, in total darkness, through tall wet grass to capture a well guarded outpost without being detected. We were sent out after being shown, on a map, where the goal was located. We did successfully complete our objective, but when we had finished, everyone was very wet and trembling from the cold.

From the very beginning, things had started out badly for us. We were beginning that night chilled to the bone and then we were given some more bad news. Because there was some mix-up, and we didn't get any poles for our tents, so naturally, we were forced to lie on the ground with the tent draped over us like another blanket. The ground was wet and very cold and even though there was no snow, the San Francisco area can get mighty chilling at night in late December.

Our sleeping bags were made out of two blankets, which were folded and snapped together between a folded up poncho. Everyone remained cold during the night making it almost impossible to get much sleep. Another problem is that when you are cold, you seem to have to urinate more often and we could only do that in designated places. For most of the night there were men roaming around with a flashlight to find there way to the latrines in the darkness. Everybody was shivering and some were wearing nothing but their underwear. Those who slept with all of their clothes on had a problem with the cold the next morning because their clothes didn't have any chance to dry out.

On the second day we were given a special canvass bag that contained a gas mask for us to wear. We were given instructions on how to use it and we practiced taking it out and covering our faces with it. We were then taken to a small building situated on top of a hill. After we were all inside we were ordered to arranged ourselves into our neat rows as tear gas came pouring in around us. During this time we had to sing the song, "Rudolf the Red Nosed Reindeer," while we were standing there with our noses itching and tears streaming down our cheeks. The song was quite appropriate because our noses were running and they did get red. After that we were lead outside to face into the wind to clear out our eyes. It would have been quite natural to rub your eyes, because they itched, burned, and watered. We were given instructions to be extremely careful not to rub our eyes, or suffer the consequences of temporary blindness that could last for several days.

We had no sooner cleared our eyes somewhat when we were marched back inside and again we stood in our neat formation. This time we were to practice using our masks. After we waited for a few minutes, someone shouted, "*Gas!*" And obediently everyone quickly removed their helmets and we slapped them quickly down to be held between our legs. I stood in the front row and I could hear somewhere behind me that a couple of helmets went tumbling to the floor. I felt sorry for those airmen that missed catching their helmets between their legs because they would not be allowed to use their mask at all. We then unsnapped the bag, took out our mask, cleared it, and put it on. We then practiced that for a few more times until we became quite proficient at it and I didn't hear any more helmets falling. I was anxious to be able to leave that building for good and breathe some real clean air.

After we had passed the tear gas test, each airman was required to march in formation on a seven mile hike carrying our M-1 carbine and a pack strapped onto his back. We were only allowed to break step when we crossed a bridge. Occasionally we were ordered to run for a short distance and then back to a march. The hike was a bit tiring and immediately upon returning from our trip, our flight had to continue on towards what looked like the entrance to a cave. The ceiling was only high enough to allow us to crawl into it.

We entered on our hands and knees as our flight, along with some other flights, had to crawl through this long low tunnel. From the moment we entered we had to move forward with our eyes closed because tear gas and smoke was being pumped in at us from the openings in round tubes that lined both sides. We were anxiously and blindly trying to make our way to the other end. The flight in front of us panicked and they started to pile up, bringing us to a complete stop in the middle. Because there was another flight coming in behind us, it was impossible for us to back out. We were trapped!

Some of the men got alarmed and did a lot of screaming and shouted things about dying. Others like me took it quite well and tried to remain calm as we just waited, but I must admit that it was quite frightening. When it was all over, more than half of the men in our flight had to be dragged from the tunnel. They were then placed into what we called the meat wagon (ambulance) and rushed to the hospital. One of the things I did observe was that it seemed that all of this bothered the larger guys the most and most of those who were hauled away were big. I wasn't one of those taken to the hospital, but I did get a bit sick, and I vomited. I had to lie down on the grass waiting for my eyes to clear and just breathe some fresh air while I was recovering. It wasn't long before I was as good as new.

During bivouac we had to eat food that was prepared from a field kitchen, which had been set up in two large tents. We were obliged to sit on the ground and eat our food out of our metal mess kits and canteens. All of this was being done with constant mix ups and the wrong amounts of the different foods were brought out and prepared for us. When we got served, we might receive double the amount that we were supposed to get of one thing and a half ration or nothing of something else. It all made for some very interesting, but not so well balanced meals. Even when everything goes well, bivouac was not intended to be an enjoyable experience. For us there were so many other things that went wrong during our encampment, that our flight was more than glad when we finally finished. It was amazing how inviting those barracks looked to us upon our return.

After we had been on the base for more than two months everyone "earned" a seventy-two hour pass to go wherever we wanted to during that time. Frank, Jose, and I were very anxious to get away from that base, so we decided to use those passes spending our time in San Francisco together.

That same dark blue Air Force bus, that brought us to our first day on the base, was now taking us back to San Francisco. The first thing Frank, Jose, and I did was to get ourselves a place to stay for the night. We got two rooms, one single and one double, on the third floor of an old brick hotel. The main thing is that it fulfilled all of our requirements. The rooms were decent and it was cheap.

It was so exciting to be getting away from that base, and we were anxious to see as much of this big city as we could. There was no logic in what we did next as we found ourselves a bar, where we could each have a beer. We were then prepared for our tour of the city as we walked on through the streets looking at everything as we went. We interrupted our walk just long enough to take a short intermission to eat a nice dinner in Chinatown.

We continued on, and the three of us had walked and talked for more than an hour. Frank seemed strangely quiet so we hadn't noticed exactly when it was that Frank was no longer with us. It seemed as though he had just vanished and we had no idea where he was and I immediately became afraid for him. Jose and I stopped and looked around as we tried to catch some sight of Frank in amongst all the other people. We then started back the way that we had come. We had only gone back about a one-half block distance when we met Frank as he was coming out of the entry way of one of San Francisco's many small diagonal shaped magazine shops. I asked him where he was and what he had been doing. Instead of answering, he showed me a brown sack and pull out the pint of whiskey that he had bought. Looking at Jose, I could see from his expression that he was just as disgusted as I about that. I then told him that the next time he had intentions to go off on some excursion on his own that he should let us know first.

We continued walking along and Frank would every so often furtively expose the top part of the bottle from the paper sack and take a quick drink. It didn't seem to take him very much time before he was handing me the bottle, and he asked me to put it under a parked car. He had already drunk the whole thing!

I was really surprised that Frank had finished the bottle so quickly, but then again I wasn't, because his personality had made a fairly rapid change and I wasn't sure it was for the worse. From the time that we got to the city Frank was his usual self and quite withdrawn and didn't talk much, but that is just what we had come to expect from him, but now he had started chattering a lot of nonsense and his speech had become slurred. The three of us just continued walking along for a little more than a half hour with Frank entertaining us with stories about his life on his father's small ranch in Montana. It was all really quite interesting but he was now telling us about things that I don't think he ever told anyone else before.

It was kind of nice to hear Frank talking a bit about his life before the Air Force but he then, for no obvious reason, he just suddenly turned quiet again. Jose and I picked up the conversation. Walking along that way we didn't notice when Frank had disappeared once again into another one of those magazine shops. As Jose and I waited for Frank and as we expected, Frank came out with another bottle. This time his brown sack was a bit larger and it contained a fifth of whiskey! Frank was quite close to what one would consider being drunk, and he surely didn't need anymore of that stuff. I was now becoming really worried about him, but I also knew that there was just no way that we would be able to stop him. Jose just seemed to accept everything as it was happening and said nothing.

The time past quickly and it became about the same time of day that we would be eating our last meal of the day on the base. Our stomachs had become used to getting hungry at that time so we were now ready to eat our supper. We had made the decision to go to a Mexican restaurant, because Frank expressed a desire to get some tortillas which, he said, were similar to flat bread that the Indians made where he came from.

We sat in a booth while Jose and I had a meal, and Frank just wanted an order of tortillas. We were talking as we ate our food. Jose and I humored Frank when he would stop eating long enough to take a drink from his bottle. Frank after taking his drink would hold the bottle out towards Jose or me and say, "*When I drink, everyone drinks!*" Jose or I would take the bottle and we would reluctantly take our turns at having a small sip of the strong liquid, but Frank was doing all of the real drinking.

When we had finished eating, Frank, like us, had to pay his bill. Because he only got the tortillas his share was less than a dollar. That's why I couldn't understand the reason Frank took off his shoe and removed a twenty dollar bill that he had hidden there to pay that small amount, because I knew that wasn't the only money he had. He then put his shoe back on before he had received the change.

By the time we left the cafe it had turned dark and the city was showing us some beauty that was quite different from what it was in the daylight. The streets were lined on both sides with lights and the different stores had their colored neon lights and the three of us just started walking aimlessly down the streets. We had plenty of time with nothing to do but take in the sights and look in every shop window.

As we continued on, Frank was becoming more and more difficult to deal with. By the time he had finished that second bottle of whiskey he was really struggling to stay on his feet. He now required our assistance just to stay upright. With Jose on one side and me on the other it had become quite burdensome for us to keep Frank moving, but he was still able to put one foot in front of the other. Traveling like this had taken the enjoyment out of the evening. Frank was no longer the friend that we had started out with and there was just no enjoyment continuing our sight seeing. It had become very tiring to go on this way so Jose and I decided that the evening was over for us and we would just take ourselves to the hotel for the night.

We had gone for several of blocks, when Frank without any warning refused to move any farther. We were forced to stop and then Frank violently pulled away from Jose and me. Frank then backed up against a store, and he leaned against the building we happened to be next to. He had managed to quickly kick off one of his shoes was able to take off one stocking, and had removed the other shoe before he fell forward into my arms as I prevented him from falling. I just had to ask him, "Frank, what in the world are you doing?"

Scarcely able to create some intelligible speech, he was barely able to make me understand what he was doing. I listened carefully to his mumbling and he was explaining to me that he had put twenty dollars in his shoe, when he left the base. I could understand his words quite clearly when he said, "It's gone. I can't find it." He seemed quite angry as he repeated, "It's gone! I can't find my money."

It was obvious that Frank was now really drunk, and without the building behind him and me pushing from the front he would surely have fallen down. Because, I had observed him taking the money from his shoe to pay his bill at the cafe, I also knew that he had his shoe on when he received the change. Therefore, the money just had to be in one of his pockets. I was able to restrain him from falling forward, by pushing my body up against him as he meekly allowed me to search through his pockets. I found the money lying loose in the back pocket of his slacks. I removed the money from that pocket and I showed it to him, but I don't think he was even able to realize the significance of it. I unsnapped the flap over the pocket of his "Ike" jacket and put all of the nineteen dollars and some change in there. I made sure that both snaps were made secure. Frank also had a dollar and some change in one of his front pants pockets, but I left that where it was.

During the whole process, I was a bit concerned about the scene that we must have created for some unknowing passerby or worse yet the police. With the money taken care of, Jose and I helped Frank move over to a nearby building which had a set of outside stairs where we would be able to get Frank to sit down. Frank couldn't even do that without our assistance. I felt that this was the only way that we would be able to help Frank put his shoes and socks back on. With this accomplished, Jose and I had more than enough of this so that now all we wanted was nothing more than to reach our hotel as soon as possible.

Progress was slow as Jose' and I were half carrying and half dragging Frank through the city streets. Then, in spite of his extreme shyness, did something I would never have expected from him. He made us stop as he unzipped his pants and then urinated right there on the sidewalk. We then proceeded slowly but we had to stop a few times along the way to rest a bit before going on until we finally, after a few wrong turns, found our way back to the hotel, where we had reserved the two rooms earlier.

We struggled up the front steps to the lobby where we were compelled to take a short rest. Our sleeping arrangements had been decided earlier when we got the rooms. After a couple of tosses of a coin, it was decided that the double room, was going to be for Jose and Frank. I was feeling quite lucky to have won the single room for myself because now I didn't think Frank would make a very nice bed mate.

Jose and I really had an enormous task as we struggled up one stair at a time to the entry of the hotel. The real job lay ahead of us after entering the lobby. We mostly carried Frank slowly up the two flights of stairs until we finally reached the third floor. When we got to the double room we took off Frank's jacket and then we laid his limp body on the bed and pulled off his shoes and socks. I figured that he would be like that for the night. I was tired, so with that done I went straight away to my room and immediately got ready for bed.

I was in bed for no more than a few minutes, but I had almost fallen asleep, when I was suddenly interrupted by Jose's pounding on my door. It startled me and I became wide awake immediately. I was in my underwear bottoms as I got up and I opened the door, for the very excited Jose. He started talking so fast, that with his accent I could hardly understand him, but he said something that sounded like, Frank was going crazy. I could also make out quite clearly that Jose was afraid of him. As soon as he told me that, I knew that the alcohol was having a terrible effect on Frank and it was also quite obvious that he was no longer lying on the bed where I had left him.

Why couldn't he have passed out like any "normal" drunk? Frank was definitely not his normal self so I really didn't know what to expect. Worst of all, the only place left for me to sleep in was the bedroom that Frank was now occupying. I quickly pulled my pants and tee shirt on and I told Jose to stay in my room. I also instructed him to lock the door and go to bed. I said that I would take care of Frank even though I wasn't certain how I would accomplish this. I really wasn't feeling that sure of myself and I was without any plan of action. I also realized that it was now up to me to do something to control Frank's behavior and keep him out of some serious trouble.

I left what had been the quiet safety of my room and hurriedly ran barefooted down the hall to the other room. Just as I was rounding my way through the doorway, I was met with a bottle of after shave lotion that zoomed past my head as I ducked. The bottle crashed against the wall on the opposite side of the hallway. Frank had thrown that bottle with enough force to make a hole in the plaster where it struck the wall.

Even though Frank was quite a bit bigger than I, there just had to be something that I could do to stop him. I immediately realized that I needed to act quickly before he could grab something else to throw at me. I rushed into the room as fast as I was able and with all of the momentum, created by my running, I was able to easily push Frank backwards onto the bed and I landed on top of him. As he lay beneath me, I shouted to him, "Frank I'm tired! I want to go to sleep!" Then I yelled at him, "Do you understand me?" And I realized just how stupid that question was and I wasn't surprised when he never answered.

Frank had been upset and he had been crying. There were tears running down the sides of his face as he now seemed to have quickly calmed down. He then started to talk a bit in a sort of whisper but all I could understand of it was him saying, "I'm sorry." He then became awfully quiet and looked quite peaceful. Since he was now lying there quietly, I just couldn't remain on top of him all night and I was quite tired. I waited for a bit longer and then I thought that it would be safe to let him get up. I very slowly and cautiously got off of him as I continued to suspiciously watch his every move.

Not making any sound, Frank sat up on the bed and he quite calmly took off his shirt. It certainly appeared to me that he was now getting ready for bed, but was I ever wrong. Instead of taking off his pants, and getting in bed, he got up and went running out of the room. I thought maybe he was just anxious to get to the toilet so I didn't bother to follow him. I thought that he would probably be heaving up some of that whiskey. The bathroom was only a short way down the hall.

I sat and waited for a few minutes and when I thought that he had enough time to get back, I set out to look for him. I had my pants and tee shirt on but I was barefooted as I walked down the hallway and then found that no one was in the bathroom. I next went down the two flights of stairs, and into the empty hotel lobby. From there I even went to the front door, walked outside and down the outside steps. I stood on the walk and looked both ways as far as I could see. I finally gave up and went back upstairs and knocked on Jose's door, but he must have been sound asleep because there was no answer and I didn't persist.

I was now quite worried about Frank. I couldn't find him anywhere, so I sadly went back to our room. I left the door unlocked for him. I went to bed, but even though I was tired, I couldn't push my concern for Frank from my mind. It took me what seemed a long time before I finally fell asleep.

At about two-thirty in the morning I was awakened, quite suddenly, by loud knocking and shouting, "Open up! It's the police!" Just hearing their loud barking gave me quite a start. My imagination was racing through all kinds of possibilities that would have brought them to our room. Frank was in every thought and none of it was good. I quickly got out of my bed, and went to the door wearing only my underwear bottoms. Before I was able to get to the door, they shouted again. I opened the door and two uniformed San Francisco Policemen were standing there, looking quite serious. One of them asked me if I had a friend named Frank Still Smoking.

As the most frightening thoughts ran through my mind, that something disastrous might have happened to Frank, I replied, "Yes, he's my friend. Why?"

One of the policemen told me, "You'd better get some clothes on."

I asked, "Is Frank all right?"

Neither policeman answered my question and just told me, "Get your clothes on and follow us downstairs."

All kinds of thoughts were racing through my mind as I quickly pulled on my t-shirt and pants. I had even imagined that I was going to be shown a corpse of my friend and that I was just being called on to identify him. My socks and shoes were still in the room with Jose. Barefooted, I followed the policemen down the stairs to the lobby three floors below. I immediately noticed Frank, with a very peculiar look on his face, just standing there barefooted in just his tee shirt, and slacks. I thought that he looked sort of stupid except he seemed to be all right apart from what looked like a big bandage wrapped around the upper part of one arm. Besides the two policemen, the room appeared well occupied this time with two Shore Patrolmen and five soldiers from Fort Ord. Everyone was in close proximity with Frank so I assumed they had something to do with what happened.

One of the two San Francisco policemen began telling me, straight away, about how they had interpreted what had happened after they had examined the window in the hotel. They told me that Frank must have left his room, went down the hallway, and proceeded down the half flight of stairs. From that landing he dived right through the window, where he luckily landed on the first story marquee where he then slid to the sidewalk below. I was standing there and listening, but I was sort of dumbfounded by what I was hearing.

At this point, one of the two shore patrolmen explained to me that they had observed the bazaar scene as it happened and they started after Frank as soon as he had landed onto the sidewalk. Frank immediately started running through the city streets in his bare feet with the two shore patrolmen in pursuit. That shore patrolman also told me the two policemen and eventually the five soldiers joined in on the chase. He said, "It took all nine of us to finally get Frank cornered."

At this point they made me understand that the two San Francisco Policemen will be taking charge of this. The policemen seemed to quite understand about servicemen on pass. He also told me that after Frank was caught he didn't resist at all. He came quietly with them and they did not even have to handcuff him. The Policeman then told me that neither they nor the hotel would be filing charges against him, but he did concede that Frank would probably have to pay for the broken window.

The other San Francisco policemen turned to me and asked, "If we let Frank go, can you see to it that he doesn't get any more to drink and that he gets to bed?"

I hesitated a bit before I replied with, "I think I can."

I believe that the other policeman sensed the lack of confidence in my answer when he said, "I think that it might be better if we just take Frank, downtown and put him in jail for the rest of the night.

It will keep Frank from doing anything crazy and it will give him a chance to sleep it off." He also said that I should be ready to let him in the room when they would be sending him back to the hotel in the morning.

It was such a relief to know that Frank was being taken care of. I was quite happy when I was finally allowed to go back upstairs to a bed that still had some hours of sleep in it for me. I anxiously crawled in and fell right to sleep.

It seemed as though I had just gone to bed, when my sleep was suddenly interrupted with the phone on the wall ringing at about 6:30 a.m. I had to get out of bed and walk across the room to answer it. The call was from the main desk with the message that my friend, Frank, was back and they were now sending him up to the room. I answered that it was no problem, but I thought to myself, "Why did they have to send him back so early?"

Frank sheepishly entered the room and I could see that he had sobered up and it was so good to see that he was his normal quiet self again. All I said to him was, "Let's get to bed. I'm tired." Without a word he took off his slacks and we both crawled into bed. I think that he fell asleep almost immediately and I don't remember much afterwards. We didn't awaken until almost 11 o'clock.

Jose had put my shoes, socks, shirt, and jacket in our room as we slept. Frank and I got dressed and met Jose where he had been waiting a long time in the lobby for us. Noticing the big bandage that was wrapped around Frank's forearm, Jose wanted to know why. He was also curious to know why we got up so late. I told him that Frank and I had a restless night of it and that I would have to tell him all about it later, because Frank seemed to have no idea about what took place during those early morning hours.

Jose wasn't aware of anything that took place, during his sleep but seeing the big bandage on Frank's arm had made him curious. He insisted that we should tell him about it and so I told Frank to tell him what happened and all that Frank said was, "I don't remember anything." I then started explaining in great detail what had been told to me by the police and the shore patrol men. Frank seemed to be surprised when I told him that he got his cut from diving through the window and how lucky he was to have landed on the marquee. The three of us then left the hotel as we continued our walking tour of San Francisco.

After walking for awhile and as I was telling Jose more about what had happened while he slept, we saw a sign that said, ***"Plane Rides - Only Eight Dollars!"***

Both Frank and Jose showed a lot of excitement about the possibility of going for a ride. I really felt that I couldn't afford to spend any more of my money. Frank then sadly told Jose, "You'll have to go without me."

I asked Frank, "If you want to, why aren't you going with Jose?"

He replied, "The police took away all the money I had left to pay for the broken window at the hotel."

Knowing that during his escapades last night, Frank did not have his Ike jacket on. I told him to look in his jacket pocket. He unsnapped the pocket and was he surprised to find more than nineteen dollars there. Of course, he wanted to know why, and I told him how that had happened last night. After my explanation, he just couldn't seem to thank me enough.

Frank and Jose got their plane rides. The hotel got just one dollar and a small bit of change for their broken window, and I know that they certainly would have taken a lot more if they could have found more money on Frank. We ended our time together with quite an experience for us to remember and also some material for me to later write about.

Everything did come out right enough, and that first night of our seventy-two hour pass was really an adventure for Frank and me anyway. By the way, Frank only received a long, but not serious, cut on one arm for his unorthodox exit from the hotel. That arm had been well cared for before he came back to the hotel that morning.

That second evening we experienced nothing more exciting than a movie and since we had already paid for them we stayed at the same hotel for that night too. I also got to sleep alone as we had planned the first night.

The next day was spent mostly in sight seeing and doing such things as riding their cable car. Actually that last day turned out to be quite peaceful and wonderfully boring. When it was all over and our pass was up, the three of us went back to the base in the same bus that had brought us there, three days before.

We had to finish our training, which was ending in the first week of February. My friend, Frank never did make it all the way to the end. Frank had told me that his father had been very sick for a long time. With less then two weeks left, he received information through the Red Cross that his father was not expected to live much longer. He was quickly given a discharge and he was sent home, straight away, to take care of his father and business at home. He would also be in charge of running their horse ranch. I missed him when he left and I will always remember him fondly. It was disappointing to have our trio broken up too soon.

Jose and I were promoted from Airman Basic to Airman Third Class when we were nearly finished with our basic training, which meant we got a small but welcomed raise in pay. I remember that Jose was sent to somewhere in England and after one letter we completely lost track of each other. I later wished that we would have kept in touch. I had the feeling that after it had all ended that in many ways basic training was beneficial for me. I received my orders to go to electronics school at Keesler Air Force Base in Mississippi.

After completing basic training everyone is given a leave of about a week to do whatever one pleased. I was taking my leave to spend that time in Wisconsin before I had to report to my next base. I really wished that there would have been more time and if I had a car I could have visited my mother in the sanatorium.

Before I left Parks Air Force Base, I was handed my orders, which was fine, but they made a mistake when they also gave me a huge envelope, that contained all of my personnel records. Those records are usually sent by mail to the next base where you will be stationed. As soon as I got away from the base and heading north toward Oregon on a Greyhound bus, I searched and read through almost everything in my records. I found the folder that contained all of the medical records, including the information about my heart and the restriction that I wouldn't be allowed to travel anywhere by plane. I was still in California, when I removed the folder containing the Electrocardiograph Record with no intention of putting it back with the rest of my records. I tore up the form that contained the information and history about my heart examinations with the restriction notice to prevent me from flying. They ended up in a trash can at the first bus stop. For some reason I decided to keep the electrocardiogram results. Even though I kept that one record with my personal possessions, I had no intention of letting anyone else at my next base see them.

I was now anxiously traveling back to see a real winter in Minnesota and Wisconsin again. I never thought that I would ever miss it and I could even think of times that I cursed the stuff, but it just didn't seem right without the snow and the cold winter weather of the north that year. I was ever so happy when that bus left California and we were somewhere in Oregon when I caught my first sight of snow. The bus made a rest stop and I just had to get out and play that lovely white stuff that I had not seen since last November when I left Minneapolis. I laid down in the snow, rolled around in it, made some snowballs to throw, ate some snow, and I even put some of it down my neck before I got back on that bus.

I spent that week of vacation, visiting with some of my relatives and my brother Tom. To conserve on my meager financial resources, I stayed at my Aunt Dorothy's place. She often allowed me use her car so I could get around a bit. I felt quite proud about being in the Air Force and I always wore my uniform everywhere that I went. The time went by quite fast and I was soon traveling by bus again on my way to my next base.

Upon leaving Wisconsin, it was an extremely long trip down the full length of Illinois that seemed to take almost forever. We were somewhere in the southern part of Illinois when I got quite tired so, I had a lie down in the very back of the bus. That seat ran the full width of the bus where I could stretch out and get more comfortable. I fell asleep, and I had been sleeping for some time, and it was about 2 o'clock in the morning, when we had just crossed over from Illinois into Kentucky.

The bus driver pulled over to the side of a completely deserted part of highway, stopped the bus, and he came to the back where I was lying. He touched me and told me to wake up. I had been sleeping soundly but I quickly awakened, and asked "What's wrong?"

I was confused because I looked out and I could tell that we were obviously in the middle of nowhere. Then he politely told me, "We have now crossed into Dixie, and you will have to get up and take another seat somewhere closer to the front part of the bus."

I knew about segregation, but this didn't make any sense to me, because I was only one of six passengers in the whole bus. Still half asleep I replied, "So what, there aren't any Negroes on this bus. It doesn't make any sense."

He then told me, "Make sense or not, it doesn't make any difference because it's the law. You've got to move towards the front." I could see that he was getting a bit irritated with me so with that I did as I was told and we continued on our way.

I was soon going to observe more about segregation in the south after riding for a few more hours, as the bus stopped again at a depot at some city in Tennessee. We were given a food and rest break and I was to get my next experience with race discrimination. I noticed, straightaway, that the bus stop was a large building which was clearly separated into two parts for eating. It was obvious that the part with the sign indicating it was to be used by whites only was also much larger, nicer and more modern than the other part. That smaller section had a sign above the entry which simply said, "Negroes."

There was something else that really caught my attention and at the time I thought it was absolutely appalling. I was standing there facing three rest rooms; one had a sign on the door that said men, another one said women, and there was a third one that said Negroes. There was also a drinking fountain that had a sign above it declaring, "Whites only!" I was already getting some real exposure to what this segregation was all about and I certainly didn't think much of it.

I finally arrived at Keesler Air Force Base which, like Parks, is another Air Training Command base. The base is located just outside of Biloxi, Mississippi, which is right on the Gulf of Mexico. It was February, but the weather was just like our warm summers in Minnesota, except the sight of palm trees and other vegetation made it quite clear that I wasn't in my more familiar north land. I would be spending my next eight months here in the Deep South, getting used to a very warm climate all year round.

The base was divided into many city blocks and each one was called a squadron. The barracks, which we had to live in, were arranged around the perimeter of that block so that they all faced towards the center of what was called the compound. At the assigned time each day, depending what shift you were on, the barracks would empty of all of their occupants and everyone would come running to that center area to assemble into a neat formation before we were marched off to school. Occasionally the compound was used for the squadron commander to make his announcements or some boring speech.

Each barracks was a two story wooden building, and instead of having a basement the foundation consisted of no more than short concrete stilts. Our sleeping quarters were in cubicles designed for two people and their possessions. Each floor of the barracks was equipped with only one huge fan, which was constantly running to cool it. Those fans weren't nearly sufficient to do the required job and many times it would be almost impossible to sleep in that very humid sweltering heat. It was quite normal to awaken each morning completely soaked with sweat. I never before took so many showers to clean my sweaty body and for that short time of relief they provided from the heat.

All of the airmen who were assigned one of the electronics' schools had to spend their first two weeks at Keesler on K.P. (kitchen police) and then they don't have to do it anymore for the rest of the time that they're stationed there. For me those two weeks seemed to take forever, working and sweating in the hot kitchens, but it was worth it, to know that you would never have to do it again during your stay. When I was on K.P., the work day was very long and extremely tedious. I think the worst jobs that one could be assigned was washing pots and pans or possibly the grease pit. At the end of the day your hands were all shriveled up and the skin would peal for a couple of days afterwards. Each day began with working at some very boring task at about 4 o'clock in the morning when it was still dark and seemed like the middle of the night. Our day would continue until sometime around 8:30 that evening. You came back to the barracks tired so you were soon in bed. We didn't have any life except that during that time. One can easily understand how happy I must have been when it was finally over and I was now going to be attending school.

With the two weeks of K. P. duty over, our daily routine completely changed to something more humane and each week day would begin the same way. We got up early each morning and we went to breakfast at the chow or mess hall. We came back to the barracks afterwards and got ready for school and leaving our building to get into formation at a certain time. They had classes divided into two shifts and I felt quite fortunate to be assigned the day shift to attend classes. We were then marched on the street about twelve blocks to the school. We moved in a very hot and sweaty parade formation, which included marching in front of a reviewing stand. It was quite uncomfortable wearing our heavily starched tan khaki's, and carrying our books. That khaki was pressed and starched so much that it seemed almost as if my clothes were made of cardboard, and I had to bend them with every step.

When we first entered the school building, it seemed too cold until we were in there awhile and got used to it. Air conditioning was quite rare back then, and I think that the schools were the only buildings on base besides the P.X., and the airmen's and officer's clubs that had it. The school was a big, white, building with a monstrous air conditioner on the roof with water constantly running down the side of it. There was not a single window in the school. Six hours each day were spent attending classes in nothing else but electronics. The training was hard, but I think it was good for me and besides I felt that it might become quite useful, for me, long after I left the Air Force. We usually had the weekends to do pretty much as we pleased.

It was also about the right time to be down there to go to the much heard about Mardi Gras celebration in New Orleans. A couple of other students from my squadron and I decided to go to New Orleans for the weekend. To save money we hitchhiked. It didn't take very long because we were quite lucky enough to make the trip as passengers in only two different cars for the total distance of about 70 miles.

I got to see probably the most colorful and largest parade that I had ever seen in my life, so that was really something special. We got to hear a lot of Dixieland jazz on Basin and Bourbon Streets. I got to see the French Quarter with the narrow streets and neat French and Spanish homes with their fancy wrought iron balconies. I did enjoy getting to see that bit of history there.

We were there at a time when people, all over the city, seemed to have really gone crazy. They were staggering, drinking, shouting, and urinating in the streets but they seemed to be enjoying themselves. Everyone seemed to be so uninhibited, and I guess they thought that it was a time and a place to let go and just have fun. It was quite an experience that I will not soon forget, but when I left I had no desire to go back there again.

In April of 1955 and about nine months after my father died, I got news that my mother got out of the sanatorium after spending more than seven long years there. This really concerned me, because it was a decision that she had made against the advice of her doctors. She told the sanatorium administrators that she wanted to get out now and be with her boys. They, probably realizing that it would be useless to try and stop her and that there really wasn't anything more that they could do for her, so against their better judgment they did release her.

I became extremely concerned as soon as I found out about what she had done. I knew that she couldn't have prepared herself very well financially for life on the outside and that she would probably need some help. I was quite certain that the only income that she would be getting to live on was a small amount of social security money. I figured that she would need much more money than that to live decently. I was also aware that my brothers would probably be in no position to provide much help, so if she was to get any help I knew that it would be up to me. I could assist by sending her a portion of the meager amount of money that I was earning, but it surely wouldn't be enough.

After some investigation, I found out that I could take out an allotment to help support her. The way an allotment works is that the Air Force takes a portion of your pay each month before you even get it and then they match it with a certain amount of money, depending on the plan you're on. I think it was set up originally for married servicemen to send money home to help support their spouse and children. Now, I thought if I could only make some similar arrangement for my mother. This would seem to be the perfect solution to my problem. I went to the proper department office and completed all the paperwork that was necessary to get the allotment started.

In 1955 an amount of $1092 was taken from my income and the Air Force matched that amount for 1955 and my mother's share from Social Security was only $516 for that year. She would now have enough money to live quite decently. As a result of this, my pay check was now going to be only a little more than $30 a month, but I knew that the money was needed for my mother and also my youngest brother Warren, who was staying with my mother. I was now providing more than half of my mother's income, so at least I could file my income tax and list her as a dependent. That did give me some tax relief, but it was just a small fraction of the amount that I was paying out.

Thank goodness that the Air Force provided me with room and board, because my pay each month was so little that I really had kind of a financial crisis of my own to deal with. Outside of the basics of life I led quite a Spartan existence, but I knew that somehow I would make it.

It was quite a coincidence that my uncle Carroll, who was an Air Force captain, was stationed at Keesler Air Force Base at the same time as I. He also bought the Packard sedan that my dad had when he died. There were many times that he let me drive it and because of the base sticker on the car indicating the car was owned by an officer, the guard would salute me whenever I left or entered the base. My airmen friends who rode with me were all fascinated by the neat car and being saluted each time as we were going to or from the base. I spent some time at Carroll's house and once in a while I got a nice home cooked meal that his wife prepared. I spent a lot of time entertaining and playing with his children. I baby-sat his children a couple of times and I even took them to an outdoor movie once.

One day my Uncle Carroll asked me if I would like to try some fishing with him on the Gulf. I was glad to go and it was to be a new experience for both of us to be fishing from a wharf in the Gulf of Mexico. I immediately noticed that the tackle we rented had really large rods and reels with the thickest fishing line I had ever seen. I remember that I was thinking that no mater what I might catch nothing would ever be able to break this line even if that catch was larger than I.

We had fished for more than an hour with no success, when suddenly I sunk my hook into something that started to pull hard and jerk about like nothing I had ever caught before. It was all that I could do to keep my place on the wooden planks of the wharf so whatever it was it had to be quite large and strong. I continued my struggle to bring it in, and every once in awhile it would even leap above the surface of the water. It was during one of those times that Carroll and I finally caught a glimpse of it as it had surfaced for just an instant. To both of us, it appeared that I had caught an enormous snake. It had taken more than fifteen minutes of constant work to bring sea creature near enough to the dock to get it into the net. It was so big that it didn't really fit into the net but Carroll was finally able to lift the heavy thing onto the dock. It was only then that we realized that I had caught myself one very large eel. The thing was over five feet long, quite fat and it had pointed teeth, which gave it quite a frightening appearance. It continued to flop around on the dock after I had landed it and we didn't know how we were going to get the hook out of its mouth. Neither Carroll nor I knew anything about this fierce looking creature, so Carol took a piece of wood and beat it to death. The eel had swallowed the hook so we gave up on that and finally just cut the line. We continued to fish for about an hour longer with no success so that was the total fishing experience for us Minnesotan's on the Gulf.

Since I lived in the barracks I wouldn't have been able to get the fish cooked and Carroll said that he didn't want it. We also didn't know if it was edible so we just left it there. We had talked about going fishing again sometime, but Carroll got transferred before we ever got another chance. He left Keesler before I did, but I felt quite fortunate to have had the chance to spend that short time with him.

There was always plenty of spare time, but I had too little money to do much with it other than an occasional movie at the base theatre. I did spend an awful lot of my time on continuing my first love which was art, because I still had my dream of going to art school after the service. When the other airmen were going to town in the evening, I devoted a lot of my time in the barracks drawing pictures. There were many evenings, especially on the weekends, that I was the only one in the whole building. Because of costs my art was mainly confined to two dimensional works using pencil or charcoal. Outside of going to school I spent most of my time being quite alone.

With my class, I finally completed my electronics training and I graduated from the Air Training Command on the fourth of October of 1955. I was given a long title of Airborne Electronics Navigational Equipment Repairman. I was now anxiously waiting for my assignment to some place, that would be more exciting, at some other Air Force Base outside of the Air Training Command.

Upon our graduation from electronics school, promotion to

Airman second Class was considered to be automatic. Another example that events in my life just can't seem to go smoothly for too long is that I didn't receive my promotion when, as the rest of the airmen in my class. The Air Force somehow got my name mixed up with another person with the last name of Brown, who had some disciplinary action taken against him which was to prevent him from getting promoted.

As things turned out the other guy got promoted, who wasn't supposed to, and I didn't. After finding that out I was terribly upset by it all because I was so counting on the badly needed rise in pay. I went immediately to my commanding officer to make my complaint. He explained to me that there was nothing he could do to get my new rank corrected to the proper date. He did assure me that he would get it straightened out, but my promotion would now be dated two months later then it should have.

That was to make a big difference later on, when I came up for my next promotion. As a result of that, it would affect my not getting my next promotion for over a year later than what it should have been. Promotion means better pay and I was certainly in need of more money. In my life it seems as though so many things just wouldn't go the way that they're suppose to. It is things like that which make me feel as if I am constantly being tested by God.

Being in the service gave me a feeling of helplessness, that I was not going to be able to give some of my time to help my mother, because I knew that she was in a terrible physical condition. I therefore made an application for a hardship transfer to a base that would be near to where my mother was living. Because of this I may have been partly to blame for my next test.

I no more than got one problem settled when I had to deal with another. All of the other airmen in my class received their orders sending them to some other base. I think that it might have been because of that hardship transfer, that I didn't get any orders.

I was told that it would be at least next two weeks before I would get assigned so I had nothing to do but wait. I spent that time as the only occupant in my barracks. Now I had lots of time for myself, but the few friends I had were gone. My art work wasn't enough to satisfy my need for something to do. I had also learned that it was usually not a good idea to volunteer for anything. I knew that I would probably be given some cleanup job that I would not like. It seemed as though my choices were limited to drawing pictures, going to a movie, going for long walks around the base, or watching television in a separated building with a day room.

Before the month of October came to an end and almost a month of waiting, I finally did receive my orders. I also had been granted my wish to be assigned somewhere near where my mother lived. It would be within driving distance for me to see her and my youngest brother in St. Cloud, Minnesota; however, I didn't have a car.

It was good news to me when I found out I was being transferred to an air base that had just recently been built near Lincoln, Nebraska. This was home to the 98th and the 307th bomb wings and it was a S.A.C. base. It wasn't very long before that when I had seen the movie "The Strategic Air Command so I was quite excited about going there.

The two bomb wings each had three squadrons of Boeing B-47 medium bombers and one supporting squadron of Boeing KC-97 refueling aircraft. The B-47 is the very same plane that is featured at the end of that movie. During the Second World War it would definitely have been considered a heavy bomber, but now it was called a medium bomber with six jet engines and a crew of three. It is capable of carrying an internal bomb load of 20,000 pounds and it also has two electronically fired 20 millimeter canons in the tail section. It was quite fast for a bomber with the ability to fly at a speed just under mach I. When that plane first came out it immediately became an example of where the future of military aircraft was going and the type of plane that would be replacing the B - 36.

Immediately after arriving at my new Base I found out that security was a serious business and I was thoroughly interrogated and examined before I was even assigned a squadron or some place to live. This was the first time that I had experienced anything like their constant security checks. I was assigned to the 98th Armament and Electronics Squadron, which was a part of the 98th Bomb Wing at Lincoln Air Force Base.

I was now in General Curtis LeMay's Strategic Air Command which had its headquarters in Offutt Air Force Base near Omaha, Nebraska, but Lincoln was equipped to handle much larger aircraft. Lincoln was also a part of Eighth Air Force that had become famous for the part they played in the Second World War and then in the Korean War. It was explained to me that this would only be my home base, and from there I would be sent on alerts or on temporary duty status to other bases throughout the world. In my case I was to get plenty of that, but I thought that I would enjoy the travel to many foreign lands. I went to such places overseas and none of it would have been possible if I had not removed certain medical records from my personnel file after my basic training.

One of the most pleasant surprises, for me, was that I would never again have any K.P. duty. This was one of General LeMay's suppositions for boosting the moral of all his military personnel in the Strategic Air Command. Civilians were hired specifically for taking care of everything in the dinning halls. The results were obvious, because the meals were much better than anything that I received, in the name of food, on those last two bases.

The menu, for each meal, always consisted of several choices of foods to eat much like a buffet. The dining halls were well decorated and provided with a nice atmosphere for eating. Instead of the compartmented trays, we had become accustomed to at the other bases; we were served on real nice white china with the Strategic Air Command symbol tastefully decorating the rim of all of the dishes in a light blue color.

As soon as they had a security badge made for me to wear I was taken to the Armament and Electronics shop and started working on the electronics equipment that I been trained on in school at Keesler. The first aircraft that I was assigned to work on was, what I thought to be, quite strange because I had never seen one like it before. It was that KC-97 aircraft I mentioned earlier, the "K" meaning airborne refueling and the "C" meaning cargo. The reason that I thought that plane was so strange is because you could observe from just looking at it that the fuselage was divided into two levels with an upstairs and downstairs and hanging underneath near the back was a glass bubble with a long refueling boom sticking out the back of it.

The first job I had consisted of going out to troubleshoot the radio and the radar equipment when there was a malfunction written up by the navigator. It was my job to trouble shoot and duplicate the malfunction which gave me the information I needed and remove the defective piece of electronics equipment and bring it into our repair facilities to have everything corrected. I then picked up a working unit and went back to the aircraft and installed it. Then I had to test it to be sure a malfunction no longer exists, and that all is put right.

Occasionally the malfunction couldn't be duplicated on the ground and I would have to go on a test hop (short test flight). I could now simulate the conditions under which the malfunction occurred and find a solution to the problem. Electronics sometimes acted differently while at a higher altitude. By the way, an airman received an extra $70 pay a month if he was on flying status. To be on flying status, one was required to have a minimum of four hours of flying time in a month, which was quite easy to do. I was able to get that during about half of the months that I was assigned there. Again removing those medical records really paid off for me.

I was unable to do all of the work included in my job description until I obtained the necessary security clearance because I would be working with some highly classified material. I had to be thoroughly investigated by the third district O.S.I. (Office Security Investigation) in Washington. I filled out all the many required forms and I had to answer a multitude of questions for them. I was told when they were done with their investigation that they knew more about me and my parents than I knew about myself. I'm not so sure that there wasn't some truth in that. We were told that they check into one's whole life from the time that he was potty trained on. After about three months, the investigation was finally completed and I now had my clearance. I was qualified to work in some highly sensitive security jobs.

Security was extremely important here and like everyone on a S.A.C. base I had to constantly wear a plastic laminated badge with my picture, my name, and other information on it. That badge had to be always in plain view and it was also marked with a list of all of the areas that I had a clearance to be in.

In order to work on any aircraft, I had to get the current passwords in the shop before I left. With my tool box, I then went out in a van or a panel truck and made my entry to the flight line at one of the check points, where an Air Policeman guard would say a number and I would have to quickly add or subtract to make the correct password number. That number was changed about twice a day, but not at the same time. After I had given him the correct number, the guard would carefully check my badge. That just enabled me to get through the gate and onto the flight line. When I got to the aircraft, that I was going to work on, I had to be checked again with another password by the crew chief of that plane. To enter the building where I worked, I even had to pass another security check for clearance. It was much nicer after being on the base for some length of time because those dreaded security checks became less frequent as one would get to know many people. We were told that, "The best means of identification for security purposes is personal recognition."

What happens if you gave the guard the wrong number or some other problem should arise? Only once in all the time I worked there did I have a problem. On this particular day I picked up a work order and I was on my way to work on an aircraft. As I was entering the flight line the guard stopped me and I gave him the password I had been given. During a 24 hour period the password gets changed several times. This time it had just been changed and I was given the wrong one.

When I gave the guard the wrong number he immediately leveled his rifle on me and told me to get out of the van. He then ordered me to lie down spread eagle with my stomach on the concrete, looking straight ahead with my chin painfully resting on the hard concrete surface. Lying in this position, it wasn't long before it began to hurt my chin and the back of my neck and I so badly wanted to turn my head to one side or the other. I was forced to wait like that for what seemed to be a long time but was really about 15 minutes and then a four by four vehicle came with four air policemen in it. They all had guns and they gave me the impression they were anxious to use them. It really felt good when I was allowed to stand up and then I was thoroughly searched before being ordered to get into the truck with them. I was rushed off to their headquarters where they luckily called my supervising officer and he came to verify my identity and I was released.

I say luckily because I knew three other airmen who told me of their experience when they first arrived on the base and they were far less fortunate than I. Dressed in their regular fatigue clothes and jacket, they were sent on some clean up detail before they got sent to an assigned squadron. The driver of the van they were in mistakenly drove them into some security area. They were about their assigned task when the got interrupted by the Air Police who like I was driven to their headquarters and they described what had happened to them. They told me that they first had their clothing searched and even had the lining partly torn out of their jackets. Next they were stripped naked and the real embarrassment of having every orifice of their body was searched. They were finally allowed to put their clothes back on, but because they had no identification on their person they were then detained for a few hours while it seemed that no one cared how long it took to find out where to send them. Besides the inconvenience, I would have found the whole process they had undergone to be so humiliating.

I think everyone on the base was familiar with a reported incident where a security guard was suspicious of an airman that had protested against the guard as he was carrying out his duty. Without showing a badge the airman continued on through the gate and then turned and joked that the guard's gun wasn't even loaded. The airman arrogantly placed a paper cup on his head and taunted the guard to shot it off his head. The guard leveled his rifle on the airman and shot him in the head which killed him instantly. The guard was fined $1, given a carton of cigarettes, and was secretly sent off to another base. I don't know if this really happened or if it was made up to just frighten us into taking this security seriously.

Another one of my jobs, soon after I had my security clearance, was changing the code in the I.F.F. Transmitter on the certain aircraft that were assigned to me. I had to memorize the many digits of the huge number that I had to enter into this black box that was the transmitter in the aircraft. It sends out a special coded signal, so that the aircraft will be immediately recognized by the control tower as a friendly aircraft. I.F.F. means Identification Friend or Foe. In time of war, the aircraft must transmit the proper code or be prepared to receive ground fire from the air base. Planes would also be sent up to intercept the non-coded plane and possibly shoot it down. The Strategic Air Command was serious about its mission to be prepared for the possibility of a war at any time.

In November of 1955, the whole 98th Bomb Wing was given orders to go to England. So I hadn't been at Lincoln very long, when I had to pack up my duffle bag and leave. I was quite excited and it was a new experience for me, because this was the first chance that I ever had to travel in an aircraft. I also thought about the caveat that was included with the results of my medical exam at Parks Air Force Base which stated that I was restricted from flying in aircraft for any reason and how none of this would have been possible for me. I had made up my mind then that I would ignore that restriction and now I was sure that I had made the right decision. I was so anxious to be able to fly and I considered it sort of an honor to be flying in a large Douglas C-124 Globemaster cargo aircraft, heading for Dover, Delaware. It was from there that my first airplane ride would be taking me across the Atlantic.

It was so exciting for me to be on such a trip. The first leg of the trip took us to Dover, Delaware with no problems. The plane was used mainly for cargo therefore we only had bucket seats to sit in and they aren't very comfortable. The only time I felt a bit of concern for my safety was when we entered a violent storm over the Atlantic. At one point, as I had been lying on the floor of the aircraft trying to get some sleep, the plane suddenly started to drop. I became alarmed as soon as I realized that the plane was descending faster than I. My body was in space somewhere above that floor. I don't think that I had spent much time in my own flight path, before the plane leveled off and my body came in contact with the floor again, but I must admit that it was more than a bit scary for this novice airman.

When we first reached England it was so cloudy that I could just barely make out the coastline, but then the clouds began clearing as we got nearer to our destination. As soon as we were in our flight path above Lakenheath R.A.F. Station I could see very well and I was amazed by how green the country side was below us. My job was to be a part of the ground crew that would have this job of servicing the radar equipment on our KC-97 and B-47 aircraft. As soon as we landed we were taken by bus to our barracks to unpack.

The base itself still belonged to the Royal Air Force, and it is located in the southeastern part of England that is called East Anglia. It is about nineteen miles north of Newmarket and from there you went almost straight west for about eleven miles to get to Cambridge. Our squadron would be assigned to fly many training missions from this base.

We were billeted in barracks the likes of which I had never seen before. They were no more than Quonset huts which were mainly constructed of corrugated steel and firmly mounted on concrete slabs to form the floors. They were the same buildings used on airbases throughout England during the "Battle of Britain" in World War II. For washing, taking our showers, shaving, and the toilet facilities were located in a separate Quonset hut that provided these services for ours and three other barracks.

All of the buildings were in decent condition and clean, but poorly heated with just one tiny gas fired pot belly stove located in the middle of the room. Fortunately the winters in England are quite mild and it rarely got below 30 degrees there. Each barracks was no more than one very long room with two rows of bunks that were stacked two high and I estimated would be adequate for about 60 men. The bunks were aligned with the head of the bed against the sloping sides of the building and there were steel lockers standing in between for hanging our clothes and storing our other possessions. The foot of the beds faced the isle that ran down the middle of the building. It all reminded me of the days that I spent in basic training except we had no foot lockers.

Our aircraft took off and landed on two runways that formed an X so this was possible from all four directions. The shops we worked in were located in between two of the legs that formed that X. Therefore the buildings were extremely close to the runways and the flight line that ran in a circle around the outside. One advantage of this arrangement was that we had no check point to drive through when going to work. We just got into a 4X4 truck and drove directly to the aircraft.

The shops were larger and somewhat nicer than the barracks, but they were also heated with those same little stoves instead of having a central heating system as we were accustomed to in the states. They were quite cold and damp most of the time. Furniture was also quite sparse and I spent a lot of free time reading with only my tool box to sit on.

The food was quite decent, but we didn't expect it to be nearly up to the standards that we become accustomed to back at Lincoln A.F.B. The quality was somewhat between what we got at Lincoln and what I received at Parks and Keesler Air Force Bases.

There was one thing that was different then any other mess hall I had been in before. As you were getting your food at meal time, there was at the end of each one of the serving lines, the ever present, large fiber drums filled with cardboard packets of cigarettes. Each little packet had just four cigarettes in it and we were encouraged to help ourselves to as many as we wanted, courtesy of the competing cigarette companies. So the cigarettes didn't cost us a penny so I always took several. I know that I haven't any right to blame making my smoking habit on that but it certainly made it easier. I never thought for a moment that the cigarette companies were giving us free cigarettes because they liked us so much or they had some honorable or patriotic motive for doing that. If one did want to buy cigarettes in the Base Exchange the cost was only 80 cents for a carton. There is no question that those companies were actually encouraging servicemen to become addicted to their product so they could sell more.

Twice during our work day there was also a little canteen truck that came out to the flight line and only if one stood outside were you able to hear its little bell ringing. It parked for about a half hour in front of the building where we worked. A man would open a wide window in the back of the truck revealing everything he had for purchase. The items included milk, orange juice, good hot tea, bad coffee, and just a couple of different soft drinks. For food they had only three kinds of prepared sandwiches; Spam, Spam and cheese, and cheese. Their potato chips (or potato crisps as my English friends would call them) never had any salt on them, but just for the American consumption they put together some special packets. In each of these packets there was small ration of salt, wrapped up in a tiny square of waxed paper, which allowed you to untwist and sprinkle that salt on the chips. I never used the salt but most of my American friends did. For something sweet they had different kinds of cookies (or what they called biscuits), some candy bars, and gum.

Not long after arriving in England, my friend George and I decided to travel to Cambridge, a city with a bit over 80,000 people. Because of their famous Cambridge University, a large share of that population was students. George and I spent a lot of time on our first visit trying to view as much of the sights as possible. In the evenings our entertainment included the pubs (with drinks at room temperature), the burlesque, movies (the pictures), cafes, and shops that were open.

Being from the United States, the word "burlesque" made me think of strippers and a low class of cheap entertainment. Burlesque in England was quite interesting and very different than anything that I had visualized. Their entertainment would be what we would call legitimate theatre including some excellent plays and musicals.

The one thing that made them different from what we would call regular theatre, was that they had beautiful nude models that posed perfectly still in the background, while all the main performances were going on in front of them. I think that perhaps they had the models to attract a more male audience.

It is essential that the background models don't make any movement and I read in their newspaper about an incident where a mouse was seen on stage and a model saw it, got frightened, and moved. Her job there was immediately terminated.

It was only our second evening, while my friend, George, and I were casually walking together along the sidewalk just looking in store windows in Cambridge, when I first met Pamela. I don't know what it was, but I was immediately attracted to her. She had been spending her time in the city shopping with, Anne, a girl friend of hers. At first the four of us just started having some casual conversation among ourselves. We then started to lazily walk along the shore of the Cam River as we paired up, Pamela with me and Anne with George. Before we left to go back to the base, we made arrangements to meet with them again at the bus stop on the next evening.

We kept our appointment with them and the four of us started that night by having a dinner together and then the girls gave us a tour of their city. After that second night, the four of us started dating quite frequently. My friend seemed to like Anne and they became friends and they dated each other for a few weeks, but as it turned out they had too many differences and their relationship didn't last. I liked Pamela, and it was soon after we met, that she and I became the very best of friends. We were almost the same age and we always seemed to like the same things, so we greatly enjoyed each other's company.

During my time off and with every chance I got, I took the double-decker tram into Cambridge, a city that I learned to love more than any other. My relationship with Pamela was developing into something much more than just a friendship and we began spending more and more time together. We had eventually developed a mutual love for each other.

One day she invited me to her home where I met her mother, father, and an older brother. I liked her family and they seemed to think well of me also. After that I spent a lot of evenings and weekends visiting with Pamela and her family. I learned from them, a lot of their customs and their way of living. I enjoyed our conversations during tea time as we drank tea and ate crumpets or biscuits at certain times of the day, besides an occasional regular meal.

Pamela also owned a very nice Triumph motorcycle, that she was quite proud of and she really knew how to handle it. She was so good with maneuvering it, that to me, it seemed as though she was overconfident and a bit too reckless. When we went somewhere on the bike, after our first time together, she always rode as my passenger. The bike had a lot of power and one could easily over drive it and get into trouble, but I soon became quite good at handling it, however I never drove it as aggressively as Pamela.

The weather in England during that winter never got to be freezing cold, but it was damp and everywhere the grass was a bright green. We did have a couple of snowfalls that melted almost as soon as it came down.

The roads, as a result of the light snow or freezing rain could be quite slippery at times and one had to be very careful with their driving, especially on a motorcycle. When Pamela had the bike she always drove it so fast and any suggestion that I made to her about being more careful and slowing down just brought a laugh, and she would call me such a "silly goose," and tell me that I didn't have a thing to fear. She said that I was always being too serious about things and that I worried too much. I did worry about her, especially during the many times when the roads were wet.

That year I enjoyed what seemed to be the most wonderful Christmas of my life with Pamela and her family. Her mother was an excellent cook and she made the most wonderful "English" meal. I enjoyed eating some of their delicious foods, such as their usual Christmas goose, plum pudding, and many other good things. I can't imagine anything that would have made it any nicer.

We also exchanged gifts. For one present, Pamela gave me the nicest red sweater which was made out of real English wool, and I proudly wore it a lot that winter and for many years after. She also gave me some beautiful handkerchiefs that were made in Ireland. They were made out of Irish linen and I could never bring myself around to using them. In fact I kept them in the original box they came in and I thought that they were too nice and I never intended to use them. She also gave me a box of good chocolates and some other nice things. I did give Christmas cards and some art work that were original creations of mine. Because I didn't have much money I wasn't able to buy her and the members of her family very much and I felt bad about it, but they seemed to quite understand my situation. They were well aware that all Americans were not rich.

I could tell that her family liked me by the cordial way they acted towards me. Her father had a job at a local plant, but he also traveled a lot. He didn't own a car but traveled by bicycle or walked but he also got to travel a lot to other countries. He was gone a lot as he went all over the world showing the birds he raised which were mainly finches.

It seemed that with each day the relationship that Pamela and I had just kept improving. Our time together was really special and when I was at the base I missed not being with her. She was now in my thought almost all of the time. I came to resent anything, such as when we were on alert, which would prevent me from leaving the base to be with Pamela.

I was still supporting my mother, at that time, with the allotment, so I really had to be careful with my finances. It strictly limited me in the things that Pamela and I could do together and what I was able to purchase. I did get a bit of extra money each month for overseas duty and because every other month I was on flying status. It wasn't very much, but it did help me somewhat. One thing that didn't cost anything, but we both seemed to enjoy was going for long walks all over the city of Cambridge and especially the park and to just occasionally sit on a bench to have a cuddle. We especially enjoyed our walks along the banks of their beautiful Cam River and watching the swans.

I really enjoyed Cambridge's many historic sites. Old over there meant much older than any of the buildings in the United States. We saw King's College that was founded by Henry VI in 1441. We also got to see the likes of King' College Chapel with its beautiful stained glass windows which was built in 1515. We walked throughout Cambridge University which is just loaded with interesting historic sites. We saw Trinity College which was founded by Henry VIII. We also saw the beautiful University Botanical Garden just off Trumpington Street. My imagination was constantly at work imaging the past events that took place so long ago as I viewed those old buildings.

We also went to the pictures (movies) quite a bit, because it was really inexpensive entertainment. They had a clever way of charging the admission price according to where you sat in the theatre and where we sat was probably the cheapest.

It didn't take me long to appreciate living in England. I liked their weather, the cities and towns, the buildings, and the food. I really did fancy the people, their customs, and their way of life. Unlike what I experienced in the United States, everything over there just seemed to work so well. It is a country one can feel safe in no matter where you went. Law and order appeared to be an important part of every person. The people seemed to have an innocence about them, and everyone I came into contact with were so polite, kind, and so unbelievably honest. In my opinion I was among a very civilized people.

Besides traveling around England the Air Force also sent me out to many other places, such as Iceland, for a short stay. Those trips seem a little less foreboding just knowing that I would always be returning to England, It created a wild anticipation within me every time that I was returning to England as I was looking down from the plane at that island. I would get goose bumps when the plane got into its flight pattern as it was getting ready to land. I was always impressed by all of the green colors that I saw from the air, and the only place that I have ever seen that may have more green was the smaller island of Ireland. I was always quite anxious to be back down on that English soil. I never felt this kind of sensation anywhere else, not even when I would come back to the United States.

We went from England to Reykjavik, Iceland in January and we got there at a very bad time. The country was having communist demonstrations against democracy and they were showing a lot of hatred towards the United States. The way they seemed to feel it was hard to understand why they even allowed us into their country. Because of the situation there, all U. S. personnel were restricted to the base. Out of curiosity, I would have liked to have been able to see more of that country. It was probably not a fair judgment but I couldn't help the negative attitude I had towards that island when I finally was able to leave.

I don't think that anyone cared too much for what we did see of the place and the weather was constantly snowy and bitterly cold for those two weeks that we were there. I was really happy when we were finally making the return trip to England. Incidentally, I am happy to report that the people of Iceland had a change of heart, less then one year later, when they saw what Russia was doing to the Hungarians during their revolt against Communism. At that time, I had no idea that those events would be affecting me personally. The people, of Iceland, then were anxious to have the Communists removed from their country.

It was near the end of March of 1956, that I had to leave Pamela and go back to the states. That evening as soon as I met her after getting off of the bus in Cambridge, she seemed to already know before I told her. That last evening together was such a sad time for the both of us and it was so hard to say good-bye and not knowing when I would be returning. As we waited for my bus to take me back to the base we continued to hold onto each other until the driver let me know that he was becoming quite impatient with us. I knew that it was impossible, but I wished that she could have come back with me and in the back of my mind that very thought was there that one day she just might return with me to the United States. I even thought about the possibility of one day returning and living the rest of my life in England.

After spending several wonderful months in England, I was now sadly leaving that country with all of my unforgettable memories. I was a very unhappy airman when I boarded the Douglas C-54, a four engine propeller driven plane used mainly as a troop or material transport, for the return trip to the United States. I was so afraid that I would never get to see that green island again.

Our trip back took us over the Azores, which is a group of islands in the Atlantic Ocean, about 740 miles from their mother country of Portugal. That was the scheduled landing for the first leg of our trip back. The severe weather, they were now experiencing at ground level created a necessary change in our plans as we circled the island. The weather, when we arrived, was quite unfavorable with ominously high winds at ground level. The tower had transmitted instructions for us to go into a flight path in preparation to land, because their forecast had indicated that the wind was suppose to subside soon. They notified us that if the weather didn't improve soon, they were going to send us on to Portugal.

We circled the island of Lajes for what seemed almost forever and the wind on the ground never did let up even a small bit. We were finally instructed by ground control that we would have to fly to Portugal. Someone screwed up, because it was now too late and we had run too low on fuel so we no longer had the luxury to choose where we would land any more and flying to Portugal now was no longer an option for us. We had to land very soon, so the control tower informed us to stay aloft for a short time as they got prepared to receive us. Instead of improving, the weather had actually got worse and the winds were considerably gustier than before. How could they have made such a mistake?

Still in our flight path, we finally got word from the tower and the plane slowly began the descent. I know that I was like most of the others, as we were praying that God would somehow get us safely on the ground. I was seated next to a window as I just had to see what was going on. I could now easily see the fire trucks and other rescue units lined up near the runway and I think that instead of assurance I now really became worried.

We started our landing right enough as we were aiming for the end of the proper runway and now we were making quite a rapid decent. The ground now appeared to be coming quite quickly towards us to meet the plane. We were over the runway but still airborne when a very strong gust of wind hit our plane from the side and turned it completely around. The plane was now moving backwards as it was being thrown, some distance, to the ground. When the plane smashed into the runway, all of the landing gear was immediately sheared off. As the plane's fuselage came crashing into the runway it began rapidly twirling around and at the same time it was sliding quite rapidly down that concrete strip with quite a bit of speed. I wondered to myself why should we want to stay on the runway and that it might be better if we would leave the runway we would be sliding on the ground which might slow up more quickly.

I could really feel the seat belt, as it painfully dug into me, while I was being jerked about in my seat. The centrifugal force held me tight against the side as I continued to watch out of the window on my left. I could see the landscape rapidly traveling by, as around and around we went. The propellers' blades were being bent and broken off and some of the blades came crashing into the fuselage. During the time all of this was happening there was the constant and terribly loud scraping noise. Our aircraft was literally being torn to pieces. Time seemed to almost stand still as it seemed to be taking forever as I anxiously waited for that plane to finally come to a stop before we ran out of island.

From the direction that we made our approach, the runway goes a bit uphill and finally ends with a high cliff that falls directly down onto rocks and the Atlantic Ocean. Our plane was heading for that cliff, but somehow, thank God, the plane did come to a stop just a bit short of that steep drop off.

It was no time at all before the helicopters, ambulances, fire trucks, and all of their other rescue equipment was near our plane ready to assist, but to their surprise, none of them were needed. There was an officer out side barking orders, that we should remove the injured first, as all of us started to walk out of the plane and no one had any visible injuries. A Portuguese General was even there to greet us as we got off the plane.

It was with great relief when I was finally able to get my feet safely on the ground. I turned round to look back at the plane, and now I understood the surprise that was being expressed by the ground crews. Much of the plane had been torn into shiny aluminum pieces of various shapes had been scattered from the beginning of the runway to where we had come to a stop. The part of the plane that we had just made our exit from was a terrible large mess of crumpled up aluminum and barely recognizable as a flight worthy aircraft. I did not have any sense of fear when things were happening, but now as I was able to clearly view it from the outside, my body did begin to tremble a bit.

The plane had been completely destroyed and it was also quite obvious that it would be only useful for some of the spare parts and equipment that may be salvaged from it. I was also thankful that God had answered my prayers for a safe landing. We realized just how fortunate we were to even be alive. It is also testimony that the Douglas Aircraft Company constructed quite a well built aircraft to maintain the integrity of the passenger part of this C-54 Skymaster to prevent casualties in this situation.

The island was beautiful and I was able to enjoy all of my forced stay there. I had probably a much nicer time of it than my other airmen friends from that aircraft, because a good friend of mine, Peter Copeland, who was a Royal Air Force (R.A.F.) pilot, just happened to be stationed there at that time.

All American servicemen were restricted to the base, but the British personnel were not. The only explanation I was able to get was that it had something to do with the fact that the island had legalized prostitution. The restriction was enforced to protect the Americans, but I guess, for some reason, the English didn't seem to need that same protection.

Peter, his friends, and I would often drive off of the base together. Since all of us wore civilian clothes, it was very easy for me to pretend that I was just another member with the R.A.F. The irony of this was that most of the time we were using a panel truck provided by the United States Air Force. The people on the island were very nice to us and the scenery was beautiful. Incidentally we never did take advantage of the prostitution. Most of the time we carried umbrellas because, even though most of the time the sky was quite sunny, one had to be prepared for the rains that would come up quite suddenly.

During the time that I was in the Azores, I wrote a letter, every day, to Pamela. In my first letter I had instructed her to send her replies to the address that I had given her for my home base in Lincoln, Nebraska. I therefore, wouldn't receive any letters while I was on this island. I also found that it was difficult to write when I wasn't getting any letters in return to reply to.

Being assigned no duties or work, I had a lot of time to myself which I spent reading or with my R.A.F. friends. We even had island boys make our beds and polish our shoes for pennies. For me it had become sort of island paradise and I wasn't overly anxious to leave when finally after almost two weeks, the Air Force was able to get us another aircraft to replace the one that was now lying on this island in ruins and was already being dismantled for any of its useful parts. It was another C-54 that finally flew us back to our home at Lincoln Air Force Base in Nebraska.

When I got home, I was quite anxious to get my mail and the letters that Pamela had written. I wasn't disappointed because that first day I picked up my mail, I was overjoyed by the huge stack of letters from her. I first arranged them in order by the date stamp and then opened each and meticulously read every single word. Each one was wonderfully written and some were replying to letters from the Azores which I had no way of knowing that she had even been receiving them. She and I continued our correspondence daily telling about the things and events in our lives and an awful lot about our feelings for each other. We kept writing our "love" letters to each other regularly, until I was back in England.

That routine would continue until the next time that I got back to England. Then when I had to leave her the next time, we were back to writing again each day. Each time I left her, I would ask her to promise me that she would be careful when riding her bike and as usual she would tell me I was a "silly goose," and that I worried too much.

We kept up this type of relationship during a period of almost four years. We even frequently discussed the possibility of some day getting married. I even saved every one of the letters that she wrote to me and each one that I received would, forever, remain so special to me. I think that I will always cherish the memory of her and most of those letters still remain with me today.

Since I got back to my home base, I spent most of my time reporting for work each day for about eight hours. My mind was still set on some day making art my career. I started spending even more time drawing and painting pictures. I also found some time for just lying on my bunk reading, and of course I did sleep some at night. It seemed that almost everything that I did, except my assigned duties, was something one does alone. Being so busy also kept me from getting lonely. I did occasionally go into the city of Lincoln to see a movie or for some other entertainment.

One day when I was in the city with a friend of mine, we just happened upon a cafe that seemed proud to be advertising a meal for only 49 cents. The meal consisted of a hamburger sandwich or a hot dog, with French fries, and a shake. We really developed a taste for their Maid Rite type of sandwich, and we thought it was like no other. Because of its special unique flavor, we always ordered their special "hamburger" sandwich meal.

My friend and I first ate at that place that year and we had their "special" each time we were in Lincoln. That continued until some time in late 1957 when one day we were disappointed to find out that the place was closed. There was no explanation but we were able to finally read about it in the Lincoln newspaper, that their business was brought to an end, because their sandwiches were made almost entirely out of horse meat. Even though I liked their sandwiches I don't think that I could have eaten them if I would have known that they were made from horse flesh.

For my birthday in 1956, I received a very special and unexpected gift. I thought that I had received the most elegant gold ring from Pamela. The ring had my initials "R B" beautifully printed on the top in a really fancy script, which has long since worn almost smooth. Engraved on the inside was the date, "27-6-56" and beneath that was "Love Pam." Pamela didn't know my ring size, so naturally with my small hands it was much too large. I immediately took it to a jeweler who made it smaller to fit me and he didn't charge me anything. He said that he got more than enough gold from it to pay for his time.

During the year of 1956 my mother received a total of $516 as her share from Social Security and she received over $2000 from the allotment money. The share that I paid into the allotment was $1039, which had been taken from my pay for that year. I gladly paid that amount to make my mother's life more decent even though that left me with only $354 remaining of my taxable income to spend for that whole year. Fortunately, for me, when I was out of the country I got $15 extra each month for overseas duty and every other month I got $70 for being on flying status and fortunately that income was non taxable.

In October of 1956, my mother died. She died mainly from complications and the tuberculosis. She weighed less than seventy pounds for about the last eight years of her life. She was only forty-one years old. My eleven year old brother, Warren, was with her at the time. He even rode with her when she was taken to the hospital on that fatal day. Warren told me afterwards that our mother acted as though she already knew when she was taken into the hospital that she would be going in there to die.

Even though I knew that it was going to happen and that it could be soon, it was still a shock for me, when I was suddenly notified by the Red Cross that my mother had died. They arranged for me to get an emergency leave to take care of things and to attend the funeral. I had a car, so I immediately packed up things and started that long sad drive to Wisconsin.

We would be having the funeral at the Big River Catholic Church and everything was very much like we experienced only two years and one month before, with my father. We were having our mother buried in one of the extra plots we bought when we buried our dad. Our mother would be just next to where our dad's body lay.

I was feeling so confused, angry, hopeless, and I thought about the injustice of it all. I even had trouble believing that a decent God could allow this to happen. Our mother was such a good person and it just wasn't right that she had to die so young. I was so confused by it all, because I was feeling a pain that was much greater than the time of my father's funeral.

As I was attending the funeral it was tearing my heart out just to be there. I really had the hope that some day, after I got out of the service, that I could afford to buy a nice house for her to live in. I would be able to take care of her properly for the rest of her life. I loved my mother so! I couldn't control my crying, so I was not a very nice person to be around at that time. I knew that I was going to miss her dearly.

Another thing, because I had just turned twenty-one years old in June of that year, I was now legally an adult. I automatically became the guardian over my four younger brothers. It didn't really mean much, but I now had a family! Being in the Air Force was a hell of a place to be at a time like this. Pat and Tom had jobs on farms for room and board. Richard was going to the Preparatory Seminary in Belleville, Illinois so thankfully, I didn't have to worry about him either. Only my youngest brother, Warren, was without a home.

Our Aunt Beth said something about taking care of Warren, but I was hoping someone else might offer to do that. I was not keen on Beth taking him, so I decided to wait. I had actually hoped that my Aunt Dorothy would offer him a home instead. I knew that she wouldn't provide him with a great place but she was at least a somewhat kinder person than Beth.

I felt so helpless being in the Air Force during this time, because I would have to go back to my home base soon. I couldn't even consider taking Warren with me, while I was still living on base. I felt obliged to do almost anything to keep Warren out of an orphanage. Because of my past experiences, I had a dreadful perception of those places! I took Warren with me and we stayed together in a hotel in Rochester, Minnesota for the time being. I even had to call the Red Cross to get an emergency extension to my leave, because I still had no home for Warren.

I finally had to admit that I didn't have any other choice. Our Aunt Beth was the only one to offer Warren a home with her and John in Saint Croix Falls, Wisconsin. In spite of the way I felt, I was somewhat relieved about that. There were papers that she and I had to sign to give her custody of Warren. I felt that she was not the best person to have him placed in her charge, because I felt that she was overly severe. I had the feeling that her husband John, who was so easy going and just the opposite of her, might modify things a bit and help make life more bearable for Warren. I also thought that Aunt Beth couldn't be too bad, because she was also a grade school teacher. I really didn't have any other choice.

Later, I would really regret my decision, to leave Warren with Aunt Beth. She was such a severe and critical person and Warren wasn't really allowed to be a child with her. It was lonely for him and he was certainly not happy there. Aunt Beth also got tired of having Warren living with her. After living with Aunt Beth for a short while she was able to get Warren placed in Boys' Town near Omaha, Nebraska.

I had seen the old movie about Boys' Town and its founder Father Flanagan and the film made it look quite glamorous. I was quite cynical and I had thoughts of it being just another orphanage. That was, until after I went there to visit my brother and got to see it with my own eyes as he proudly showed me around. Another thing that did appeal to me was the fact that Boys' Town was located only about 60 miles from my home base at Lincoln.

This chapter that began with a ***detour into the skies*** to loosely paraphrase another author, I felt had its beginnings with the best of times but now I felt it was ending as the worst of times for me.

- XVII. My Name -

AND NOW I COME to the reason for my choice of a title. It is soon after most people are born, that they receive their first, middle, and last names by which they shall be known for the rest of their life, but I was not that fortunate. One look at my original certificate of birth, as it was recorded in the Capital at Bismarck, North Dakota in 1935, something strange is immediately noticeable. What one sees is: Full Name of Child William Joseph Brown. The name William had been clearly crossed out so according to the certificate I was just "_____" Joseph Brown. My parents had agreed that Joseph would be my middle name, which was also my grandfather's first name. My mother and father were going to have a legal first name given to me later, when both of them could finally decide on one. Time past by quickly and that task would just never be accomplished.

When I wrote letters I never used sincerely yours or yours truly; instead I developed the habit of closing my letters with, (I am, Roy). All of my assignments since I first entered school would be identified with the name, Roy. The teachers and my classmates would always address me as Roy. During all of those years that I was attending different schools, I was conscious of only two other boys by the name of LeRoy, but I never once met another Roy.

It was obvious to me that my name wasn't a very common one. During the time that I was being called Roy I didn't really like the name or even the sound of it. It was not enough that my dad's name was Roy. I just wished that my parents would have given me one of the more common names such as, John, David, or Mike.

My mother, father, my brothers, and all of my relatives only called me Sonny. In fact, some of those relatives even thought that Sonny was my only real first name. At home with my family and when I was with my relatives, it had become more natural and much more pleasant for me to be simply called Sonny rather than Roy.

I never felt that Sonny was the solution to my first name problem either. I always had a strong feeling that there was something not quite right with being named Sonny. I never had the experience, like my brothers, of being called by my first, middle, and last name when I had done something wrong. As an example if Pat did something wrong our mother would start admonishing him with, "Patrick James Brown." No matter what I did, I would always be called nothing but Sonny!

I did not know that I was not legally given this first name of Roy. I just felt that I was called that because I had the same name as my father. It wasn't until many years later, when I had begun the fourth grade. It was when we were alone one night that my mother related the circumstances that created the problem for me. She told me she dearly loved my dad, when I was born, and that she wanted me to have his first name as my first name. She also told me that my dad did not want me to have his name, because he said he hated the idea that he might be called big Roy and that I would be called little Roy. Furthermore, he made the remark that he wanted to leave no monuments to himself. She explained that they had considered calling me William but decided against it and time just seemed to slip away and they never did get around to giving me a legal name of my own.

After my mother had finished explaining this to me, she made me promise not to tell my dad or anyone else, not even my brothers.

Until that day, I always thought that my real name was Roy and that Sonny was just my nick name and now I wasn't sure that it really did me any good to know differently because I still continued to label my assignments until I graduated from high school with "Roy." When I joined the Air Force I enlisted with the name of "Roy."

It wasn't until one day when I was in the ninth grade, that I broke that promise to my mother. My brothers and I were with our dad in one of the surrounding towns near Winona delivering, from door to door, handbills for his insurance company. I hated that job so much that when I had to go back to replenish my supply of handbills that I thought of a way to get away from it for awhile. I thought I would distract my dad by asking, "How come I was never given a first name?"

He immediately asked, "Who told you that?" I told him what mother had said and he finally admitted everything. He explained it to me in almost the same way that my mother had told me. My father then asked me if I had told Pat or any of the others. I answered that I hadn't said anything, to anyone about it. He then told me, "Well don't! They wouldn't understand."

It wasn't until I was twenty-one years old and both of my parents were now dead and I was in the Air Force that I decided to take matters into my own hands. Since my father didn't want me to have his name, but my mother did want it to be Roy, I made up my mind that I would take the French spelling of that name.

I had in my possession a Notification of Birth Registration from the Department of Commerce Bureau of the Census. I had always used it as my birth certificate when one was required. It had my name recorded as simply a big space and then Joseph Brown. I found a typewriter that had the same type as the document. I first practiced on a plain piece of paper before doing anything with the certificate. When I was feeling sure of myself I used that typewriter and carefully typed in "Roi" in the proper place and it was lined up quite well with the rest of the lettering on the certificate. One would have to look at it very carefully to see that it wasn't originally that way. It was then, that I proudly considered my first name Roi to be official. I do, however, expect people, in the United States, to use the English pronunciation of my name.

It is difficult for me to understand my motives for doing certain things at times, when I considered that one of the reasons that I had never liked the name Roy was because it was so uncommon. Then I had my name changed to a spelling of that name that is even more unusual, in the United States at least. Nevertheless, the name, Roy or Roi, also has the same proud meaning of "king" in both languages. Another thing, it is something that is mine and no one can take it from me.

The "oi" in French is pronounced like "wa" which is hard for most to say so instead of the French pronunciation "Rwa," I usually answer to the English pronunciation, "Roy." I have no longer any feelings about the sound of it.

Besides that Notification of Birth Registration, my name has also been, long since, changed to Roi with my social security card, the Internal Revenue Service, my drivers' license, credit cards, and all other forms of identification.

Therefore -

I am,

Roi

– XIX. Afterward –

As the author of this I feel obligated to inform you what has happened in the lives of my brothers after all of those years. It would have been impossible, for me, to write my story without including something about them. I consider that I certainly am justified in feeling proud of each one of them. My brothers and I traveled an extremely difficult and disconcerting road, sometimes together, but separately far too often. I suppose that one might consider us to be good examples of, what some would call, survivors. I would like to think that we inherited some of our best qualities from both of our parents.

With too much regularity my brothers and I, during our formative years, were each exposed to entirely different environments. I have come to accept, as a reality, that it forced upon us a diversity that must have been of some benefit. We did not use our past as any excuse, but there is no question that we must have been influenced by it. We, according to the old saying, "Played the cards that we were dealt." We each achieved a certain amount of excellence in our chosen fields of endeavor. I believe that each one of us was able to contribute, in some positive way, to the country that we were born into.

Patrick, who is mentioned in the book more often than any of my other brothers, was only a little more than a year younger than I, so naturally we experienced more of our lives together and, as a result, I was closest to him. He is the only one of us brothers that never spent time on active duty in any branch of the service, but he did serve time with the Army National Guard. After experiencing a successful profession in photography for several years, he later became a mechanical engineer with the I.B.M. Company in Rochester, Minnesota. He traveled to work, each day, from his small farm that was near Lewiston, Minnesota. He also demonstrated to all, the neighboring doubters, that he was a far better than the average part time farmer.

Pat retired from I.B.M., but he is still busy doing some volunteer work for the local high school. He also has, quite seriously, taken up running as a sport and he successfully competes in many races and marathons. Patrick now lives in Lewiston with his high school sweetheart and wife Teresa. They had five children, two boys and three girls.

Thomas served a tour of duty with the United States Marines. After he returned to civilian life, he worked at various jobs, which usually required a great deal of physical skill. Besides his strong physical abilities, Tom is also quite bright and very creative. He is well suited to his job, because he has always preferred working outdoors. He is now employed with the Empire Gas Company in Kingdom City, Missouri. Thomas and his wife Sharon raised their three daughters spending most of those years living in Waukon, Iowa.

Richard after his tour of duty with the United States Marines, worked at several jobs requiring his outstanding electronics skill. Richard never did graduate from high school, but his genius didn't allow that to become any handicap. He was employed by Control Data Corporation in Minneapolis on their research and development team for a couple of years. Then he moved to California, where he worked again in research and development, but this time with the

Ratheon Company. He has always been in high demand for his skills. Even Radio Shack has made considerable use of his invaluable assistance, at times, as a consultant.

Richard is now the manufacturer of some extremely fine high end audio equipment for a wealthy consumer with an extremely discerning ear and a demand for excellence. His products have received world wide acclaim as the most exemplary in the industry. His company is located in San Jose', California and it is simply called B. E. L. or Brown Electronic Laboratories. Richard and his wife Sue reside there and they have no children.

Warren, the youngest and a full ten years my junior only completed the ninth grade, before he joined the United States Navy and served three different tours of duty in Vietnam. He attended college and earned his Bachelors' Degree in accounting from Saint John's University in Collegeville, Minnesota. He successfully completed the difficult test to become a Certified Public Accountant (C.P.A.) which had become his chosen profession now, for the last several years. He later got his Masters Degree in Business Ed and does some teaching at Cardinal Stritch University. In addition to his expertise in finance, he has become quite knowledgeable about law, and understanding our legal system. Warren and his wife Julie live in Buffalo, Minnesota where they raised their one son and two daughters.

Note: Our half brother Bobby died at the age of fifty-five years. Our other half brother Billy, who was originally given a life expectancy of only about fourteen years, died at the age of sixty-five years.

After serving 4 years and 8 months in the Air Force, Roi got married and started to raise a family. He also got a teaching degree and he enjoyed teaching 6th grade during the day for more than 30 years and teaching four nights a week at a Community College. He presently makes his home in Rochester, the home of the Mayo Clinic and he is quite proud to be a Minnesota author. Today he is retired and he enjoys playing tennis, riding his bike, going for walks, dancing, and day tripping.

ISBN 1425106508

9 781425 106508